Software Project Management

A Process-Driven Approach

BOOKS ON SOFTWARE AND SYSTEMS DEVELOPMENT AND ENGINEERING FROM AUERBACH PUBLICATIONS AND CRC PRESS

Design and Safety Assessment of Critical Systems
Marco Bozzano and
Adolfo Villafiorita
978-1-4398-0331-8

Implementing and Developing Cloud Computing Applications
David E. Y. Sarna
978-1-4398-3082-6

Secure Java: For Web Application Development
Abhay Bhargav and B. V. Kumar
978-1-4398-2351-4

Scrum Project Management
Kim H. Pries and Jon M. Quigley
978-1-4398-2515-0

Engineering Mega-Systems: The Challenge of Systems Engineering in the Information Age
Renee Stevens
978-1-4200-7666-0

Certified Function Point Specialist Examination Guide
David Garmus, Janet Russac, and
Royce Edwards
978-1-4200-7637-0

Enterprise Systems Engineering: Advances in the Theory and Practice
George Rebovich, Jr.
and Brian E. White
978-1-4200-7329-4

Process-Centric Architecture for Enterprise Software Systems
Parameswaran Seshan
978-1-4398-1628-8

Secure and Resilient Software Development
Mark S. Merkow and
Lakshmikanth Raghavan
978-1-4398-2696-6

Real Life Applications of Soft Computing
Anupam Shukla, Ritu Tiwari,
and Rahul Kala
978-1-4398-2287-6

Product Release Planning: Methods, Tools and Applications
Guenther Ruhe
978-0-84932620-2

Process Improvement and CMMI® for Systems and Software
Ron S. Kenett and Emanuel Baker
978-14200-6050-8

Applied Software Product Line Engineering
Kyo C. Kang, Vijayan Sugumaran,
and Sooyong Park
978-1-42006841-2

CAD and GIS Integration
Hassan A. Karimi and Burcu Akinci
978-1-4200-6805-4

Applied Software Product-Line Engineering
Kyo C. Kang, Vijayan Sugumaran,
and Sooyong Park, eds.
978-1-4200-6841-2

Enterprise-Scale Agile Software Development
James Schiel
978-1-4398-0321-9

Handbook of Enterprise Integration
Mostafa Hashem Sherif, ed.
978-1-4200-7821-3

Architecture and Principles of Systems Engineering
Charles Dickerson, Dimitri N. Mavris,
Paul R. Garvey, and Brian E. White
978-1-4200-7253-2

Theory of Science and Technology Transfer and Applications
Sifeng Liu, Zhigeng Fang,
Hongxing Shi, and Benhai Guo
978-1-4200-8741-3

The SIM Guide to Enterprise Architecture
Leon Kappelman
978-1-4398-1113-9

Getting Design Right: A Systems Approach
Peter L. Jackson
978-1-4398-1115-3

Software Testing as a Service
Ashfaque Ahmed
978-1-4200-9956-0

Grey Game Theory and Its Applications in Economic Decision-Making
Zhigeng Fang, Sifeng Liu,
Hongxing Shi, and Yi LinYi Lin
978-1-4200-8739-0

Quality Assurance of Agent-Based and Self-Managed Systems
Reiner Dumke, Steffen Mencke,
and Cornelius Wille
978-1-4398-1266-2

Modeling Software Behavior: A Craftsman's Approach
Paul C. Jorgensen
978-1-4200-8075-9

Design and Implementation of Data Mining Tools
Bhavani Thuraisingham, Latifur Khan,
Mamoun Awad, and Lei Wang
978-1-4200-4590-1

Model-Oriented Systems Engineering Science: A Unifying Framework for Traditional and Complex Systems
Duane W. Hybertson
978-1-4200-7251-8

Requirements Engineering for Software and Systems
Phillip A. Laplante
978-1-4200-6467-4

Software Project Management

A Process-Driven Approach

Ashfaque Ahmed

CRC Press
Taylor & Francis Group
Boca Raton London New York

CRC Press is an imprint of the
Taylor & Francis Group, an **informa** business

AN AUERBACH BOOK

CRC Press
Taylor & Francis Group
6000 Broken Sound Parkway NW, Suite 300
Boca Raton, FL 33487-2742

First issued in paperback 2019

© 2011 by Taylor & Francis Group, LLC
CRC Press is an imprint of Taylor & Francis Group, an Informa business

No claim to original U.S. Government works

ISBN-13: 978-1-4398-4655-1 (hbk)
ISBN-13: 978-0-367-38198-1 (pbk)

Library of Congress Cataloging-in-Publication Data

Ahmed, Ashfaque.
    Software project management : a process-driven approach / Ashfaque Ahmed.
        p. cm.
    Includes bibliographical references and index.
    ISBN 978-1-4398-4655-1 (alk. paper)
    1. Computer software--Development--Management. I. Title.

QA76.76.D47A3965 2012
005.1068--dc23   2011047045

**Visit the Taylor & Francis Web site at
http://www.taylorandfrancis.com**

**and the CRC Press Web site at
http://www.crcpress.com**

Contents

PART II SOFTWARE LIFE-CYCLE MANAGEMENT

PART IV   PEOPLE MANAGEMENT

Preface

When I was searching for good books on software project management, I found many interesting ones that had been written by experts in this field. These books contained valuable information on many topics covering software project management and related subjects. I was therefore surprised when a friend of mine who is a professor at a renowned Indian university told me that his students find it difficult to get good books on this subject. On going through the syllabus, though, I realized that none of the books available in the market covered more than 50% of the syllabus. My friend agreed that this was the case and that is why his students had to refer to several books to cover their syllabus. Based on my friend's suggestion, I decided to write a textbook that would cover the entire syllabus of software project management. This book is the result of that effort. Thus, students need not refer to other books for their courses any longer.

When I started writing this book, I wanted to ensure that it covers most of the syllabi prescribed for software project management at major Indian universities. In the process, the book has become comprehensive enough to cover most of the syllabi at major universities around the world. I have ensured that major topics have been covered in depth. I have also provided a case study that runs through the book covering most of the topics.

Structure of the Book

Most of the books available in the market are written with the intent of covering siloed information. Chapters are grouped in broad areas such as "quality control," "measurements," etc. This book has been written in the same flow as any software project. Part I covers project management and Part II covers the software life-cycle management. Part III covers topics such as process improvement, process selection, etc. Part IV covers people management and Part V deals with technology management.

One of the most important aspects of large, modern software projects to build industry strength and reliable software products is to continuously improve software engineering processes so that cost can be reduced and schedules realized. At the same time, the quality of software products should continuously be improved. Part III elaborates on how these goals can be achieved.

Any software project management book should cover the areas of software engineering management, project management, people management, and technology management. If any of these areas are not covered, the book will not be of much use.

Scope of the Book

This book covers several areas, including human resources, software engineering, and technology. All the topics covering these areas are discussed up to the level required for software project management. For advanced studies in these areas, the reader should refer to books written exclusively for these subjects. In this book, we will focus on areas that apply to managing software projects.

Part III focuses on software engineering processes and various software engineering processing models devised by organizations like the Software Engineering Institute, the International Organization for Standardization, and the Institute of Electrical and Electronics Engineers. Part IV deals with the human side of project management and contains chapters on team management, supplier management, and customer management. Part V deals with technology, techniques, templates, and checklists that help project teams in accomplishing their goals.

Work on software projects is primarily done by people. They take help from technological tools and techniques to improve their productivity. Software engineering helps the project team in accomplishing their work in a more organized, consistent, and efficient way by providing a structured and well-defined process to do their work. This book is structured in such a way that Part I describes how to do project management with detailed information on project and process management using skills and experience needed (described in Part IV) with the help of tools (described in Part V) in a structured manner (described in Part III) to develop work products through processes described in Part II.

Case Study

I have purposely chosen a case study that pertains to a company that is developing a software product. Agile development models are currently the rage, and this is for good reason. For product development, agile methodology is truly amazing. Nevertheless, this methodology has some shortcomings, one being difficulty in adapting it for geographically scattered teams that may be working in different time zones. In such a situation, the most challenging aspect of project management is to be able to communicate effectively. Agile methods demand that all team members be co-located so that high-bandwidth casual communication can take place among them. This makes offshore teams a complete no-no. The other shortcoming of agile methods is lack of documentation. Five years down the line, when the product has grown enormously and most of the original team has moved elsewhere, it will truly be a daunting task for a new member to understand all that code and make required changes. It will be simply impossible! To understand what I mean, look at the codes of some of the largest software products like Linux, which was built as an open source project using some sort of agile methodology. It is indeed extremely difficult to change any code inside the Linux kernel. The third shortcoming of agile methods is their inability to adapt to parallel and concurrent development. This means that if a large product is needed to be developed quickly, it will not be possible to do this with agile methods. So if a product containing one million lines of code is needed to be developed in a short time of 1 year (that is right, 1 year to be exact), then the total effort required for this project will be 500 months for one person to write it if we take productivity figures of 2000 lines of code per month per person (which is quite reasonable). This means about 42 years. Now if we want to do this in 1 year, we will need 42 people to do it. Managing 42 people on an agile project is impossible. At the most any agile methodology permits 20 people. Many projects are even bigger than one million lines of code. Most government, banking, and large corporate software products consist of more than 10 million lines of code.

In these cases, agile methods will not work. You need to adapt some method that will permit parallel development where many teams can work on the project concurrently so that the product can be developed within 1–2 years instead of, say, 10 years.

The case study presented in this book is a good example of how to adapt to given situations and be successful. After all, offshoring provides several benefits and cannot be ignored. Documentation too is a very important aspect of software product development and should be adhered to. This case study provides a good insight as to how to address the challenges of communication management, documentation, and concurrent development even when the development methodology is to take the benefits of agile methods.

Students reading the book will have a chance to look at the inner workings of a real, successful project. All aspects of a regular software project are covered in the book. To make it more beneficial, the case study has been divided into several parts, and relevant parts are provided at the end of most of chapters. Therefore, after getting a good grasp of the concepts provided in a specific chapter, students can go through the case study and get a feel of the practical aspects of those concepts.

I hope this book will be useful for the intended readers. For any suggestions to improve the book in future editions, please write to me at ashfaque.a@gmail.com.

Author

 **Ashfaque Ahmed** has more than 22 years of experience in the software industry. He has a BSc in engineering and an MBA in information systems. He has worn many hats during his career, including that of a project manager, test manager, system analyst, and business analyst. He has managed projects of sizes varying from a few thousand dollars worth to projects worth millions of dollars. Some of the larger projects ran for a span of more than two years. He has also worked on software product development projects that typically run for decades and that keep adding new features and modifying existing product features almost endlessly.

Ahmed is a popular author. He has recently authored a book titled *Software Testing as a Service*, which was published by CRC Press, Boca Raton, FL, in September 2009. He has written more than 15 research papers for Technology Evaluation Centers and Tech Target. He is also a contributing author at Technology Evaluation Centers (www.technologyevaluation.com) and an expert at Tech Target Application Development Media Group (http://www.techtarget.com/).

PROJECT MANAGEMENT FUNDAMENTALS

Chapter 1

Introduction to Software Project Management

In Part I, we will learn

- What is software project management?
- What are various components of a software project?
- What are various processes of a software project?
- How are effort estimate, project plan, risk plan, etc., made?
- How are projects monitored and controlled?
- What is the impact of software development model on software project management?

In this chapter, we will learn

- What is a project?
- What is a software project?
- What processes are involved in a software project?
- How are people, processes, tools, and technology integrated in a project?
- What are the characteristics of a good project manager?
- What are the subprocesses in the area of project management processes?
- What management metrics are measured in software projects?

1.1 Introduction

As per data from Gartner and other research agencies, about 25% of world gross product is spent on various kinds of projects. More than $10 trillion were spent on projects out of world gross product output of $40.7 trillion in 2008. Most of the expenditures in information technology (IT) and software are considered as expenses in IT and software projects. More than $2.7 trillion were spent in 2008 on IT and software projects. That means out of all expenditures in all kinds of projects, IT and software projects represent more than 25%.

In major economies of the world, millions of people are employed in the IT and software sector. In 2008, more than 4 million people were employed in this sector in the United States.

Indeed the IT and software sector is one of the biggest employers in major world economies. Moreover, more people are expected to be employed in this sector in the future as it is growing fast.

1.2 What Is Project Management?

Project management can be broadly defined as starting an activity to achieve some stated goals using limited resources, budget, and time. During the project, resources and budget are consumed in a limited span of time (Figure 1.1). After the project is finished, the unconsumed resources and budget should be released. Since each project is started for a customer, a fourth dimension in the project is also added. It is customer satisfaction. The customer must be satisfied with the goal achieved by the project. This goal could be the creation of any product or service.

So we can see that there are inputs to the project in terms of resources, budget, and allocated time duration, and the output of the project is the achieved goal. A project must be initiated. To execute the project in a systematic manner, it is better to have a project plan. During project execution, some risks may arise, which may end up jeopardizing the project plan and in fact the entire project. So we should have some controlling measures, which can be employed to tackle any risks arising in the project successfully to avoid the project getting jeopardized. By the time project execution ends, we must have a proper project closure so that we can end the project. In Figure 1.2, you can see these project processes.

1.3 What Is Software Project Management?

Before moving to software projects, let us first discuss IT projects. But even before discussing IT projects, let us understand IT and software and their differences. IT is a field where an IT system refers to a complete system comprising many parts like hardware systems, software systems, and any other components from some other fields. A complete IT system can be used for any purpose like running a business, doing research, use in robotics, use in automation systems, etc. For instance, a robot is

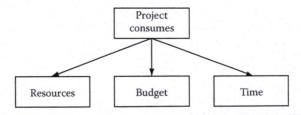

Figure 1.1 Any project consumes resources, time, and budget.

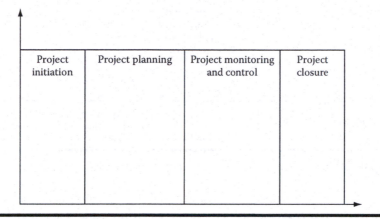

Figure 1.2 Project management processes.

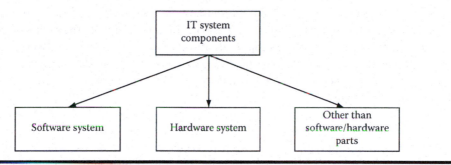

Figure 1.3 IT system components.

mostly a hardware device, but the information or instructions given to it to do some things are done using a software system. In other words, we can say that the brain of the robot is a software system and other parts of the robot like its limbs and sensing devices attached to it are hardware parts (Figure 1.3).

Generally, when we refer to IT, we mean the combination of software system and the computer hardware in which the software system will be running. For example, a business software application for doing transactions may be a complete IT system when the software system is installed in the computer hardware system and is ready to be used by end users.

Since software is being used in many new industries and we use more and more software systems in our daily lives, it is now becoming part of most things we see or interact with. Our vehicles now have computers. (Computers were not part of automobiles up until the 1970s, but after the 1980s, they slowly started appearing in many car models.) Our gadgets of daily use (music systems, air conditioners, washing machines, etc.) now have some sort of computer built into them. In manufacturing industries, industrial robots have been used since the 1950s. Now these robots are becoming sophisticated with more advanced software systems to control them. More recently, the ubiquitous mobile phone handsets have been the major beneficiaries of advancement in software system capabilities. In fact, more than 40% of all spending on IT budgets now goes to the telecom sector (mostly mobile and communication applications), which is a part of the IT industry (Figure 1.4).

So an IT project could be for setting up an enterprise-wide software system (along with the hardware to run it) to get business intelligence capability, manage store operations, or manage warehouses, etc. Tasks involved in such a project could be building (developing) the software

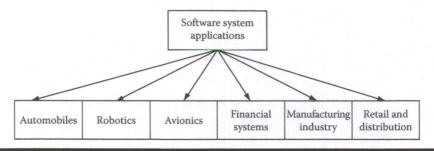

Figure 1.4 Application of software systems in many industries.

system, buying the computer hardware to run it, installing the software in the computer hardware, preparing the network of computers (if it is an enterprise-wide system), and finally configuring the software system so that it can run on the network of computers.

A software development project on the other hand is making software design based on customer requirements and implementing it into source code. This source code is then tested to make sure that it is defect free so that end users can use the software system without running into many problems. In software maintenance project, an already existing software product is modified to remove software defects, add new functionality, port the software product on some other operating system, etc. Software development and software maintenance projects together are referred to as software projects (Figure 1.5).

Software projects demand not only general project management skills but also good software engineering skills [1]. A goal of any software project management is to develop/maintain a software product by applying good project management principles as well as software engineering principles so that the software project is delivered at minimum cost, within minimum time, and with good product quality. Good project management principles will ensure good productivity. Good productivity in turn will ensure that the project is delivered in minimum time at minimum cost. Good software engineering principles will ensure good product quality. Even though how software engineering principles are formulated may not be in the domain of software project management, adopting those principles in their projects definitely comes under the purview of the job of a software project manager. For instance, a project manager responsible for managing a civil construction project must have knowledge and experience in civil engineering. An electrical engineer managing a civil project will not be a suitable fit. Similarly, a project manager responsible for managing a software project must have knowledge and experience in software engineering.

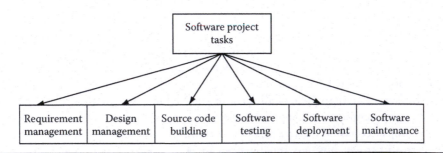

Figure 1.5 Tasks in software projects.

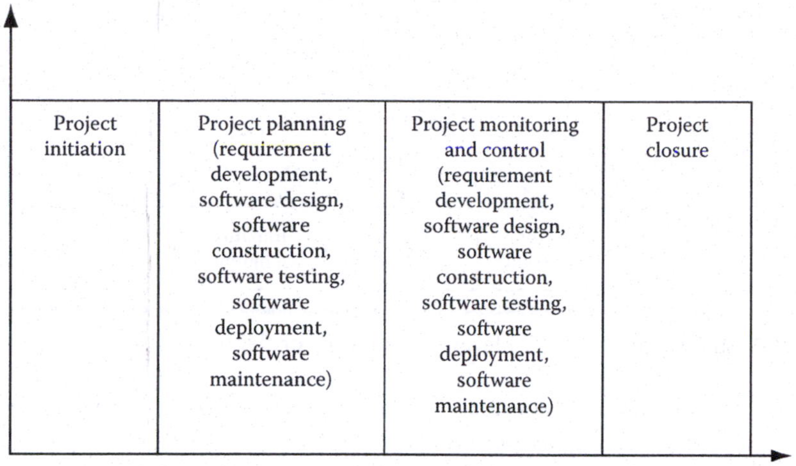

Project initiation	Project planning (requirement development, software design, software construction, software testing, software deployment, software maintenance)	Project monitoring and control (requirement development, software design, software construction, software testing, software deployment, software maintenance)	Project closure

Figure 1.6   Software project management processes with software engineering processes.

Project management processes may include project initiation, project planning, project monitoring and control, and finally project closure. The software engineering processes may include requirement development, software design, software construction, software testing, and software maintenance. These software engineering processes have to be somehow accommodated in project management processes (see Figure 1.6).

In a nutshell, software project management can be defined as applying project management and software engineering methods to develop/maintain a software product so that the goal of developing/maintaining a software product can be achieved using minimum possible resources and money and within the minimum time possible.

1.4 Importance of Software Projects

Importance of software project management can never be emphasized more when we observe that it is the single most influencing factor that is touching our lives in many ways day by day. The pace of software products used in many walks of life is increasing every day. This necessitates the development of software products in new areas, which would not have been imagined 10 years back. That is why the number of software projects and volume of work performed in these projects are increasing tremendously. On average, money spent on IT and software projects has been increasing on the order of 10% or more annually for the last 30 years worldwide. This increasing pace of spending on IT will continue in the foreseeable future. Clearly, the software and IT industry is the most significant change agent that is shaping our lives. In this context, people who are building and managing software and IT systems are playing an increasingly important role in our society.

1.5 Problems in Project Management

In the previous section, we discussed the importance of software projects and the important role played by the people who are managing these projects. But these people are also facing unique problems. Unlike other industries where engineering practices are well established due to the vast

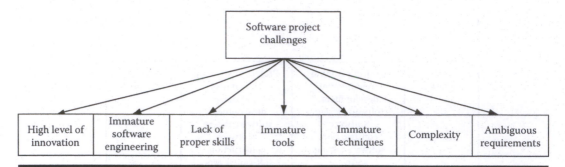

Figure 1.7   Typical challenges encountered in software projects.

amount of research and development done for hundreds of years, the software industry is relatively new. Software engineering has been in existence only for last 60 years or so, starting from the 1950s. Lack of sound engineering practices makes software project management a difficult proposition. Requirements and software design specifications in the software industry are still immature. Tools, technologies, and models for software projects are still evolving. Education and training required to work on software projects are also still evolving, resulting in people working on software projects with less than desired skills. A person responsible for managing a software project thus truly feels inadequate due to less than perfect circumstances under which he is supposed to perform (Figure 1.7).

Project management for any kind of project is a complicated matter. When the project size is big and the nature of the project is complex, managing the project becomes a daunting task. Project managers have to comply with government regulations, meet deadlines; deal with suppliers, staff, and customers, report to higher authorities, and tackle issues and myriad tasks planned or unplanned on a regular basis.

When it comes to big software development projects, some more complexities get added. In the software industry, finding and retaining skilful and experienced resources is a big challenge. Software projects are often outsourced. Software projects often involve teams located at many sites. These sites may be scattered over geographically far flung locations. There may be large time differences due to different time zones of these sites. People working on these projects are from different cultures. They may have different work ethics, may have different productivity levels, and may speak different languages.

Another highly important factor that makes software development/maintenance projects ever so different from other kinds of projects is the level of innovation and creativity required to deliver [2]. Software professionals are not only required to deliver as per specifications given to them but they need to use their intuition and capability to think out of the box to deliver software design or software prototype or software code. So software building is not only a science but also an art.

Due to these factors, communication, effort estimation, work distribution, reporting, work tracking, team management, etc., get affected (Figure 1.8).

How can a software project manager handle his project successfully, given the difficulties mentioned earlier? It may seem like a superhuman effort to manage modern day large software development projects. Yet, a large number of software development projects are being executed successfully even though these challenges always pose huge threats for these projects.

How do successful project managers manage their projects? What tools help them in their job? What kind of preparation do they do for the project? What kind of processes do they adopt?

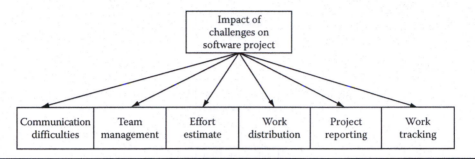

Figure 1.8   Impact of challenges on software projects.

What kind of experience is required to be a successful project manager? What makes them a successful software project manager?

Any software development project has one goal: To develop a software application or product. A given software application or product could be for internal use or sold to customers. When software is developed for use by the organization itself, it is known as a software application. When software is developed for the purpose of selling to customers and not for use by the organization itself then it is known as a software product. The organizations who develop such software products are known as software vendors. Now a business can decide to outsource development of the software product or application instead of developing it in-house for many reasons. The software vendor can outsource part or full software development activity to some software service provider. This way, the outsourcing and supplier management angle gets added to project management.

Whatever the situation is, the development team that builds the software application or product needs to focus on developing the application or product and not on any peripheral activities. But modern day software applications and products are large and complex. Building them involves a lot of things, and in the process, the team may easily lose its main purpose, that is, to develop the software application or product. One way to avoid this kind of drifting away from the focus is to have a defined project process and use this process map to chalk out a project plan as to which tasks will be done at what time, in what sequence, who will be responsible for these tasks, etc. This kind of planning based on a process structure is extremely useful for large and complex projects.

1.6 Processes in Software Projects

What is process? Process is a defined way of doing things. Any task we want to do in our daily life needs to be done by taking a series of action steps that results in completion of the requested task. That means a process to do a task can be broken down into certain series of steps. For instance, if you want to withdraw money from your bank account using an automatic teller machine (ATM), you need to first find a nearby ATM machine, then you need to insert your debit card in the slot in the machine, enter your password, specify the amount you want to withdraw, take the money, and finally remove your card from the machine.

In Figure 1.9, you can see all the steps involved in the process of withdrawing money from an ATM.

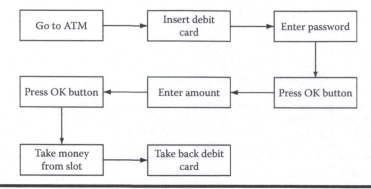

Figure 1.9 Process of withdrawing money from ATM and the process steps involved.

Coming to software projects, there are many processes going on in any software development project [3]. We can classify these processes under the following categories based on their priorities:

1. *Evolving processes beyond a project*: As can be seen from evolving software engineering practices, software projects are no longer seen in isolation. Software engineering is striving to make sure that software projects should be completely predictive and measurable. Based on project size and productivity, a project manager should be able to calculate project cost and schedule for a software project easily. At the same time, software engineering also allows for continuous improvement in project and organizational processes to improve quality and productivity. So a continuous improvement process also runs above projects at the organizational level. These processes are discussed in Part III.

2. *Project management processes (project initiation, planning, control, monitoring, and closure)*: These are the processes that get influenced by top-level processes and govern lower-level processes related to software development. Project management processes are the ones that help the management to see what is going on in the project and also allow them to control the project. So these are management processes. These processes also include the processes for project risk management, effort, cost estimation, etc.

3. *Software development life-cycle (SDLC) processes (requirements, design, build, testing, maintenance, etc.)*: These are the development processes that actually build the application (Figure 1.10). These processes are discussed in Part II.

1.7 Project Processes, People, and Technology

Organization level processes are the top-level processes that influence working of a project from outside while subprocesses in an SDLC process are the lowest-ranked processes. The other processes come in between these processes. The way these processes are set up and implemented impacts the way a software development project is handled [4].

Apart from these processes, there is a direct impact on the project by the customer, whether external or internal. That is why customer expectation management is a complete subject in itself as the customer has the most important influence on any project. Style of functioning of the project manager also influences the way the project is executed. Then of course, it is a matter as to how to deal with the project team members. Software developers are highly skilled people and they need to be provided with the best environment to get maximum output from them. Then comes the case of

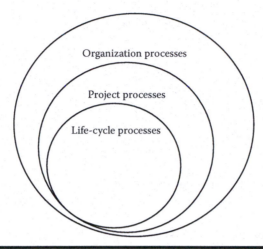

Figure 1.10 Processes involved in software development projects and their boundaries.

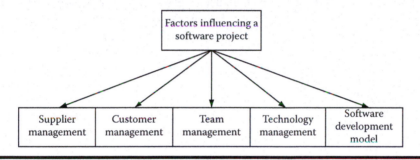

Figure 1.11 Influencing factors in software projects.

suppliers (service providers) who are increasingly deployed to get leverage in terms of getting skilled manpower and expertise. Project managers need to get maximum value from every buck they have to spend on these suppliers. So supplier management is an essential ingredient in projects where the entire project or part of it is outsourced to software service providers (Figure 1.11).

Software projects are also greatly influenced by technology. What technology best suits a project depends on a large number of factors including productivity, capability, reliability, technology availability, technology maturity, technology skills, etc. Managing the technology in software projects thus also becomes important. Each technology has its own limitations apart from the benefits it offers. So choosing the right technology for the job in hand is a very important consideration for any project manager. Technology selection will be based on considering the best fit in the perspective of job requirement, skill availability in the project team, and productivity.

1.8 Successful Software Project Manager

A successful software project manager [5] should be able to understand not only how a project should be planned and executed but also the processes beyond the project itself. He should learn the environment in which he should be planning and executing the projects. No doubt, software projects are extremely challenging; nevertheless a good framework to plan and execute

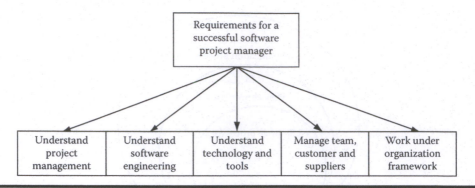

Figure 1.12   Requirements to be a successful software project manager.

a project definitely helps. Human beings can think and can be creative; but they also make mistakes unlike robots or machines. But unlike robots and machines, human beings can do creative things. Software project tasks require a lot of creativity and that is why they are very human-intensive activities. At the same time, compliance to good framework ensures that these human mistakes are avoided or at least minimized. Frameworks also ensure that there is a good way of working on assigned tasks and outputs are measurable (Figure 1.12).

Software project managers should understand these practical aspects and should plan and execute their projects accordingly to be successful.

More detailed information about the role of a software project manager, project management skills, etc., are discussed further in Chapter 18.

1.9 Project Management Processes

Project management processes form the basis on which a project can be initiated, planned, monitored, controlled, and closed. On the other hand, software engineering processes define structure, steps, and procedures to do various tasks in software development. But these processes lack the ability to schedule, plan, and control themselves. It is the project management processes that do the job of scheduling, planning, and controlling software engineering processes.

1.9.1 Software Project Initiation

As we have seen in an earlier discussion, there are three kinds of processes running in an organization that develop software products or applications, namely, software life-cycle processes, project management processes, and organization level processes. Next, we will learn project management processes. The first among project management processes is the project initiation process.

We can further divide the initiation process discussion into processes for application initiation, product initiation, and product implementation initiation.

1.9.1.1 Software Application Development Project Initiation

A software development project not only involves huge costs but also much resources and time even if the software project or a part of it is outsourced. Large software projects have great impact

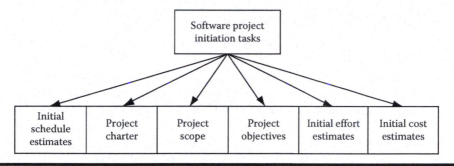

Figure 1.13   Software project initiation tasks.

on the company that will be using the software product, which is either developed in-house or outsourced. So a large software development project carries many high risks. It becomes one of the most important points on the agenda of the top executives.

All these things imply that large enterprise level software application development projects are very important. They carry this tag and everybody can see it and feel it.

This also means that the project must have a give-away sanction from top management. If this sanction is not there and if the top management is not able to back the project fully, the project cannot move ahead. Even before its start, the project dies.

Now if the top management is excited and gives approval for the project and a project team is being formed, then the project may start (Figure 1.13).

During the initiation phase of a software application development project, the project charter, project scope, project objectives, and initial risk planning and effort estimate are prepared.

1.9.1.2 Software Product Characteristics

Before we move on to project initiation for building software products, we should know that they are very different from software applications. Throughout this book, terms like software application, software products, and software systems have been used interchangeably. If any of these terms are used anywhere, please note that the subject matter discussed there applies to all of these three things equally. Software applications are specifically built based on a limited set of user requirements. So they have limited features to fulfill the specific needs of end users.

Software products on the other hand are built with a large number of features to take care of the needs of different kinds of users. Mature software products built over several years contain many varied features so that end users with varying needs can use these features. Software vendors also keep building new features, and over the years, the enterprise resource planning (ERP) and big commercial off the shelf (COTS) systems become massive in size (ERP and COTS systems are examples of large software products).

These COTS systems are also very robust. They can be run on all supported platforms without any problem. Robustness is a special feature built into software products.

They are also reliable. They are thoroughly tested before they are introduced on the market. Software vendors test thoroughly to make sure that their product does not have many bugs because if the released product has many bugs, it will fail on the market and also will create a bad reputation for the vendor. So they make sure that their products are defect free.

Most of these COTS systems have open interfaces so that they can be integrated easily with other systems.

1.9.1.3 Software Product Development Project Initiation

With increasing popularity of COTS systems [6], a large number of software vendors are developing their software products. Some software vendors are developing large enterprise level software products like ERP, supply chain management (SCM), customer relationship management (CRM), and many other large software products. Recently, some other kinds of software products have also become popular. These are known as software as a service (SaaS). Most of these applications are smaller in size and they are not general-purpose applications. Instead they provide very specific functionality, which can be used by any other software product or application to complement some aspects of their own features. For example, an online flight reservation application provided by one service provider can have links where they can get information about fares offered by different airline companies. This online reservation system will be a hosted application with a Web site interface. Users of this application can use the Internet to access the Web site and use this application to book their air tickets online. The fares of these airline companies keep changing. To provide end users with currently offered airfares, these fares must be shown in real time to end users. Some service providers get this information from airline companies and provide this information to the online airline reservation Web sites through the link provided in the reservation application. The real-time information provided by these service providers is through an SaaS application. This application cannot be used directly by any end user. But in conjunction with some other application, they provide a useful service.

SaaS applications [7] can be used by end users on a subscription basis. If the application is big and involves creating and maintaining databases, the service provider creates these databases for its customers. Examples of large scale SaaS applications include Salesforce.com (a CRM application), OneNetwork.com (a retail management application), etc. These are large service providers that provide their own application to customers using the SaaS model. Some other smaller SaaS service providers provide services like market research, customer support, and many other specialized services (Figure 1.14).

How are these software products made? After all, development of these software products does not start with end-user requirements. The software vendor sees a market opportunity of developing such a product. He develops the software product and sells it or provides services using this software product to customers. So basically, software product development starts when a software vendor sees a market opportunity and then decides to develop this product. He uses market research data to decide which features will go into the product. Accordingly, he forms a project team and hands this information to them so that they can develop the software product.

So whereas a software application is created based on end-user requirements, a software product is made using market research data.

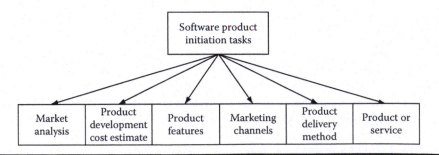

Figure 1.14 Software product development initiation tasks.

During the initiation phase of any software product development project, the project scope, risk planning, and effort estimate are made. But unlike a project that develops custom software, effort and time estimates are also done beforehand. In fact, time to market for such a product is a crucial factor, and thus, instead of time estimate calculation, team size calculation for boxing the project under a tight time schedule is done. As per product development roadmap, a product release plan is also developed.

1.9.1.4 Software Product Implementation Project Initiation

Small COTS applications do not need implementation. Mostly, they are installed from a CD or downloaded from the Internet and installed. But bigger COTS applications like ERPs, SCM systems, CRM systems, etc., require much effort to implement either at a customer site or at a hosted site [8]. They are huge consisting of large modules. Their database layer is totally detached from the application layer. In fact, the entire software product may consist of many layers.

Implementation of these huge packages is a different ball game altogether. If the product is implemented without customization, then the project involves system installation, configuring the application as per user requirements, database creation, data population, data migration from legacy system, etc. It also involves integration between different modules of the application. This kind of implementation is also known as plain vanilla implementation or bespoke implementation. This kind of implementation is done fast and can be completed in 1–3 months depending on the size of individual tasks.

But most often, the application is implemented with some customization. Nowadays, an application contains most of the business logic, which needs to be correctly configured. Customization takes place more in reports. The application also needs to be integrated with other enterprise systems. A typical large-scale ERP system implementation takes somewhere around 1–3 years. But this implementation time is shrinking due to increase in productivity of project teams as well as advancement in technology.

During the initiation phase of any software product implementation project, the project charter, project scope, project objectives, and initial risk planning and effort estimate are prepared (Figure 1.15).

1.9.2 Software Project Planning

Depending on the characteristics of a project, detailed project planning is done either after project initiation or after completion of project requirements. Generally, detailed project planning can be done only after the project team has complete requirements for the project since the requirements together with project scope determine effort, cost, and quality required. If complete details about these things are not available, a baseline for the project cannot be made. In project planning the main tasks that are to be planned are software life-cycle processes (refer to Part II for details about these software life-cycle processes), which actually build the software product.

Any project faces external and internal risks. Software projects face risks related to people, technology, process, and other areas. Due to these risks, the project schedule, cost, or quality may get affected. Recognizing these risks and making proper plans to mitigate negative impact on the project are taken care of by making a risk planning and executing them when they arise.

Depending on the software life cycle chosen, the project plan may vary. In the linear waterfall model, the software engineering processes are executed linearly, and thus, in a software project, each of the software engineering processes occurs just once. But in the case of an iterative life-cycle

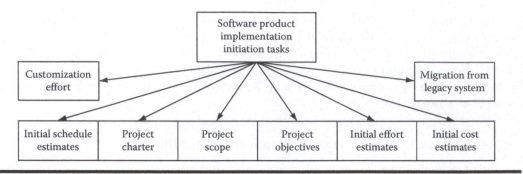

Figure 1.15 Software product implementation initiation tasks.

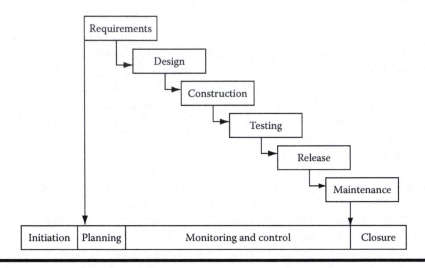

Figure 1.16 Project management in waterfall model environment.

model, the individual software engineering processes can occur more than once. In some iterative models, the iteration occurs between construction and testing. So these two processes can occur as many times within the project as the number of iterations. At the extreme end of iterative software development model, iteration can happen for all of the software engineering processes. So all software engineering processes will occur as many times within the project as the number of iterations. These variations are depicted in Figures 1.16 and 1.17.

1.9.2.1 Components of Project Planning

Software projects need many inputs for making project plans. They also produce numerous outputs in the form of separate plans for risks, communication, configuration and version control, schedules, resource requirement and allocation, etc. All of these project planning components in fact are complete plans themselves. A separate chapter has been devoted for each of the planning activities of risk management, effort and cost estimation, and configuration and version control management in this book.

You will learn about software project planning in detail in Chapter 6.

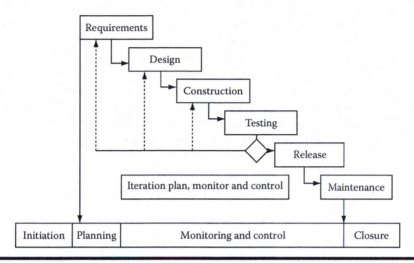

Figure 1.17   Project management in iterative model environment.

1.9.3 Software Project Monitoring and Control

There have been many methodologies for planning, monitoring, and controlling software projects like waterfall, agile, iterative, and many other models (refer to Part III for details about these models). Software development and maintenance is still an evolving discipline, and so the way a software project is handled differs from one project to another. Software technologies also keep evolving. So it is difficult to plan, let alone monitor or control, a software project.

Due to the inherently risky nature of software projects, constant monitoring and control is required to rectify any event that may jeopardize the project.

To monitor and control effectively, the project manager needs measurement data. The measurement data come from measuring processes and product. So first project processes should be planned such that their measurement can be taken, and secondly, it should be ensured that proper measurements are taken. Only then effective project monitoring and control is possible.

You will learn about software project monitoring and control in detail in Chapter 7.

1.9.4 Software Project Closure

With the increasing use of statistical process control, project closure has become an important activity in projects. During project closure, all project artifacts are analyzed and completed. Data from these artifacts are transferred to central project repository so that these data can be used for future projects. It has to be ensured that all project data are normalized so that the data are useful.

You will learn about software project closure in detail in Chapter 8.

1.10 Configuration and Version Control Management

The most prominent aspect about software projects is the change in requirements during almost the whole product development life cycle. Due to changing requirements, work done in software development life-cycle processes also needs to be changed accordingly. This leads to many versions of work products in all phases of the development life cycle. Managing all these work products is done using configuration and version control.

A project manager will be well equipped and prepared if he acknowledges the fact that requirements will keep changing. Once this need is established, the action plan for tackling it can be established. The foremost need is to manage changes in requirements as and when they arrive. Once this process is well established, the tasks affected due to these changes can be identified. Once these tasks are identified, then a proper replan will have to be made.

The best solution for managing various requirement versions is to have a central repository where all versions of requirements can be stored. All the team members working on the project must have access to the requirements, irrespective of their scattered geographical locations. The version control rights can be set as per requirements. People who have rights to change the requirement documents can make changes in documents and check in the documents back to the repository. Other team members may have only viewing rights.

In organizations that are developing products, there could be many projects going on at the same time. In those cases, it is the best policy to have many branches of the main requirement folder. Each project team will have access to its respective requirement branch. Each team will be responsible for managing its own branch.

You will learn about software configuration management in detail in Chapter 5.

1.11 Management Metrics

A business unit must keep improving its business processes over time; otherwise, it will become extinct by the forces of fierce market competition. Improvement in business processes is important because only through these improvements, a business unit can improve productivity of its processes and improve quality of its products or services. If it is not done, the business unit will become uncompetitive in comparison to its competitors and thus will face the danger of becoming extinct. Better productivity provides means to cut costs and time, and better product quality provides a chance to increase business as customer appreciation is the best marketing tool.

Process improvement can only happen if you can measure it, compare it with best practices, and then bring about changes in your processes. In the case of software development projects, the management metrics are the productivity data for the projects [9]. The software work product quality data are the technical metrics [10]. Throughout this book, both management and technical metrics are discussed in detail at each level where it is possible to collect and analyze them and can be used for making management and technical decisions (Figure 1.18).

Measurement of project processes during execution at regular intervals makes sure that the product quality is always under control. These measurements also enable the organization to improve its processes by assessing effectiveness of processes and making certain modifications in these processes. When selecting any of the measurements for a project, the essential point should be that they should be relevant to the project. It is also of utmost importance that the selected measurements should have certain inherent characteristics so that they are meaningful to the project. Again these measurements should be practical, should be calibratable, and should be done at a minute level and not at a gross level. Gross level measurements fail to point to the root causes of problems.

Over the years, several metrics have been defined and used in projects. Many of these approaches use statistical process control (SPC) methods.

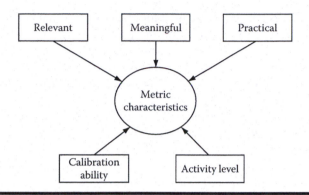

Figure 1.18 Quality characteristics required of software project metrics.

One SPC approach is popularly known as the Seven Tools of Quality [11]. Essentially, it is made of seven distinct techniques developed by different organizations and individuals. These quality tools are either used in isolation to each other or used in conjunction with other tools. These are as follows:

1. *Check sheets*: Check sheets are used to count the number of occurrences of issues over the entire project or during specific phases of the project. If the same problem resurfaces during a project or within a phase of the project many times, it is an indication of bad project management. Check sheets are a good measure to know whether project execution is smooth or it has many issues. Check sheets are also useful during recording of lessons learned from the project.

2. *Histograms*: Histograms basically depict variance of outputs on either side of a central tendency for a process output. Histograms are great tools for knowing whether any project attribute or characteristic is falling within acceptable norms or it is deviating from standard acceptable norms.

3. *Pareto charts*: Pareto charts are used to identify problematic areas in the software development process. If analysis is done for the occurrence of problems encountered in a project, it will be found that 80% of the problems are encountered in only 20% of the project area. That means 80% of the project area contains only 20% of problems. If we concentrate our efforts on the problems in the 20% of the project area, we will solve 80% of the problems. This strategy is far better compared to putting effort on the entire project. This is what Pareto charts are all about. Pareto charts are one of the most popular metrics in the software industry to measure process as well as product characteristics to find out problematic areas and subsequently to fix them.

4. *Cause and effect diagrams*: These diagrams are also known as fish bone diagrams because they look like fish bones. They are also known as Ishikawa diagrams after the name of the inventor Kaoru Ishikawa. These diagrams are used to find the root causes of a problem in processes which results in a single identifiable problem and then list these causes in the diagram against the identified problem. All the root causes are arranged and depicted in the diagram based on the level of their impact on the problem area. This results in a hierarchy of causes. From this kind of diagram, it is easy to compare different causes of problems and finally find the right solution, which will help in tackling the root problems and the corresponding causes effectively.

5. *Scatter diagrams*: These diagrams are used for identifying correlation and suggesting causation. Scatter diagrams are as well used for finding root causes of problems in projects. Thus, they are similar to cause and effect diagrams. Each effect (end result or problem caused by a root cause) can be plotted against the root causes, and their relation over a series of inter-related data can be found out. This will help in eliminating those root causes of problems from the project.

6. *Control charts*: These charts are used to identify processes that are out of control so that they can be fixed. For example, a temperature measurement device (for any temperature-sensitive process) is attached to a device that records temperature on a control chart. If the temperature goes either above or below the acceptable limits, it can be easily traced using the control chart. Similarly, a control chart can be used to measure defect density in different phases of a software project, and if the defect density is observed to be going higher than acceptable limits, corrective action can be immediately taken so that defect density can be brought under control. Control charts are very popular in many industries.

7. *Graphs*: Graphs are used to depict information about processes in a suitable manner. Basically, graphs do not provide decision-making software metrics. However, they help in conveying the bigger picture about the project.

1.12 Case Study

This case study is taken from the projects done by a software vendor who is building a state-of-the art software product, which is used as a SaaS by its customers. We will cover the project consisting of four iterations for the release of its 6.0 version. Project management–related processes are covered in Part I. These project management processes include project initiation, project planning, project execution, project monitoring, project control, project closure, risk management, effort estimate, and cost estimate.

Elaborate project initiation is done only for the project for the release 6.0. At the four iterations contained in this project, project initiation is minimally done at the iteration level. The minor releases of 5.3, 5.5, and 5.8 coincide with iteration 1, iteration 2, and iteration 3. Iteration 4 and major release 6.0 coincide with each other. (Minor releases of 5.4, 5.6, 5.7, and 5.9 are merged with other releases.) Project planning, project execution, project monitoring, project control, project closure, risk management, effort estimate, and cost estimate are done at the iteration level. Aggregated project cost and project effort are done at the project level.

1.12.1 Project Introduction

The SaaS software vendor has some of the largest grocery retailers in the United States and European countries as their customers, who have used the services of the SaaS software product for quite some time. A market need was felt to have a functionality that could enable third-party logistics service providers (3PL) to get instant information about the need to have trucks for transportation of goods by its customers (manufacturers/distributors). This information should be in advance so that the 3PL can plan for sending the required trucks to the desired locations at a specified time. The customers at the same time can plan for picking and packing of required goods at the requested warehouse and make the load ready so that the goods can be picked by trucks at the required time. The retailer (who will receive the goods) on the other hand can make preparation at its desired warehouse (from advance information about the incoming truck) so that these goods can be received without any delay.

In fact, to enable such functionality, a mechanism known as appointment scheduling is employed. The complete details about this functionality are given in next section.

1.12.2 Software Functionality

A retailer has many retail outlets. Goods are sold at these outlets. The retail outlets keep a small stock on the shelves and some more in store rooms located in the same retail outlet premises. When the stock of a particular item becomes low in quantity, the outlet orders a fixed quantity of the items from its own warehouse for replenishment. The replenishment order is received at the nearest warehouse. The warehouse collects the required quantity of the item from the warehouse and waits for a truck to arrive and dock. Then the warehouse staff loads the goods in the truck. The truck then moves and reaches the retail outlet. The outlet staff unloads the goods from the truck and fill their shelves and store rooms. The movement of truck from retailer's warehouse to retail outlet is known as outbound logistics (Figure 1.19).

The retailer's warehouse orders goods from manufacturers/distributors when the stock of particular goods in the warehouse becomes low. When a warehouse belonging to the manufacturer/distributor receives order for goods, it collects the goods from its warehouse and waits for a truck to arrive and dock at its dock doors. Once a truck docks, the manufacturer/distributor staff loads the goods in the truck. The truck moves and reaches the retailer's warehouse. The warehouse staff unloads the goods and stores it in their warehouse. The movement of truck from manufacturer's/distributor's warehouse to retailer's warehouse is known as inbound logistics.

For inbound logistics, the trucks usually belong to 3PLs. 3PLs charge the retailer or manufacturer on the basis of distance the truck travels, its capacity, and fuel cost. Generally, they charge on a full truck basis regardless of whether the truck is fully loaded or not. For this reason, the warehouse that loads the truck makes sure that it has enough orders for goods from the retailer warehouse to make the truck full.

In the software product up to release 5, functionality was provided for calculating transportation cost, basic appointment functionality at warehouse for loading of truck, and appointment at the other warehouse for unloading of truck. Functionality for what goods are loaded in the truck is also provided.

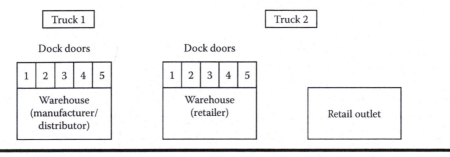

Figure 1.19 **Retail outlet, warehouses, and movement of trucks.**

1.12.3 New Functionality in Release 6.0

The most important feature that is added in release 6.0 is a very sophisticated appointment scheduling of trucks at both receiving and shipping warehouses. In a fast-paced work environment, waiting for trucks for loading and unloading is a waste of time. It was felt that on an average, the trucks were waiting for 5 h at each warehouse. This situation was a cost-effective proposition for all the parties including the manufacturer/distributor, 3PL service provider, and the retailer. A mechanism was needed that would ensure that this waiting time can be reduced drastically. It was when a decision was taken to have a very sophisticated appointment scheduling functionality in the software product.

Appointment scheduling is a complex concept. There are many factors to be considered to realize this functionality. When a truck arrives at a warehouse for unloading, a quality control check is performed for the received goods at the dock door. Quality control inspectors must be present at the dock doors at the time of receiving. To unload the goods, labor should be available at the dock doors. All dock doors at a warehouse are not the same. Some of them can receive a particular type of goods while some other dock doors can receive some other types of goods. Similarly, all dock doors cannot dock all kinds of trucks. Some dock doors can dock only a particular type of truck while some other dock doors can dock some other types of trucks. The same considerations need to be made at the shipping warehouse.

When orders are received at the shipping warehouse, they need to get a truck from a 3PL service provider fast. They also need to pack goods in the warehouse as per the orders received. When the truck arrives, the warehouse staff must inform it as to which door it has to dock at. On the other hand, if just by processing orders, all these details become available at the warehouse automatically, the warehouse staff just has to execute as per available details. They will pack goods and then place the goods at the dock door from where it has to be loaded in the truck. The 3PL service provider already has been informed in advance by the software system as to when a truck is required at the designated dock door at the particular warehouse. Once the goods are loaded, the truck leaves for the retailer warehouse. The retailer warehouse already has information as to when and where the truck will arrive. So at the designated time, everything is ready at the retailer warehouse. So theoretically, we can see that there is no loss of time anywhere right from truck arrangement for loading to unloading of truck. However, in reality, there could be instances when a suitable dock door is not available for loading or unloading, due to various reasons. These reasons could be an already busy dock door, a dock door closed for out of operation hours, the unavailability of quality control inspectors or labor, etc. But all of these are valid reasons for delays. Overall, this functionality will help in cutting unnecessary delays.

We will discuss details about this project in most of the chapters throughout this book.

1.13 Chapter Summary

Work on projects constitutes a major proportion of world GDP (close to 25%). Software and IT projects are in turn are important activities, which constitute close to 25% of all project works. Software project management is all about managing diverse activities involved in typical software project. A software project manager needs to manage project team, suppliers, customers, and project tasks on a daily basis. To manage these activities in a controlled and consistent manner, he needs to make a good project plan and then execute it effectively. He also needs to work in the environment provided by the organization. All his activities and the project itself will be influenced to a large extent by this environment. In modern software project management practices, role of this organization-wide environment is increasing day by day. This factor is significantly influencing software project management.

Exercises

1.1 It is said that government spending on IT is increasing as government departments take initiatives to improve customer service or have a wider reach of services. Find out what factors are responsible for the increase of IT spending by government agencies. Also list and explain the three biggest IT projects undertaken by the federal government in recent times?

1.2 What you think are the major characteristics of a project?

Review Questions

1.1 How do you define the word, "project"? How are software projects different from other kinds of projects?

1.2 Why do software development projects fail?

1.3 What remedial measures can be taken so that software development projects do not fail?

1.4 What is software project management?

1.5 What are typical project management processes?

1.6 What are the essential qualities of a software project manager?

1.7 What are software project management metrics?

1.8 How are project management and software development processes related to each other?

Recommended Readings

1. F. F. Tsui, O. Karam (2006) *Essentials of Software Development*, Jones & Bartlett Publishers, Sudbury, MA.

2. M. Hamilton (1999) *Software Development: Building Reliable Systems*, Prentice Hall PTR, Upper Saddle River, NJ.

3. E. McGuire (1999) *Software Process Improvement: Concepts and Practices*, IGI Global, Hershey, PA.

4. A. Bahrami (2008) *Object Oriented Systems Development*, McGraw-Hill Education (India) Pvt Ltd., New Delhi, India.

5. D. Philips (2004) *The Software Project Manager's Handbook: Principles That Work at Work (Practitioners)*, Wiley-IEEE Computer Society Press, New York.

6. R. Kazman (2008) *COTS Based Software Systems: Third International Conference, ICCBSS 2004*, Redondo Beach, CA.

7. K.-J. Lin (2007) *Service-Oriented Computing—ICSOC 2007: Fifth International Conference*, Vienna, Austria.

8. C. B. Tayntor (2005) *Successful Packaged Software Implementation*, CRC Press, Boca Raton, FL.

9. D. D. Galorath, M. W. Evans (2006) *Software Sizing, Estimation, and Risk Management*, CRC Press, Boca Raton, FL.

10. A. Kossiakoff, W. N. Sweet (2002) *Systems Engineering Principles and Practice*, Wiley-Interscience, New York.

11. S. H. Kan (2002) *Metrics and Models in Software Quality Engineering*, 2nd edn., Addison-Wesley Professional, Boston, MA.

Chapter 2

Project Initiation Management

In the previous chapter, we learned

- What is a project?
- What is a software project?
- What processes are involved in a software project?
- How are people, processes, tools and technology integrated in a project?
- What are the characteristics of a good project manager?
- What are the subprocesses in the project management processes area?
- What management metrics are measured on software projects?

In this chapter, we will learn

- How is a project initiated?
- What is a project charter?
- What is project scope?
- What are project objectives?
- What project activities are performed during project initiation?

2.1 Introduction

Software projects are notorious for initial hiccups and false starts. This usually has to do with an unclear project charter, an unclear project scope and unclear requirements. While many project stakeholders (mostly top management) realize that they are in need of a software system badly, they hardly know exactly what they are looking for. This situation leads to chaos. Even though a project team is formed at this stage, nobody is clear as what is to be done. This has led many projects to fail even before they started.

However, if the project manager is adept and experienced, then he can handle such a situation. He can chart out some plan of action and can do some hard bargaining to get things going. He can identify who exactly the stakeholders are and their needs. For this to happen, the project manager must have a good idea of the business situation and what causes are exactly plaguing the business. He also should strive hard to think about the software solution that can pave the way for the business to help the management to come out of the morass. Generally this is not the typical role of a project manager, but if this kind of situation is encountered, and if the project manager is experienced to deal with it, then definitely it can boost chances of the project going forward. He can then engage a project team for the task.

This is the scenario at most of the in-house software projects. In the case of outsourced projects, things are different. The project manager from the service provider's side may have participated in project negotiation along with the marketing team to bag the project. In such cases, the project charter and project scope are much better defined as compared to the previous situation, and thus, the project has much better chances of going forward.

During project initiation, the project manager has to do a lot of ground work where he will provide initial and rough effort estimation, identify risks and make risk mitigation strategies, define the project scope, prepare a project charter, etc., after consultation with the project stakeholders. Most of these initial artifacts, which are just sketches at this stage, are refined and developed further in later stages of the project whenever more understanding about the project is realized or when project objectives get changed.

2.2 Define Project Charter

Most projects start on a high note. Stakeholders have high hopes. Accordingly, lofty project charters are made. Unfortunately, as the project progresses, all the enthusiasm vanishes quickly. So what could be done to avoid such situations?

The project stakeholders need to set their expectations with grounded realities. All their hopes should be aligned with practical limitations and achievable goals. If this is not done right from the inception of the project, the project is going to falter all the way. The project charter [1] should include things like project goals, project objectives, major responsibilities allocation, etc. But a simple project charter may be a simple statement from the top management (Table 2.1).

The project charter is the place where a big picture of the effort, even beyond the project, is captured. For instance, say, the project is part of a product development effort in which the product is being developed incrementally. The product development consists of many small projects for which a small set of features are being developed and added into the product each time a project gets completed. The project charter will capture information for the entire effort to build the ultimate product through these small projects, and in fact, during all of these projects, the project charter may remain the same with not many changes. Similarly, the project charter should also

Table 2.1 Sample Project Charter

The project will provide a cutting edge software solution to our sales team to provide excellent customer service for our customers so that all customer issues can be solved within 24 hours of lodging of a complaint.

include the business goals for which the software project is being initiated, and also state that the software project will help in achieving those business goals.

2.3 Define Project Scope

After analyses of failed projects, it has been found that most of the projects fail because of an increase in the scope of the project over time. An increase in project scope [2] happens primarily due to two factors. One factor is that as the project progresses and features are being built in the application, the user community, after seeing the partially made application, may feel that some additional functionality is also needed to do their job using the newly built application. So they keep making change requests throughout the development cycle. This not only disrupts development activity, it also makes the application susceptible to defects. But the most important impact over the project is the increase in the volume of the project work [3], which results in the escalation of costs and an elongation of the schedule. The other factor that results in change in the project scope is a poor requirements definition. A poor understanding of requirements or a poor definition of requirements leads to changes required later on in the software design or software build to rectify this problem. In any case, the project scope increases due to these factors. Table 2.2 shows a simple project scope.

To deal with scope creep, it has to be ensured that the requirements are lucid and clear from the very start so that project effort estimation and project schedule are accurate. If any changes are to be made in requirements, then there should be a proper change request mechanism that will identify the impact of the change on the project and this should be communicated to the stakeholders. All these aspects should be clearly defined during the initiation stage itself.

There is one more aspect about project scope, apart from the volume of work, in terms of the number of features that has been discussed in the previous paragraphs. It is the fact that the software product to be produced needs to have a specific level of quality [4]. This level of quality needs to be frozen during the project initiation phase. Suppose you need to build a defense application for national surveillance for detecting attacks by an enemy. This kind of system requires confidential and limited access control, a sophisticated and bullet-proof information system, fast and accurate access to information, and extreme reliability. Definitely, such a software system needs to be of very high quality in terms of reliability, security, correctness, and efficiency. A high level of quality for such a software system translates into high effort required for building this application. In contrast, a game built for kids does not need to have such quality requirements, and thus, the effort required to build that game will be much less.

So, a combination of a number of features and the quality level determines the total volume of work. It is very important, early on in the project, to clearly lay out these aspects so that the volume of work can be determined.

Table 2.2 Sample Project Scope Definition

The project will be delivered within 15 months from the date of start of the project. The software product that will be made through this project will have features for customer complaint logging, issue resolution, and issue closure. The software product should have the capability of supporting our customer base of 10,000, who will be using the service through an Internet connection by logging into our web portal.

Table 2.3 Sample Project Objectives

The organization will be able to increase customer satisfaction to 99.5% from the existing level of 92%. This will help in reducing customer attrition, increasing repeat business from existing customers, and enhancing our brand value.

2.4 Define Project Objectives

The project should have a set of well-defined objectives [5] that must be met. If any of these objectives are not met upon completion of the project, then the project will be considered to be a failure. The stakeholders state and set the project objectives. The objectives should be stated in clear language and the set of objectives should be kept as small as possible. Examples of project objectives could be reducing/completely eliminating paper-based transactions in the organization after implementation of the proposed software application to reduce transaction processing time, centralization of marketing function across the organization to reduce costs, etc. (Table 2.3)

If clear project objectives are set at the project initiation, it would help the project team to understand the importance of the project and will help the team to do its best to achieve the goals.

2.5 Practical Considerations

One size does not fit all! You cannot have a cookie cutter to create a project plan from a simple template. Different kinds of projects need different approaches. If you have a Web project, then you have entirely different activities and tasks required to be completed for the project, compared to a project to make a software application for a mainframe computer. Similarly, the quality required for making a surveillance application for a defense project will be of higher quality, compared to an application made for viewing information on the Web.

Some of the factors that make project management vary for different projects are as follows:

- *Project size*: Project size is the single-most important factor that makes the approach to handling one project different from another. Smaller projects need less formal project management than the larger ones.
- *Product quality*: If the software product to be made requires stringent quality measures, then an elaborate quality control mechanism will be required throughout the project process to ensure that defects are prevented in the product at each stage of development. On the other hand, if the software product to be made does not need stringent quality norms, then a cursory quality control mechanism will be enough.
- *Technology*: Technology plays an important role in determining productivity on any project. If the platform is some older technology, like a client server, and the programming language is, say Ada, then the project effort will be considerably more than if a newer and more productive technology, say Java, is used.
- *Code reuse*: Code reuse can considerably reduce the required project effort. So, the effort on two projects will be very different if one project code reuse has been extensively used, compared to some other project where code reuse has not been used.

Due to these factors, each project has different needs for quality levels and has different productivity levels. Understanding these factors and taking them into account when project initiation takes place will give a proper start for the project.

Project initiation is the right time when project expectations, project scope, project deliverables, quality standards, cost estimates, etc., should be correctly set so that a good project plan can be made, which in turn can lead to smooth project execution.

2.6 Estimate Initial Project Size

At the project initiation stage, a rough project size [6] should be estimated so that a sketch of the initial project plan can be realized. From the initial requirements (as available in a Request for Information quote), a rough design estimate can be made. The rough design can include details about how the product can be broken down into parts. These parts can be sized from estimating, either the estimated number of lines of code required to build them or by using an estimated number of function points. After the size of each part or module is determined this way, the complete size of the software product can be determined. Since at the initiation stage detailed information about project parts is not clear, the estimate of the product size is also rough. However, this can be taken as a starting point, and the product size estimate can be refined as the project progresses.

Especially on outsourced projects, a rough product size estimate should be made during the initiation phase so that a general idea about the project can be made and passed on to the stakeholders. This information will be helpful for them to make crucial decisions about the project.

In Figure 2.1, the software product to be made is shown as consisting of six main features. These six features together constitute the entire software product to be made. To make the software product, the software project will involve tasks consisting of project and software development life-cycle-related tasks. Rough estimates about project and product size can thus be made on the preliminary data available.

A study of data available for previously executed projects can throw some light while estimating the size of the software product to be made. So, if data is available for a similar sized project, use it to show the customer how big the current project should be.

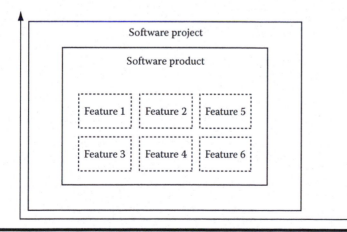

Figure 2.1   Initial software product and project size estimate.

2.7 Estimate Initial Project Effort and Costs

Initial project cost estimates [7] can be determined from the productivity of the members of the project team, the effort estimate, the number of hours put in by software professionals, and the prevailing hourly rate of software professionals who will be working on the project as project team members.

The cost of the project is one of the most important considerations of stakeholders. If the project is going to cost more than they had anticipated and budgeted for, then most probably, the project will be called off. In some cases, the stakeholders may agree to a reduction in the size of the project so as to reduce the cost of the project.

From Figures 2.1 through 2.3, we have some initial data available for a project. The initial stage data suggests that requirement specification development will take 2 months of time, and software design, software construction, software testing, and software deployment will take 2, 6, 2, and 2 months, respectively. That means, the total schedule for the project is 14 months. For requirement development, two people are required, and for software design, software construction, software testing, and software deployment two, six, four and two people are needed, respectively. That means,

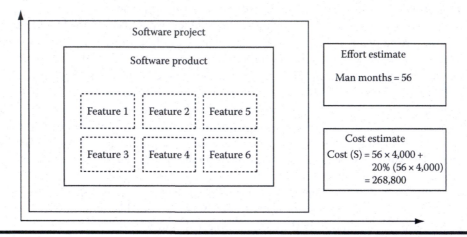

Figure 2.2   Initial software project effort and cost estimate.

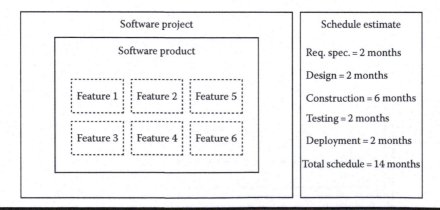

Figure 2.3   Initial software project schedule estimate.

the total effort required is 56 man months. On an average, the salary of each project team member is $4000 per month. Overhead costs for the project are taken as 15% of the cost of salaries of the project team members. So tentative development costs will be $268,800 for the project.

Data from previously executed projects can be used for estimating the cost for the current project. Customers will love to know just how much their project will cost them very early in the project, at the initiation stage itself.

2.8 Estimate Initial Project Schedule

Like project cost, the project schedule is one of the most critical aspects of the project. Stakeholders may have the objective of gaining a marketing edge over the competition by implementing the proposed software application. Many of such objectives are time sensitive, and the stakeholders may like to see the new system implemented before a specified date.

During project initiation discussions, stakeholders may ask the project manager to reduce the project schedule [8] that has been presented to them, even if project costs rise because of this. In such cases, the project manager may have to adjust his project schedule to suit the needs of the stakeholders. He will have to adjust his project plan, resource allocation, etc., accordingly.

2.9 Create Initial Project Plan

The project manager needs to create a tentative project plan [9] during the project initiation stage to demonstrate to the customer what kind of resource requirements, effort required, and timelines could be expected for the project. This will be one of the selling points for the project. The most important aspect of this tentative project plan is to let the customer feel confident about the project. If timelines, costs, or effort figures are not as per customer expectations, then discussions can be held with the customer to win on some points and negotiate on others.

Nowadays, the time window of opportunity for businesses is limited, and the customers look to utilizing this time window to the utmost. So, they need the fast development and implementation of the software system to utilize this time window. Hence, even if costs are on the high side, they will like to go in for faster software product development so that it is implemented quickly, and they can start using it to tap the business opportunity within the time window. For this reason, the project manager has to make a project plan that will enable software development at a faster speed and thus realize customer expectations. So, it may often happen that the project manager may need to revise his project plan and present a revised plan to the customer.

2.10 Project Initiation in Iterative Model

One of the goals of the iterative model is to reduce project size and to make a number of smaller projects instead of going in for a large project and building the entire software product in one go. Project size is reduced by dividing the set of complete requirements into many smaller sets and developing smaller software products out of these smaller sets of requirements, taking one set of requirements at a time. So the big software project becomes a set of smaller projects. These smaller projects are known as iterations. The first iteration starts from scratch as each building block for this iteration is developed from scratch. Once this iteration is over and approved by the customer, the next iteration begins. This time, the product is built over what was developed in the first iteration.

In the iterative model, planning the project is done at three levels. At the top level, the project plan for the development of the entire product is conceived. The time span for such a plan could run into several years. At the middle level, project planning is done at major releases of the software product. The time span for such plans could be at the year or half year level. The lowest project plan is the plan for each iteration. A better term for it could be the iteration plan. At this level, the project plan could run from a few weeks to a few months. Many software vendors have minor releases per quarter, and the iterations can coincide with these minor releases.

The product developed in each of these iterations could be a complete standalone product; different from products made in other iterations. But in general, products made from these iterations are partial products and not fully functional products. However, the product made from the first iteration is a fully functional product that can be run and whose features can be seen. In subsequent iterations, more features will be added on top of this product.

So, we can see that project initiation is a very low-key affair at the iteration level. The project team decides/picks the next set of requirements to work on after they are through with delivering the previous iteration. Even at project level, initiation is not a big and formal affair. At the most, it is an informal and low-key affair. But at the top level, where the product is conceived and development is planned, project initiation definitely plays a big role. It is indeed a big decision to start building a software product whose market potential may be excellent; nevertheless, it is a big risk to invest money and time in building a new product. At that level, management commitment is more than just the product itself. It has to do more with benefiting from market opportunity, planning for the successful launch of the product in the market, planning the market strategy, etc.

In the example discussed in Figures 2.2 through 2.4, the project in an iterative environment will have some differences compared to the traditional development model employed on a project. The same project will not be completed in one linear progression. The requirements will be so divided as to be covered over many iterations. If six requirements were decided upon (the same as the number of features depicted in Figure 2.2), devoting one full iteration to each of these main features, we end up having six iterations during the project. Suppose it was decided that the entire project needs to be completed in 18 months, then each iteration will run for approximately two and a half months. Each iteration will have requirement development, software design, software construction, software testing, and software release phases. In the agile world (all iteration-based software

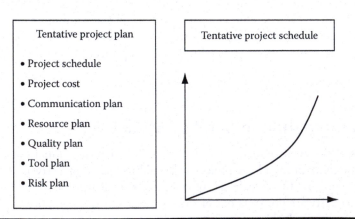

Figure 2.4 Tentative project plan.

product development models), the development phases are called and operated in a different manner compared to the traditional waterfall model. So, we have phases such as storyboard development, design, test driven development, module integration, testing and release. Before an iteration starts, the requirements to be worked on are chosen from the list of requirements. But even before that, each requirement is given a priority. The highest priority requirements are reserved for the first iteration. The other phases of the iteration will be planned accordingly. All activities for the first iteration will be firmed up before the iteration starts. But for other iterations, no concrete plan will be made. They will be tentative at the most. In fact, the requirements themselves will be tentative in nature and can be changed when more understanding and insight about that particular requirement is gained.

On other kinds of projects, there will not be a large list of requirements to start with. Even though there is the intention of building a large product, the stakeholders may first like to test the waters. In those cases, a few initial iterations can be treated like a feasibility study. The stakeholders may first seek feedback from end users on, for example, the necessity of building the software product, and then try to portray an overall picture. If the feasibility looks good, then the stakeholders signal a go-ahead for the project. If not, they will decide to scrap the project. The cost of scrapping the project at this stage will be small, and thus, the risk of losing large sums of money on a failed project can be avoided.

2.11 Stakeholder Influence

For a project to be successful, it is very important that it has strong support from the stakeholders [10]. Generally, stakeholders are personally interested in the project, and estimate the value the project will deliver to their organization on completion. If, for some reason, the stakeholders do not have confidence in the project, the project is bound to fail. Stakeholder interest is the paramount factor for the life of any project. Therefore, their involvement in the project must be ensured. To make a success of the project, they must take initiatives and influence its progress. Generally, stakeholders have very high influence at the beginning of the project. As the project progresses and stakeholders see that it is going in the right direction, they slowly start distancing themselves from the project. So their influence on the project diminishes. This is natural. Once they see some good progress and status reports on the project, they are assured of the success of the project and so divert their attention to other issues in their organization. But if the project falters, and stakeholders see that the project is going in the wrong direction, they are forced to attend to the project more closely. They start giving more time to the project and try to influence it more (Figure 2.5).

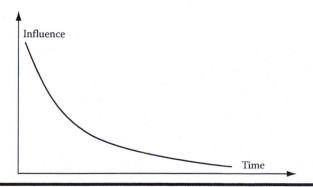

Figure 2.5   Stakeholder influence on the project over project life.

2.12 Quality Planning

From the start, quality planning [3] should be made an integral part of all activities associated with the project. This will ensure that the product being developed has the right quality. Large projects have a large number of project activities, and many of them are very complex. During the execution of their tasks, people may forget about quality, or due to time constraints, may be forced to ignore it.

Quality planning during project initiation could include a broad framework of how the quality of each and every work product, developed during the life cycle could be ensured. It may involve defining the process map and deciding on how the quality of work products will be measured and ensured. Some of the time-tested process frameworks for ensuring quality include, measuring work product attributes often and comparing them with the desired quality levels to know if the quality of the work products is good or bad.

2.13 Feasibility Study

For most projects, initiation is the stage when a make or break decision about the project should be made. If a project is allowed to keep going despite getting wrong signals, then at a point far downstream, it may prove to be a very costly mistake when the project is forced to be abandoned. It will be far better if a feasibility study [11] is conducted at the beginning of the project to know what chances the project has of achieving the desired goals. Once the feasibility study is completed and a report is made, then a review can be done to ascertain if the project should be continued or abandoned.

2.14 Project Division

In instances when it is felt that the requirements are not clear enough to proceed with the later stages of the project, it makes a lot of sense to divide the project into two parts [12]. The first part will deal with developing the requirements to the point where they can be taken for designing the application, and the second part will deal with the development of the software application. This is a good way to remove all uncertainties from the project. The requirement development part of the project may not have a fixed deadline denoting completion (as there is no previous knowledge as to how many requirements are there in the first place), but when the requirements are crystal clear, the other part of the project to develop the software application will have a lot of clarity, and thus, timelines and cost can be predicted with some good accuracy.

One alternative to project division is also available. It can be done this way. First, the customer can ask for open bids from service providers with just the preliminary information which is available about the project. At this stage, price or any monetary information for the project is not included. Once a suitable service provider is chosen, he can be asked to make detailed requirement specifications. These specifications are then handed over to a third party expert who provides project size information based on the requirement specifications. He hands over the project size information to the customer and the service provider. The customer in turn can calculate the required budget for the project given the prevailing market rates for software development costs. The service provider calculates the schedule and the number of people required to do the software development on the project based on its productivity level. So at this stage, project budget, project duration, and the number of people on the project is fixed. Later, if the requirements are modified, then the impact of the change on project schedule, project budget, and project team size can be calculated, and the project information can be adjusted accordingly (Figure 2.6).

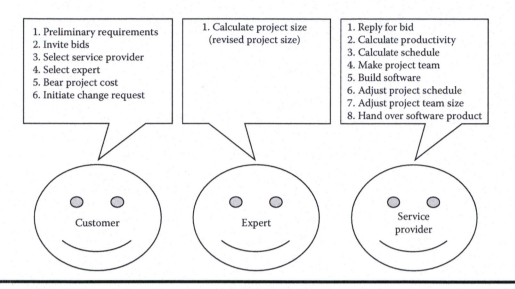

Figure 2.6   Alternative model for project division.

On paper, this arrangement looks good. But what are the weaknesses of this model? Well, one point of contention is how good the bidding process will be. After all, without detailed information being provided for the bid, how can service providers make good bids? Then, how is the customer going to know which bid is good and which one is not in the absence of vital information on bid responses like project cost, project schedule etc. So the bid selection will be mostly arbitrary. This is the weak point in this model.

2.15 Artifacts of Project Initiation

Since project initiation forms a very early part of the project, much project information is still not clear. Even customer requirements are not complete. So, it is too early to expect all details of the project, including project plan, project schedule, resource allocation, etc., to be developed. But we can definitely freeze the project scope, project charter, and project objectives at this stage. Similarly, if a feasibility study has been conducted, then the feasibility report may be one of the artifacts for the project.

2.16 Case Study

In Chapter 1, we saw the introduction of the project of our SaaS vendor. We will now continue with our case study and discuss how the project initiation part of the case study was done for the release 6.0 of the product of our SaaS software vendor.

2.16.1 Project Charter

In the industry there are no good solutions available for appointment scheduling. By creating this functionality, the SaaS vendor wants to become a leader in this arena. Existing as well as potential customers are also eagerly waiting for a good solution that could substantially cut the waiting time during the shipping–transporting–receiving operations of goods. After building and implementing the appointment scheduling solution, the SaaS vendor will be able to effectively satiate the needs of its customers.

2.16.2 Project Scope

Appointment scheduling functionality is the biggest feature for the 6.0 release. It could not be completed in one iteration. So, it was divided among four iterations. Calendars were created separately for dock doors, warehouses, organization, etc. in the first iteration (release 5.3).

The existing functionality of appointment scheduling up to the release of 5.2 was limited only as a mechanism to announce the arrival of the truck for either shipping or receiving at the warehouses. It was not actually making an appointment, as no constraints were considered for making an appointment.

For truck appointments at dock doors for loading/unloading, there are a lot of constraints to be considered. Therefore, it was decided to create the functionality over many phases. Thus, in release 5.3, only constraints of truck type and goods types were considered for making appointments. At this juncture, calendars were also used for dock doors (if for instance, a dock door is open from 6 AM to 6 PM on Mondays, then if any truck arrives after 6 PM its appointment will be considered only for the next day). In release 5.5, the functionality was enlarged to consider constraints of labor availability, quality control inspector availability, expected arrival time of truck, time window for making an appointment, and dock door type. In release 5.8, the functionality was enlarged to consider constraints of business partner preference, truck capacity, reservation frequency on a dock door, and reservation lead time. In the final iteration, the functionality was enlarged to consider the constraint of time gap between appointments. In this iteration, more time was given for testing than for development as the vendor wanted to make sure that all the functionalities work well, and that the software product do not fail. Instead of having a large number of poorly made features, it is better to have a software product with a limited number of features that are robust and will not fail. Reliability was the top priority.

After the four iterations and the entire 6.0 release, the software product should be able to be implemented with the new functionality by all existing customers as well as new customers who will sign contracts during this period.

2.16.3 Project Objectives

The software vendor could see that there was a large gap in the market for supply chain management software solutions in the grocery retail segment. The software vendor's flagship software product already had functionality for transportation management, inbound logistics, outbound logistics, fleet management, transportation rate calculation management etc., up to release 5.6 of the software product. The project charter for the project to release 6.0 (through minor releases of 5.3, 5.5, and 5.8) was to create additional functionality, such as appointment scheduling for warehouses with incoming trucks and an audit trail for all transactions.

Most software planning systems use complex logic to implement solutions which could be used in real world planning systems. Unfortunately, most of the systems fail miserably in delivering on promises. One reason is that real world happenings are far from ideal. There is always some unplanned risk lurking around the corner that can upset the rhythm of even the most meticulously planned activities. Then the planning logic is error prone.

A good algorithm was needed in the first place. Secondly, it had to be implemented in such a way that it would provide a real world solution. So, it was decided to go in for hard as well as soft constraints for making the appointment scheduling of an incoming truck for loading/unloading at a dock door. The soft constraints could be overridden if some other constraint that is higher in hierarchy is satisfied in the current situation. But the hard constraints are such that they will never be overridden. All the constraints are thus put in a hierarchy, with some of the constraints higher up in the hierarchy and others lower.

2.17 Chapter Summary

Project initiation most often happens with a kick off meeting involving the project manager, the stakeholders, and some key project members. They define the project charter, project scope, and project objectives. A preliminary effort and cost estimate is chalked out. A preliminary sketch is also made for the project schedule so that a tentative duration for the project can be established.

At the initiation stage, everything about the project is tentative. But the goal is to see if the project is itself feasible or not. For this purpose, a feasibility study can also be conducted in case the confidence level for the project is still uncertain. If the project is found not viable after the feasibility study, it can be abandoned. Abandoning an unfeasible project at this stage is less costly than abandonment after investing large sums of money and effort. In cases when it is felt that the requirements from customers are not clear or complete, then the project can be split so that the requirements can be made clear and complete in the first phase of the project. In the second phase of the project, the software product can be built on the basis of complete customer requirements.

Exercises

2.1 Project initiation is always fraught with the possibility of developing misunderstanding between the project stakeholders and the project teams. Provide a list of actions that the project team can take to avoid building such a situation.

2.2 Go to some open source projects and find out about their project charters. Find out why they have those project charters.

Review Questions

2.1 What is a project charter? How can you ensure that the project charter is useful for the project?

2.2 What things should go on the list containing project objectives?

2.3 How can you ensure that the project scope for a given project is well defined at the initiation phase so that it does not get over stretched later?

2.4 What are the difficulties faced by software projects during project initiation?

2.5 What is the relation between quality level and project scope?

2.6 What other activities are performed during project initiation apart from defining project charter, project objectives, and project scope?

Recommended Readings

1. H. Kerzner (2009) *Project Management: A Systems Approach to Planning, Scheduling, and Controlling*, Wiley, Hoboken, NJ.
2. J. P. Lewis (2002) *Fundamentals of Project Management: Developing Core Competencies to Help Outperform the Competition*, American Management Association, New York.
3. É. Verzuh (2005) *The Fast Forward MBA in Project Management*, 2nd edn., Wiley, New York.
4. A. Ahmed (2009) *Software Testing as a Service*, CRC Press, Boca Raton, FL.
5. R. J. Muller (1997) *Productive Objects: An Applied Software Project Management Framework*, Morgan Kaufmann, San Francisco, CA.
6. E. Miranda (2003) *Running the Successful Hi-Tech Project Office* (Artech House Technology Management and Professional Development Library), Artech House Publishing, Boston, MA.
7. C. F. Gray, E. W. Larson (2002) *Project Management: The Managerial Process*, McGraw-Hill/Irwin, Burr Ridge, IL.
8. Q. Wang (2008) *Making Globally Distributed Software Development a Success Story: International Conference on Software Process, ICSP 2008*, May 10–11, Leipzig, Germany.
9. H. A. Levine (2002) *Practical Project Management: Tips, Tactics and Tools*, Wiley, New York.
10. J. McManus (2004) *Managing Stakeholders in Software Development Projects* (Computer Weekly Professional), Butterworth-Heinemann, Amsterdam, the Netherlands.
11. J. Sanchez, M. P. Canton (2007) *Software Solutions for Engineers and Scientists*, CRC Press, Boca Raton, FL.
12. S. Donaldson, S. G. Siegel, S. Siegel (2000) *Successful Software Development*, Prentice Hall, Upper Saddle River, NJ.

Chapter 3

Software Project Effort and Cost Estimation

In the previous chapter, we learned

- How is a project initiated?
- What is a project charter?
- What is project scope?
- What are the objectives in a project?
- What project activities are performed during project initiation?

In this chapter, we will learn

- How is an effort estimate for a project made?
- What are the different effort estimation techniques?
- How is a cost estimate for a project made?
- What are the different cost estimation techniques?
- How is a schedule estimate for a project made?
- How is a resource estimate for a project made?

3.1 Introduction

Effort estimation for any software project is very important. However, for outsourced projects it is even more crucial. Effort estimate along with the schedule indicate to the customer what the cost impact will be and when the software can be realized. The management in customer organizations typically expects a lot from software projects. Software projects are seen as strategic tools to compete in the market. Therefore, a successful software implementation is regarded as a market edge and can influence the fortunes of that organization.

Software projects are costly as software professionals are expensive to hire. The optimal usage of time of these high-salaried people requires careful project planning to minimize wastage of time of these high-cost resources. At the same time, the service provider should be able to bill its customer for the actual effort put forth in delivering the project so that neither the customer nor the service provider is at a loss for wrong billing in the costs involved. Therefore, an accurate effort and cost estimate is of paramount importance for software projects.

With regard to effort for a software project, there are two aspects. One is to provide a good effort estimate and present it to the customer. The other aspect is to use it to form the project team based on the skills required for the project and the kind of budget that will be available for the project so that the right kind of people can be staffed for the project within the specified budget. Tight budgets and tight schedules are the general norm for most projects today and this makes good and reliable effort, schedule and cost estimates for projects even more important.

3.2 Effort Estimation Techniques

Effort estimation is an evolutionary phenomenon. The beginning of any project sees an initial effort estimate which is rough and mostly inaccurate at best [1]. The more the information available about the project, the more accurate will be the estimate. As more and more information becomes available for any project as it progresses, it makes sense to revise project estimate regularly to make the estimate more accurate (Figure 3.1).

Statistical effort estimate techniques are extremely useful for effort estimation [2]. Actual effort data from past projects provide good guidance as to what the effort required for the given project could be. Comparing data available for current project with past executed projects should provide this valuable estimated effort information. Thus, historical projects data come in handy for effort estimation. But how can one make estimates for projects in cases when no information or no relevant information is available for the current project or past projects? Here we have the following scenarios:

1. Much relevant project data are available for the current project but not much information about previous projects.
2. Previous project data are available for the project but not much information about the current project.

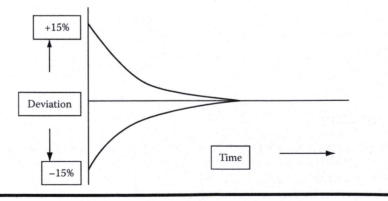

Figure 3.1   Effort estimate deviation with elapse of time.

3. Project data are available for the current project as well as that of previous projects.
4. Some project data are available for the current project.
5. No project data are available for both current as well as previous projects.

3.2.1 Choosing a Suitable Effort Estimate Technique

Different effort estimation techniques can be used depending on the situation [3]. If you have good information available for the current project but no data available for previous projects, the best technique for effort estimation will be the COCOMO model, because this model uses project size information from lines of code (LOC) as well as project attributes available from current project information. COCOMO also uses industry averages for environment factor calculations. Therefore, if no previously executed project information is available then the COCOMO model is the best.

If we have data available for both current as well as previous projects then the function point analysis (FPA) technique is a good option. This is because FPA technique uses historical project data for deriving adjustment factors. It also uses historical project data to derive productivity for projects. Therefore, in cases where we have both project as well as previously executed projects data, FPA can be used. Otherwise this technique is difficult to use if both these pieces of data are not available.

If we have some or all data available for the current project, then the Wide Band Delphi model is the best. Wide Band Delphi technique essentially is an experience-based technique. People who will be doing the actual project tasks along with other project team members derive effort estimates for various project tasks after many brainstorming sessions (Table 3.1).

If we have no project data available for the current project then it is simply impossible to estimate effort.

3.2.2 Function Point Analysis

FPA [4] considers two things for effort estimates. First, it determines size of the project in terms of the number of function points (FPs). Second, it determines productivity of the project team. Project size is derived from customer specifications. Based on customer requirements, an estimate is made for the number of functions to be built. These functions are contained in either internal or external files. Each of these functions has interfaces for communication with internal and external files. These functions also have interfaces for communication with devices. The number of parameters for each of these functions is determined. The complexity of these functions is also determined. Based on function complexity and number of parameters inside each function, the number of FPs is determined for each function. Totaling all these FPs gives the total number of unadjusted FPs for the entire system to be built and then the adjustment factor for the system is determined (Figures 3.2 and 3.3).

Table 3.1 Estimation Technique Selection Based on Project Information Availability

	Project Details	Estimation Technique
1	Historical project data + current project data	FPA
2	Current project data	COCOMO, Wide Band Delphi
3	No data	No technique can be used

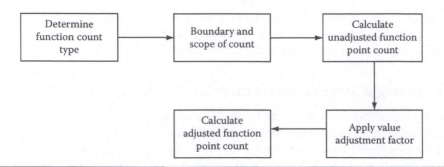

Figure 3.2   Function point count process steps.

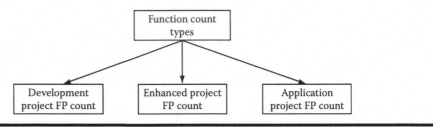

Figure 3.3   Function count types.

The process for calculation is as follows:

1. Determine type of function count
2. Identify scope and boundary of count
3. Determine unadjusted FP count
4. Determine value adjustment factor
5. Calculate adjusted FP count

For function count calculations, three types of function count are defined: development project FP count, enhance project FP count, or application FP count. Depending on the type of project in hand (development, enhancement, or application type of project), the suitable function count type (FP count type) is chosen. FP count type is used for determining how the number of FPs will be summed up. The scope of count is determined from the data, screens, and reports which will be used by the application. The boundary is determined by the integration needs of the application with other applications. If the application is a stand-alone one and will not be integrated with other applications, then the boundary value will be zero. But if some integration is required then using the integration interface, function counts for integration will be calculated. Calculation is done on the basis of the number of external interface files and the complexity of the functions contained in those files.

An unadjusted FP count consists of five function types. These types are grouped into two, namely, data functions and transaction functions. Data functions are internal logical files and external interface files. Transaction functions are external inputs, external outputs, and external inquiries. These functions are defined with descriptions like User Identifiable, Control Information, Elementary Process, Data Element Type (DET), and Record Element Type (RET). For each file, the complexity is determined using these descriptions. You make a table and calculate the complexity values of Low, Average, or High depending on the values for DETs and RETs present in the file (Table 3.2).

Table 3.2　Complexity Calculation for Files (Internal Logical Files and External Interface Files)

RET	DET		
	1–19	*20–50*	*51+*
1	Low	Low	Average
2–5	Low	Average	High
6+	Average	High	High

Based on the complexity, a value of FP is assigned for the file. A complexity of Low yields a value of 7, for Average it is 10, and for High it is 15 for internal logical files. For external interface files, the values are 5, 7, and 10, respectively. You also notice that FPs for external files are less than those for internal files, because internal files are used more often during system operation than external files. Hence, more FPs are assigned to internal files.

The FP calculation for transaction functions is similar (Table 3.3).

Based on the complexity, a value of FP is assigned for the external input. Complexity of Low yields a value of 3, for Average it is 4, and for High it is 6 (Table 3.4).

Based on the complexity, a value of FP assigned for the external output. Complexity of Low yields a value of 4, for Average it is 5, and for High it is 7. In case of external inquiries, it is 3, 4, and 6, respectively.

Once we have the number of FPs for the entire system, we can derive the effort estimate for the project by multiplying this number with productivity.

Table 3.3　Complexity Calculation for External Inputs

RET	DET		
	1–4	*5–15*	*16+*
0–1	Low	Low	Average
2	Low	Average	High
2+	Average	High	High

Table 3.4　Complexity Calculation for External Outputs

RET	DET		
	1–5	*6–19*	*20+*
0–1	Low	Low	Average
2–3	Low	Average	High
4+	Average	High	High

$$\text{Effort (in man months)} = \text{No. of Function Points} \times \text{Productivity}$$

The calculation for productivity is yet another time-consuming process. Based on the experience and skills of project team members, productivity is calculated. There is no fixed formula for productivity calculation. Mostly it is calculated using statistical process control data from previous projects. The industry norm for productivity calculation is arrived at in terms of effective LOCs generated per month per person. This figure includes work done in other phases of the development life cycle as well (requirement management, design, testing, etc.). So even though in the construction phase, actual LOCs generation may be 6000 per month per person, the effective LOCs for the project may come to less than 600 since effort for work done in other phases is also included. The industry norm for productivity in software development industry is 300–1000 LOCs per month per person. When SPC data are not available, productivity has to be calculated from scratch or an industry average figure has to be taken for effort calculations.

There are also some other formulae to calculate schedule and staff size required to execute the project. These were derived by luminaries in software engineering like Barry Boheim.

Project duration = $2.5 \times (\text{effort})^{1/3}$
Minimum duration = $0.75 \times (\text{effort})^{1/3}$
Optimum staffing size = $(\text{effort})^{1/2}$

3.2.2.1 Function Point Analysis Usage

The FPA technique can be used at early stage of the project when only the customer requirements are available. It is a standard effort estimation method and is recognized by many customers. FPA is, therefore, widely used in the industry. On the flip side, it is a difficult and time-consuming technique and only experts can use it. Hence, it is not advisable to use the FPA technique when the project estimators do not have the requisite experience.

3.2.3 Wide Band Delphi

The Wide Band Delphi technique [5] is based on conducting brainstorming sessions with the project team and arriving at consensus figures for effort estimates. When effort estimates are made by people who will actually work on the assignments for which they give the estimate, then figures are likely to be close to the actual effort that will be required. The raw effort figures by the project team members about their own assignments are then normalized when other team members debate about these figures and any inconsistencies in the raw figures are removed. There are two to three such brainstorming sessions. In the first session the raw estimates are discussed just to get the basis on which the estimate was made. In the next two sessions, estimates are taken from other team members. Finally, the estimate for each task is normalized.

One practical way of coming to a consensus effort estimate using the Wide Band Delphi technique is through the following formula.

Effort estimate = (pessimistic estimate + likely estimate × 4 + optimistic estimate)/6

Here pessimistic estimate is the one where a team member's estimate is the highest (in terms of number of man months). The likely estimate is the average of the most common estimate figure. In most cases, the likely estimate is the estimate given by the person who has been assigned to the task for which the effort estimate is being made. The optimistic estimate is the one where a team member's estimate is the lowest (in terms of number of man months).

The Wide Band Delphi technique is commonly applied on small to medium-sized projects and where the project team is composed of people who have been around and have worked with each other for some time. The project manager also knows that in such a situation some team members make good estimates and some are not able to do it with that much precision. So the effort estimate figure thus derived has a good backing by the team and the project manager. At the same time, taking into consideration all effort estimate figures from all team members makes the figure rather objective and reliable.

3.2.4 COCOMO

COCOMO [6] is one of the original effort estimation models developed by software engineering experts. It is also a very popular technique for effort estimation for software projects. Since COCOMO does not use SPC data, it can be used in cases where past project data are not available. Rather COCOMO uses industry averages for inputs in providing effort estimation calculations.

COCOMO uses project assumptions, definitions, and many cost factors in assessing an estimate for any project. It uses source LOCs required to build the software as the volume of work to be done for which the effort estimate is made. Apart from source LOCs, there are cost drivers and scale drivers which influence effort. Cost drivers include software safety, developer skill, usage of tools, etc. All of the cost drivers are categorized into personal factors, product factors, platform factors, and project factors. Personal factors include analyst capability, application experience, programmer capability, language and tool experience, etc. Product category includes database size, required software reliability, product complexity, required reusability, documentation needs, etc. Platform factors include execution time constraint, main storage constraint, virtual machine volatility, platform volatility, platform difficulty, etc. Project factors include use of software tools, modern programming practices, required development schedule, multisite development, requirement volatility, etc. The scale drivers include precedentedness, development flexibility, architecture/risk resolution, team cohesion, and process maturity.

3.2.4.1 Basic COCOMO

There are many ways COCOMO calculations can be made, as variations of the original COCOMO model have been improved upon or adapted to suit many environments. For a quick effort calculation, a variation of the COCOMO model is used which is known as basic COCOMO.

The basic COCOMO calculation equation is as follows:

$$Effort = 2.94 \times EAF \times (KLOC)^E$$

where
  EAF is the effort adjustment factor derived from cost drivers
  E is the exponent derived from scale drivers
  $KLOC$ is the kilo lines of software code

Values for EAF range from 1.0 to 2.0. Values for E range from 1.0 to 1.5.

Schedule duration is calculated as

$$\text{Duration} = 3.67 \times (\text{effort})^{SE}$$

where *SE* is the schedule equation derived from scale drivers.

Staffing needs can be calculated by dividing effort with duration.

In the basic COCOMO model, hardware constraints, use of modern tools and techniques, personal productivity, etc. are not taken into account.

Basic COCOMO is most suitable for making estimates at early stage of any project.

3.2.4.2 Intermediate COCOMO

In intermediate COCOMO, we make an effort estimate for the project with the product size along with the cost drivers. The cost driver set includes assessment of attributes for product, project, hardware, and the project team's experience and skills. These attributes are categorized as product attributes, which include required reliability, application database size, and application complexity.

Hardware attributes include run-time performance constraint, memory constraint, virtual machine environment volatility, turnabout time requirement.

Project team attributes include analyst capability, software engineer capability, application experience, virtual machine experience, and programming language experience.

Project attributes include software tool usage, software engineering methods usage, and development schedule requirement.

How each of the cost drivers impacts the effort estimate is assessed by assigning appropriate weights to these attributes. To assign these weights, first a six-point scale is created with scales of very low, low, nominal, high, very high, and extra high. The values for these scales vary from a low of 0.70 to a high of 1.60. For any project, each of the attributes is given relevant values based on this scale. These attribute values are industry standard but at what scale value any attribute falls is decided by the estimating person (Table 3.5).

The formula for intermediate COCOMO is given as $E = a(\text{KLOC})^{(E)}$. EAF, where *a* and *E* are a coefficients whose values depend on the kind of software project (organic, semi-detached, or embedded) for which the estimation is being made (Table 3.6).

3.2.4.3 Detailed COCOMO

In basic and intermediate COCOMO, the effort estimate is a gross estimate at the project level. But a project is further divided into many phases. Each phase may need to have a separate effort estimate calculation. This is done in the detailed COCOMO model.

In the initial stages of the project, when a rough estimate is needed for each project phase, the basic COCOMO model is used. In later stages in the project when all project details are clear and an effort estimate is needed for each project phase, the intermediate COCOMO is used to calculate the effort estimate for each phase. The same values that are used for calculation at the project level can be used for calculations at the phase level. The only difference will be that at this level, the effort estimate will take values for relevant cost driver attributes and not for the entire project. For instance, for the design phase, the effort estimate will take attribute values only for cost drivers that will influence the design phase.

Table 3.5　Scale and Scale Values for Attributes of Cost Drivers

Cost Drivers	Ratings					
	Very Low	Low	Nominal	High	Very High	Extra High
Product attributes						
Required software reliability	0.75	0.88	1.00	1.15	1.40	
Size of application database		0.94	1.00	1.08	1.16	
Complexity of the product	0.70	0.85	1.00	1.15	1.30	1.65
Hardware attributes						
Run-time performance constraints			1.00	1.11	1.30	1.66
Memory constraints			1.00	1.06	1.21	1.56
Volatility of the virtual machine environment		0.87	1.00	1.15	1.30	
Required turnabout time		0.87	1.00	1.07	1.15	
Personnel attributes						
Analyst capability	1.46	1.19	1.00	0.86	0.71	
Applications experience	1.29	1.13	1.00	0.91	0.82	
Software engineer capability	1.42	1.17	1.00	0.86	0.70	
Virtual machine experience	1.21	1.10	1.00	0.90		
Programming language experience	1.14	1.07	1.00	0.95		
Project attributes						
Use of software tools	1.24	1.10	1.00	0.91	0.82	
Application of software engineering methods	1.24	1.10	1.00	0.91	0.83	
Required development schedule	1.23	1.08	1.00	1.04	1.10	

**Table 3.6   Coefficient Values *a* and *E*
for Various Project Types**

Software Project Type	a	E
Organic	3.2	1.05
Semi-detached	3.0	1.12
Embedded	2.8	1.20

3.2.4.4 COCOMO Model Conclusion

Over the years, the COCOMO model has been refined by many experts. At the same time due to changes in technology and growth in maturity of software development teams, the formulae for calculation of effort, duration, and manpower requirements needed to be adjusted for many factors so that the formulae remain relevant and can be effectively used. One popular variant is known as COCOMO II. Many organizations have developed their own versions of the COCOMO model based on the unique environments under which they operate. While some of them have added or deleted more dimensions in calculation of effort estimate figures, some others have modified the values of these dimensions to correspond to their environment.

3.2.5 Effort Estimation for Waterfall Model–Based Planning

Software projects with the waterfall or traditional development model have to plan for everything in advance including making elaborate effort estimates [7]. But effort estimation cannot be made without proper identification of project tasks that will be involved in making the estimate for the project. The best way is to first break the project into phases and milestones and then estimate which tasks will be involved in each phase. In traditional software development projects, a waterfall model is adopted. So the project will have major phases and milestones of software requirements management, software design, software construction, software testing, and finally software release. A software maintenance project may have reverse engineering, software construction, software testing, and release phases. Sometimes a project could be small, consisting of a partial set of activities, for instance, one needs to provide only the design of the software application, while other services are provided by some other service provider. In any case, once phases of the project are identified, then individual tasks of the project can be identified. Once these tasks are identified, then the size of these tasks can be measured from specifications such as quality level and phase-specific information. For instance, suppose for the coding task in the construction phase, a component needs to be developed using Java. The size of the component will depend on the number of functions that will be built for this component. The complexity of the component will depend on what kind of functions these will be. Will these functions have interfaces for other functions? Once you have all details about the component, then you can make a size estimate for the component precisely. Now you need to know who will code this component. Does this person have prior experience of coding similar components and are they good at it? From here you can estimate productivity. From size and productivity one can figure out how many days it will take to develop that component. Estimates for all tasks in the project can be made likewise (Figures 3.4 and 3.5).

One important consideration for effort estimation for a project with the waterfall model is calculating effort estimation for different phases of the software life cycle [8]. This can be done in two ways. Effort estimate for a phase can be calculated by summing up effort required for all

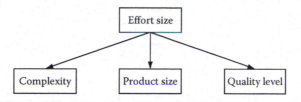

Figure 3.4   Factors influencing effort size.

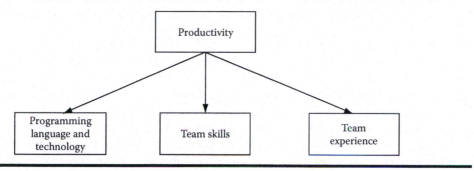

Figure 3.5   Factors influencing productivity.

tasks associated with that phase. An effort estimate for all phases can also be calculated from total effort required for the project by allocating percentage of effort for each phase. Thus, if total effort required for the project is 1500 man hours, and if requirement management comprises 15% of total effort, then the effort estimate for requirement management will be 225 man hours (1500 × 15/100). Likewise, an effort estimate for other phases can be calculated.

3.2.6 Effort Estimation for Iterations Model–Based Planning

Agile, iterative, extreme programming, and many other forms of alternative models for software development are fundamentally different from the waterfall model in that they have iterations over one phase or many phases of the SDLC life cycle. Effort and schedule estimates for these projects differ significantly compared to the waterfall model [9]. Many authors of books related to software engineering and software project management have tried to explain differences in effort and schedule estimation for different models. The agile model is best suited for projects where the risk of software development is very high. That is why from the beginning, it was adopted for projects where the software product to be developed was small or the software requirements were not typical (no similar type of software products existed before due to new technology or new industry). These kinds of projects are more like research and development projects with a high degree of innovation and creativity required. Thus, instead of a fixed price/fixed duration model, a time-and-material–based contract suits such projects. In this kind of arrangement, making an effort and cost estimate for the project is difficult (Figure 3.6).

However, with the increasing maturity of iterative models, increasingly varied kinds of projects are being executed with any of the iterative models. It is not uncommon for even large projects with a size exceeding 1 million LOCs these days to use an iterative model. In such cases, an effort and cost estimate for the project becomes necessary. However, empirical methods for effort and cost estimation for such projects have not sufficiently developed and standards are not available that can be used. Therefore, most organizations have developed their own methods for these calculations.

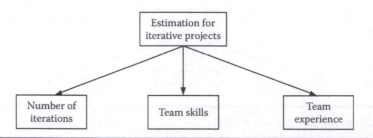

Figure 3.6   Factors influencing effort estimate for agile and iteration-based projects.

Essentially, the iterations of tasks over different phases in the project make an effort estimate difficult. For instance, suppose the design of a component needs to be iterated three times (which is not known at the start of the project) then effort for designing the component normally should be three times that of effort required for designing that component once. However, this is not the case. In each iteration the effort required will be different, because the component details will be different in each iteration, there will be different sets of tasks in different iterations, and the volume of work in each iteration for developing/modifying the same component will be different. Therefore, the effort estimate will be different in each iteration. Moreover, since it is not known how many iterations will be there in the first place and how much work will actually be involved until each iteration starts, effort estimate simply becomes impossible to calculate.

One more aspect in an iteration-based model is that iteration is done either for modifying the same component or a complete iteration is made over all the phases of the product development life cycle for developing a new functionality in the software. In the latter case, each iteration is completely different from the other. Effort and cost estimates for each iteration will be different and have to be computed separately.

One positive aspect about computing effort and cost estimates for iteration-based projects is that the duration of each iteration is short; usually 2–8 weeks. In the few initial iterations, effort and cost estimates may be wrong to a great degree. However, since the volume of work does not much exceed that of any waterfall model–based project (may be 1/20 or even less), this variance is not significant in terms of the amount of time and cost even though it may be large in percentage terms. In subsequent iterations, since the team has gained experience, estimates will be more accurate and will not be a major risk factor.

Due to these reasons, for iteration-based projects, effort and cost estimates are not a major concern for customers and thus, not a critical element of project management.

Again, effort and cost estimation is good only when the project activities can be well defined and estimated measurements can be taken with some precision. When a software product is to be developed using a new technology, it is extremely difficult to predict project activities and their measurements in terms of duration and costs involved. Similarly, when a new software product is to be developed using any agile model and since there is no significant body of knowledge available that can be applied for effort estimates, then again effort and cost estimate is difficult. At the same time, using established models like the waterfall or rational unified process is not practicable as these types of projects are very risky (as outcomes of these projects are largely unknown). Iteration-based product development models are extremely useful in such cases as they reduce exposure to high risk by dividing it into many smaller risks in terms of small iterations. If the project outcome after a few iterations is not encouraging, then the project can be abandoned with lesser impact in terms of revenue and effort loss.

3.3 Cost Estimation

Once you have the effort estimate for the project, calculating costs for the project is required [10]. Here we are assuming that the project is based on a fixed cost–fixed duration basis. The most popular method involves first converting the effort estimate into man months if it is not already done. Then a standard man month rate is applied for the project. Suppose for a project the effort figure is 13 man months and a man month rate of $4,000 is applied. The project cost comes to $52,000.

If the project is outsourced, then the service provider may top this cost figure with some overhead costs that are typically a percentage of this cost figure. Suppose the service provider applies a 15% effort cost as overhead cost. Then in our case, the overhead cost will come to $7,800. Thus, the total cost for the project will be $59,800.

Software projects have many kinds of associated costs, including expenses for hardware, management costs, software tool acquisition costs, training costs, etc. But the most expensive item on the project budget is the salary of software professionals who will be working on the project. Salaries of project staff comprise more than 70% of total project costs.

The biggest cost driver for any software project is the effort required to complete the project. Increased effort drives up salary expenses for project staff. Therefore, the project manager always has to keep an eye on the productivity of the staff so that the money spent on salary has a good return value.

Moreover, the salary of software professionals is not directly linked to their productivity; two software professionals with the same years of experience and same skill sets but with different productivity levels may get the same salary. Similarly, the salary for different professionals with same productivity may be different. This creates a problem in calculating project expenses.

If the salary structure of staff were as simple as depicted in Figure 3.7, cost calculations could have been easy. But due to the fact that the salary, for example, of two junior developers is different from each other makes cost calculation difficult. In that case, compared to the average effort put in by the two junior developers, the payment for the same effort is different. This becomes an anomaly if the project manager calculates project costs based only on designation (Figure 3.8).

Similarly, some other factors are to be considered when costs are calculated. We can conclude from the earlier discussion that effort and project costs can vary due to variance in salaries and

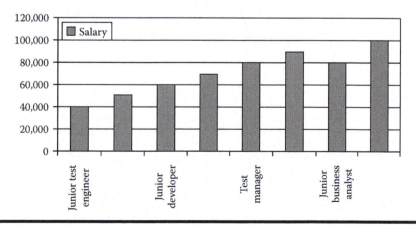

Figure 3.7   Salary of project staff.

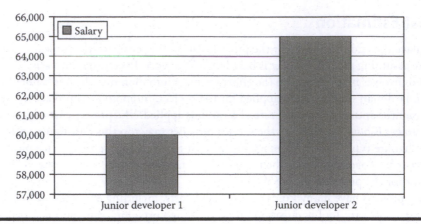

Figure 3.8 **Salary of two junior developers.**

thus in such cases, correlating effort and project cost will be difficult. This is why you simply cannot replace one resource with another (with different pay) without properly accounting for change in project cost.

3.3.1 Cost Factor Analysis

Suppose a project manager has a project budget of $450,000 (+15% – 10%). The estimated effort for development is 500 hours (including requirement gathering, design, and construction) and 300 hours for testing. The assumed overhead cost is 15%. So the budget range for the project is from $517,500 to $405,000. Of this amount $77,625–$60,750 is earmarked for meeting overhead expenses. From $439,875 to $344,250 is available as budget for spending on staff salaries. The hourly wage for average development staff is $70 and for testing staff is $60. The hourly wage for a test manager is $80 and for a project manager is $90. Effort required for project planning, controlling and monitoring is 10% of development effort. Effort required for test project planning, controlling, and monitoring is 10% of test effort. Table 3.7 presents the cost analysis.

Table 3.7   Project Cost Analysis for Salaries of Project Staff

Effort Type	Hours	Costs/Hour	Costs
Development effort	5,000	70	350,000
Test effort	3,000	60	180,000
Project management	500	90	45,000
Test management	300	80	24,000
Total cost			599,000

But from the project cost data mentioned earlier, only $439,875–$344,250 is to be spent on salaries. What could be done in this situation? One option is to ask the stakeholders (customers) for a revised budget. Or one may have to cut some features from the software to reduce effort required. This situation must be communicated to the stakeholders as soon as possible.

On most projects costs play a vital role. Talent costs money and companies have no option but to hire talented professionals to keep their crucial projects running successfully. How does one balance talent versus costs? One option is to utilize the time of your staff intelligently. Do not waste any money by not properly loading your staff with project assignments. Use any good software which will allow you to track how your staff is loaded with assignments. Plan ahead for future assignments so that staff has assignments all the time and they do not sit idle between assignments. Pay particular attention to assignment loading on highly paid staff, who should be assigned work that is crucial and where the hourly rate for project work is high.

Use PMO (Program Management Office) to share staff hours diligently. PMO should ensure that no overloading or underloading of staff hours are done on any project or across projects. To deal with extreme cases when either project work is less than staff hours available or project work is more than available staff hours, use flexible teams. The flexible team can include contracted staff who can work when needed and can be removed when no work is available. These measures can go a long way in ensuring proper staffing needs.

There are two types of projects: time and material based and fixed schedule–fixed costs based. Fixed cost–fixed schedule based projects are the ones where requirements are concrete and most of the project details are clear. Costing for such projects is also clear in the beginning of the project. But not all projects have enough clarity to start with. Many projects start with lots of doubts, ambiguities, and uncertainties. In such cases, costing and scheduling is very difficult to make. Hence, these projects are executed on a time and material costs basis. The customer agrees on recurring payment of time spent by a project team on his/her project. Generally, the recurring payment is in the form of a monthly fee.

Many projects are a mix of the two forms of projects. For a certain period in the beginning, a project is formed on the basis of time and material. Once certain amount of clarity is achieved on the project, the project is converted into a fixed cost–fixed duration basis.

3.3.2 Activity-Based Cost Estimation

Accurate costing in any business scenario is a difficult task. Even when a reliable system is employed for costing, it is often difficult to attribute a cost to a certain head. Accounting being a difficult task, often it turns out that after much adjustment here and there, costs are attributed to certain heads of expenses at a gross level.

Activity-based costing tries to ease this situation [11]. For each individual activity on the project, all costs are calculated from starting of the activity to its finish. Whenever accounts are prepared, all incurred costs are accounted for all activities on the project. This ensures there is no irregularity in the accounts and the account reports are accurate. This helps the management know how expenses are being incurred and whether there are any undue expenses incurred on tasks. Coupled with activity-based costing, if baseline planned costs for activities can be compared with actual costs for tasks, then it will be of immense help for the management to know which project activities are not proceeding in the right direction, and thus necessary steps can be taken to bring those activities on track (Table 3.8).

Table 3.8 Cost Analysis Based on Activities

Activity	Start Date	Schedule (Months)	Effort (Months)	Average Staffing	Cost ($)
Planning					
Management					
Requirements					
Prototyping					
Configuration management					
Functional design					
Design review 1					
Detail design					
Design review 2					
Quality assurance					
Coding					
Reuse acquisition					

3.3.3 Cost Estimation for Iterations-Based Planning

There is not much difference when it comes to making cost estimates for iteration-based projects compared to waterfall model–based projects. Total effort may determine the costs for the project regardless of schedule and number of iterations. Costs are determined for each iteration separately as well as for the major release of the software product being developed. Costing for the entire product can also be made by summing up costs of each major release. So we have three levels of costs each at the iteration level, major product release level, and at the entire product development level.

3.4 Schedule Estimation

The amount of effort and schedule put in terms of time is not equal [12]. There may be many parallel processes where project tasks are being completed. In such a situation, effort will be greater than the schedule. In cases where there are floats or slacks in the schedule, the schedule will be greater than the effort. Therefore, the effort for the project is calculated first, followed by the schedule.

Once the schedule is made, the schedule duration will be the difference between the date when the project starts and date when the project ends. From the PERT/CPM view, the project duration will be the difference between start date of the earliest project task and end date of the latest project task.

3.4.1 Schedule Estimation for Waterfall Model–Based Planning

The effort for the entire project is based on adding all efforts required for each and every project task. Of these tasks, one has to determine which tasks will be done in parallel. For instance, much of the work in the construction phase is done in parallel as modules are distributed to different

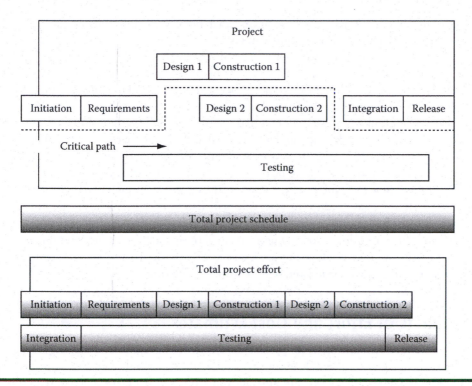

Figure 3.9 Project effort and project schedule for a project.

teams who will be developing their modules in parallel to modules being developed by other teams. Similarly, much of the software testing is done in parallel as many testers test their own modules in parallel to modules being tested by other team members. Also it will have to determined if there will be slacks and floats between tasks.

Using PERT/CPM or network diagrams you can find the critical path for the project, and thereafter, its schedule and duration (Figure 3.9).

For projects that have no parallel tasks (classical waterfall model), the schedule is the same as the effort (if there are no slacks in the schedule). This is because the length of the critical path for the project is the same as the duration of all project tasks (i.e., effort). But this is rare. In most cases, some parallel tasks take place on the project and thus effort and schedule for the project are different. Schedule and effort will also not be the same in cases where there are gaps between the end of one task and the start of the next task in sequence even when they are in sequence. When the schedule is calculated, the idle time (time gaps) between tasks is also added but in effort calculation these time gaps are not added.

3.5 Resource Estimation

After making the schedule, we estimate the resource requirements [13]. In order to do this, we should first get the list of tasks on the project. For each task, we need to identify the required skills and level of experience. A list of all skills and minimum necessary experience required for each task should be marked. For each task we need to identify the resources available in the organization. So we will be matching task skills and minimum experience requirements with skills and necessary experience possessed by resources. The names of "resources" that possess all skills and necessary experience required for the task should be listed against that task.

The next step is to find the availability of resources for doing those tasks. From the list of names of resources, identify resources that will be available between the task start and finish dates. The other dimension is the amount of work involved in each task. How many resources will be required for that task should be calculated. The productivity factor for the organization will come in handy here. The number of resources required for the task will be the volume of tasks divided by the productivity and time duration under which task is to be completed. For example, if volume of work is equivalent to 2000 KLOC and productivity for the organization is 1000 KLOC per person per month, and if the task has to be completed in 1 month, then we need two resources for this task (2000)/(1000 × 1). Sometimes we may need less than one resource to do the task. In such cases, a resource may be assigned to the task, who will also be doing some tasks on other projects. Generally the loading factor for a resource should be kept at 1 (loading factor is the amount of work which a resource can do in working hours on a working day). But sometimes due to unavailability of resources, we may need to increase loading for a particular resource to more than 1. In that case, the resource is overloaded and will be working overtime.

3.6 Artifacts of Effort and Cost Estimates

Essentially, an effort estimate provides project costs, project duration, and staffing needs. But it does not provide a detailed schedule. A detailed schedule is derived from the work breakdown structure. The actual staffing needs are also derived from the work breakdown structure after staffing requirements are attached to the schedule. What we get from effort estimates are average staffing needs for the project, which helps in deriving project costs. In most cases, customers need project cost and project duration to sanction the project. The project manager needs to provide these details early on in the project. In cases where the project is being outsourced, the bidders for the project provide estimated costs and duration in their bid details. The more details about costs and duration provided on the estimate sent to the customer, the better it will be. Details will help the customer to understand how the project will progress and how costs are derived. This builds customer confidence in the project team that the team is capable of delivering the project. This goes a long way toward making a success of the project.

3.7 Practical Considerations in Effort and Cost Estimates

When the effort and cost estimates are derived using formula-based techniques like COCOMO or FPA, it gives a raw estimate. The risk factors are not included. Any estimate should have a risk factor as an essential ingredient. So the project manager should include some reserve in the project for covering risks in the project. For details about risks please refer Chapter 4.

As has been repeatedly argued by Brooks, Boheim, and others, effort estimation for software projects is a tricky affair. Only after the software design is well established that effort estimate can be calculated with some accuracy. The best approach for effort and cost estimation for a project should be to do it frequently after each major milestone is achieved. Adjust these figures when you come to know more about the project as it progresses.

Generally we measure size as source lines of code (SLOC). The source code is written when the project is in the construction phase. But we also have other phases when no source code is written (requirement specification, software design, software testing, documentation, etc.).

Working in these phases takes time and effort. So how do we account for this effort and time when we are reporting the effort and time in terms of SLOC? One good solution is to account for the effort and time taken in these activities along with the one in the construction phase and then calculate the effort and time required in terms of SLOC. For instance, suppose it took two business analysts 2 months to develop requirement specifications; a system analyst developed the design in 2 months; and five developers developed the application in 5 months. Out of these 5 months they spent around 2.5 months doing unit and integration testing. The two test engineers took 1 month for doing the system testing. Code fixing for developers again took 15 days. Supposing the system developed contained 30,000 SLOC, then what are the figures for effort?

Time spent by business analysts = 4 months (2 × 2 months)
Time spent by business analysts = 2 months
Time spent by developers on development = 12.5 months (5 × 2.5 months)
Time spent by developers on code fixing = 2.5 months (5 × 15 days)
Time spent by developers on testing = 12.5 months (5 × 2.5 months)
Time spent by testers = 2 months (1 × 2 months)
Total time spent by team members on the project = 35.5 months
Total code written on project = 30,000 SLOC
SLOC per month on project = 30,000/35.5 = 845 SLOC/month

3.8 Effort and Cost in Product Development

In the case of product development for software vendors, the effort and cost estimate does not have much significance for just one iteration or one project. Their product development effort is continuous in nature, as they continuously keep working on new releases of their product. When one release (whether minor or major) is over, they immediately start working on the next release. Sometimes they employ more than one team simultaneously to do their product development faster in a time-boxing environment. Due to their continuous operation, they rather calculate their development costs at quarterly, half yearly, and yearly bases and do not bother about costs for just one iteration or one project. They have a constant-sized team and this team does not get disbanded after each iteration or project. They may expand or contract team size due to long-term market conditions, and not due to demands of any iteration or project. The software vendors rather concentrate on the effort and cost involved in the entire product development that spans many years. They make estimate for this entire cost and effort requirements when they decide to go for building the software product. They keep revising this estimate at their yearly or half-yearly plans.

3.9 Case Study

In Chapter 2, we saw how the project of our SaaS vendor got initiated. We continue our story of the software product vendor (or rather, SaaS service vendor).

3.9.1 History

When they decided to build the software product; they estimated that the size of their product will be around 500,000 SLOC when they can start marketing their software product. They had also decided that they will go for incremental software development so that they can sell their product with a bare minimum of features and can keep developing their product and keep adding new features, and at the same time they can keep selling their product in the market with the already developed features.

They had estimated that they will be able to develop the initial product in 2 years time. That meant they needed to develop the product at 21,000 SLOC per month (including the time required to develop requirement specifications, software design, and software testing. In all of these activities, no source code lines are added but they take time. This time is added along with the time required to write the source code.). They had estimated that a good project team consisting of around 22 people could do the job. On average, the salary of each project team member would be around $6,000 per month. That meant the quarterly cost will be around $400,000. So over a 2-year period, $3,200,000 will be the development cost. Later, when they were established in the market and realized that they wanted a larger team to develop the software at a faster rate, they thought about their options. They wanted a team of 50 people to speed the development at two and half times compared to the present speed of product development. If they had hired the additional staff locally, it would have cost them $1,000,000 per quarter for a development team of 50 people. The option of hiring contractors would have cost more than this figure and, hence, it was not an option. Moreover, they wanted to hire permanent staff instead of temporary staff as they were looking for a long-term goal instead of short-term staffing. Thereafter they thought of offshore service providers. Offshore development staff would cost one-third of what it costs if they hired locally. They evaluated a few service providers and finally zeroed-in on two of them and made contracts with both of them. Now they had a staff of more than 50 people and the total development cost of $730,000 per quarter.

3.9.2 Current Project

The current project could be broadly categorized as developing the appointment scheduling engine, developing search functionality, integrating the appointment scheduling functionality to existing features, and finally testing the whole application thoroughly. Since a very complex logic was to be implemented, the logic first needed to be thoroughly tested and, subsequently, integration of the logic with the rest of the application was to be tested. Therefore, the testing part was crucial for the success of the project. At the same time, since this logic was being implemented for the first time, the testing component for the project was comparatively large.

3.9.3 Effort and Cost

Over the proposed four iterations (minor releases) and the complete appointment scheduling functionality to be achieved by end of the major release, it was estimated that the effort required to complete the functionalities associated with appointment scheduling will be approximately 300,000 SLOC. This approximation was derived after using a bottom-up effort estimate. First the functionality was broken down into lowest-level components. Effort for these components was estimated. Summing up of efforts for component gave the overall effort for the entire functionality.

Exercises

3.1 Find the relationship between effort and cost. What cost factors have more impact on effort and which cost factors have lesser impact?

3.2 Agile projects may have less effort required compared to traditional projects. What factors are responsible for this phenomenon?

Review Questions

3.1 Describe the Function Point Analysis technique for deriving effort and cost estimates for software projects?

3.2 Describe the COCOMO technique for deriving effort and cost estimates for software projects?

3.3 Which estimation technique will you use for a project where data for past projects are not available and why?

3.4 How are cost and schedule for a project related to each other?

3.5 How do project scope and quality level affect the effort required for a project?

Recommended Readings

1. P. Jalote (2002) *Software Project Management in Practice*, Addison-Wesley Professional, Boston, MA.
2. J. C. Goodpasture (2003) *Quantitative Methods in Project Management*, J. Ross Publishing, Boca Raton, FL.
3. D. Brandon (2005) *Project Management for Modern Information Systems: The Effects of the Internet and ERP on Accounting*, IRM Press, Hershey, PA.
4. F. P. Deek, J. A. M. McHugh, O. M. Eljabiri (2005) *Strategic Software Engineering*, CRC Press, Boca Raton, FL.
5. D. D. Galorath, M. W. Evans (2006) *Software Sizing, Estimation, and Risk Management*, CRC Press, Boca Raton, FL.
6. M. Zelkowitz (2004) *Advances in Computers, Volume 62: Advances in Software Engineering* (Advances in Computers), Academic Press, Amsterdam, the Netherlands.
7. G. Lenz, T. Moeller (2003) *Net—A Complete Development Cycle*, Addison-Wesley Professional, Boston, MA.
8. J. Love (2007) *Process Automation Handbook: A Guide to Theory and Practice*, Springer, Berlin, Germany.
9. D. J. Anderson, D. Anderson (2003) *Agile Management for Software Engineering: Applying the Theory of Constraints for Business Results*, Prentice Hall, Upper Saddle River, NJ.
10. E. Verzuh (2005) *The Fast Forward MBA in Project Management*, 2nd edn., Wiley, New York.
11. C. Jones (2007) *Estimating Software Costs*, McGraw-Hill Osborne Media, New York.
12. R. T. Futrell, D. F. Shafer, L. I. Shafer (2002) *Quality Software Project Management*, Prentice Hall PTR, Upper Saddle River, NJ.
13. J. Greene, A. Stellman (2007) *Head First PMP*, O'Reilly, Sebastopol, CA.

Chapter 4

Risk Management

In the previous chapter, we learned

- How is an effort estimate for a project made?
- What are the different effort estimation techniques?
- How is a cost estimate for a project made?
- What are the different cost estimation techniques?
- How can a schedule estimate for a project be done?
- How can a resource estimate for a project be done?

In this chapter, we will learn

- What is a risk on a project?
- What kinds of risks exist for a project?
- What kind of impact may risks have on a project?
- What strategy is needed to deal with risks?

4.1 Introduction

Risks are unforeseen or unplanned happenings, which, when they occur, devastate or at least adversely affect our future plans. When we analyze any software project, what kinds of risk come to our mind? Basically, a project has these components: budget, time, resources, quality, and technology. If any risk occurs that might affect any of these components, then the project may fail. What is the best way to reduce or mitigate the risks? There could be many aspects to any project. But a project manager must develop a comprehensive risk mitigation plan so that if any risk arises

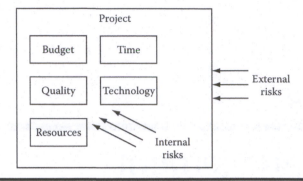

Figure 4.1   Internal and external risks for a project.

during execution, he will be able to handle it comfortably. If he has not made a proper risk plan, then if anything wrong happens, he will not be able to handle it (Figure 4.1).

Risks can be categorized as external and internal. If a risk to the project arises due to an aspect being dealt with by the project team, then it is an internal risk. All other risks are external risks. Suppose a project is to be coded using a particular programming language, and one developer on the team is not conversant with it. In this case, he is given training so that he can pick up this language. However, if even after training, this team member is not able to use the programming language, he will not be able to do the task assigned to him, and his inability will be considered an internal risk. Now, suppose that this particular training is not available from any training service provider, then in that case, the risk becomes an external risk (Figure 4.2).

Many environmental factors affect a project. If any of these environmental factors impact a project, then though the impact on the project is external (as environmental factors are external to the project), it can still be substantial for that project. Some of the external risks can be managed by a proactive approach. But many external risks cannot be managed. One good example is the obsolescence of a technology. When the project starts, a particular technology is chosen (a prebuilt vendor component, for instance) little realizing that the vendor will not support that component by the time the project finishes. Similarly, the customer may go out of business due to economic recession and the project may need to be scrapped.

At the project level, risks impact any of these project deliverables: schedule, quality, or budget (risks affecting resources or technology ultimately impact budget, quality, or budget) [1]. At the beginning of the project, the project manager is given (or he makes them after consultation with the customer) limits for these three things, that is, to deliver the project within the stipulated time limit, within the budget, and with the product quality of a stipulated standard. If any of these three are not delivered, then the project is considered to have failed. So, the project manager has to ensure that these limits are

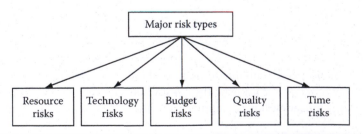

Figure 4.2   Major risk types.

communicated clearly to the project team. The project manager should make sure that the project team understands these limits and delivers its part of the project within these limits. At the same time, he also needs to work out his plan well, so that he and his team are ready to face any surprises if they arise and handle those situations with ease.

4.2 Causes of Risks

What are the probable causes of risks on a software project? What can be done to prevent or minimize the impact they can have on the project? How much impact do they have on the project? What is the probability that they may occur and might impact the project?

For any good project manager, it is of utmost importance that he first of all makes a list of risks which his project faces. After that, he can find solutions for tackling them. So here is a discussion of some of the risks that may occur in any software project (Figure 4.3).

4.2.1 Quality Constraints

These days, quality is one of the major concerns for software products, as the high cost of supporting these products is well understood, and thus, avoidance of providing product support for bad quality products is a top policy among software vendors. Software vendors realize that it is much cheaper to make a good quality software product with low support costs than to produce a software product of poor quality and end up with high support costs. So an elaborate set of quality constraints are imposed from the start of the project to the finish [2]. In fact, nowadays, a separate software process group is formed that oversees the quality of projects. Indeed, meeting quality requirements is a big risk for all projects.

4.2.2 Resource Unavailability

Resource unavailability is one of the major risk factors, as software professionals are in great demand the world over [3]. Finding and procuring a good software professional is a complete project in itself. Retaining him within the organization is yet another challenge.

4.2.3 Disinterest

Lack of interest is a concern that needs to be mitigated by project managers as it severely affects productivity [4]. A good motivation program for individuals who lack interest in the project can be organized.

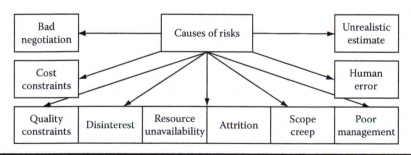

Figure 4.3   Major causes of risks.

4.2.4 Attrition

Due to the high demand for software professionals, most professionals have many job offers in hand at any given time. When they find a lucrative offer, they quit an organization to join another organization, thus leaving a project midway. Attrition has become such a big issue that managements at big corporations have specialized programs to tackle it [5].

4.2.5 Scope Creep

Scope creep is one risk that affects most software projects, and it always impacts the project severely. Requirements keep changing and new requirements keep piling up even after the project has completed the testing phase and is into the implementation phase. A good change management mechanism can tackle this menace effectively.

4.2.6 Cost Constraints

Once a project is approved for commencement, a budget is allocated and procured for the project. But due to unavoidable reasons, the budget can be constrained. In such situations, the project cannot proceed as sources of funds have dried up and project expenses cannot be met. There is no solution for this problem, but if this risk is known in advance (an unlikely occurrence), then the project could be cut short and scrapping of the project could be avoided.

4.2.7 Bad Negotiation

If the project manager has good negotiation skills, then he can procure an additional/modified budget, support, and resources, whenever the need arises. But sometimes due to bad negotiation skills or for lack of foresight on the part of the customer, this kind of support is not provided and the project lands in troubled waters [6].

4.2.8 Unrealistic Estimate

An unrealistic estimate is yet another risk that is very common on most projects [7]. It is also a fact that effort estimates for software projects are difficult to make because of the uncertainties involved. So, it is always possible that it is understated. It is always better to keep a buffer when an estimate is made, to take care of uncertainties.

4.2.9 Human Error

The human brain has a processing power that no computer can match, but it has a limitation. It cannot do repetitive work without making errors. These human errors are caused by the distractions of the brain because our brain keeps processing all signals sent by our sensory organs continuously, and thus, the work we are doing gets less attention, which results in errors in the work [8]. Due to human error, the requirements or design, or the construction may get injected with defects. To overcome this, we must have review processes for the work done to remove any defects.

4.2.10 Poor Management

Poor management is yet another human risk factor. Not all project managers are naturally talented. Many of them learn managing things from experience. If a project manager lacks experience in managing a project, then it is a big liability for the project and it will show up in project results [9]. Even if a project manager has experience, personal traits dictate whether he can handle the project well or not. So the project manager for a project must be chosen carefully, taking into account his experience and personal traits.

4.3 Risk Categories

All of the risks mentioned in the previous section can actually be broadly grouped into categories of budget risks, resource risks, quality risks, schedule risks, and technology risks. How can these categories of risks be tackled? Let us discuss this point in the following section.

4.3.1 Budget Risks

Risks that impact the project budget need the foremost consideration, and they need to be controlled throughout the project [10]. If for some reason the budget goes above the permissible limit, then the project manager must do something to control it. It is common practice for the project steering committee to decide to cut short some product features to contain the project within the budget. But this is not a good practice. Instead, remedial action must be taken as soon as the project shows the risk of cost overrun, so as to prevent the problem from actually happening. That is why, at all times, project expenses should be tracked and controlled.

Then there are cases when project cost control is not in the hands of the project manager. For instance, due to market forces, the salaries of team members have to be increased, otherwise they might leave the project to get a better salary. In such instances, the management may decide to increase salaries so that they do not leave. In such a case, the project manager has no choice but to revise the project costs and inform the customer about it. This fact can adversely affect the project.

To reduce the impact of budget risks, the budget allowance should include reserve funds. So when such risks occur, allowances can be taken up from the reserves to avoid the project from failing.

4.3.2 Time (Schedule) Risks

The opportunity time window for businesses is slowly shrinking in today's fast-paced and changing business environment. So, if the project looks to be slipping away from the targeted date of deployment, then it will be a great business opportunity loss for the customer. For this reason, the project should never be allowed to cross the targeted release dates [11]. Nevertheless, due to unforeseen circumstances, the project dates may get affected. Sometimes, unexpected rework to be done on software construction will lead to the slippage of the task schedule. There may also be instances when due to a lack of proper communication, customer requirements are completely misunderstood, resulting in an inappropriate product being delivered to the customer, and thus, complete rework is required to prepare the software. This will again lead to project schedule slippage.

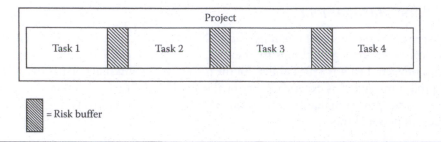

Figure 4.4 Schedule risk buffer provisions in a project.

To reduce the impact of schedule slippages, a schedule allowance should be taken for each time-related risk (Figure 4.4).

4.3.3 Resource Risks

Project team members are the most costly resources in software projects [12]. So, creating reserved resources for the project is a difficult proposition. On one hand, the project manager needs to keep project costs at the bare minimum, and on the other, he has to make a provision for reserved project resources as contingency for any risk of losing any project team member at any time during the execution of the project. It is a reality that software professionals are in great demand, and most projects run the real risk of team members leaving the project for more lucrative offers. In such a situation, a project may suffer if any team member decides to leave the project midway. Whatever tasks the member had finished on the project is fine, but what about the remaining tasks that have not been started yet, or have only been half finished? Generally, it is not a good idea to keep a paid reserve on the project as it would add to the cost of the project. But keeping a pipeline open for probable replacements is a good idea. When a replacement is needed, the project manager can tap this pipeline and get the replacement. But sometimes getting the right replacement takes time, and thus, the project suffers. This risk can be mitigated by keeping a reserve in the project schedule for any delay in resource replacement. This reserve pool can consist of people sitting on the bench or list of people who are working on other projects and the dates on they will be available (Figure 4.5).

Project team members leaving in the middle of the project is one of the biggest risks any project may face. Such team members take the project task (the task he was working on) knowledge with them as well. This results in a big loss to the project. This risk can be mitigated to some extent by implementing a knowledge management system that will store all the knowledge acquired by team members during the project. It will also store all the work performed by the project team. So, when a team member leaves the project, the knowledge acquired and the work

Figure 4.5 Resource risk strategy.

done by him is in the knowledge management system. Thus, the project team will not lose all the work that has been done and the knowledge acquired by the person who is leaving.

Knowledge management is discussed in further detail in Chapter 19.

4.3.4 Quality Risks

Industry strength software needs a rock solid reliability so that during operations, the support costs can be kept at a minimum [13]. Otherwise, supporting a poor quality software product becomes a losing proposition. So, the quality of the software product is always a concern and a big risk. The quality of the product may be poor due to bad software design or bad software construction. Even if it is good, there is still a chance of defects inadvertently creeping in due to complexity, large integration interfaces, or due to the large number of changes in the design when the requirements are altered.

To deal with quality risks, the best policy is to have a check for quality integrated in the project schedule itself (quality planning). This will ensure that the quality at the work product level is on par with the desired level, which in turn will ensure overall product quality. Peer reviews, code reviews, and other formal quality review processes should be strictly followed for all work products (Figure 4.6).

In fact, ensuring quality of the software product being developed has become so critical these days that quality planning must be integrated tightly in the entire project plan to reduce quality-related risks.

4.3.5 Technology Risks

Technology obsolescence is a fact of life [14]. With the rapid introduction of new products into the market, older products quickly become obsolete. So, many projects face the prospect of having an outdated technology on which the software product is being built. In such cases, the software product becomes unusable even before it is implemented. Similarly, if any hardware component that may have been integrated with the software and the hardware becomes obsolete, the software product becomes unusable. An appropriate selection of programming language, hardware platform, and user access methods will make sure that the software product does not become obsolete during the expected lifespan usage of the product. When selecting technology tools and techniques, contact the vendors to make sure that they will be providing support in future as well for the tools you are buying from them.

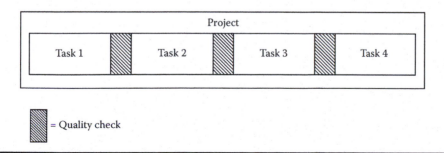

Figure 4.6   Quality checks at the end of a project task.

4.4 Risk Analysis

Dealing with any kind of risk requires some risk analysis [15]. The analysis should consider the kind of impact risk can have on the project as well as the chance of it happening. Based on the analysis, you then need to sort risks and put them in order. Risks with high probability and high impact will be put on top of this list, while risks with low impact and low probability will be put at the bottom. The project manager will then be better prepared to deal with all kinds of risks in a systematic manner (Table 4.1).

Different risks occur at different times in the project. For instance, the product quality may not meet the expected standards during the design stage, and the design may need to be reworked. The rework may stretch the project schedule and the project plan may need to be redone. So, this is a risk that can occur at the design stage. Similarly, during testing, a lot of unexpected defects might be found, and the time taken to fix these defects will overshoot the budgeted time. Sometimes, it may so happen that a team member may fall sick and it may take time to replace him. This may cause a delay in finishing the assignment that was given to the team member (Figure 4.7).

In a nutshell, project risks are dynamic in nature. They can occur at any stage of the project. So the project risk matrix where the project manager has listed risks and their impact as well as their probability needs to be revised at regular intervals and the risks that are likely to happen at that moment in time need to be assessed and remedial action should be taken.

Table 4.1 Matrix of Risks: Their Impact and Probability

Risk Category	Risk	Probability	Impact
Budget	Task budget overrun	High	High
Budget	Wrong budget estimate of a task	Medium	High
Resource	Not available	High	Medium
Resource	Skill training	Medium	Medium
Schedule	Wrong estimate of a task		
Project scope	Scope creep		
Quality	Bad quality of product		
Quality	Product reliability issues		
Technology	Technology obsolescence		

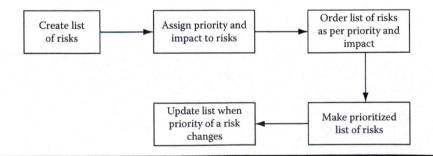

Figure 4.7 Risk analysis life cycle.

4.5 Balancing Act

No project can be executed 100% as per the project plan. There is bound to be something different than planned due to the occurrence of any kind of risk and the subsequent impact it has on the project. How can the project manager justify whatever has been delivered? Can he justify any schedule or budget overrun? What about deviation in the quality level? What about a less-than-agreed on set of features being delivered?

There are no easy answers. Each project is different. It depends on the importance of each deliverable on the project compared to the other deliverables. This is not an easy choice. At the top level, quality level considerations come from the kind of application being developed, and for what purpose. If the application is meant for a general purpose information displaying system, and the end users do not mind occasional bugs, then the quality level for the project can be compromised in preference for costs or schedules. On the other hand, if the application needs accurate transactions without any compromise, then quality cannot be undermined. In that case, costs or schedules can be allowed to overrun to get the desired level of quality (Figure 4.8).

These are all subjective considerations. The project manager must decide what limits to cross and what limits to abide with. In doing so, he also should have consent from the project stakeholders.

The project manager may also come across situations (which are very common) where requirements as well as priorities are ambiguous. In those cases, it will be in the best interest of the project manager to remove those ambiguities as much as possible. Clear, well defined, and feasible requirements lead to a better control over the project. At the same time, priorities should also be set appropriately. Delivering low priority requirements at the cost of high priority requirements will lead to unsatisfactory project performance.

From a software engineering point of view; clear requirements are the most vital inputs to a project. But every experienced project manager knows that clear requirements are not enough to do the job. Priorities are equally important.

It is this balancing act that each project manager must perform to succeed in the project at hand.

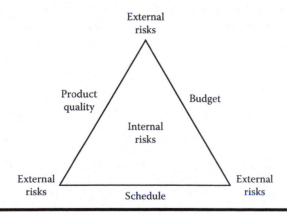

Figure 4.8 Internal and external risks, and balance in product quality, project budget, and project schedule.

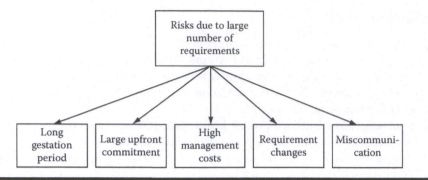

Figure 4.9   Major risks in traditional software development.

4.6 Project Risk Management in Agile Models

Using a waterfall model to execute your project is a big risk. It is because the outcome of the project (the software product) is ready only after the whole project is completed after a prolonged period of time. Suppose the project duration is 6 months, then the outcome of the project is known only after investing time and money for these 6 months. The outcome could be positive or negative. Waiting for such a long time to get the result is a big risk indeed. To reduce this risk, iterative approaches to software development have been tried. Instead of taking all the requirements and doing the entire product development in one go, requirements are broken into small sets of manageable requirements. Each small set of requirements is then used to develop a small product. The duration for making these small products (software features) is kept at 4–6 weeks or even less. After each iteration, there is a demonstrable product that can be tested to see if it works as intended, and as per the requirements. This approach reduces the big risk into a set of small risks (Figure 4.9).

All the risks associated with the waterfall model are either miniaturized or totally eliminated in the iterative model. They can be managed in a better way as well due to the small size of these iterative projects.

4.7 Artifacts of Project Risk Management

Risk management deals with defining probable risks, their impact on the project, and the ways of dealing with them to minimize their impact on the project. The outcome of risk management planning is the risk management document. It contains the list of risks, their impact, probability, and what measures are to be taken to overcome them if they occur. Since risk can occur at any time during the entire course of the project, and their chances of occurring vary from time to time, they are dynamic in nature. So the risk management document should be updated regularly to keep risk information current.

4.8 Practical Considerations for Risk Management

All of the risks on a project can be categorized as manageable and unmanageable. The project manager must make mitigation strategies for all manageable risks. The unmanageable risks at hand cannot be managed, and thus cannot have a mitigation strategy. A good example of an unmanageable risk is a natural calamity, such as an earthquake. If an earthquake strikes, then you cannot manage the earthquake. What can be managed to some extent, are the consequences. The fire brigade, police, and volunteer teams can try to find people who are stuck in the debris and try to save them. For human and capital losses, insurance companies can shell out insurance benefits.

So for all unmanageable risks, the project manager can at best rely on external help if possible. But for all manageable risks (that he can manage), he should make mitigation strategies. These strategies will help him when these risks occur and impact the project in any way.

4.9 Case Study

In Chapter 3, we saw how effort and cost estimation were done for the project of our SaaS vendor. In this chapter, we will see how risks on the project were identified and how risk mitigation plans were made to tackle those potential risks.

Every business is constantly trying to find out what the current market size for the products and services it sells, and where it stands in the market vis-à-vis its competitors. What is the total market potential for the software product it wants to produce? Who are the other players in the market? What are their market shares? How does it want to carve a share in the market for its products and services? What strategies are other players making? What are the future prospects and where is the future heading?

Based on these findings, the business makes its own strategy. It makes a market plan and prepares a detailed roadmap to achieve the market position it wants to hold. It also assesses the risks associated with its venture and formulates a strategy to deal with these risks. The survival of the business entirely depends on how it perceives the risks and how it successfully mitigates these risks.

For any software vendor, the biggest risk is whether its software product will become as successful as envisaged by the market potential for the product, from its market research. Once market potential is assessed, the vendor then starts implementing its strategy by commencing building the software product, which is a costly affair. The development costs are determined in advance, and an appropriate budget is allocated. A development team is formed, and the team starts developing the software product. The development of the product itself may encounter several risks.

4.9.1 Risks on This Project

Our SaaS vendor underwent many challenges and risks while developing its flagship software product. The foremost risks envisaged by the development team were

- Viability of offshore teams and relationship with service providers
- Attrition
- Communication gaps (languages, understanding of tasks, understanding of messages, etc.)
- Development costs
- Development schedule
- Software product quality

For the 6.0 release, the development team formulated the following strategies to tackle these risks:

■ First of all, a thorough check was made for competency and maturity of the offshore service providers. Subsequently, a comprehensive service level agreement (SLA) was drafted, and then the service providers were made to sign the agreement. As per the SLA, the service providers would make a detailed weekly report for all tasks performed by its employees and details of these tasks. These reports would be reviewed by the software vendor. The hours spent on tasks and progress status on assignments per week will be checked by the vendor. Only after review would the hours of work reported be cleared.

■ To tackle attrition, the software vendor made sure that its own employees were not only given the best salary in the industry, but were also provided with a working environment that satisfied their personal aspirations. Each employee was counseled, and based on his aspirations and his ability, was given assignments. During performance review, if performance was not up to the mark, then suggested measures were taken in consultation with the employee. Likewise, the vendor had made sure that the staff at the service providers was also treated in a similar manner.

■ Communication gap between the onshore and offshore teams was a big challenge due to distance, different time zones, and culture differences. To mitigate this risk, it was decided to have a standard template for all communication among teams. Virtual meetings were decided for knowledge transfers and issue resolutions. It was decided to use Webex (Cisco Systems Inc.), Skype, Yahoo Instant Messenger, Microsoft Net meeting, and other media for virtual meetings. VOIP phones were also used. Due to time zone differences, meetings could take place either early in the mornings or late in the evenings (even if it meant working nonoffice hours).

■ To make sure that project and iteration schedules were on track, the development team decided to keep a buffer in the schedule of 10% of the schedule estimate. If the schedule was going to be affected due to the occurrence of any risk, then the schedule buffer could be used. This strategy worked fine throughout the project related to release 6.0 of the software product. At the same time, for each iteration, the project manager would assign a priority value to each feature, which was to be taken into the iteration. The most prioritized features would be developed first. If the iteration permitted time, then lesser prioritized features could be taken for development. So, if due to the occurrence of any risk, a feature took more time for development than planned, then at least all prioritized features were developed in the iteration even if some nonprioritized features could not be taken up.

■ To make sure that the unavailability of any project team member for short durations did not affect the project schedule, each team manager was authorized to ask for overtime work from his team. In the absence of a team member for short durations, the other team members performed those assignments to finish them on time. Similarly, if the schedule was being affected for any other reason, then the project manager would ask for overtime from his team to finish any pending assignments on time.

■ To ensure that the quality of the software product was always high, reviews and checks were incorporated into the process after each work product was completed. When the requirements were completed (in the form of requirement specifications), they were tested to make sure that they did not have any deficiencies or defects. Similarly, the design and source code were also reviewed thoroughly before wrapping up these tasks.

4.10 Chapter Summary

Software projects are a huge risk for stakeholders as their interests are at stake on the success or failure of the project. Once they approve a project, then the burden of carrying the risk falls on the shoulders of the appointed project manager. Each activity and project task has its own share of risk. During project execution, risks that might adversely hamper the project lurk at every corner. So, before starting execution, the project manager must ensure that he has a sound risk management plan to tackle any risk that might crop up.

Any of the risks can impact schedule, cost, or quality. So all the risks should be categorized by the kind of impact it has on any of these project components.

To make a sound risk mitigation plan, the project manager should first identify the risks that can occur during project execution. He should make a list of all these potential risks. Then he should find out the severity of impact each of these risks can have on the project. He can also then make a priority for each risk for tackling it. Based on impact and priority, he can sort out this list to come up with the risk with the most urgent need for tackling, and at the end of the list, the risks that are the least likely to have any impact on the project and those that have the least priority as well. For each risk, the project manager can find out the cost and effort required to tackle them. Based on the cost and effort required for tackling probable risks, the project manager can make buffers in the project plan. In this way, if any risk appears, the project manager can save the project schedule or cost from going out of hand by consuming the budget or schedule from the buffer.

To tackle risks that can impact quality, quality assurance measures must be ensured throughout the project. All work products during the project must be checked for quality. Only when quality norms are met with, should the project be allowed to proceed to the next phase, so that in the next phase of the project, the input work product is defect free. For this arrangement, the project schedule must have tasks for work product inspections as well as some time allowance so that the work product can be reworked to make it defect free.

These risks can happen anytime during the project execution, and they may not crop up at the expected time. So the project manager should keep revising his list of risks, so that they are always arranged and ordered as per their probability of occurrence.

Exercises

4.1 Find out all the reasons why risk management in the iterative development models is different compared to the traditional waterfall model.

4.2 Find out all the risks that cannot be managed on a software project. List the reasons why these risks cannot be managed.

Review Questions

4.1 List all the kinds of risks that can occur on a project.

4.2 What strategy is adopted to minimize the impact of any risk on the project?

4.3 Describe in detail the steps taken in preparing a risk management strategy.

4.4 Why is risk management so important for any project?

4.5 What strategy is adopted to minimize the risk of changing requirements?

Recommended Readings

1. J. Smith, P. McKee (2001) *Troubled IT Projects: Prevention and Turnaround* (IEE Professional Applications of Computing Series, 3), Institute of Electrical & Electronic Engineers, Hertfordshire, U.K.
2. K. Heldman (2007) *PMP: Project Management Professional Exam Study Guide*, Sybex, Alameda, CA.
3. D. Lock (2007) *Project Management*, Ashgate Publishing Company, Aldershot, U.K.
4. M. D. Lewin (2001) *Better Software Project Management: A Primer for Success*, Wiley, Hoboken, NJ.
5. F. Tsui (2004) *Managing Software Projects*, Jones and Bartlett Publishers, Inc, Sudbury, MA.
6. P. C. Tinnirello (1999) *Project Management*, CRC Press, Boca Raton, FL.
7. D. D. Galorath, M. W. Evans (2006) *Software Sizing, Estimation, and Risk Management*, CRC Press, Boca Raton, FL.
8. R. T. Futrell, D. F. Shafer, L. I. Shafer (2002) *Quality Software Project Management*, Prentice Hall PTR, Upper Saddle River, NJ.
9. J. E. Tomayko, O. Hazzan (2004) *Human Aspects of Software Engineering*, Laxmi Publications, New Delhi, India.
10. R. J. Muller (1997) *Productive Objects: An Applied Software Project Management Framework*, Morgan Kaufmann, San Fransisco, CA.
11. R. E. Fairley (2009) *Managing and Leading Software Projects*, Wiley-IEEE Computer Society Press, Hoboken, NJ.
12. J. T. Marchewka (2006) *Information Technology Project Management*, Wiley India Pvt. Ltd., New Delhi, India.
13. J. W. Horch (1996) *Practical Guide to Software Quality Management*, Artech House, London, U.K.
14. K. Bittner, I. Spence (2006) *Managing Iterative Software Development Projects* (The Addison-Wesley Object Technology Series), Addison-Wesley Professional, Boston, MA.
15. P. Jalote (2002) *Software Project Management in Practice*, Addison-Wesley Professional, Boston, MA.

Chapter 5

Configuration Management

In the previous chapter, we learned

- What is a risk on a project?
- What kinds of risks exist for a project?
- What kind of impact may risk have on a project?
- What strategy is needed to deal with risks?

In this chapter, we will learn

- What is a configuration management system?
- What are the parts of a configuration management system?
- Why is a configuration management system required on a software project?
- What strategies can be made to deploy a configuration management system successfully for a project?

5.1 Introduction

Configuration management is needed on software projects because numerous artifacts are produced during the entire product development life cycle. There needs to be a place where these artifacts can be kept safely and from where they can be accessed easily and securely whenever required. Configuration management is in fact a supporting process that runs alongside the development process.

During the entire software development life cycle, requirements keep changing. This results in many versions of work products. Each team member is supposed to work on the right version of any work product. If these versions are not managed properly, there may be the possibility that

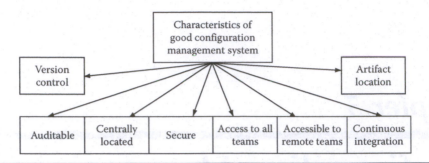

Figure 5.1   Characteristics of a good configuration management system.

team members start working on wrong versions of work products. It is therefore very important that documents and work products be kept at the right place and that project teams be aware of the right locations of documents in the configuration management (Figure 5.1).

Continuous integration is adopted for many software development projects. A build of the software product is kept at a central location and each new piece of software being developed is integrated with the existing build. Thus, in a single day there could be more than 50 or more revisions or more of the same build due to new codes being added by developers throughout the day. There could also be many versions of the build at any given time. The new code must be checked in the right software build. If a proper configuration and version control system is not provided, this kind of software development (continuous integration) is not possible.

5.2 Configuration Management

The driving force behind configuration management is the need to store, archive, identify, retrieve, and release work products and information items for the entire project team [1]. Change control for different versions of information items is what makes configuration management a difficult area. Each information item can be identified using tags associated with the information item. Some common tags for item identification include

- Project name
- Year and time stamp
- Document name
- Document number
- Author
- Activity identifier
- Document type
- Version number

A configuration management system is used by the entire project team, which may consist of one's own team as well as contractors and service providers. To manage who can have access to what information, a secured access system is required. To achieve this, we can define roles and permissions centrally. Information items are stored inside folders. Each folder can have multiple sub-folders. Each of these sub-folders can, in turn, have multiple sub-folders. This hierarchy is maintained for each major classification of items. The items are then created and stored at the appropriate place in the hierarchy (Figures 5.2 and 5.3).

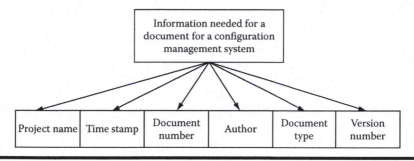

Figure 5.2   Information required for keeping a document or work product in a configuration management system.

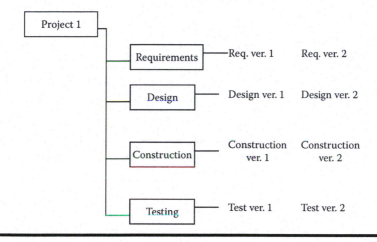

Figure 5.3   Folder and item hierarchy structure inside a configuration management system.

Each folder then has an access permission for each defined role. Each role may have edit/view or view-only roles. Roles with proper access permission can only view or edit any item inside that folder, or any sub-folders inside that folder. An account for each individual project team member is created on the configuration management system. Each of these accounts is then linked to appropriate defined roles. Team members can then create/access documents and files on the system as per their access rights.

5.3 Configuration Management Techniques

As has been mentioned previously, keeping track of the right versions of information and work product items is very important in any project. So version control is one of the most important aspects of any configuration management system. As most software projects are executed with teams at different locations, which may be under different time zones, a central configuration system is required that would allow smooth working of all teams from all locations. Consider the problems this type of development work can face if a central configuration system is not available and a decentralized system has to be followed. Each team would have its own configuration management system. The setup would vary between teams, with the same item being named and known differently in each system (Figure 5.4).

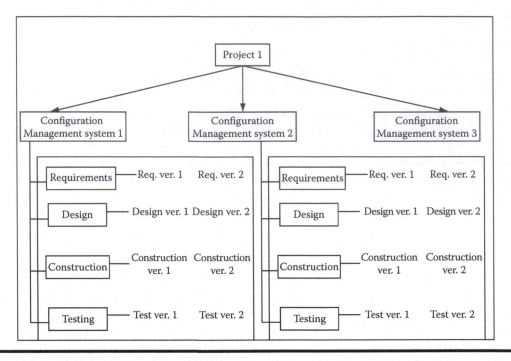

Figure 5.4 Folder and item hierarchy structure inside a decentralized configuration management system.

This kind of arrangement would create chaos. It would be difficult to control versions of documents and would make it harder for teams to manage their work. If integration were required between two components developed by two different teams, it would be difficult to know if they were the right versions for the integration. In short, it would create a great many problems. Moreover, synchronizing different versions of documents over different configuration management systems is a tedious and error-prone task. It also adds unnecessary overhead.

In light of things we have seen so far related to different aspects of configuration management systems, it makes sense to stick to some best practices that are relevant to these kinds of systems. Following are some techniques and best practices [2] that are extremely useful:

1. Centralized configuration management system [3]
2. Secured access mechanism with role-based access control [4]
3. Continuous integration of software build with smoke test facility [5]
4. Easy branching mechanism to branch out an entire software version [6]
5. Audit facility

As discussed earlier, a centralized configuration management with a role-based access mechanism will allow smooth functioning of the system.

When it comes to managing the central source code build, some critical considerations need to be made, especially if we are in continuous integration mode. Generally, when the project is in construction phase, developers will write code and will check their code with the existing software build whenever they complete a unit of a component on which they are working. If, for some reason, the build gets broken due to faulty code, the configuration system will not allow other

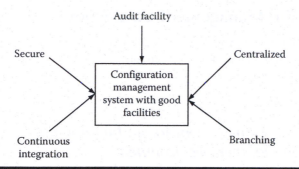

Figure 5.5 Facilities required of a good configuration management system.

developers to check their piece of code until the build is rectified by the developer who had checked in the last piece of code. (This functionality can be achieved by installing an automatic smoke testing tool such as Cruise Control, which will keep generating error messages whenever a piece of source code is checked in to the software build as long as the wrong piece of source code is not rectified and checked in.) The current developer then rewrites his piece of code and checks his code again. If the build is successful, other developers are allowed to check in their piece of code. This kind of mechanism is important to maintain integrity of the software build. For a better management of this build management; an automated smoke test facility is usually provided. Whenever a new piece of code is checked in to the build, this test facility runs automatically. It checks integrity of the build. If the build is fine, a success message is sent via e-mail to the current developer. If the smoke test fails, a failed message is sent to the current developer and any other person whose e-mail address is defined in the list of e-mails. This mechanism is indeed very useful. Together with other good characteristics, this facility forms a good configuration system (Figure 5.5).

Generally, after a software product version is fully developed and tested, development work is stopped on that version. The project team then starts working on the next version of the software product. The person responsible for managing the configuration management system creates a new work space on the configuration management system for the new version of the product. There are thousands of folders and files on a typical software development project. Creating all of them from scratch will take an inordinate amount of time. It is far more effective to create a branch of the existing folders and files of the project and copy them in the new branch. So a new work space will become ready quickly.

The configuration management system should also have a good audit facility. Whenever any documents stored on the system are needed for verification, they should be easily available. If any changes are needed on any archived document, both the new and the old versions should be available on the system. A time stamp should also be available for the changes made on any document.

5.4 Artifacts of Configuration Management

A configuration management system holds software build files, work products, and documents generated at each phase of the software development life cycle, and reviews, reports and other information documents. All of these documents and files have many versions. Whenever there is a change required in any document or artifact, a new set of new versions of files are created and saved on the system. Thus, for each project, there will be requirement specification documents, design documents, software builds, testing plans, testing cycle documents, training manuals, review documents, etc. on the system.

5.5 Configuration Management Case Study

In Chapters 2 through 4, we learned about project initiation, effort estimation, and risk management for the project undertaken at our SaaS vendor. Here is a case study on how to set up and arrange a central configuration management system that can be used by internal, external, and offshore teams at the same time.

5.5.1 Configuration Management for an Incremental Iteration Development Environment

A U.S.-based mid-market software vendor built a software system that allowed retailers, distributors, and manufacturers to manage their orders, inventories, shipment of goods, third-party logistics service providers, warehouses, etc. This system is being used by many large customers in the U.S., Europe, and other markets.

For development of this software system, they adopted the incremental iteration development model. They have their own internal project team that works on developing the software. They also have employed service providers at offshore locations in India, Russia, and other locations to reduce their development costs and to shrink the development cycle. This arrangement is working very well for them. Thanks to the efficient and reliable configuration management system that they have deployed centrally and that is accessible to all teams regardless of their locations, they have been able to do all their development work without encountering too many hurdles. The configuration management system is available 24 h a day, 7 days a week, and there is virtually no downtime. It is also very secure, and no hacks have occurred since it started working.

The access rights were of two types. Administration rights (edit, delete, add) were given only to team members who were either owners of documents or responsible for maintaining documents. Others were given view-only rights to download and view these documents. One super-user role was also created—this could be used to create new branches and to add, delete, or modify any folders or documents in the entire configuration management system.

The main branch of the version control contains the main build of the software containing all the major updates that have taken place since the product was developed. This main branch also contained all related artifacts for the main build (Figure 5.6).

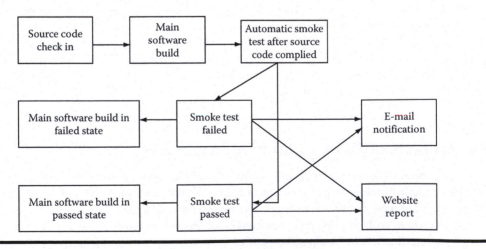

Figure 5.6 Workflow for smoke test on the main software build.

An automated smoke testing software was installed on all branches where developed software code was being checked. Whenever any fresh code is checked in the build by any developer, this software will run automatically. It will check the compatibility of the new code with the existing build. If any inconsistency is found and the build fails, it will show a failure notice on a status page and also send this page to the designated people on the e-mail list, including the person who checked in the fresh code. If the status page shows success, the developer can start working toward his next assignment. If the build fails, he receives a failure notice and starts working to fix the problem. He can either check back the code with which he checked in or can check in the corrected code again. This practice ensures that the build is available for all developers located at any geographical site most of the time. If, for some reason, the developer cannot rectify the build even after checking back his code or is not aware of the failure, the problem is escalated. If any build is not fixed within 1 h, the configuration tool will send an e-mail to the global program manager. He can then take any appropriate action.

Each developer also keeps a local build and smoke test application on his personal computer. He keeps this local build in synch with the build located at the central configuration tool. Before checking his code in the central configuration tool, he runs his code on this local version. If the code is built successfully and the smoke test application shows a success status, he checks his code in the central build. This ensures that the central build does not fail often.

5.6 Chapter Summary

On software projects, many versions of the work products are developed due to defect fixing, pending changes, change requests, etc. Configuration management on software projects plays an important role in making sure that all these versions of work products are correctly maintained and that project team members have access to all these work products and project documents.

Particularly, source code builds are very sensitive to version control. Source code build is the repository where each developer checks in his source code after developing it. These check-ins can be done several times during the day by each developer. If the source code checked in by a developer has defects, it will fail when the build is run. Finding and fixing the cause of failure becomes a tedious and difficult task.

The configuration management system should have a good security mechanism in place so that it is not hacked by unauthorized persons. Unauthorized access to the system may result in loss or theft of vital project information. At the same time, the project team should have easy access to the system so that they can archive, retrieve, edit, or remove project work products and documents without any problems.

Apart from the regular role of configuration and version control management, these systems also play an important role as keepers and providers of project information.

Exercises

5.1 For any open source project, try to find the configuration management system log. Find significant features of the maintained configuration system for the project. (You can find many open source projects at www.sourceforge.net.)

5.2 From requirement change request logs for any accessible project, find out the complete change log for each work product.

Review Questions

5.1 Why is a configuration management system required on software projects?

5.2 What are the essential ingredients of a good configuration management system?

5.3 What is a smoke test?

5.4 Which is a better configuration management system: a centralized system or a decentralized system? Explain the benefits and drawbacks of each.

5.5 What is branching on a configuration management system?

Recommended Readings

1. J. Estublier (1995) *Software Configuration Management: ICSE SCM-4 and SCM-5 Workshops. Selected Papers* (Lecture Notes in Computer Science), Springer, Berlin, Germany.
2. J. Keyes (2004) *Software Configuration Management*, CRC Press, Boca Raton, FL.
3. A. Mette Jonassen Hass (2002) *Configuration Management Principles and Practice*, Addison-Wesley Professional, Boston, MA.
4. B. Barkley (2007) *Project Management in New Product Development*, McGraw-Hill Education (India) Pvt Ltd., New Delhi, India.
5. S. P. Berczuk, B. Appleton (2002) *Software Configuration Management Patterns: Effective Teamwork, Practical Integration*, Addison-Wesley Professional, Boston, MA.
6. M. E. Moreira (2004) *Software Configuration Management Implementation Roadmap*, Wiley, New York.

Chapter 6

Project Planning

In the previous chapter, we learned

- What is a configuration management system?
- What are the parts of a configuration management system?
- Why is a configuration management system required for a software project?
- What strategies can be made to deploy a configuration management system successfully for a project?

In this chapter, we will learn

- What is software project plan?
- What are the parts of a software project plan?
- What are the types of software project plans?
- What inputs go in making a software project plan?
- What techniques are used in making a software project plan?

6.1 Introduction

Project planning for any software project involves making the best trade-off among quality, schedule, cost, and organization benefits which can accrue from the project. In in-house projects, the benefits to the organization from the software are related to management gains in the form of increasing market share, reducing operational costs, reducing risk exposure, complying with government regulations, etc. Benefits to the end users include ease of work, reducing labor-intensive work, increasing work performance, etc. Often the project manager may not be aware of these benefits; nevertheless, if he has information about these things, it will help him to satisfy his customers' needs in a better way.

For instance, if he knows that the main objective of the project is to enhance the productivity of the staff, then he will choose a software design where the user input required in doing transactions is kept to a minimum, thus increasing user productivity.

In outsourced projects, one important goal of the service provider is to make a profit from the project. They keep a profit margin on top of estimated project costs. Accordingly, while doing resource planning, the project manager should plan it in such a way that costs of resource for the project do not impact the profit margins of the project.

There are so many details that the project manager has to be aware of; only then, can he make a good plan for the project.

6.2 Project Planning Fundamentals

During project initiation, high-level project planning is done. But at that stage, not many of the project details are available. So the project planning is at best a rough one. The effort estimate done at that stage is also a rough one. Both these plans need to be refined at a later date when all or most of the project details become available so that it becomes more usable for the project.

Depending on time frame requirement of a project, it can be either a top-down project planning or a bottom-up project planning [1]. Generally, in the case of product development by software vendors, the project management is a top-down approach, and in the case of custom software development, it is a bottom-up approach. The market forces dictate the software vendors to release new versions with desired features within a specified time period. In this case, the release date is fixed, and so the software development team is given a specified time period within which they have to incorporate the desired features in the software and have to make it available on the market. Since the time and the features are fixed, the development team has no choice but to develop the product within that specified time frame. This is known as the top-down approach. In contrast, in custom software development, the project team is given the software requirements, and from these requirements, they estimate how much time it will take to develop the product. Then the development team decides on the release date of the project. This approach is known as the bottom-up approach.

For large outsourced software development projects, which are instituted to make industry strength large software products, software engineering plays an instrumental role along with service level agreements (SLAs), project scope, etc. Using software engineering will ensure that the project and product development processes will be well defined and will ensure good product quality at competitive cost and acceptable schedule. Project scope defines the volume of work to be done on the project in conjunction with requirements. SLAs define deliverables, frequency of status reports, legal and commercial liabilities, etc. (Figure 6.1).

The project plan itself consists of a large number of planning components [2]. It includes risk planning, resource planning, task planning, effort estimation, cost estimation, communication planning, configuration management planning, tool planning, supplier management planning, quality planning, and scope planning. We will study all of these planning components in detail later in the chapter.

6.2.1 Top-Down Plan

The product development company (software product vendor) always has product release dates planned in advance. Similarly, any company who needs a software system for meeting the market demands needs the system within some stipulated time. In fact, a large number of companies are

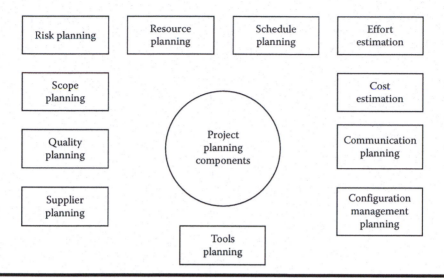

Figure 6.1   Software project planning components.

operating under acute market pressures and they need software systems within a certain time window to accomplish their business goals. If the software system is not provided within this time frame, then the business may experience severe losses. Under these circumstances, a software project should be instituted with a top-down approach.

As you can see in Figure 6.2, there are a large number of inputs in the case of planning top-down projects. Here, apart from project scope, SLAs, and chosen software engineering model and requirements, we have project start date, project end date, project duration, and project budget. All of these details are available to the project team before the start of the project.

In the case of top-down projects, the plan outputs include supplier management, configuration management, communication management, defect prevention strategy, WBS structure, resource allocation, tool management, scope management, effort estimate, and risk management (Figure 6.3).

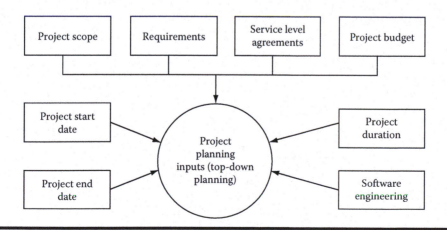

Figure 6.2   Software project planning inputs for top-down approach.

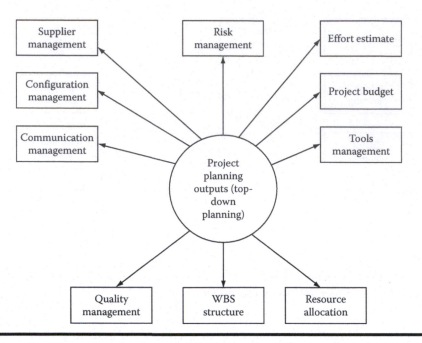

Figure 6.3 Software project planning outputs for top-down approach.

6.2.2 Bottom-Up Plan

Large software projects devoid of much clarity at the beginning of the project tend to have a bottom-up approach for their project planning. At the beginning of the project, effort is made to find out what tasks should be involved in the project and how the project may span out. Obviously there will be no sufficient information available at the beginning of the project, and the project team has to strive to gather as much information as possible to make a reasonable plan for the project. They collect information about project scope, requirements, and SLAs. Using any appropriate software engineering model, they define the development strategy (whether to use waterfall, agile, or any custom approach) and accordingly settle for the kind of development tasks they will employ in the project. Once these inputs are in place, then the project team can chalk out the project plan, including the complete output (Figure 6.4).

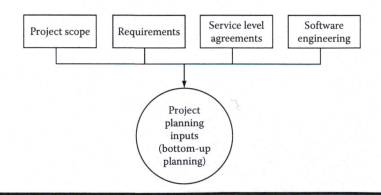

Figure 6.4 Software project planning inputs for bottom-up approach.

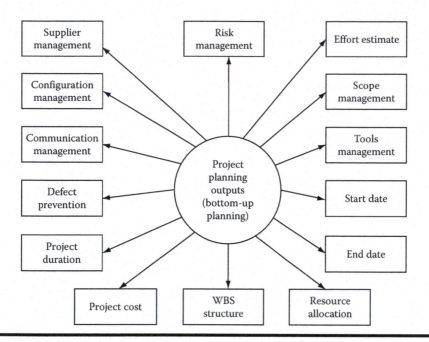

Figure 6.5   Software project planning outputs for bottom-up approach.

Project planning requires inputs based on which outputs will be created in form of project plan. Inputs for project planning for bottom-up approach include project scope, SLAs, and chosen software engineering model, along with the all important software requirements (Figure 6.5).

In the bottom-up project, the project plan output includes supplier management, configuration management, communication management, defect prevention strategy, project duration, project cost, work breakdown structure (WBS), resource allocation, project start and end dates, tool management, scope management, effort estimate, and risk management.

6.2.3 Work Breakdown Structure

When a project plan is made, all project tasks are included in the plan [3]. Each of these tasks has a start date and an end date. When all the tasks are listed in the plan, it will be difficult to identify which task is dependent on another task, which task is on the critical path, which task signifies a milestone, etc. It is also necessary to group the tasks that are part of the same phase in the project and put them under a pseudo task with the name of the phase. The last tasks in each of these pseudo tasks will be the milestone tasks, which are also pseudo tasks. In Microsoft Project and other project management software, all tasks pertaining to the same group can be expanded or collapsed at the parent task. This makes reading the WBS easier and manageable (Figure 6.6).

6.2.4 Resource Allocation

Software projects have variable staff requirements over the project [4]. While construction and software testing phases need a large pool of resources, the requirement and design phases need a far smaller number of resources. One more aspect about software projects is that skills are not usually transferable. So a software architect who makes software design is usually not associated

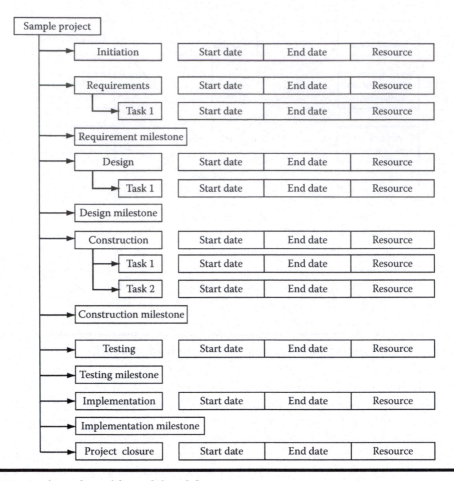

Figure 6.6   Project plan with work breakdown structure.

with software construction. Once he designs the software application, his job with the project is complete and he can be assigned to some other projects. In general, about 50% of the resources are required during the construction phase. For software testing, it is about 30% (Figure 6.7).

This uneven resource requirement over the project phases has led to the evolution of concurrent engineering models. Many teams are formed for software construction and testing who work in parallel, and thus, project cycles get reduced.

6.2.5 Supplier Management Plan

If the entire project or project parts are to be done by outsourced project teams, then a supplier management plan is needed for the project [5]. It will include creating the SLA, its compliance, etc. (Figure 6.8).

It is important to manage suppliers so that parts developed by them are not inferior to the parts made by your team. Similarly, if there are two or more suppliers, then the quality of work products/products provided by them should be of the same level. One major area of concern is the integration of software parts made by suppliers to the main software build. To mitigate this risk, the central build should be employed so that from the start of the build, the outsourced team can

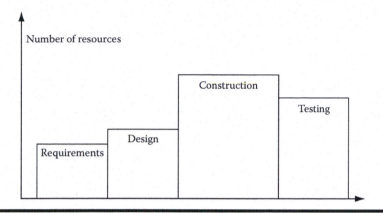

Figure 6.7   Resource (staff) requirements for a software project over different phases.

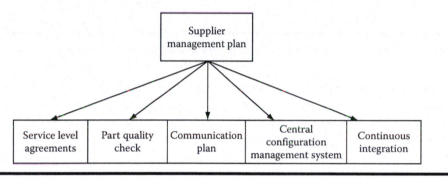

Figure 6.8   Supplier management plan.

keep checking their code. This will make sure that integration problems will not arise. Detailed information about supplier management is provided in Part III.

6.2.6 Configuration Management Plan

With many scattered teams working on the same project in many cases, it is most important that configuration management is done carefully. It should be ensured that all teams have the same version of source code and document files; otherwise chances of rework will increase. It is the best policy to have a centralized configuration management system used and maintained by all the teams. Security and access control for this system should be of high quality so that project team members can do their work securely and without any fear of losing their work. Detailed information about configuration management is provided in Chapter 5.

6.2.7 Communication Management

Communication management depends solely on project organization structure, customer management strategy, and supplier management needs [6]. For effective communication among all of these parties, it is essential that a proper communication management strategy is in place. The project manager must define what needs to be communicated to whom, in what

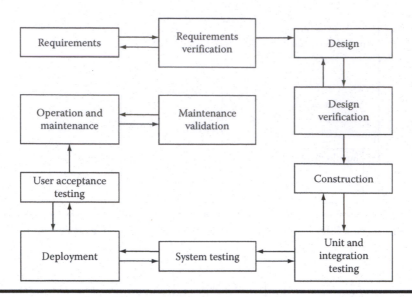

Figure 6.9 Defect prevention mechanism (quality assurance) in the project.

manner, and when. A good way to promote a uniform communication channel across all the scattered project teams is to use a good set of project templates. A set of standard templates will go a long way in establishing a smooth and uniform communication among all the project teams. Detailed information about communication management is provided in Chapters 19 through 21.

6.2.8 Defect Prevention Strategy (Quality Assurance)

Quality assurance and control is the most important aspect of any software project [7]. Without having a defect prevention strategy (quality assurance), the project will be doomed to fail. Defect prevention strategy should be an integral part of the project (Figure 6.9).

After each project phase, the work products should be validated and verified, and only if they pass the expected quality level, the project should be allowed to proceed further. Otherwise the work products should be reworked until a satisfactory quality level is achieved.

6.2.9 Project Duration

Project duration is calculated using the critical path along the project tasks. The longest path is the critical path of the project, and its length is the project duration. Detailed information about the estimation of project duration can be found in Chapter 3.

6.2.10 Project Cost

Estimation of the project cost begins with effort estimation. Once we have effort estimate, productivity, and hourly salary rate information about project team members, we can calculate resource costs. Adding overhead expense to this figure will amount to project costs. Detailed information about the estimation of project cost can be found in Chapter 3.

6.2.11 Tool Management

Planning should be done for making selections for programming languages, software and hardware platform, productivity tools, configuration management system, testing tools, project tracking, communication systems, etc. Detailed information about tool management can be found in Part IV.

6.2.12 Scope Management

Requirement scope management is one of the most crucial aspects of any software project. It along with a number of requirements and quality level determines the volume of work to be done. Detailed information about scope management can be found in Chapter 10.

6.2.13 Effort Estimate

Effort estimation is discussed elaborately in Chapter 3. Please refer to that chapter for more details.

6.2.14 Risk Management

Risk management is discussed elaborately in Chapter 4. Please refer to that chapter for more details.

6.3 Project Planning Techniques

6.3.1 Critical Path Method

The critical path method (CPM) or program evaluation review technique (PERT) is a project planning technique devised at Remington Rand Corporation by J. E. Kelly & E. I. Du Pont De Nemours & Company in 1957 [8]. This technique is also called network analysis. This technique establishes the schedule of a project. Generally, if a project has tasks that are to be executed mostly in a linear fashion, then project planning for that project is easy. Problems start when parallel tasks have to be planned. When there are a large number of parallel tasks, it is certainly very difficult to plan and manage the tasks. The issues such as which task is dependent on which task, when a task has to start and when it has to finish, how much slack/float is there between two tasks, etc., make the planning and managing of the project a tough call. The CPM/PERT method allows tackling these issues. All the tasks are first laid out on a sheet in an order based on their start dates. Then the order in which tasks must be carried out is identified. Similarly tasks dependent on other tasks are identified and a relation is made between the tasks. Tasks with no relation among them are put in parallel. When all the tasks are thus laid out, a path is made, which runs along the longest path of execution. This is the critical path for the project, and it defines the duration of the project. The start date of this path is the start date of the project and end date of this path is the end date of the project. The length of this critical path is the duration of the project (Figure 6.10).

6.3.2 Goldratt's Critical Chain Method

Eliyahu Goldratt has recognized that the CPM/PERT method proves to be insufficient for planning and tracking projects [9]. Earned value management is also not worthwhile. In the CPM/PERT method, tasks are scheduled and a critical path is defined, which denotes the duration of the project. See Figure 6.10 to understand it better. To take care of uncertainty and risks, tasks

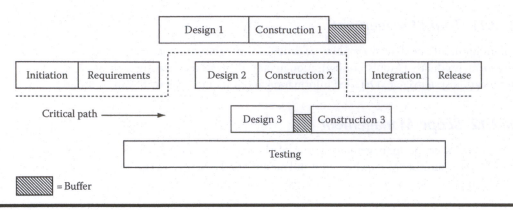

Figure 6.10 Critical path for a software project.

are padded with some buffer. When people who are assigned these tasks, they always tend to take their tasks lightly until the last minute. So even when ample buffer is provided for their tasks, this entire buffer is lost without any gain for the project. They defer carrying out their tasks to the last moment of the deadline, which invariably results in either poor quality or late completion of tasks.

To help project management practitioners, Eliyahu Goldratt introduced the theory of constraints. Due to constraints present in the environment, projects are always under threat. To protect projects from failing, it is important that these threats are understood and proper planning, monitoring, and controlling are done so that when projects diverge from a planned course of action, immediate action can be taken to put them back on track and make them emerge as successful products.

Basically, these constraints (risks) can impact a project in terms of either cost or schedule or content. In any project, there are some tasks that can be considered fixed while some others are variable. These fixed tasks are the ones that are well defined, and they can be scheduled with certainty. On the other hand, variable tasks lack concrete details, and even though they are scheduled with some probable time frame, the time frame for their completion is not certain. So a buffer is provided for these tasks to take care of uncertainty (Figure 6.11).

Goldratt proposed that buffers for well-understood tasks should be removed (as effort required for them can be easily calculated), but a buffer should be provided for uncertain tasks.

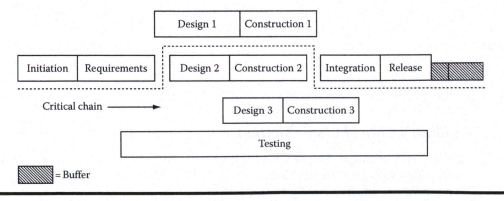

Figure 6.11 Goldratt's critical chain for a software project.

Buffers for uncertain tasks should be detached from those tasks and restored at the end of the project. When monitoring the project, the project manager should actually monitor the buffer and not the task durations. He should see if the buffer is getting consumed or not while the project executes. Whenever he sees that the buffer is getting consumed, he takes action to control the project.

The critical chain method is extremely useful for managing projects. It helps in reducing the uncertainty in projects and thus helps in delivering projects with much better certainty.

6.4 Project Planning Artifacts

Project planning is a large subject and generally it is claimed that it constitutes 10% of total project effort. It is here that most of the project details are chalked out and a detailed project plan is made. Project planning is the stage when most of the project documents are made. So we have a large number of project artifacts here. The artifacts include project plan, risk management, effort estimate, cost estimate, resource allocation, communication plan, configuration management plan, WBS structure, supplier management plan, tool management plan, etc.

6.5 Project Planning in Agile Models

Agile models are best suited when either requirements are not clear or the customer wants small deliveries at short intervals. Risk associated with agile or iterative models is negligible as small deliveries require small efforts, and if delivery is not on a par with expectation, only a fraction of the effort gets lost in rework as the rework itself will be small.

For details about software life-cycle models, waterfall method, agile methods, etc., please refer to Part III.

Iteration occurs up to a certain level in the software development life cycle with different agile models. At one extreme are the Scrum and eXtreme Programming models where there is a complete iteration from requirement to release. The other extreme is where the least amount of iteration occurs only from just one phase to another, or within one phase there could be some iterations. This kind of behavior can be seen in models like open unified model or rational unified model.

Project planning with iterative models differs significantly compared to the waterfall model [10] (Figure 6.12).

At the top level, a roadmap is created for the complete product. It is known as a product plan. It is tentative in nature and lacks concrete details as all of it is planned in advance before the actual product development starts. It can be made for 2–3 years or more and will have the input from the top management as to what customer requirements that product will fulfill when it is completely made.

At the middle level, we have a major product release plan. This plan includes several iterative plans. Generally, most of the software vendors have major releases once in a year. So this plan spans 1 year. It includes details as to what new product features will be developed in that major release.

At the bottom is the iteration plan. Iteration plans correspond to the minor release of a software product. Iteration plans have all the details as to what activities will be performed in that iteration (Figures 6.13 through 6.15).

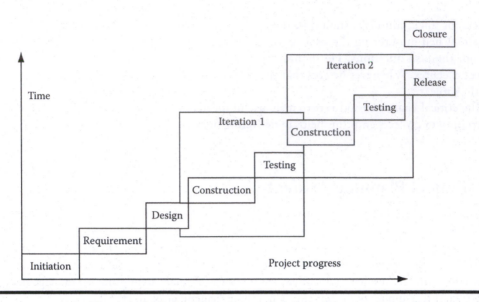

Figure 6.12 Project life cycle in limited iteration model (iteration occurs only for construction and testing activities).

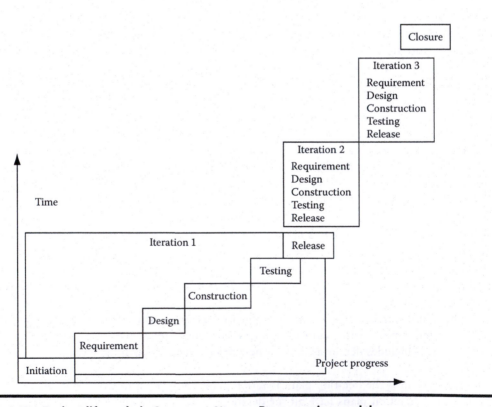

Figure 6.13 Project life cycle in Scrum or eXtreme Programming model.

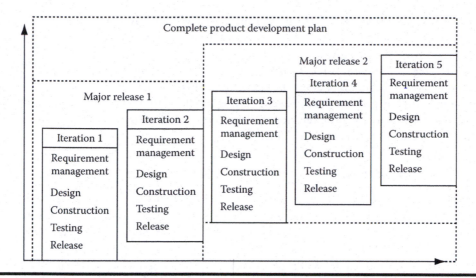

Figure 6.14   Iterations, major releases, and complete product development plan.

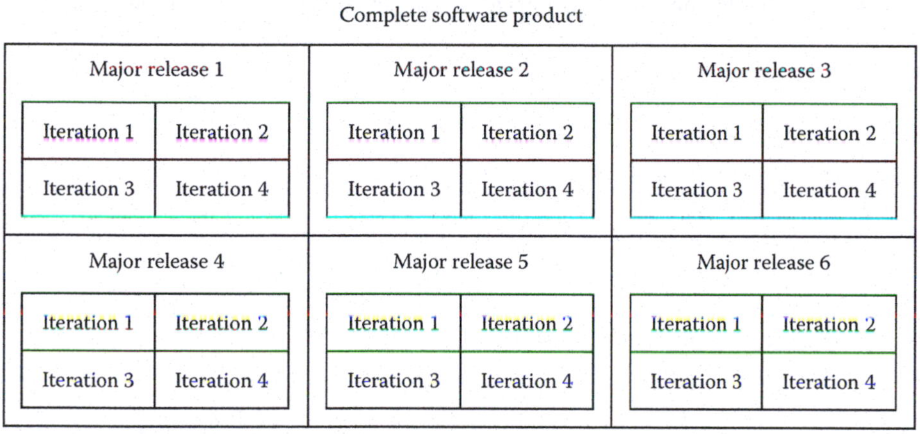

Complete software product

Major release 1		Major release 2		Major release 3	
Iteration 1	Iteration 2	Iteration 1	Iteration 2	Iteration 1	Iteration 2
Iteration 3	Iteration 4	Iteration 3	Iteration 4	Iteration 3	Iteration 4

Major release 4		Major release 5		Major release 6	
Iteration 1	Iteration 2	Iteration 1	Iteration 2	Iteration 1	Iteration 2
Iteration 3	Iteration 4	Iteration 3	Iteration 4	Iteration 3	Iteration 4

Figure 6.15   Complete software product, major releases, and iterations.

Some of the salient features of extreme agile models:

- Customer feedback after each iteration.
- *Adaptive rather than predictive*: This means iteration planning and effort estimate are not meant to be the most important things about the project. The ability to handle change request is the most important aspect.
- *Constant resource requirements*: In waterfall models, each type of work product is worked on by specialists. The moment they finish their tasks, they are no longer needed in the project and they move to some other project. In the case of agile projects, project team members keep working on the project continuously. This is because each iteration is of very short duration (sometimes as small as 1 week). Once each team member finishes with his assignment on one iteration, he starts working on the next assignment on the next iteration without much idle time between these two assignments.

■ *Easier resource management*: The project manager need not pay much attention to resource allocation as each project team member is kept busy by work assignments in iteration after iteration without any significant idle time.

■ *Refactoring*: Since there is no elaborate design effort while developing software features in each iteration, the software design becomes ungainly over many iterations. When the design becomes unmanageable (when you start getting problems in integration of new features with old features), it needs to be refactored. Planning for refactoring is an important consideration while making plans for iterations.

6.5.1 Iteration Planning

Iteration planning is done based on a concept called velocity. Velocity is measured in terms of building a number of feature points per iteration. Any software feature is analyzed for its size and complexity. Accordingly, it is assigned some feature points. Based on team size and skill and experience of team members, it is determined how many feature points the project team can make in an iteration of, say, 1 week. So the number of feature points developed per iteration becomes the velocity of the project team. Based on the velocity, the project manager (or sprint master, if you are in a Scrum project) can determine how many iterations will be there in a minor release, major release, or the complete product development. For example, suppose the complete product to be developed has 10 features.

Feature 1 has 3 feature points.
Feature 2 has 2 feature points.
Feature 3 has 5 feature points.
Feature 4 has 6 feature points.
Feature 5 has 4 feature points.
Feature 6 has 2 feature points.
Feature 7 has 7 feature points.
Feature 8 has 3 feature points.
Feature 9 has 5 feature points.
Feature 10 has 4 feature points.

So in total we have 41 feature points in the project. There are nine people in the project and each iteration will last 1 week. If velocity of the project team is determined to be four feature points per 1 week iteration, then the gross number of iterations will be 11. Some risk factors can be added here. One risk is refactoring time. Other risk factors could be sick leaves, attrition, wrong velocity calculation, etc. To tackle wrong velocity calculation, it is advisable not to promise a commitment for the entire project to the customer. Let two to three iterations get executed. After that, you will have a pretty good idea of the velocity of the project team. This is especially true if the project consists of people who have never worked with each other before and the project manager is not aware of their pace of work. To tackle other kinds of risks, the same kinds of strategies can be taken that have been mentioned for waterfall projects.

6.6 Planning at Project Management Office

Many business organizations create an IT division that takes care of all software and information technology needs. Other organizations, instead of creating a division, create a central organization that takes care of their IT projects. This organization is known as the project management office

(PMO) [11]. The PMO takes care of organization level management for all projects. It helps in providing resources for projects, monitoring and controlling projects, providing infrastructure, providing funds, etc.

The PMO can take many forms. Organization structure of program management can become very complicated in software service organizations. For some large corporations, the PMO can include many programs (clustering of projects related to each other), project portfolio management divisions, etc.

Planning at the PMO level includes resource planning, business planning, infrastructure planning, etc. At one level, these plans are aimed at fulfilling the business needs of the parent organization. At the project level, these plans help the projects plan for adequate project staff, infrastructure, and budget.

More information about PMO organization structures can be found in Chapter 19.

6.7 Case Study

So far in previous chapters, we have seen how some of the essential planning components such as risk planning, effort and cost estimation, and configuration planning are handled at our SaaS vendor projects. In this chapter, we will see how planning for schedule and resources is made at the iteration and project levels.

At the project level (coinciding with major release once per year), the following planning is done:

- Identify and prioritize features. (Feature set should be continually revised throughout the project.)
- Identify iterations and loosely allocate features to each iteration.
- Plan for time-boxed iterations (if followed).
- Calculate cost and effort. Since the project is very stable, there is not much variation in cost and effort from year to year.

At the iteration level, the following planning is done:

- Plan for iteration.
- Identify tasks to implement features.
- Allocate tasks to resources.
- Implement iteration.

6.7.1 Feature Selection

Which feature is to be taken for development in an iteration is often a bone of contention between the marketing team and the development team. The development team has its own technical reasons for feature selection. The marketing team, on the other hand, wants everything to be developed based on the requirements that they identify through interaction with customers and the market feedback they receive. Our SaaS vendor has a mechanism for sorting out this tussle. Their chief technology officer is the final authority in feature selection. During the yearly project plan, he makes a list of probable features that will be developed and added to the core software product in the coming year after consultation with marketing department. At this stage, the features are not marked with any priority. It means that all features have equal importance at this stage. Before the start of an iteration, the marketing team gives priority for each feature. The top priority features are taken for the iteration. The project manager estimates the effort required for each feature. He then tries to make a balance between availability of resources, who will work on the project and how much time should be allocated to each team member. Based on this information, he can find out how many features can be taken for the next iteration in the 3 months during which the iteration will run (iterations are taken on a quarterly basis). He also takes into account some contingency allowances in case any risk or issue arises during the iteration. This list of features is then locked for the iteration. In essence, in a time box of 3 months, these features will be developed and integrated into the core software product.

6.7.2 Heart of Planning

The waterfall model of software development is completely plan driven. In contrast, pure agile models are not plan driven. They are rather implemented in an "As you go!" spirit. The features demanded by customers are implemented, and thus, nothing is planned in advance about any project or iteration activity. Iteration planning is done only after the customer spells out a list of features they want in the iteration. Without a plan, the project team is not able to provide a clear picture to the customer, and at the same time, the team is not able to plan its own activity in advance. This is a drawback. So how can our SaaS software vendor cope with its project and iterations when there is virtually no planning done in advance?

We have discussed top-down and bottom-up planning in previous sections. In our case, since the release date is fixed, we follow top-down planning for iterations. A complete list of features for the major release of 6.0 is fixed. But at the iteration level, which feature out of the listed features is to be implemented in the next iteration is not fixed. That means there could not be any iteration planning in advance, and the project planning is hazy at best. So we have some problems here. First, iteration plans are not easily possible. Second, even though the agile model is flexible, effort, schedule, and budget are not able to be drawn in a situation where nothing is fixed. So essentially, we have a conflict between flexibility and responsiveness on one hand and allocating resources and budget for the iteration on the other hand.

The vendor is able to cope with this problem using a time-boxing concept. The release date is fixed for iterations. Their marketing team comes up with a list of features that are to be implemented in the next iteration. The list can be ordered according to priority. The top priority features can be taken for implementation in the iteration first. Once they are implemented, and if time permits, the low-priority features can be taken for implementation in the iteration. Remaining low-priority features, which could not be implemented in the iteration, can be taken in future iterations.

In this arrangement, we have a cushion. If the iteration plan goes well, we take up more features. If some issues arise during the iteration and if some high-priority features take more time than planned, then some of the low-priority features cannot be implemented. So the low-priority features act as a buffer.

This arrangement is good as it provides both flexibility and responsiveness. At the same time, it allows for making plans and allocating resource and budget to the iterations.

For planning components related to effort and cost estimates, risk management, configuration management, communication management, and resource management; see the relevant chapters. These topics are covered in their respective chapters in detail (Table 6.1).

Table 6.1   Documents Planned and Generated during the Project

Use Case Model	
Supplementary Specification	*Nonfunctional Specifications*
Risk assessment	
Effort estimate	
Master test plan	
Phase plan	Iteration plan with schedule
Software architecture document	

6.8 Chapter Summary

Project planning is a very important step in the software project. Any large software project has a large number of important project tasks. Without proper project planning, it will be impossible to manage such a large number of complex tasks when it is time for execution. So a detailed project plan is mandatory.

In the case of agile and iterative kinds of projects, project planning is less important, and in fact it should not have minute details. It is because the entire process is agile and these process models work on the premise of responding to change quickly. Nevertheless, when an iteration is firmed up and requirements for that iteration are clear, a project plan is needed to carry out the project with clear goals. The other iterations in the future as well as the overall plan encompassing all the iterations should have a project plan with fewer details. Generally, at these levels, it is best to have a project plan without firm dates for project tasks.

The project plan has many components to manage different aspects. For managing communication, the project should have a communication plan. For managing efficient resource utilization, the project should a resource plan. For managing quality aspects of the work products, there should be a quality plan. For managing suppliers, a supplier plan is warranted. For managing configuration and version control, the plan should have a configuration management plan. For managing tools and technology aspects, the plan should have a tool and technology plan. Finally, the most important aspects such as cost, schedule, and effort for the project should have respective plans.

There are many methods that help in making project plans. For making project schedules, Gantt charts, network diagrams, PERT/CPM charts, etc., are very important. For effectively tracking and controlling projects, earned value management and Goldratt's critical chain methods are very important. During project planning, it is important to keep the requirements of these methods (base budget, base schedule, etc.) in mind when the project planning is done.

There are many good tools available on the market that help in making project plans, for example, MS Project, Primavera, etc. Some of the project planning tools are online and are available on the Web so that project teams that are located at many geographical sites can access the tool and work collaboratively.

Exercises

6.1 Find some examples of project planning for a construction industry. Find how project planning is done for that industry and what the planning components are. Compare it to that for a software project.

6.2 It is said that software project planning consists of tasks that are not elastic and their schedule cannot be stretched or shrunk. Find out why it is so and if some remedies exist.

Review Questions

6.1 What do you understand by a software project plan?

6.2 Why is a software project plan needed?

6.3 What are the components of a software project plan?

6.4 What are the inputs for a top-down project plan?

6.5 What are the inputs for a bottom-up software project plan?

6.6 What precautions are taken while creating a project plan to tackle different risks?

6.7 What kinds of project plans are devised for iterative models of software development?

Recommended Readings

1. M. E. McGrath (2004) *Next Generation Product Development: How to Increase Productivity, Cut Costs, and Reduce Cycle Times*, McGraw-Hill, New York.
2. R. Wysocki (2006) *Effective Software Project Management*, Wiley India Pvt. Ltd., New Delhi, India.
3. D. A. Gustafson (2002) *Schaum's Outline of Software Engineering*, McGraw-Hill, New York.
4. J. Taylor (2003) *Managing Information Technology Projects: Applying Project Management Strategies to Software, Hardware, and Integration Initiatives*, American Management Association, New York.
5. C. Ebert, R. Dumke (2007) *Software Measurement: Establish–Extract–Evaluate–Execute*, Springer, Berlin, Germany.
6. R. Muller (1997) *Productive Objects: An Applied Software Project Management Framework*, Morgan Kaufmann, San Francisco, CA.
7. J. W. Horch (1996) *Practical Guide to Software Quality Management*, Artech House, Boston, MA.
8. J. P. Lewis (2004) *Project Planning, Scheduling & Control*, McGraw-Hill Education (India) Pvt. Ltd., New Delhi, India.
9. H. A. Levine (2002) *Practical Project Management: Tips, Tactics, and Tools*, Wiley, New York.
10. R. E. Fairley (2009) *Managing and Leading Software Projects*, Wiley-IEEE Computer Society Press, Hoboken, NJ.
11. C. J. Letavec (2006) *The Program Management Office: Establishing, Managing and Growing the Value of a PMO*, J. Ross Publishing, Boca Raton, FL.

Chapter 7

Project Monitoring and Control

In the previous chapter, we learned

- What is a software project plan?
- What are the parts of a software project plan?
- What are the types of software project plans?
- What inputs go into making a software project plan?
- What techniques are used in making a software project plan?

In this chapter, we will learn

- What is project monitoring?
- What techniques are there for project control?
- How is project monitoring done in iterative projects?

7.1 Introduction

Projects are inherently dynamic in nature. They also have unpredictability about them. These two factors call for continuous monitoring and control of projects lest they go haywire. In manufacturing, pace of work is fast, but all the activities are more or less predictable. You can plan the order of tasks to be carried out; and depending on material, machines, and labor availability, you produce goods without much consideration to worldly or not so worldly things. Routine machine inspection, work product (work in process) samples for quality control, and skills training are all

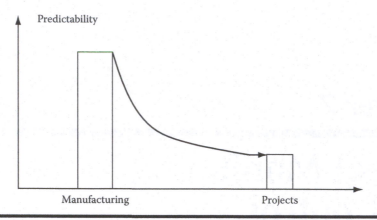

Figure 7.1 Process predictability for projects against manufacturing.

it requires to produce goods with good quality. It is not so with projects. There are surprises and there is something new about each project. More so with software projects (Figure 7.1).

To control and manage this element of unpredictability, you need to have tools and techniques that can be employed to make the journey comfortable. For software projects, first of all you need to have a well-defined process model, the application of which will help in reducing uncertainty and in achieving consistency. The process model will set steps to be followed for completing all project tasks and thus help in planning the project. A good process model also allows measuring both project processes and the work products. Measuring project processes and comparing them with those from best practices will provide information about productivity, costs and schedule, and where the project is heading. Measuring the quality of product/work product and comparing them against those achieved with best practices will provide information about the quality of the work products developed as compared to what could be achieved using best practices. When you have a good project plan in hand, you can execute your project with much ease.

In this chapter, we will discuss everything related to project monitoring and control for software projects.

7.2 Project Monitoring

A project plan consists of a project schedule and project budget apart from other plan components like communication plan, quality plan, configuration plan, resource plan, etc. To track the project execution against the plan, there are major and minor milestones defined in the project schedule [1]. When the execution reaches any of these milestones, costs and schedule can be compared to know how the execution is faring against the project plan. Then there are tools like status reports, Goldratt's critical chain method, Gantt charts [2], earned value management (EVM) [3], etc. that help in monitoring and controlling the project.

7.2.1 Monitor against Project Plan

Monitoring against the project plan is the most obvious method to get project progress reports. The project plan is treated as a baseline against which the actual progress is measured. Major and minor milestones are provided in the project plan for dividing the whole project plan for easy tracking. If for some reason a milestone is not achieved as per plan, then the project manager has to explain to

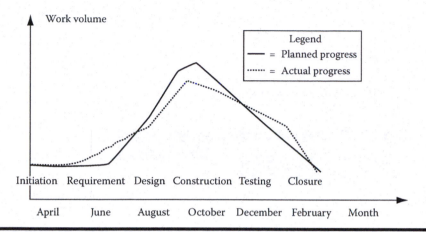

Figure 7.2   Project plan vs. actual progress.

the customer why the milestone could not be achieved as per plan. And if this occurs, what should be done to achieve the next milestones on time? There are some techniques available like resource leveling [4], resource optimization [5], schedule optimization [6], etc., which can be applied to put the project on track (Figure 7.2).

7.2.2 Measure Task Progress and Status Reports

How can you measure the progress of a project task? If you have a task and you want to measure it, then you need to have information about planned task and actual start dates, planned volume of work, actual volume of work, and task duration. From the planned and actual volume of work, one can figure out the remaining work to be done to complete the task (Figures 7.3 and 7.4).

If the volume of work is ignored and only dates are taken into consideration, task progress calculation will be wrong. Suppose a task starts on April 11 and finishes on April 20. That means the duration of the task is 10 days. If the project manager is asked to provide a status report of the task up to April 16, then without measuring the volume of work if he says it is 60% (since 6 days of work has been done out of 10 days) then he is wrong. This figure is only the planned work

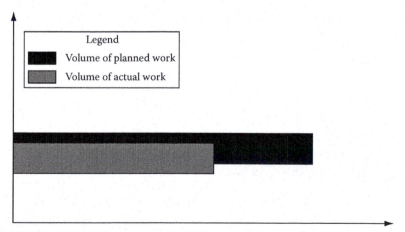

Figure 7.3   Progress tracking of a task.

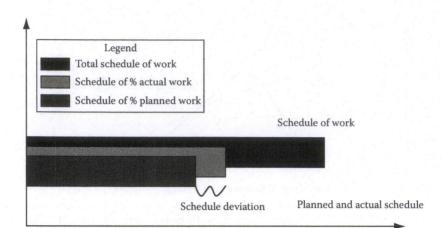

Figure 7.4 Project schedule deviation.

and not the actual work. Now suppose the work involves writing source code of size 5 KLOC (kilo lines of code). That means his team should be writing 0.5 KLOC of source code per day. Now if he measures and finds that up to April 16 his team has written 3.5 KLOC. That means his team has completed 70% of work. Compared to the planned completion of 60% of work (0.5 × 6/5% = 60%), his team is actually ahead of schedule.

This calculation is done for projects where volume and cost of work per day during the entire project period are constant. But this does not happen in reality. To have meaningful calculations, this aspect also has to be taken care of.

7.2.3 Identify Deviations

When project monitoring is done, the focus of the measurements is to find the deviations from the planned schedule and costs [7]. In the example given earlier, the schedule performance achieved is 70% compared to planned 60%. That means the team is ahead of schedule by a +10% margin (Figure 7.4).

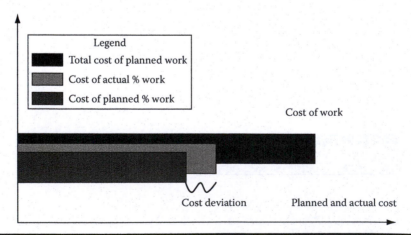

Figure 7.5 Project cost deviation.

Now suppose total planned cost for the task is $100. If you break the cost on a daily basis then it comes to $10 per day. In our example, up to April 16, planned cost is $60. Now suppose the actual cost comes to $65. So we have a deviation of +5%.

Again these calculations are based on constant volume of work and cost per day, which does not happen in reality (Figure 7.5). In the EVM explained in a later section, we will see why it is so.

7.2.4 Performance Indicators

Performance indicators are used to know the performance of project in terms of cost, schedule, and quality [8]. EVM is a good tool for creating and monitoring performance indicators. Performance indicators work only if baseline information is available. If for some reason, baseline information about cost, schedule, or quality could not be kept or is not accurate enough to be reliable, these indicators do not work. It is because there is no accurate planned data available against which the actual execution data can be compared.

EVM is explained in a subsequent section.

7.2.5 Monitor against Project Schedule

A project plan is generally a high-level plan for a project and it does not include details like resource allocation to tasks, task details, etc. A project schedule includes these things, and thus, project schedule tracking and monitoring means measuring the progress of tasks as well as evaluating the performance of resources in the tasks on a daily basis. So while project plans are tracked at the milestone level, project schedules are tracked at task level. Project schedule tracking and monitoring may include information like resource utilization percent, resource loading, task progress, etc.

7.2.6 Periodic Measurement

As has been emphasized throughout this book, projects are extremely dynamic and unpredictable in nature. It is very important that project progress at task level is tracked and measured very frequently to know if everything is progressing well or if there are problems at any time [9]. Actual measurements should be always compared with planned figures, and if any deviations are found, a plan should be made to fix these deviations. In good organizations, each project team member logs his daily activity in a centralized project monitoring system. Reports from this kind of system can be used to track task progress in terms of schedule. For cost tracking, the project manager can make a simple sheet and keep it updated with the number of hours the resources have worked on the project tasks. Multiplying these hours by their hourly pay rate will give the expense of each task. If more than one resource is working on a task, adding expenses for all the resources working on that task will give the figures of expense of that task. You can then compare the actual expense of the work done so far against the budgeted cost for that work.

7.2.7 Earned Value Management

For any project, specific time duration and specific budget are allocated while making the project plan. In ideal conditions, execution of the project will be completed at exactly the same time and at the same budget. In reality, this never happens. Sometimes, the project may be completed before the stipulated time duration or at less cost. But these cases are rare. Most often, the project overruns both the time duration and cost. Large projects warrant huge budgets, resources, and time.

It is very important that they are tracked and monitored closely, and timely reports are given to the stakeholders so that they know how the project is progressing. Their reputation and very often jobs are at stake based on the success or failure of the project. So they must get timely status reports about progress of the project. During reporting, if proper project monitoring information is not communicated to the stakeholders, they may not know how the project is progressing. They may be reported only about the percentage of project completion against planned schedule or about the percentage of budget spent so far. But from this information, it is not clear if the project is actually progressing as per plan or if it is lagging behind.

This is because there is a third dimension that has not been accounted in these calculations. This dimension is the volume of work performed over different periods of time during the project are not the same. Similar is the case for budget. For example, in software projects, when software design work is in progress, the volume of work per day is low. But during software construction, a great volume of work is accomplished per day as a lot of developers work on the project. Clearly, a volume of work done per day at different phases of the project is very different. Similarly, budget consumed per day over the project will vary considerably due to different pay rate for differently skilled people and even for the same skilled people and the fact that at different phases of the project, differently skilled people work on the project.

As you can see in Figure 7.6, it is difficult to conclude whether the project is progressing well or not as the actual schedule and cost cannot be compared against any value.

However, if you look at Figure 7.7, the actual cost and schedule figures can actually be compared against planned data. It is because this time, we are tracking the project progress using earned value (EV). The project duration and the project budget are outlined at the beginning of the project. When the project execution starts, we will be recording actual project progress in terms of budget and time consumed by project tasks. Based on the budget consumed by a task, task progress is measured and we also record how much task progress should have been done after consuming that much of budget. This is known as EV. So we have three values here: planned value (PV), EV, and actual value (AV).

As per definitions of EVM,
Schedule variance (SV) = EV – PV
Cost variance (CV) = EV – AC

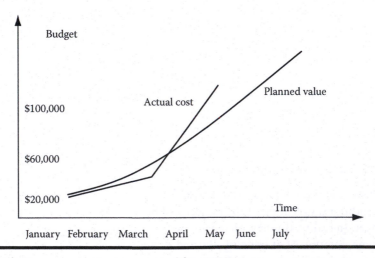

Figure 7.6 Project progress measurement without EVM.

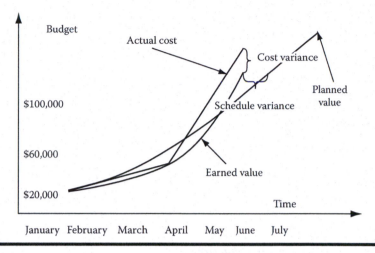

Figure 7.7 Project progress measurement with EVM.

Apart from variances in cost and schedule, there are two more indicators available in EVM. They are the cost performance indicator (CPI) and the schedule performance indicator (SPI). They are calculated as follows:

CPI = EV/AC
SPI = EV/PV

Let us see an example to observe how EVM works.

Suppose we have a project with the schedule of 100 days. The budget for the project is allocated at $100,000. After the elapse of 60 days, project measurements are taken. It is found that a budget of $50,000 has been consumed up to this point in the project. Suppose at this stage, 40 days' worth of project is actually complete. But from the planned schedule, it should have been 50 days' worth of project completed. So how is the project progressing?

In Section 7.2.3, we have seen a simple scenario where project schedule and project budget are allocated linearly (project budget and schedule are consumed linearly in proportion to total budget and schedule). That means the project progress should be linear. Alas! It does not happen that way. There is no linear progression of the project in reality. It is because a project has many tasks and each of these tasks has its own volume of work to be performed at different rates over a period of time. For instance, a software design task may be completed over a period of, say, 20 days. If the work is performed linearly, then each day, the percentage of work to be completed is 5% so that in 20 days, 100% of the work will be completed. In reality, however, on some days the planned work may be 3%, 5%, or 6% or could be just any other value. It all depends on the availability of resources on a particular day and the dependency of a task on another task. Similarly, the budget consumption is not linear. Some tasks cost less to perform than other tasks. So in a unit of time, a volume of work done for some tasks can be higher than that for other tasks with the same budget. So far we have discussed the nonlinear behavior for a planned budget and schedule. Likewise, the actual budget and schedule consumption will also be nonlinear. Once we understand the nonlinear relation between percentage of completion of any task vis-à-vis completion of total task for both planned and actual progress, it will be easy to understand the concept of EVM.

Coming back to our example, we have actual cost (AC) of $50,000 and PV of $55,000 (corresponding to the planned days of work performed up to this point). The project manager has also been tracking the earned value of the project on a weekly basis. On this basis, he has been plotting the earned value of the project as it progresses. From this figure, he has an EV of $45,000.

Now let us do some mathematics with the figures we have:

SV = 45,000 – 55,000 = –$10,000
CV = 45,000 – 50,000 = –$5,000
CPI = 45,000/50,000 = 0.9
SPI = 45,000/55,000 = 0.82

For both CPI and SPI, the ideal values are 1. In case CPI is 1, it means that the project budget is consumed as per project plan. Similarly, if SPI is 1, the project schedule is progressing as per project plan. In our example, we can see that at the point of measurement, the project is lagging behind both in schedule and in budget consumption (as both are less than 1). The project manager can do well to find out why the project is lagging behind and how the project can be put back on the right track.

7.2.8 Measure Resource Utilization

Resource utilization is a measure of efficiency with which available resources within an organization are utilized in projects. Resource utilization is evaluated more frequently at program or line of business level [10]. For instance, suppose a software service company has a practice division for application development services for financial services. It has a total IT staff of 80 people. It has five projects running. In these projects, a total of 76 people are engaged. That means there are four people who are not assigned to any project. That means this practice division has 95% of resource utilization.

7.2.9 Measure Resource Loading

Resource utilization in projects can be tracked using information as to how many hours of project work is allocated to the resource and how many hours of actual work the resource has put in. So if a resource is allocated 20 h of work and he actually puts in 25 h of work, the resource utilization is 125%. From other points of view, resource loading also comes into picture [11]. Suppose a task requires 20 h to be completed. A resource allocated to this task works 8 h a day. So under normal loading conditions, he will finish this task in 2.5 days. Now suppose as per schedule, this task needs to be completed in 2 days (16 h). In this situation, the resource can only complete 80% of the work under normal loading conditions. The project manager then has two choices: he can assign additional resource to this task to complete it in 16 h or he can increase the workload of the existing resource. To complete this task within the schedule, the resource should be loaded with 125% of workload. He may need to work some extra hours every day (overtime of 2 h per day in addition to his 8 h of regular work).

7.2.10 Monitor Skills and Knowledge of Project Team

During project planning and detailed scheduling, resource matching to project tasks is done. When there is some gap in required and available skills, a training plan is made to bridge this gap. During execution, this training part is also to be tracked to ensure that the planned training has been successfully completed and that the resource who has received the training now can do his task competently. Sometimes it may also happen that during planning, some tasks and the required skills to do them are not properly planned. During execution, it is realized that training may be needed. In such cases, arrangement should be quickly made for training. If there is a delay in starting that task, the project plan should be adjusted accordingly. The additional time may either be taken from the schedule buffer or be adjusted against any slack in the project schedule.

One more possibility may be regarding resource skills. Sometimes, a resource may leave the project and the project may need to find a replacement. In such a situation, the project manager may need to do resource skills matching and find a suitable replacement.

7.2.11 Monitor Risks

Everything to be done in a project comes with a risk. If a software design is to be made, there is a risk that the design is faulty. When doing software testing, there is a risk that the testing is not good enough. When doing a particular project task, there is a risk that it may not be completed on time due to resource shortage or underestimation of the effort required for the task.

For each kind of risk that may arise, a contingency plan is needed so that the project does not get affected. Risk identification has to be done and its impact and probability has to be assessed at all times during the execution of the project. A detailed study about risks is provided in Chapter 4.

7.2.12 Monitor Issues

Several kinds of issues keep arising during the execution of the project [12]. These issues need to be addressed and solutions to be found and applied so that project progress is not affected. There may be some doubts about the design for which a developer needs a clarification. That clarification is to be provided on time so that the developer's time is not wasted. At the peer review meeting, it is felt to refactor a source code construct, but there are still some team members who want to keep the existing source code. Then there are team members who want to finish their work faster to take a break later but the project manager feels that quality may go down.

All kinds of issues keep arising and the project manager needs to resolve them satisfactorily and in time. Issues are time sensitive and thus require solution within a certain time frame. But all issues are not same. Some have more impact on the project while others do not have much of an impact. So if there is more than one issue at hand, then the project manager should first analyze the impact and accordingly make a list of issues with set priorities and assigning top priority to resolve the issues that have most severe impact on the project. He can defer attending to the issues that do not have much impact on the project and can address issues immediately that may have severe impact. In this respect, issue resolution is similar to mitigating risks.

7.2.13 Status Reports

The customer needs status reports to know whether the project is progressing well or lagging behind in some respect. The project manager needs to prepare status reports and send them to the customer. Generally, these status reports are sent after completion of any milestone in the project [13]. These milestones could be anything and could be set after discussion with the customer. But most often, these milestones denote completion of one phase of the project (requirements, design, construction, testing, etc.). The status report should contain information about cost, schedule, and quality as to how the project execution is faring against the project plan. If the project is lagging behind in any of these aspects, then a good explanation should be included as to why it happened. The report should also contain a remedy plan to put the project on track. The report should also contain information regarding achievements, challenges faced, and issues resolved during the report period. Depending on the requirements of the customer, the report can be detailed or succinct. Many project managers make a mistake of not making a good rapport with the customer.

If no rapport is made with the customer, the customer will never appreciate the effort and hard work put into assignments by the team. So it is required that the project manager establish a good rapport with the customer.

7.3 Project Control Techniques

Projects have so many risks and uncertainties that managing and controlling them is a tough task. The project manager has to keep balancing many trade-offs to keep the project on track.

7.3.1 Resource Leveling

Resource leveling is one technique that is employed to resolve resource conflicts during project execution. Sometimes, it so happens that a resource is to do more than one task. Now it is found that one task will get delayed due to the delay in the other task. If there is a slack found in the schedule, the other task that has not started yet can be taken to some other time frame so that it will not be affected due to delay in the first task. Or if this is not possible, then adding some more resources to the task can resolve this issue (Figures 7.8 and 7.9).

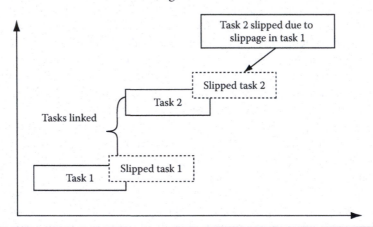

Figure 7.8   Slippage in a task leads to slippage in the dependent task.

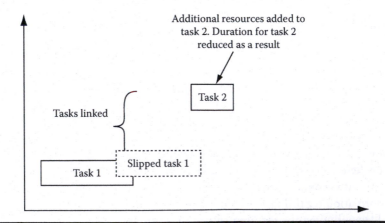

Figure 7.9   Additional resources allotted to a dependent task to complete it faster in less time.

When using software such as Microsoft Project for making the project schedule, the software has tasks that conflict with other tasks in the schedule. These conflicts could be due to impractical start or finish dates for tasks, resource overallocation, or dependency of tasks on each other (so that if the first task gets delayed, the other will also get delayed). Adjusting those tasks manually or automatically will resolve the conflict.

7.3.2 Schedule Optimization

Using PERT/CPM methods, we can determine the critical path of the project. But before drawing the critical path, the project manager should ascertain that there is no unnecessary slack in the project plan. If there is any slack anywhere on the critical path, it should be removed to make the project plan optimized. Similarly, as there could be many critical paths for the same project plan, unnecessary slack on all paths should be identified and removed. Now the longest path out of these will be the critical path for the project (Figures 7.10 and 7.11).

Schedule optimization can also be done during execution. If during execution, any task on the critical path is found to be done earlier than planned, then the critical path can be shortened.

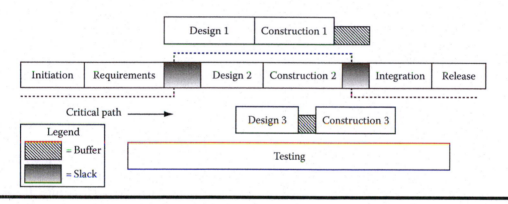

Figure 7.10   Slack in the critical path of a project plan.

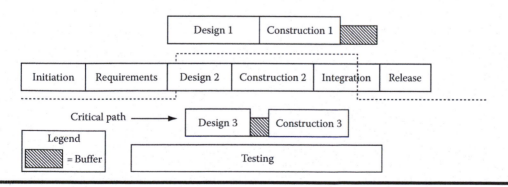

Figure 7.11   Optimized project plan after removal of slack on the critical path.

This way schedule for the project can be collapsed or the extra time available can be used for starting dependent tasks earlier than planned schedule.

One more technique of schedule optimization is to find if any tasks can be put in parallel that are currently in sequence. This way the schedule can be collapsed by a big margin.

Then we can also optimize the schedule by checking if any task can be split and then putting these split tasks in parallel so that the schedule can be collapsed.

In fact, using concurrent engineering methods, we can successfully optimize a project schedule. In the concurrent engineering technique, activities for downstream processes are planned ahead during a previous process step. In software projects, we can design the software product in such a way that the construction and/or testing work can be split easily. So when the project progresses to these stages, the work can be split and these split assignments can be assigned to many teams. These teams can work on these assignments in parallel to the work carried out by other teams. This way the project schedule can be collapsed by a large margin.

7.3.3 Corrective Actions against Deviations

From the project monitoring status reports, if it is observed that the project is deviating from plan, then corrective actions are to be taken by the project manager. For taking corrective action, the situation is to be analyzed and root causes are to be identified. Once root causes are found, solutions to fix them can be thought of and then action can be taken accordingly. It is also advisable to have a good measurement of all process- and product-related attributes that are relevant to the project. Good measurements will help in decision-making process.

Some of the reasons for increased project cost include increase in overhead (higher cost of procuring tools, infrastructure, etc.) or salary. It could also be due to schedule overrun. So cost increases could either be schedule dependent or schedule independent. If procurement costs are going higher, management can find alternatives to keep the cost from increasing. If the cost increase is due to schedule overrun, then immediate action should be taken to correct the schedule deviation.

Schedule deviation (almost always overrun) can happen due to faulty effort estimate, faulty scheduling, resource unavailability, loss of critical resources midway in the project, requirement creep, etc. Requirement creep is the most cited problem attributed to schedule overruns. The best policy regarding requirement creep is to bargain with the customer whenever any requirement change request comes. The customer should be made aware of the consequences of the change request in project schedule. Accept a change request only after the customer understands and agrees on the consequences in the project schedule. Risks of resource unavailability or loss of resources pose a serious threat for the project. To deal with such risks, proper resource planning is needed.

The third deviation that can occur in the project is the quality of the work products. Bad quality cannot be forgiven even if schedule or cost overruns can be accepted. Software engineering techniques help in ensuring that work product quality can be improved by means of improved project and product processes. The software development life cycle should be divided into well-defined phases, and at the end of each phase, there should be a list of defined work products. There should always be a gate that will allow the project to proceed to the next level only after the work products are verified to have the expected quality level by measuring them and comparing with the expected quality levels. If any deficiency is found in any part of the work product, then it should be rectified and only then should the project be allowed to proceed to the next phase. This will ensure that quality of the work products is good. This in turn will ensure that quality of the finished product is good.

7.3.4 Corrective Actions against Issues

As we have seen in Section 7.2.12, issues should be classified into many categories and top-priority issues should be tackled first. Issues are also time-sensitive, and if they are not tackled in time, they will impact the project. How severe the impact will be depends on the kind of the issue itself. When many issues are in hand at a given time, it is difficult to identify their priority. All of them seem important. In such cases, it will be best to list them and put a weight against each of them. Time sensitivity should also be considered (e.g., in how many days the issue should be sorted out). Now sort out your list with these two values against each issue. If an issue with more weight has a bigger time window and if an issue with lower weight has a smaller time window, then if time permits, both should be tackled in parallel so that both can be resolved within their time windows. However, if the project manager does not have much time to tackle both simultaneously, then it will be best to tackle the issue with the higher weight. So if a lower-priority issue cannot be resolved, it will not have much impact on the project, and at the same time, a bigger impact on the project can be avoided by resolving a higher-priority issue.

7.3.5 Resource Optimization

in outsourced projects, the project manager from the outsourcing company may have to think about benefits to his organization from the project. For instance, the service provider will have a profit motive. When the company bid for a project, it would have taken the profit margin for the project. During project execution, however, there are many factors that threaten to eat into the profit margin. The project manager has to keep an eye on the expenses so that profit margin could be kept intact. In this regard, one known source of threat is an increasing wage of employees. To handle this issue, the project manager may have to make sure that productivity of the employees gets increased commensurate with the hike in salaries.

There are many practical ways of optimizing your resources in projects. The best option is to use project portfolio management to utilize your available resources to the best possible way. When you have a pool of resources and a list of projects, you can staff the projects in such a way that your pool of resources are utilized in such a way that no or least resources are sitting idle. Even within the pool of resources, some are costlier than others. It definitely makes sense that time of these higher-paid staff should be utilized to the maximum.

7.4 Project Monitoring and Control Artifacts

Project monitoring provides project process and work product data that we can use to make decision and control the project so that later on it can be kept on track despite derailings in the past. The cost could have gone up from what was budgeted, the schedule could have overrun, or the work product quality could have gone down from what was expected. So basically we have three attributes of a project that should be monitored and controlled: schedule, cost and quality.

The artifacts belonging to the schedule include PERT/CPM charts, network diagrams, resource charts, EVM, etc. The artifacts belonging to cost include budget analysis, resource optimization, EVM, etc. The artifacts for quality include requirement document review, design document review, source code review, test cycle logs, etc.

The most important artifacts of project monitoring and control are actual project cost, product quality and schedule data. The overall project cost and schedule data in relation to project size and quality level determines productivity on the project.

7.5 Project Monitoring and Control in Iterative Model

Software project planning for iterative development projects has been discussed in Chapter 6. As discussed there, most of the action happens at the iteration level, and thus, most of the planning is also done at this level. Since duration of each iteration is small (a few weeks to 2–3 months), impact on an individual iteration due to any unforeseen circumstances is not that severe. Most of the project risks are tackled by dividing the entire project into small iterations. Thus, for iterative projects, the risks are manageable because their sizes are reduced, and they are distributed throughout the project by means of breaking the project into small iterations. However, sometimes it may happen that the customer demands some drastic change in his requirements, which may force an iteration to undergo a large change from the planned activities. In such cases, the project monitoring and control will be out of control, and thus, the project plan (iteration plan) will become invalid. A new project plan will have to be made (Figure 7.12).

But in general, a project plan (or iteration plan) can be controlled using typical controlling techniques. A good technique to control an iteration is using a priority system for requirements or features. All the high-priority features will be completed in the iteration, and the low-priority features can be kept as options if time permits in the iteration.

7.5.1 Performance Measurements

Unlike waterfall-based models, performance on agile projects is measured in different parameters. Some of these measures include the following:

- Feature points delivered per iteration
- Number of defects found per iteration
- Productivity of team in terms of delivering features per person per iteration

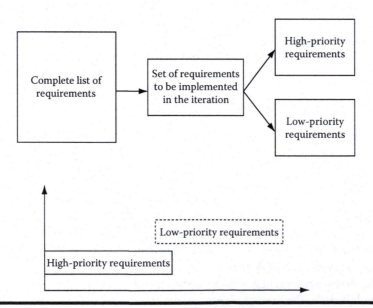

Figure 7.12 High- and low-priority requirements and keeping their schedule accordingly.

7.5.2 Risks

Iterations are generally time boxed. You need to complete a certain number of feature points (feature points are a number assigned to a feature depending on the size of the feature and its complexity) in the iteration duration. If you are not able to complete them, it may be due to inaccurate effort estimation, some issues arising, or some other risk that is responsible for problems in the project. But these problems arise during the first few iterations. Otherwise agile environments are pretty stable and devoid of risky propositions. There is no such thing as resource allocation in these projects. Each person in these projects has his role well defined. He keeps on working on successive iterations without being told by project manager what he would be doing in subsequent iterations. From the stories to be worked on in a particular iteration, the developers write unit tests and then start building the features. Whenever time permits, they also keep refactoring the old source codes. In fact, refactoring is one of the most risky affairs in agile projects. If refactoring is not done properly, subsequent iterations can face problems in writing code for new features as design issues prevent old source code form integrating with the new code.

7.6 Case Study

In the previous chapter, we have seen how project and iteration planning is done at our SaaS vendor. In this chapter, we will see how project and iteration control and monitoring are done.

Our SaaS vendor has major and minor releases of software coinciding with yearly project plan and iterations within the project plan, respectively. During the execution of iterations, there are bound to be issues and risks arising due to various internal and external factors. In such cases, risk and issue mitigation strategies come in handy if they exist.

Luckily, the SaaS vendor project team has such contingency plans. They have weekly iteration review meetings, led by the project manager and attended by project team members. Most of the issues and risks encountered in the previous week are known to the team members before the meeting takes place. In addition, any risk that has not affected the plan so far but is lurking around the corner is also discussed. These potential risks are not on the meeting agenda and are discussed after the agenda is discussed and a plan of action is taken for these risks.

Some of the risks encountered in the project include sick leaves, unplanned holidays, technical problems encountered in implementing a design, a rush call from the marketing department for an unplanned feature to be added, etc. An action plan generally consists of causal analysis of the problem, finding root cause of the problem, finding a suitable solution for the problem, implementing the solution, checking if the solution works, and finally eliminating the risk. The analysis of impact of the risk is also done. Generally, the resources are fixed and additional resources are not added in the project for mitigating any risk. So the impact the risk has had on the schedule is considered. The schedule is readjusted if necessary, and the rescheduled plan is made. If change in the affected task also impacts other tasks, then those tasks are also rescheduled. If the impact is severe and the entire iteration plan is going to be affected, then one more possibility is explored. It is the option of working overtime to cover for the extra time required to finish the tasks.

7.6.1 Tracking Tools Used

The project manager uses Microsoft Project to track project plan, resources, and schedule. The Gantt chart generated by Microsoft Project is used for project monitoring and control. For defect tracking, Seapine Software's TestTrack Pro is used.

7.6.2 Problems Encountered

The most complex and large component which was being developed in release 6.0 of the software product was a feature called "Appointment Scheduling Engine." The logic is complex and implementing it was tough. Even testing this solution was a big challenge. Developing it required first implementing the logic and then modifying the behavior of the component by using software and hard constraints. For testing it, an elaborate plan was made.

When actual testing got started, it was found that the engine was failing in most of the cases. It did not recognize any of the constraints. Initially for testing it, two test engineers were assigned. But later, it was found that the engineers lacked experience to test such a complex component. So they were replaced by two experienced business analysts who had also worked on product management of the product, and they knew about the architecture and requirement specifications well. They set up an elaborate suite of test cases and decided to do exploratory testing of the component.

The business analysts found that the requirement and design documents were not up to the mark. They decided to first make a pseudo logic for the component. They took some time in assembling some documents and getting information from developers and software designers so that they could make this logic. Once it was built, it helped them to make the strategy to test the component. The junior analyst did the testing for load time calculations and the senior analyst did the appointment scheduling part of the component. When the junior analyst finished his testing for load calculation, he was assigned to test the user interface part including the calendars, searches for appointments, shipments, etc.

Overall, the effort paid off and the appointment scheduling engine started working as per requirements. It was the biggest success story of the project.

7.7 Chapter Summary

Software projects are indeed difficult to monitor and control. Difficulties arise due to the fact that many specifications for work products are not clear even after the project begins. So the project team takes some assumptions about the work products into consideration that are yet not so clear. As the project progresses, some clarity is achieved. So before this happens, the project team tries to manage the project work with some vagueness. This aspect is the most difficult problem in software projects. In such a scenario, project monitoring and control thus become a difficult proposition.

There are many tools and techniques available for the project team to monitor and control the project. For controlling purposes, the project plan has some schedule and budget buffers. So when any risk occurs, a certain amount of budget and schedule are adjusted in the project by dipping into the buffer. On the other hand, there are some tools that help in overcoming setbacks in the project without consuming any buffers. Some of these techniques include resource leveling, schedule optimization, taking corrective action against deviations, etc. Then of course, we have the EVM technique, which can be employed to take corrective action. The EVM technique also provides the facility to have a project dashboard with performance indicators. If any of the indicators goes the wrong way, then the project manager can easily recognize it and take prompt action.

Exercises

7.1 What should be the best course of action if many quality issues arise? How can you deal with a situation when the work products are found to have more than an expected number of defects?

7.2 A project has three software components developed by two teams. One team turns out to be faster than the other team. What effects it will have on the project?

Review Questions

7.1 What attributes of a software project are considered for monitoring and control?

7.2 Explain what you understand by resource leveling.

7.3 How can you measure progress of a task?

7.4 What measures can be taken if it is found that the project schedule is deviating from the planned schedule?

7.5 What measures can be taken if it is found that the project cost is deviating from the planned budget?

7.6 What measures can be taken if it is found that the product quality is deviating from the expected quality level?

Recommended Readings

1. H. Kerznerd (2009) *Project Management: A Systems Approach to Planning, Scheduling, and Controlling*, Wiley, Hoboken, NJ.

2. C. F. Gray (2005) *Project Management*, McGraw-Hill Education (India) Pvt Ltd, New Delhi, India.

3. J. D. Frame (2003) *Managing Projects in Organizations: How to Make the Best Use of Time, Techniques, and People*, Wiley, New York.

4. T. Kendrick (2004) *Project Management Tool Kit: 100 Tips and Techniques for Getting the Job Done Right*, American Management Association, New York.

5. M. Marchesi (2003) *Proceedings of Fourth International Conference on Extreme Programming and Agile Processes in Software Engineering, XP 2003*, Genova, Italy, May 25–29, 2003, Springer, Berlin, Germany.

6. R. J. Muller (1997) *Productive Objects: An Applied Software Project Management Framework*, Morgan Kaufmann, San Francisco, CA.

7. P. Jalote (2002) *Software Project Management in Practice*, Addison-Wesley Professional, Boston, MA.

8. F. A. Goodman (2006) *Process Based Software Project Management*, Auerbach, New York.

9. T. D. Wells (2002) *Dynamic Software Development: Managing Projects in Flux*, Auerbach, New York.

10. R. A. Morris, B. McWhorter Sember (2008) *Project Management That Works: Real-World Advice on Communicating, Problem-Solving, and Everything Else You Need to Know to Get the Job Done*, AMACOM, New York.

11. J. M. Nicholas, H. Steyn (2008) *Project Management for Business, Engineering, and Technology*, 3rd edn., Butterworth-Heinemann, Oxford, U.K.

12. D. D. Galorath, M. W. Evans (2006) *Software Sizing, Estimation and Risk Management*, CRC Press, Boca Raton, FL.

13. P. C. Tinnirello (1999) *Project Management*, Auerbach, New York.

Chapter 8

Project Closure

8.1 Introduction

After successful execution of a project, things come to a close. How satisfying the journey has been is determined from all the status reports and feedback from the customer. All along, there could have been moments of anxiety, discovery, joys, and sorrows. There could also have been moments when everything looked haywire and the project looked like a failure. But you have come to the stage where the project will be closing soon, and this signifies that ultimately things worked and things could be achieved even after going through some adverse situations.

A software project could be a software development, software customization, software integration, software maintenance, or just one phase of the software development life cycle (requirements, design, construction, or testing a software product). As per the contract, the final deliverables have to be handed over to the customer before the project deadline. While we can discuss project

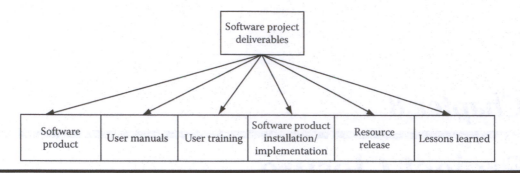

Figure 8.1 Software project deliverables before project closure.

closure formalities for any/all of these types of projects, it may become a large text. So we will limit the discussion to project closure formalities and tasks for a typical software development project (Figure 8.1).

Before the closure of the project, you need to check if all deliverables are going to be achieved before the set deadline. The deliverables include the tested software product, user/training manuals, user training, and installation/implementation of the software product at client site. It may also include product release information if the project is to develop a software product with many iterations and is built incrementally.

Do not forget that you need to keep a record of what happened during the execution of the project. If your company has a software engineering group and data from all projects that need to be kept in a central repository for statistical process-control purposes, then you also need to make sure that all relevant project data available before the closure of the project are fed into this repository.

8.2 Source Code Management

Many versions of the source code get generated as requirements, and designs get changed during the software development life cycle. During testing, many bugs are discovered and they are fixed. The final source code thus has seen a lot of change, and which version will be shipped to customer needs to be identified (Figure 8.2).

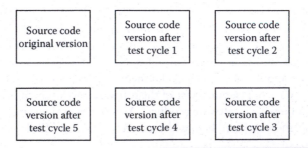

Figure 8.2 Many versions of source code.

The configuration management system should be kept up to date with all source code changes [1]. Sometimes, developers keep a local copy of the source code on their machines and forget to update the configuration management system with the changes they have made in the source code. Similarly, the user manuals and documents are sometimes not updated with the changes in code, which results in shipping wrong documentation to the customer. So it should be made sure that the correct version of the source code along with the documentation is shipped to the customer.

8.3 Project Data Management

Software service providers as well as internal teams maintain a large pool of project data for new projects [2]. So when an existing project comes to an end, it is very important to archive project data. The archived data help in estimating effort, schedule, costs, and quality level for new projects. This information is very valuable for new projects. Providing project data as a performance indicator to the customer not only boosts customer confidence about ability of the project team, but it also helps in increasing productivity, project goal clarity, and reducing schedule and costs when future projects actually get executed (Figure 8.3).

Statistical process-control quality methods work on the principle that collecting sample data and comparing it with a trend or norms tell whether the quality is improving or going worse [3]. Similarly, having historical data about similar projects helps in setting goals for and estimating the new project. Then when the project is executed, the trend data help in correcting any problems in the project.

Just keeping project execution data in the archive is not of much help. When you need to compare or use data, it should be clean and relevant. So before sending project execution data into the repository, it should be made sure that the data are clean. Similarly, irrelevant project data are not of much use. For any project, relevant data are the execution data from similar projects. This similarity is in terms of project size, industry for which the software product was made, programming language used, life-cycle methodology used, etc. So the repository should be categorized accordingly. Depending on these variations, there will be many different types of projects. When a new project is to be initiated, the repository should be searched for similar projects. Data from these projects can then be used for the new project. This cleaned and filtered data then will be very much relevant for the new project and thus will be extremely useful.

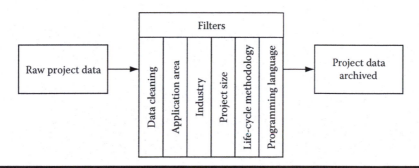

Figure 8.3   Strategy for project data archiving.

8.4 Project Closure in Iterative Model

The iterative development model is very popular in software product development these days. Software vendors are always keen to launch new versions of their software product in the opportunity time window lest the opportunity is lost. This results in some problems on the software development front. Iteration closure is often a messy affair if care and restraint are not exercised. Due to market pressure, top management is under pressure to incorporate all the requested features in the release. But it is clearly not feasible to do so. It is better to prioritize features based on market demand and effort required to make them. So release planning should be a part of the iteration planning at the beginning of the iteration. Features with high demand but requiring lesser effort should ideally be included first in the iteration. If time permits, then go for adding another feature. Keep doing it until you do not have any time left for adding any more features. Care should also be taken not to compromise on quality.

8.5 Lessons Learned

In life, people learn from doing things, and when they become older, they become much wiser as they accumulate all the learning over the years. Now when they apply this learning in their assignments, they are much more effective. They tend to do things better and are generally more productive.

Learning is a continuous process, and it should be done whenever someone gets a chance to do things or see others doing things. Projects are an excellent platform for learning. Each project has many new things that people may not have done earlier in their lives. Not only the project team members but also the organization learns from a project. Such learning should be documented so that it can be referenced for future projects [4] (Figure 8.4).

Some examples of lessons learned on the projects could be

- How to do a task in a better way
- How to manage the project in a better way
- Finding good solutions for issues faced
- How to negotiate with the customer
- How to mitigate an imminent risk
- Which techniques work and which do not in particular situations

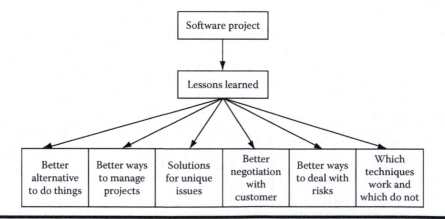

Figure 8.4   Lessons learned on a project.

Differences between a good organization and a bad one could boil down to the learning, which is wasted or used effectively on projects.

In a software project, we have many kinds of documents. We have project management-related documents such as project plan, communication plan, project schedule, effort estimate, cost estimate, resource plan, and resource allocation. Then, we have requirement documents, design documents, user manuals, and maintenance manuals from life-cycle management. We also have contract documents, statements of work, and legal documents from contract management.

Due to change requests, we will have many versions of different life-cycle documents. All of these documents go in the configuration management system. But most documents from contract management and project management do not go in the configuration management system. At the most project plan, project schedule, work breakdown structure, and resource plan go in the configuration management system.

Communication documents are the ones that contain the most unstructured and informal documentation. Nevertheless, e-mails and instant messages contain very useful pieces of information. Once the project is over, all these good pieces of information get lost. There should be some mechanism to extract this information and store it on the configuration management system, or rather knowledge management system, so that it is permanently available to the entire organization and not just one project. This information should be stored as lessons learned on a project.

8.6 Resource Release

The moment the project appears to be winding up, the project manager should make a release plan for resources so that the moment they are no longer needed on the project, they are immediately absorbed in other projects running at their organization [3]. Similarly, if any hardware or licensed software is being used specifically for the project, then a plan to release them should also be made. Many project managers are so absorbed in their project that they do not realize that their project will be winding up shortly, and the costly resources may not be utilized properly if they are not released immediately.

8.7 Data Structures

Discussion on any project management topic may not be complete without a discussion on unstructured data [5]. Let us admit it. Almost all project data come under the unstructured data category. On the other hand, good examples of structured data are manufacturing process data. In the manufacturing world, the manufacturing process is structured. That is why most manufacturing activity can be successfully automated. The boundaries of each and every manufacturing activity are well defined, and the limits for process variations are short. In fact, all manufacturing data can be easily digitized and thus can be easily used in computations. That is why they are amenable to automation easily. Coming back to projects, do you think any project process step can be precisely quantified? Well, it is difficult to do so. Even after implementing a strict process model, there will be variations in process steps from one project to another. So process measurements taken on one project will not be precisely the same compared to some other project. And this is the crux of the problem. One futuristic solution to this problem is when code reuse will become close to 100%. In that case, we will not be writing source code at all. In fact, we will have software components available in the market, which we can buy and use to assemble a software product, very similar to the case when a manufacturer assembles a car. In such a scenario, project data will be highly structured, and thus more and more project tasks can be easily automated.

Until this becomes a reality, we have to keep writing source code whenever we have to develop a new software product. Currently, what we have is some software components available in the market that can be used, but the rest part of the application is to be developed from scratch by designing the software system and then writing source code per this design. While we design software product and write source code, we come across a jungle of unstructured data. And this is where pitfalls lie. But then if projects become manufacturing, then they are not projects any longer!

For use with statistical methods, past project data must be qualified before it is quantified. As discussed in previous paragraphs, most project data are unstructured. All these data are subjective as well [6]. For instance, even though a project is shown to be completed on time without problems, in reality, there would have been some amount of overtime to complete the project on time. Now, this overtime data are not shown anywhere in the project data. Thus, the project data as shown formally on records are not true. If the person evaluating that project does not have any idea about this fact, then he may assume a wrong impression about the project. The bottom line is that each and every data must be qualified before it is stored in the repository and be subsequently used. It is the task of the project manager to ensure that he qualifies the project data at the closure of his project.

8.8 Case Study

In previous chapters, we have seen all of the things associated with the way projects and iterations are initiated, planned, and executed. In this chapter, we will see how project and iteration closure takes place with the projects at our SaaS vendor.

Since product development is a continuous process, resources released from a project are immediately absorbed in subsequent projects. Of course, resources finish their work on a project, and then they have nothing to do with that project. But their time is already planned for future projects by the global program manager. The configuration manager also plays a crucial role in saving all project documents and source code in a separate branch on the configuration management system. This branch serves as the complete new version with back integration with previous versions of the software product. Now, this branch is ready to be saved as the concrete version of the software product, and a new branch can be created on the configuration management system from this branch for the next version of the software product. Once the project is declared as complete, the branch of the configuration management system containing the source code and project documents is made read-only, and no changes are allowed in any of the source code or project documents.

For knowledge management and lessons learned on the project, these same project documents available on the branch of the configuration management system are used. In release 6.0, the greatest lesson learned was that even when elaborate planning is done for project tasks, things can turn nasty. The appointment scheduling functionality was really complex, and all plans to design, construct, and test it failed. It was only after some hard and long brain-storming sessions and much thinking that the functionality could be designed, constructed, and tested properly.

Due to the difficulties faced on the project, the original plan was at risk of going out of hand. Even the 10% schedule buffer was not sufficient. Finally, a compromise was made to do away with an additional feature that was also planned in the same release. This feature was moved to the next release. The resources allocated for designing, constructing, and testing this feature were also pulled and used for the appointment scheduling feature.

8.9 Chapter Summary

Before project closure, many activities remain on the project. Many loose ends are to be knotted before closure. In fact, the project team may be involved in many unfinished activities if the project execution has not been smooth. However, the main tasks of closure include resource release, preparing lessons learned on the project, source code management, and project data management. Once project data and lessons learned are prepared, then they should be archived to be used for future projects. Source code control is important, because during system testing, much defect fixing would have been done, and thus a lot of changes in the source code would have occurred. At this time, which version of the software should be deployed at customer site has to be determined.

For project data, care must be taken to make sure that it does not contain any extraneous data. During archiving, care has to be taken to archive the project data correctly in the right place so that this data is useful in the future.

Exercises

8.1 In iterative projects, find out how project closure is different compared to project closure in traditional projects.

8.2 What are typical project tasks in project closure phase?

Review Questions

8.1 Why are project data useful?

8.2 What care should be taken before archiving project data?

8.3 What tasks are done before closing a project?

8.4 What strategies are taken to ensure that lessons are learned?

8.5 Why is resource release important?

Recommended Readings

1. A. Stellman, J. Greene (2005) *Applied Software Project Management*, O'Reilly Media, Sebastopol, CA.
2. R. E. Fairley (2009) *Managing and Leading Software Projects*, Wiley-IEEE Computer Society Press, Hoboken, NJ.
3. P. Jalote (2002) *Software Project Management in Practice*, Addison-Wesley Professional, Boston, MA.
4. G. Ruhe (2001) *Learning Software Organizations: Methodology and Applications: 11th International Conference on Software Engineering and Knowledge Engineering, Seke*, Springer, Berlin, Germany.
5. A. Griffith, A. King, Engineering and Physical Sciences Research Council (2003) *Best Practice Tendering for Design and Build Projects*, Thomas Telford Ltd, London, U.K.
6. P. Jalote (1997) *An Integrated Approach to Software Engineering*, Springer, New York.

SOFTWARE LIFE-CYCLE MANAGEMENT

Chapter 9

Introduction to Software Life-Cycle Management

> **In Part II, we will learn**
>
> - What is software engineering?
> - What impact does software engineering have on a software project?
> - What are various life cycle models for software development?
> - What are various phases in a software development life cycle?
> - How are quality assurance and quality control done in the software life cycle?

> **In this chapter, we will learn**
>
> - What is software engineering?
> - What are software development life-cycle phases?
> - What development metrics are measured?
> - What are the work products in a software life cycle?
> - How is quality assurance done during software development?

9.1 Introduction

Suppose we are living in a world where software development is done automatically. There are robots that gather the software requirements and feed it into a software program. This software program designs the software and generates the code. Since there are virtually no defects in the requirements (robots do not make any mistakes!), there will not be any defects in design and construction. So, there will not be any need for testing the built software product. The design and construction of the software product will be done in a matter of minutes. Don't you think this will be utopia!

Sadly, we are living in a world where it has not become a reality yet. We still have people who visit customer sites and elicit customer software requirements. The customer happily dictates requirements. The requirement gatherer documents these requirements in the best possible way he understands them. Then, he converts these requirements into software features and hands it to the software design team. The software designers convert these features into designs in the best possible way they can do it. Then, they hand these designs to the construction team. The construction team works on these designs tirelessly to convert them into a beautifully constructed software build. Now, this build is tested to remove the defects introduced during design and construction. Finally, the product is implemented at the customer site.

Again, sadly, due to low quality of the software product, users start finding defects when they start using it in their daily work. Due to rapid changes in business and work environments, the software product they are using becomes unusable and may need changes after some time. Also due to changes in business environment, some new functionality may need to be added to the software product to make it more useful. Due to rapid changes in technology, the hardware or software platform may become obsolete, and thus the software product may need to be ported to a new platform.

To perform these activities successfully requires highly skilled, trained, and experienced people. At the same time, all of these activities are resource intensive. So software personnel have to toil hard and apply their skills creatively to perform these activities. But even then, the desired software products take a long time to develop, and the customer may need to wait for many months if not years to see the product in action.

So until we reach utopia sometime in the future, all software professionals need to toil hard and perform the activities of the software development life cycle (Figure 9.1).

At the same time, some progress has been made in the field of software engineering. Software engineering is not yet fully evolved and matured, but still, it has come a long way in the last 50 years or so. Using any current software engineering framework, it is possible to design and construct industry strength software products that are of reasonably good quality. Time and effort required to build software products has gone down by a magnitude of more than 20:1, thanks to rapid advancement in software engineering, increasing code reuse, development and adoption of high productivity software design and coding platforms, improvement in development life-cycle management, etc., which help software development projects tremendously in all the three parameters of time, effort, and quality.

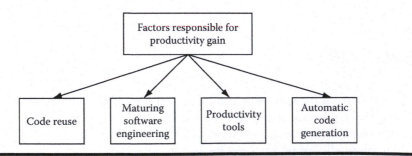

Figure 9.1 Factors which helped in improving productivity on software projects.

In this chapter, we introduce software engineering concepts related to development life cycles on software projects. In later chapters in this part of the book, detailed discussions about each and every activity involved in different phases in development life cycle are discussed.

9.2 Software Engineering Management

Software engineering is a vast field. It is also fast evolving. At the same time, it is currently more art than science or engineering. It is because software engineering still does not have theories that are based on solid applied science. Software engineering currently is based on best practices derived after observations made on thousands of software projects.

For practical purposes, software engineering can be divided into two parts: software engineering management and software technical engineering (or software life-cycle management). The technical aspects related to software engineering include good software design and good software construction (Figure 9.2). Software engineering management, on the other hand, deals with concerns with four primary areas. The first one is to how to build a software product with minimum cost, within minimum time and with required quality. The second concerns maintaining a consistent quality across all projects within an organization. But, the most crucial aspect is how to keep improving productivity and quality on software projects with increasing organization process maturity. The organization processes should keep maturing with experience gained on executing projects. The last concern is how to choose an appropriate software engineering process for different software projects (Figure 9.3).

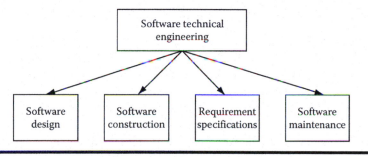

Figure 9.2   Software technical engineering (software life cycle).

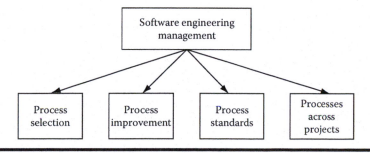

Figure 9.3   Software engineering management.

All these areas discussed about software engineering have a very important role in software project management [1]. Without these inputs, it is difficult to manage modern large-scale software projects.

In this book, we will be discussing software engineering management aspects in Part III and technical aspects in this part. The software engineering management topics include process improvements, development process selection, developing and implementing mature life cycles. The technical software engineering concerns different phases of development life cycles, work products developed in these phases, and activities carried out within different phases. In this part, we will concentrate on all these aspects related to technical software engineering (software development life cycle). Process improvements and process selection are discussed in Part III.

9.3 Software Life-Cycle Management Processes

Most projects involve requirements, design, testing, and construction activities. Software development projects are no exception. Customer requirements are gathered and developed, and then an appropriate software design is made that fulfills the needs of these requirements by converting these requirements into a suitable software design. Software design is further converted into a software product through software construction activities. During the entire development life cycle, quality control and quality assurance activities are carried out to ensure that quality of the end products is within agreed upon norms.

Let us discuss various software development life cycles in this section.

9.3.1 Software Life Cycle in Waterfall Model

The waterfall model is still a widely used methodology for software development, though some other development models are also gaining wide acceptance. Some variations of the waterfall model include concurrent development, incremental development, and prototyping. Standards like CMM, CMMI, ISO, and IEEE introduced comprehensive quality assurance activities in the software life cycle, and thus the waterfall model has incorporated many of these aspects.

The waterfall model is best suited for large software development projects for government, military, and other industries. Again, the waterfall model is best suited for projects where well-developed software requirement specifications (SRSs) exist [2]. The entire software development/maintenance project is divided into well-defined phases. These phases are requirements management, software design, software construction, software testing, software release, and software maintenance. These phases are tightly divided and are phased out in time sequence, and once one phase is complete, development moves into the next phase (Figure 9.4).

9.3.2 Software Life Cycle in Iterative Model

As can be seen from many discussions on software development project problems, it is a fact that software projects are different from other kind of projects. Requirements are best captured in many iterations and not in one go. In most cases, after end users see a working prototype, only then they are able to provide inputs regarding their exact requirements. Then, there is the huge risk a software project faces when the software product gets ready only after a long period of time and when the product development goes from converting requirements into software design, which,

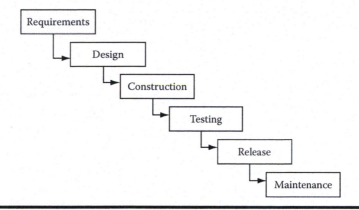

Figure 9.4   Software life cycle in waterfall model.

in turn, is converted to construction. What if after this hard toil that goes on for months only to be found out that what has been developed is not what end users expected. Definitely, it is a huge risk.

One solution to deal with this kind of situation is to adopt an iterative model for software development [3]. Instead of taking all requirements and begin designing and developing the software, we can take a few of the requirements and start designing and then building the software only for this set of requirements. Once the software is built, it is delivered to the end users. They can ask for some changes, and these changes can be done quickly. So the cycle for all these activities may last a few weeks (1–6 weeks). Once this is over, some more requirements can be taken and again this cycle is repeated. This cycle is repeated until all requirements are converted into the software product. In this way, the huge risk of delivering wrong software product at the end of a long period of development can be avoided. Customers also like this kind of model as they keep getting deliveries at short intervals, and so their confidence with the development team is high.

To do things this way, some methodologies have been developed over the years. Some well-known methodologies include Scrum, eXtreme Programming, incremental iteration model, and spiral development. There is one more iteration-based model, which was developed by Rational Corporation (part of IBM). It is known as the rational unified process model. This model is discussed at length in Chapter 16 along with the other major agile models like Scrum and eXtreme Programming. At the heart of all these methodologies is the concept of using only a few of the requirements developing the software product, and delivering it after a short cycle of development. The goal is to iterate until all of the requirements are converted into a software product (Figure 9.5).

There are some negative aspects about this kind of software development as well [4]. Not all software products can be developed this way. The iterative model is suited only for lightweight or smaller software products. For large software products, the waterfall model is still the preferred model, though iterative models are also catching up in this space. In fact, many large software products need to be developed using concurrent engineering, where many development teams participate simultaneously on building the same software product. For large software products, you need to build a large base framework on which the product has to be developed. This base framework includes creating data model, conceptual model, logical model, and physical model. This base framework corresponds to the complete software design phase as depicted in the waterfall model of software development. If the base framework is not done, then the software product can be unstable. Once the base is ready, then software functions can be developed using any suitable software development process model. At the same time, it is difficult to create the complete

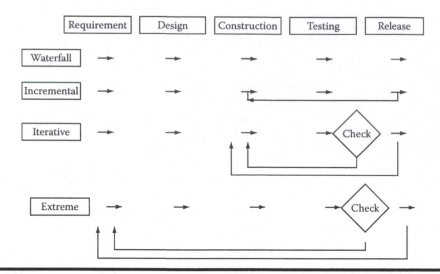

Figure 9.5 Software life cycle in various software development models.

software design when your requirements themselves are not crystal clear, and in fact many of the requirements are not even properly understood either by the end users or the project team. Some agile models tackle this problem of making elaborate and complete software design by resorting to a technique known as refactoring. This concept is discussed in detail in Chapter 11.

Iterative software development models are still evolving though. One good framework has been developed by the open source community of Eclipse (see http://www.eclispse.org). They have developed a software development framework similar to the rational unified process and called it unified process framework [5]. Using this framework, even large software products can be developed. The basic building blocks in this framework are the development of software components. The architecture is known as "service oriented architecture" (SOA). More about SOA is discussed in Chapter 11.

9.3.2.1 Moving from Waterfall Model

Sometimes, due to problems faced in the waterfall model, a project needs to move to an iterative model [6]. In such cases, a complete change may be needed not only with the project organization structure but with the top layer, which controls at the organization level as well. The project management has to be done at three layers, as compared to two levels in waterfall model. In the waterfall model, there is a project level and a program management level (program management office [PMO]). In an iterative model, there is an organization level where the complete product management is taken care of. The lower level structure concerns major releases of the product, and finally, the lowest level where most of the actual product development is done using iterations. More details about organization structures can be found in Chapter 19.

9.3.3 Software Life Cycle in Concurrent Engineering Model

Concurrent engineering is a field that espouses the cause of rapid product development using many teams that work on product development simultaneously [7]. The most labor-intensive phases in the software development process are software construction and software testing. If tasks involved in these phases can be broken into smaller parts and if many teams can be employed to do these tasks

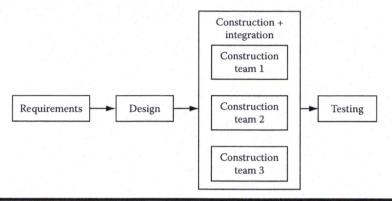

Figure 9.6   Many construction teams in a concurrent engineering environment.

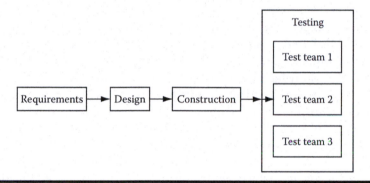

Figure 9.7   Many testing teams in a concurrent engineering environment.

in parallel, then the software development life cycle can be shrinked substantially. The task of product development is divided into smaller tasks in such a way that each of these tasks can be executed independently of each other. So unrelated teams can work on completing each part of the product without the need to know what other teams are developing. This mechanism makes it easy for concurrent working of many teams. Once these parts of the product are complete, they are assembled to make the complete product (Figure 9.6).

In software development, dividing the software product is difficult. Decision about division of the software product to be developed is taken during the design phase so that many parts of the software can be constructed or tested parallely. To enable concurrent development, the software product is divided in such a way that each of the parts has defined interfaces through which they can be integrated with other parts. To test these parts, dummy parts are used for these interfaces so that the part can be tested (also known as test oracles). Once these parts are developed by each independent team, they are integrated to make the complete software product. Similarly, for testing, each test part is assigned to a different team so that they can test their own parts in parallel and thus the length of the testing cycle can be reduced (Figure 9.7).

9.3.4 Software Life-Cycle Processes

Even though different process models have different process phases or steps defined, neverthe-less, process steps are best represented by the waterfall model. In the case of the rational unified process, phases are represented in matrix with workflows. These workflows do not get completed within one phase but instead they cross more than one phase. This is true in most life-cycle cases as many processes are completed in cycles, and thus they are nonlinear in nature.

Here, we discuss the life-cycle processes in detail.

9.3.4.1 Software Requirements

After the project initiation is over and statement of work (SOW) is signed, the project team starts gathering software requirements from the customer. After the requirements are gathered, they need to be developed to make them suitable for system modeling. Some of the techniques used for software requirements include elicitation techniques and analysis techniques.

To produce a software product, you need to get good requirements. A problem starts here. Requirements for software products are never very clear. Most of the time, the requirements are to replace processes that are currently done manually with those that use software. But this is not all. Management wants to use software to get a strategic advantage. For instance, management believes that by using software, they will be able to reduce substantially inventory from current levels. Now, this kind of expectation cannot be clearly defined. It could be a fact that software can provide visibility and tools to better manage inventory, but it cannot be said that using software will help in reducing inventory by a certain percentage. Similarly, people expect that their workload will get reduced after the software product is implemented. It is true in most of instances, but, initially, a lot of master data must be entered in the software system, and this needs a lot of work in the early stage when the software product is being implemented. In such cases, false expectations are not met, and users start blaming the project team for not meeting their expectations.

Requirement gathering and subsequent requirement management is a difficult task. A good process must be defined so that both these tasks can be done in a good and consistent manner. The requirement gathering differs from one place to another. At some places, user interviews and many formal methods are employed to get requirements. At other places, informal methods are used. Also, the size of the software product also influences as to what methods are to be deployed for requirement gathering. To reduce variability in processes involved in requirement management, a good requirement gathering template can help.

Some of the challenges in requirement gathering include unclear requirements, difficulty in getting requirements, difficulty in understanding requirements, and translating those requirements into a suitable software design. Requirements changes take place throughout the project. This makes software development difficult. Incorporating changed requirements is a difficult proposition. Suppose a design has been made and the project is in the build phase, and then imagine a change request arrives. The software architect feels that a large change will be required in design. He has no option but to do it as the change request has been accepted. He takes time to make changes in the design. The build team will have to stop their work as this change in design will cause many of changes in code. In effect, much rework has to be done by the project team. This kind of rework can take place many times during the project. This makes design and code changes vulnerable for failures. So more defects can be expected in such a software product that has experienced many rework requirements.

This scenario is not an isolated case. But in fact it is a prevalent malady in most software projects.

Traditionally, a waterfall model has been adopted for software development projects. There is a strict division of phases in the project. The requirements phase comes first and when it gets completed, a sign off is made supposedly to mark the end of requirements phase (though in reality requirement change requests keep coming). Next comes the software design phase. When it gets completed, a sign off is made. Then comes the building phase. Here, coding is done. Then, in the testing phase, the built software is tested. Once testing gets completed, the go live phase (also known as deployment or release phase) comes, and after completion of this phase, the software is implemented at customer site. Once the go live phase is over, software goes into the production phase.

This approach is good in many respects. It assures good quality in the software being produced. It is well organized. But there is one great disadvantage with this approach. This approach cannot incorporate changing business requirements. In today's turbulent business environment, things change fast. So even if a software requirement looks very good today, it may not look so good tomorrow. Without incorporating changes required tomorrow, the software being developed may prove to be a sitting duck.

So what could be a good approach for countering the malady of requirement changes? Over the years, many organizations proposed and practiced some new approaches for software project management to tackle this perennial issue. Some of them include the iterative model, agile methods, spiral method, and extreme programming. In all of these approaches, the fundamental shift to requirement management is that the requirements should be collected and developed iteratively so that unclear or unknown requirements can be incorporated once they become clear. Collectively, we can term them as iterative development models.

The iterative model suits software projects, because only a small set of requirements is taken for starting the software project instead of collecting the entire set of customer requirements. So even if end users are not clear about their exact requirements, the project can be started with a handful of known requirements. The software can be designed and built for this set of requirements and delivered to the end users. All of these activities are performed in a short cycle of a few weeks or a few months. Then, the next set of requirements can be taken, and the next iteration can be done based on this set of requirements. Users are happy to see the results so early and thus have more confidence in the project team. This definitely makes a good business sense.

We will learn about requirement management in Chapter 10 in detail.

9.3.4.2 Software Design

Software design follows the software requirement phase. Based on the requirements, software is designed in such a way that the features required in the requirements document can be implemented in the software design. Apart from how the features as per functional requirements can be implemented, design also considers factors such as reliability, robustness, security, ease of use, internationalization, localization, and compatibility. All of these are collectively termed as nonfunctional design requirements.

Large enterprise systems have many kinds of users. They use the system to do their everyday tasks. To make a good user experience, it is important that the user should be presented only the information that he needs to do his job and not everything that the software product can do. So software features should be linked to roles, and these roles should be linked to software features that are required by these roles. Similarly, the information presented to the user should be in a manner that is easy for the user to use the information and be able to perform his everyday activities easily. All of these aspects should be part of the software design.

Some of the challenges in software design include difficulty in modeling due to changes or unclear requirements, limitations of representation of requirements into system design, etc.

Software design plays an important role in software development. If the design is good, software will have fewer defects and may be considered reliable. Due to requirement creep as mentioned in a previous section, the design may get unstable, which may lead to a poor quality product.

Enterprise software products though may have a lot of features; nevertheless, they need to have open interfaces so that they can be integrated with other software products. This is because even big ERP products may not have everything an enterprise may need, and so it must be integrated with other software products that may be providing the other needed features.

There are good processes available that help in designing different kinds of software products. For instance, software applications to be deployed over the Web need a different kind of design than an application that will have to be deployed offline.

New discoveries in the software engineering field are also forcing software design to change. The latest discovery of SOA is forcing project teams to design their products as per requirements of SOA. SOA indeed is an exciting field that is paving the way for software reuse on a mass scale. We will discuss SOA and related technologies in Chapter 25.

We will study more on software design in Chapter 11.

9.3.4.3 Software Build

Software coding (also known as building or construction) is the most labor-intensive task in software development projects. For good coding management, a well-planned approach needs to be adopted for configuration and version control, sticking to good coding standards, and using a good object-oriented approach.

Software building (construction) requires a team effort to build a software application. Some of the challenges in software construction include lack of team work, rework due to changes in design, lack of clarity in design, bad allocation of work, and bad component structure.

Whether it is waterfall or agile development, rework in the coding phase should be avoided as far as possible. Software coding is characterized by a large team of developers for large projects. How the project is divided and how developers are assigned their task, and how these tasks are tracked is a major decision in the project. It is very important that proper planning for these tasks is made well. It is also important that a very good version control management tool is deployed so that each version of the software being developed can be maintained and development can happen without any interruption due to version issues, etc.

We will learn more about software construction in Chapter 12.

9.3.4.4 Software Testing

Software testing is very important area, because most critical bugs should be trapped here. Otherwise, fixing bugs in the maintenance phase becomes very costly. Software testing is undertaken as a separate project on many software development projects as it provides a lot of additional value. In such cases, it is known as independent verification and validation (IV&V). IV&V helps in trapping defects at all phases and in all work products during the entire development life cycle. These defects are subsequently removed. Making a separate project for testing thus helps in increasing reliability of the software product.

Some of the challenges for software testing include too many defects in the software application that increases load on software testers, lack of test strategy, lack of test planning, etc.

Software testing has been gaining importance over the years. Customers now expect much better quality from their software products than was the case a few decades back.

Software testing includes unit testing, integration testing, system testing, user acceptance testing, performance testing, and usability testing. IV&V includes requirement specification review, design inspection, construction inspection, and integration inspection. So scope of testing has increased on software projects manifold after the advent of IV&V.

Developed software contains many bugs introduced due to faults in requirements, software design, and software coding. The purpose of software testing is to find these bugs so that they can be removed. This kind of software testing is known as functional testing. Functional testing is of two types: white box testing and black box testing. When developers check their own code for testing logic of the conditional statements or checking formatting of data, etc., then this kind of white box testing is known as unit testing. In integration testing, developers test whether data are passing correctly between functions. So most white box testing revolves around testing at the function level.

When it comes to testing at the system level, black box testing techniques are used. Black box testing is also used for user acceptance testing. In black box testing, requirements and design documents are referred to assess whether the built system adheres to customer requirements.

Apart from the functional aspects, the built system is also to be checked for many other aspects, for instance, whether the built system can withstand load of transaction requests made by users on the server on which the application is installed. Then, usability, system integration, and many other kinds of aspects are to be tested to verify if the system is working as per these expectations.

The software system may contain a large number of bugs. It will be very difficult to detect all of the bugs. Even if you employ a large testing team, it may take a considerable amount of time to detect a fraction of all bugs. This kind of exercise will not be of much use. If we are testing a software product, then the marketing team cannot wait for long, as they need to put the product in the market within a specified time frame. If we are testing a software application specifically built for an organization, then that organization cannot wait for long to get to use the application. Moreover, the cost of such a large testing effort will be huge. This kind of testing activity is simply not acceptable.

A better approach is to have an effective testing. There will be a time limit under which all testing activities have to be performed. There will also be a cut-off quality level that is acceptable to the customers. So a compromise between quality level and time to test the application has to be made. For example, we can have a schedule of 15 days to test the application and acceptable quality level of 100 critical bugs to be fixed after the system goes live.

For all kinds of testing to be effective, a comprehensive framework is needed. As has been stated previously, user acceptance testing needs a requirement document and a good understanding of what exactly the customer needs in the system. The system testing is based on the system design document. The integration and unit tests are also based on the design document, but they are done at much lower levels. System testing is done at the system level whereas unit and integration testing is done at the function level.

Testing should also be prioritized based on needs of the project. For instance, of all the requirements, some are of high priority and some others are not. Definitely high priority requirements should be tested first so that they are covered even if time does not permit further testing. In such cases, low priority requirements may not get tested, but the impact on the project in such instances will be much lower compared to cases when high priority requirements could not be tested due to time constraints.

Similarly, when it comes to system testing, the testing team should have a very good idea about the design and architecture of the system. Only then they can do testing effectively.

These things can happen only when the testing team gets involved early in the development life cycle.

9.3.4.5 Software Release

Some of the challenges in the release phase include too many bugs found in user acceptance testing, incomplete, or superficial testing due to a limited testing phase, poor documentation, and poor user training due to unplanned release.

When software is made ready for released, then you not only need to make sure that the software application runs per customer requirements, but also it should be easy to maintain after production. Processes involved in the software release phase include preparing user manuals, user acceptance testing, user training, system configuration, and installation. A software release can be an alpha, beta, or final release. Depending on the kind of release, the processes may vary. In an alpha release, the software is released only to internal users and not to the public or customers. Even if it is released to customers, it is offered for free just for testing purposes. In case of a beta release, the software is released for free to the public and customers before the final release so that the product is thoroughly tested by the users themselves, and all defects found by them are removed. This ensures that there are no defects in the final release.

9.3.4.6 Software Maintenance

Software maintenance is an area that can be more demanding than software development. It is because, most of the time, it is done by a team that is different from the team that developed the software. Even if they did a good documentation job during development, understanding those documents and the code is a difficult for anybody. That is why it is best if the software development team also do maintenance; but in practice, it is difficult if not impossible.

Some of the techniques used for maintenance include reverse engineering and re-engineering. Some of the challenges in maintenance include inadequate maintenance plan, inadequate strategy, and inadequate technique.

Software maintenance is often neglected when software is developed. This leads to many problems when it goes into production and then needs maintenance. So it is of utmost importance that maintenance is kept in consideration during software development. Some of the issues that arise in software maintenance include

- Software code is not readable
- Design and construction documents are either outdated, nonexistent, or insufficient
- Unstructured code
- Maintenance personnel having insufficient knowledge of the software application

If any of these problems exist, then the software application is difficult to change during maintenance.

9.4 Software Life-Cycle Metrics

When it comes to measuring work product and process attributes in the development life cycle, what comes to mind? Definitely, all the work products and the final product that are produced during the development life cycle. Then, there are different steps that are involved in producing these work products [5]. During the requirement development and specification stage, the work product being worked on is the SRS document. The SRS must have attributes like testability, maintainability, completeness, and nonambiguousness. The size of the SRS does not make any sense itself because there is no relationship of SRS size to the size of the software product. Similarly, during design, construction, and testing, there will be a large number of work products being produced. Measuring quality of these work products will provide good insight as to how the project team is faring against benchmarks or any other standard against which the measurements are to be compared. For producing these work products, there will be a large number of processes undertaken. Measuring productivity of these processes will provide good insight as to how the project team is faring against benchmarks or any other standard against which the measurements are to be compared [8].

9.5 Work Products

In manufacturing, intermediate products created during product manufacturing are known as works in process (WIP). These WIP products result after a processing step done during manufacturing. In the software industry, these intermediate unfinished products are known as work products. During the software development project, each software development process produces work products. It is important to identify these work products, and there should be a mechanism that will measure quality of the work product. This will ensure that defects are trapped and removed before development proceeds to the next phase (Figure 9.8).

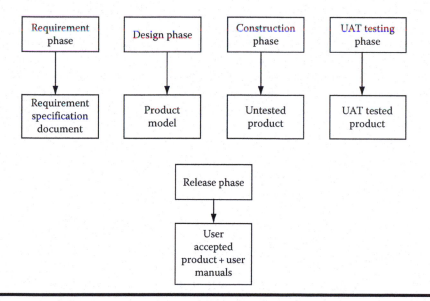

Figure 9.8   Work products from various software life-cycle phases.

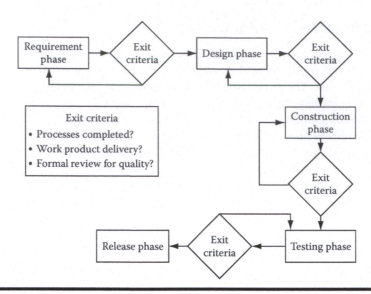

Figure 9.9 Quality assurance mechanism for software projects.

9.6 Quality Assurance

There is an inherent drawback in waterfall and other models of software development. Software testing had been relegated to be done after software construction. There was no mechanism to find out if requirement specifications were correct. Similarly, no mechanisms were provided to check whether the software design was correct. What if there were faults in the requirement specifications or in software design? Obviously, if there were faults in requirement specifications, then the software design will be faulty. Similar will be the case with software construction, because it will be based on faulty software design. A faulty work product as an input to a process step will always result in a faulty work product output. Instead of building subsequent work products based on faulty input work products, it makes sense to check the input work products to verify if they are correct and do not contain any defects. The downstream activities in the development life cycle should start only after verifying that the input work products do not contain any defects.

After each phase of software development gets completed, there should be exit criteria that will ensure that all work has finished per project plan and that these work products are defect free. Only then, the project can move on to the next phase. The exit criteria should include completion of all processes for the phase, completion of work products, and finally acceptable quality of work products. For quality control, formal review processes should be included in each phase (Figure 9.9).

If any of the three exit criteria is not met, rework may be needed, and, thus, instead of the project moving forward, it will move back [9].

9.7 Case Study

We discussed project management-related aspects with our SaaS vendor in Part I. In Part II, we will discover how the development life cycle evolved and was being used by the SaaS vendor. We will discover how the requirement specification was prepared, how software design was made, how software code was written, how software testing was done, how user training was conducted, how the product was deployed, and how maintenance was performed.

9.8 Chapter Summary

In introduction to software development life cycles, we have learned what constitutes a software development life cycle. We have also learned some of the techniques employed for rapid development such as concurrent engineering. We have also learned about software measurements and how a good set of software metrics helps in achieving a good software product. We have also learned about software quality control and what exact measures are required on software projects. We have also learned about work products that are made during different phases of the software life cycle. This chapter will prepare us for the next chapters of Part II, where we will learn about various major phases in the software development life cycle: software requirements, software design, software construction, software testing, software release, and, finally, software maintenance.

Exercises

9.1 Find out which software development life-cycle model was adopted for any open source project. What are significant aspects about the adopted model?

9.2 Find out the rationale for selecting the development life cycle on that open source project?

Review Questions

9.1 What are the phases in the software development life cycle?

9.2 What statistical process control methods can be employed on software development projects?

9.3 What is concurrent engineering? How can concurrent engineering be used in software development projects?

9.4 What are work products in the software life cycle?

9.5 What metrics are utilized on software projects?

Recommended Readings

1. J. Keyes (2002) *Software Engineering Handbook*, Auerbach, New York.
2. M. Silver (2004) *Exploring Interface Design*, Thomson Learning, Australia.
3. D. Leffingwell, D. Widrig (1999) *Managing Software Requirements: A Unified Approach*, Addison-Wesley, Boston, MA.
4. J. Lind (2001) *Iterative Software Engineering for Multiagent Systems: The Massive Method* (Lecture Notes in Computer Science), Springer, Berlin, Germany.
5. Q. Wang, D. M. Raffo (2008) *Making Globally Distributed Software Development a Success Story*, Springer, Berlin, Germany.
6. C. Larman (2003) *Agile and Iterative Development: A Manager's Guide*, Addison-Wesley Professional, Boston, MA.
7. P. Ghodous, R. Dieng-kuntz, G. Loureiro (2006) *Leading the Web in Concurrent Engineering: Next Generation Concurrent Engineering*, Volume 143 Frontiers in Artificial Intelligence and Applications, IOS Press, Amsterdam, the Netherlands.
8. S. Datta (2007) *Metrics-Driven Enterprise Software Development: Effectively Meeting Evolving Business Needs*, J. Ross Publishing, Fort Lauderdale, FL.
9. J. Parnaby, S. Wearne, A. K. Kochhar (2003) *Managing by Projects for Business Success*, Wiley, London, U.K.

Chapter 10

Software Requirement Management

10.1 Introduction

Software requirement development and management is one area where the project team needs to do a lot of work. Requirements are one of the most important parts of the software project. After all, the software application or product is to be built based on these requirements.

For government projects, requirements come with all the details. It is simply because at government offices, everything should be accounted for, and so they need minute details of everything including information about why and how the software will be developed and exactly what are the requirements for which the software will be developed. These requirements are sometimes documented more than required. But they always come with correct and complete details. Requirements for internal software projects come with fewer details. In the case of commercial and business software development for external customers, the details of requirements can vary. For outsourced software projects, great details are available. But in case of offshore outsourced projects, complete requirement details are needed and hence are provided by customers.

10.2 Software Requirements Development

Consider this request from the marketing department of a software vendor: "We need to develop an online access system for our banking application by next month." Yes, this is a requirement with the timeline from the marketing department's point of view. The project manager may just get bewildered, but this is what happens to software project managers. If you get requirements like this, then you need to pay attention to find out actually what is required and then develop the requirements accordingly.

Developing the requirement is done by software engineering folks. Even if detailed requirements come from a customer, analysis of these details must be done [1]. Some of the requirements may need to be elaborated further. Some of the requirements may not be feasible. In those cases, some alternative solution has to be suggested to the customer and approval obtained from him.

Once most of the requirements are made clear and approved, then software design processes can begin.

Requirements can be broadly grouped into two categories: functional requirements and nonfunctional requirements [2]. Functional requirements pertain to those requirements that state the

Figure 10.1   Software requirement types.

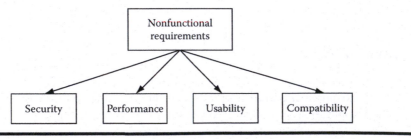

Figure 10.2   Nonfunctional software requirement sub types.

functionality required in the software system that the customer is looking for (Figures 10.1 and 10.2). A functional requirement could be, for instance, to have a transaction ability so that the user can purchase certain goods from the Web site using a credit card.

Nonfunctional requirements are those requirements that do not belong to the core functional requirements. Instead, they state how the software system will behave in certain conditions. Some of the nonfunctional requirements include security, performance, usability, compatibility, etc. A customer requirement may be stated that the software system should be secure so that unauthorized access to the software system is not allowed. In that case, a comprehensive security mechanism should be incorporated in the software system so that unless a user has been provided privileges for access, he cannot access the software system. In the requirements, if it is stated that the response time for a page loading should be less than 10 s, then the software system and the hardware on which it will run should be made load pages within 10 s even during expected peak loads.

Some of the considerations associated with requirement development include

■ Well-defined required functionality (both functional and nonfunctional) to make an appropriate software product.
■ Defined details of the operational environment in which the software system will operate.
■ Maintenance and final retirement plan should be in place.
■ All limitation factors should be stated before the development life cycle starts, including limitation factors for design, construction, maintenance, and testing activities. Otherwise, during development, unpleasant surprises may crop up.

Limitations and constraints to be considered for developing the software product during the requirement development stage itself should be considered. They should include

■ Cost and cost drivers
■ Risks associated with requirements (incomplete/ambiguous/wrong requirements) that can have impact on the project
■ Factors related to customer's unique business considerations, regulations, and laws to better relate requirements to software design
■ Time constraints and schedule drivers
■ Consideration of issues implied but not explicitly stated by the customer or end-user
■ Technological limitations

During requirement development, the customer requirements are analyzed, and a detailed software requirement is developed. If complete information is not available at this stage, then some assumptions are made. These assumptions are noted down for further discussion with customer and to get their approval. At this stage, care is also taken to view requirements, constraints, and limitations of design, construction, maintenance, and testing of the proposed software product. Due to these considerations, some additional requirements may also need to be added [3].

All the requirements need to be converted into software features (logical entities) [4]. All these features need to be categorized under some major heads (top level features). All other features that are dependent on the main feature should be put under these heads in hierarchical order. Whenever new requirements are added, they are refined, derived, and allocated to these

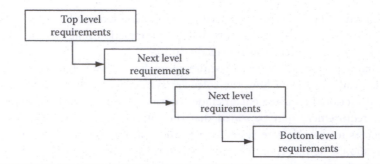

Figure 10.3   Software requirement hierarchies.

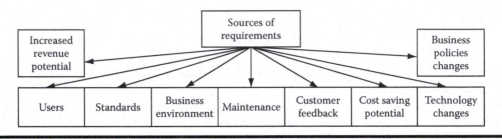

Figure 10.4   Sources of software requirements.

logical entities. These logical entities are then allocated to products, product components, people, or associated processes (Figure 10.3).

Involvement of relevant stakeholders in both requirement development and analysis gives them a view into the evolution of requirements. This activity continually assures them that the requirements are being properly defined.

There are many techniques employed to elicit requirements from customers or from other sources [5]. Some of them include interface control working groups, interim project reviews, operational walkthroughs and end-user task analysis, technical control working groups, technology demonstrations, prototypes and models, brainstorming, customer satisfaction surveys, quality function deployment, market surveys, questionnaires, interviews, and operational scenarios obtained from end users, beta testing, extraction from sources such as documents, standards, or specifications, observation of existing products, environments, and workflow patterns, use cases, business case analysis, and reverse engineering (Figure 10.4).

Examples of sources of requirements that might not be identified by the customer include the following:

- Standards
- Business environmental requirements (e.g., laboratories, testing and other facilities, and information technology infrastructure)
- Technology
- Business policies
- Legacy products or product components (reuse product components)

10.2.1 Develop Requirements

The initial requirements, whether from customers or from other sources, need to be made usable as input for making software requirements. Any irrelevant information from the gathered information must be purged. Any information missing should be sought from responsible sources. Conflicts between any pieces of information should be resolved. Once the collected information looks complete, it should be consolidated.

10.2.2 Requirement Development Tasks

Some of the tasks done during requirement development include

- Customer requirements are refined and elaborated to develop product and product component requirements.
- Establish and maintain product and product component requirements that are based on customer requirements.
- Allocate the requirements for each product component.
- Identify interface requirements.
- The requirements are analyzed and validated, and a definition of required functionality is developed.
- Establish and maintain operational concepts and associated scenarios.
- Establish and maintain a definition of required functionality.
- Analyze requirements to ensure that they are necessary and sufficient.
- Analyze requirements to balance stakeholder needs and constraints.
- Validate requirements to ensure that the resulting product will perform as intended in the user's environment.

For a large enterprise application development, a large number of requirements may be found in specific areas. In such cases, a team of business analysts may be required who may gather the requirements and later develop them. For instance, if an enterprise system requirement is to have functional areas like finance, supply chain management, customer relationship management, and human resources, then we can have at least four business analysts who will gather and develop requirements specific to their areas. Once these requirements are developed, then they may need to be consolidated. Once the consolidation is done, then a system model may need to be developed. In fact, it is possible that functional models for each functional area may be developed separately and later consolidated. These models need to be developed using a standard language like UML (unified meta language). For a user interface, some UI flow model is also to be developed.

10.3 Software Requirements Management

As has been stressed throughout this book, requirement change requests are the order of the day. Even when the project team initially feels that all requirements are clear, during design, or test strategy process, some confusing points may arise relating to any of the requirements.

When that happens, then that particular requirement has to be discussed, and only after clear understanding between the customer and the project team may that requirement be incorporated into design.

A very good requirement change management and version control is definitely necessary for a successful software development project. When analyzed, most failed software projects reveal that the failure was due to unclear requirements or too many requirement changes. In the case of unclear requirements, the development team assumes certain things in the absence of concrete details and that assumption may be wrong. In that case, the developed system may not match customer expectation and so the project may fail.

10.3.1 Requirement Change Control

Whenever requirements are changed, there must be a system that will notify each person whose work is affected due to change in requirement. How the change will impact their work also must be assessed. How much rework will be involved should also be calculated and documented [6].

Most of the impact on late requirement change is on construction and testing. This is because they are the two most labor-intensive activities. It is estimated that more than 40% of all effort in software development life cycle is done in construction phase. In software testing, this comes to 25%–30%.

One more aspect of requirement change is the severe impact it has when the development and testing are being carried out by distributed teams. With a distributed team scenario, communicating the change request immediately and effectively so that rework can be avoided is a big challenge. If some of the distributed teams are located in different countries and are service providers instead of in-house teams, then many other issues also get involved [7]. Understanding the change becomes difficult.

One more issue with requirement changes pertain to version control. It is difficult to know whether all distributed teams are working on the correct version of the requirements or not. There will be instances when some of the teams may be unaware of the latest requirement changes, and so, unknowingly, they may be working on the wrong version.

10.3.2 Requirement Problems Diagnosis

When distributed teams are working on a project, the best option is that requirements are kept in a central repository with access permissions to all project teams. Whenever any changes happen, then there should be provision for automated e-mails to be sent to all concerned teams. People with less experience should be identified, and care should be taken that they understand these changes and do their work accordingly.

The configuration and version control system should be located centrally and should be easily accessible to all teams. Requirement allocation should be done in such a way that each team and their individual members are always aware of what requirement they are working against, and where on the configuration management server the relevant work products are located. In case of any doubts, there should be a responsible person who can clarify any issues immediately within an agreeable timeframe.

10.4 Requirement Life-Cycle Management

Software requirements are the first phase of any software life-cycle management [8]. The journey of any software application starts from here. Refer to figures of software life cycle for different software development process models provided in Chapter 9. Here, we will discuss processes involved in requirement development (Figures 10.5 and 10.6).

10.4.1 Requirement Development and Management in Waterfall Model

The waterfall model is modeled on the fundamental notion that software development is done in phases, and each phase commences after the previous phase gets completed, and they follow each other in time sequences. So in one software project, there is just one iteration of each phase, and once it is completed, there is no option to come back to this phase. In real life, most organizations use a modified version of the waterfall model. So once requirements are developed, a review process is initiated to check whether the requirements are incomplete, ambiguous, or are otherwise faulty. A check is also done to ensure all requirements meet characteristics like maintainability and

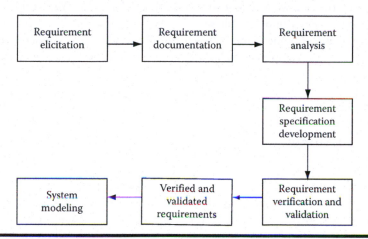

Figure 10.5 Software requirement development life cycle.

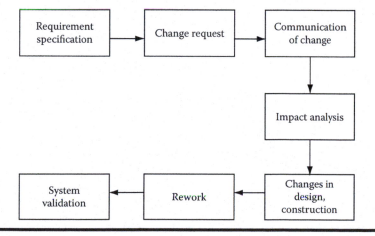

Figure 10.6 Software requirement change management life cycle.

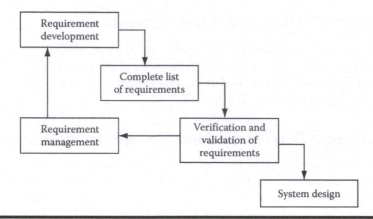

Figure 10.7   Waterfall model—requirement management and verification life cycle.

testability. If, during review, it is found that either some work is not complete or there are defects in the work product, then a rework is done to remove that defect. Once the work is approved, then the project is allowed to enter into next phase.

In the requirement development and management phase, the work product is the requirement specification document. The complete list of requirements is verified and validated during review meetings. If any requirements do not meet the validation criteria (e.g., testability), then requirements should be reworked, and only then system design phase can be allowed to start (Figure 10.7).

10.4.2 Iterative Model

In iterative models (including eXtreme Programming, agile methodology, and Scrum), complete requirements may be gathered but not used for product development in one go. Instead, a subset of requirements is taken, and development is done for those requirements in any iteration. Once that iteration gets completed, then a new set of requirements is taken for development (Figure 10.8).

In Scrum, the list of requirements is kept in a repository, which is known as the "backlog." Whenever any requirement becomes available, it is stored in this backlog. When a sprint (iteration)

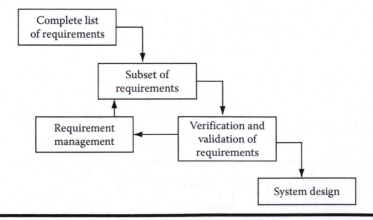

Figure 10.8   Iterative model—requirement management and verification life cycle.

is planned, the relevant requirements are pulled from this backlog. Most requirements in the backlog are not fully developed. So, when some requirements are pulled from the backlog, they are developed to be complete, and then the iteration or sprint proceeds. When any change request comes, generally, it is taken in the next iteration.

In agile models like Scrum and eXtreme Programming, the sources of requirements are the customers, customer feedback after iteration completion, found defects during development, and many other sources mentioned earlier in this chapter.

Requirement management on agile projects is much better. There are generally no incidents when a change request has to be incorporated during the course of an iteration. Change requests are generally taken in the next iteration, and thus there is no rework involved due to change requests.

10.5 Software Requirements Practical Strategy

Making requirement specifications from diverse and unstructured documents from many sources is a challenging task [9]. Here is a list of best practices for gathering and managing requirements.

1. Requirements come in many forms (e-mail, chats, customer request, meetings, reviews, etc.). So initial form varies. Use a standard template to get all requirements so that requirement format is consistent and that it is easy when they are to be incorporated in design. Capturing all requirements is also possible this way.
2. Requirements should be verified with the source so that there is no communication gap and requirements are captured as accurately as possible.
3. Requirements should be complete, and no requirement should be incomplete. Also, delivery dates should also be captured.
4. Requirements should be prioritized based on urgency, ROI, etc.
5. Communicate requirements as early as possible across all teams especially to distributed teams.
6. Trace dependency among requirements so that if one requirement is important but is dependent on another requirement that is not a priority, then it has to be made sure that both requirements are delivered.
7. Track requirement changes.

No matter how much attention is paid in collecting requirements, some omissions or mistakes do happen. This results in delivering an inadequate software product to the customer.

Nonstandard requirement specifications are the most dangerous aspect of software development projects. Consider an instance when the customer has specified that the software application should be used by sales department to take orders from customers. It does not provide details about various options while taking orders. The design team from the software project simply designs the system with the assumption that any person in the sales department takes the orders over the phone and has a list of products against which he books the orders. When the software is developed and presented to customers, they expect other options to be available to the sales staff while booking orders. It turned out that the customer was looking for a solution for configurable items that it sells. For configurable items, each main product has options for subitems to choose from. Any configurable item can have options at many levels. For instance, a desktop system can be bought with options for processor model, memory card, sound card, network card, hard

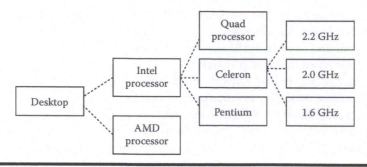

Figure 10.9 Configuration options for a desktop computer.

disk, CD ROM drive, etc. The customer can choose company name, specific brand, and then specific model for each of the computer parts while giving the order.

See Figure 10.9 to better understand configuration items. A desktop computer can have options to choose either Intel or AMD processor. The Intel processor can be a quad processor, Celeron, or Pentium processor. A Celeron processor can be of 2.2, 2.0, or 1.6 GHz capacity. The order management system must have the capability to choose the specific options provided by the customer. If configuration capability is not present in the ordering system, then it will be of no use to the sales department as they cannot book any customer orders using the software application (Figure 10.9).

Understanding the requirement and finding the correct solution for that requirement is the most important aspect of software development projects.

10.6 Software Requirements Artifacts

Software requirements are among the most unstructured data in a software project. They need to be converted into a good structure in the form of software features (requirement specifications). Only then, this data becomes useful to the project team. So the software requirement specifications document (SRS document) must contain specifications in the most structured form. For the test team, a verification and validation document for the SRS document is the artifact of this phase.

10.7 Software Requirements Quality Control

Software requirements can be checked or tested for defects. Found defects can subsequently be removed, and, thus, quality of the software requirements can be improved. Some kinds of defects in the requirements may include incoherent specification, wrong specification, wrong assumption, incomplete specification, and wrong relationship between requirements. Through a thorough check, these defects from requirement specifications can be removed.

The requirement development team itself can do these tests, or a test team can perform these tests.

10.8 Case Study

We continue our case study in Part II with the way our SaaS vendor's development team develops and manages software requirements in this chapter.

The SaaS vendor decided to build the appointment scheduling functionality only after existing customers, and market surveys revealed that there was a market gap for this functionality. So a business analyst was recruited to visit existing customers and gather the requirements. Already during interaction and user feedbacks from customers, there was some idea about the features required by them. Based on this existing knowledge and further interaction with customers, the business analyst completed the requirement gathering. Later, he built the requirement specifications.

10.8.1 Major Components of Appointment Scheduling

An appointment of any truck to a dock door of any warehouse even before arrival of the truck at the said warehouse can be made if some advance knowledge about the truck and what it contains is available. Here is a list of information needed to create this kind of appointment.

Information about the arriving truck includes truck capacity, truck type, kind of goods loaded/to be loaded, and expected arrival date (time) at the warehouse.

Information about the origin warehouse includes warehouse site information, warehouse company information, and distance from target warehouse.

Information about the target warehouse includes warehouse site information, warehouse company information, and number of dock doors.

Information about the dock doors of the target warehouse includes number of doors, types of trucks, which can be docked at each door, types of goods, which can be unloaded at each door, dock door calendars, partners whose goods can unloaded at specific doors, labor availability, quality assurance personnel availability, already docked trucks, already scheduled trucks, and unavailability of dock door at specific times.

The most important aspect about the appointment scheduling engine is that the user can first search a shipment (truck) that is not scheduled yet and then run the engine, so that a suitable schedule can be made for the shipment at any dock door of the target warehouse. There are so many factors to be considered for this appointment that humanly it is not possible to make a suitable schedule. The appointment engine is provided with all possible and practical constraints, and it honors or ignores those constraints depending on the rules defined for them in the engine. All these constraints are divided into two groups, soft and hard constraints. The soft constraints can be overridden if a hard constraint does not permit it to be made applicable. For instance, if a soft constraint does not allow a shipment to be made at 3:30 PM on October 10, 2010, at dock door 1 of warehouse A for a duration of 2 h, and if a hard constraint does allow this time window for appointment then the soft constraint will be overridden and an appointment will be made. Then, inside each of the category of hard and soft constraints, there is a hierarchy. Suppose a higher ranked constraint is applicable for a shipment, and that a lower ranked constraint does allow a shipment to be made within a time window. However, due to this higher ranked constraint, an appointment cannot be made. On the other hand, if no higher ranked constraint is applicable for a shipment, then a lower ranked constraint will determine if an appointment can be made for a shipment.

The appointment scheduling engine is used to calculate two things. First, it would determine the start date and time for an appointment. Then, it would calculate the duration of the appointment if the appointment duration is variable and depends on many factors.

Here is the requirement specification for the loading/unloading calculation part of the requirements.

10.8.2 Loading/Unloading Time Calculation

1. For some dock doors, a fixed load/unload time is mentioned. Even if the actual time is more or less than this fixed time, this fixed time should be recorded and not the actual load time.
2. There is a maximum and minimum time allowed (reservation time) for each dock door for specific business partners, in which all load/unload activities should be performed. If any load/unload time calculation is coming above or below this set, then the reservation time is the allowed time (maximum or minimum whichever applies), and this time should be recorded for making reservation at the dock door. If the calculated load time is less than the reservation time, then the calculated time should be recorded.
3. A default load time should be provided for each dock door group. If no fixed or variable load/unload time is defined for a dock door in that group, then this default load time should be recorded for all loading/unloading on that dock door.
4. The variable load/unload time should be calculated by the number of quantities of pieces of goods to be unloaded/loaded multiplied by loading/unloading time per piece of goods.

There were also requirements developed for calendars for dock doors, dock door groups, warehouses, organization, and enterprise. Requirements for search functionality for specific shipments based on origin, destination, shipping date, expected arrival date, etc., were also developed. Finally, the requirements for appointment scheduling functionality were also developed. This functionality also included options for manual appointment, cancellation of appointment, and grouping of appointment.

Overall, there were some 560 requirements for the entire project for release 6.0.

10.8.3 Quality Assurance

Quality assurance is an integral part of all software development activities at our SaaS vendor projects. The requirement specifications or software features to be developed are thoroughly tested (reviewed) before software design and architecture activities start. Each requirement specification is reviewed for completeness, flaws, maintainability, and testability. For example, there was a requirement that any shipment can be searched by providing partial information like shipment number and partial shipping address information. The complete address information consisted of street, county, state, country, and zip code. The partial address information could be a combination of any of the pieces of these address parts. To search a shipment with partial address, it is important that these pieces of information are linked loosely with each other. A zip code of 10994 belongs to New York state. So the search result should not show any shipments with this zip code belonging to some other state. There could be more than one city with the same name belonging to different states. In that case, all shipments with that city name (belonging to more than one state) can be displayed in search results if zip code and state are not mentioned.

Apart from the functional completeness aspect for a requirement, testability, maintainability, and other kinds of flaws also need to be checked and reviewed. Performance issues should also be checked if the requirement specifies that a large number of users will be using that software feature simultaneously.

10.9 Chapter Summary

In this chapter, we have learned all about software requirement gathering techniques, requirement management, change management, version control, etc. Change in requirements and unclear requirements are the two pitfalls that affect most software projects. To deal with this problem, there are two methods. One method is to take only a few requirements at a time and do the entire development for these requirements. This will mitigate the risk of change in requirements. The other technique is to manage the entire development process so that the changes can easily be incorporated in the entire development process.

To ensure that the requirement specifications built are defect free, we must go through a review process. All requirement specifications should be checked to see that they are not ambiguous and are indeed properly defined. They should be checked to see that they can be easily tested. They should be checked for maintainability.

Review Questions

10.1 What methods and means are available for requirement gathering?
10.2 What is the process flow for requirement development?
10.3 What quality control mechanism can be employed during requirement development and management?
10.4 Why is requirement management important? Why it is needed?
10.5 What is the process flow for requirement management?

Recommended Readings

1. A. Jaaksi (1998) *Tried and True Object Development*, Cambridge University Press, Cambridge, U.K.
2. L. Chung, B. A. Nixon, E. Yu, J. Mylopoulos (2000) *Non-Functional Requirements in Software Engineering*, Springer, Berlin, Germany.
3. P. C. Tinnirello (2001) *New Directions in Project Management*, CRC Press, Boca Raton, FL.
4. A. Aurum, C. Wohlin (2005) *Engineering and Managing Software Requirements*, Springer, Berlin, Germany.
5. S. F. Ochoa, G.-C. Roman (2006) *Advanced Software Engineering: Expanding the Frontiers of Software Technology*, Springer, Berlin, Germany.
6. S. E. Donaldson, S. G. Siegel (2001) *Successful Software Development*, Prentice Hall PTR, New York.
7. R. Sangwan, N. Mullick, M. Bass, D. J. Paulish (2006) *Global Software Development Handbook*, CRC Press, Boca Raton, FL.
8. H. Jonasson (2007) *Determining Project Requirements*, CRC Press, Ann Arbor, MI.
9. J. Dyché, E. Levy (2006) *Customer Data Integration: Reaching a Single Version of the Truth*, Wiley, Hoboken, NJ.

Chapter 11

Software Design Management

In the previous chapter, we learned

- What are customer requirements?
- How are customer requirements gathered?
- How are customer requirements managed?
- What is the role of a configuration management system in requirement management?
- How is quality assurance done during software requirements management?

In this chapter, we will learn

- What is software design?
- What are the considerations for making a sound software design?
- What techniques are used to design software?
- How is quality assured during software design?

11.1 Introduction

Software design development can be likened to designing a physical product. Suppose a new car model is to be developed. The car design is broken down into separate components and in the end assembling them will become a complete design for the car model. Various factors are considered during the design of the components. Suppose one factor to be considered is that during a car accident, the car body should take most of the impact and the passengers should get the least impact, so that injury to car passengers can be minimized during accidents. For this to happen, the car body should be made of material that can collapse on impact and thus take most of the impact.

So during design, when selecting the material of the car with safety in mind, the body is one of the prime considerations. Similarly, an aerodynamic body helps in keeping the car from rolling over during accidents, and thus it is a prime safety factor that the car body should be aerodynamic.

During design, one consideration is also made that though each component is developed separately, after assembly, the components should work with each other without any problems. That means assembling does not create any problems in the product itself.

Similar considerations are also done when software products are designed. In fact, in designing software systems, consideration is given to things like how well the system will be maintained during operation and how easily the system will be actually developed and tested [1].

Software design is done using modeling languages like UML and using notation methods like use cases and activity diagrams.

We will learn all about software design considerations, workflows involved in design, etc.

11.2 Software Design Fundamentals

When a building is constructed, a good foundation is laid out for the building, so that the building will have a long lifespan and will not collapse. Similarly, it is given a strong and resilient structure, so that even in case of an earthquake, it will not fall down. Similarly, software design provides the foundation and structure upon which the software system is constructed. The design should provide a sound, resilient, and scalable structure to support the software system (Figure 11.1).

In these days, most software systems are built incrementally. In the beginning, a software system may consist of only a few features. The feature set is expanded in future releases as and when it becomes necessary to include them in the system. If proper structure is not provided from the very beginning, the addition of these new features will make the system unstable. To deal with this problem, a technique called refactoring is used on these agile projects where incremental software development is done. Some of the design techniques that help make good software design include open architecture, modularity, and scalability [2].

The current trend of service-oriented architecture (SOA) has also helped tremendously in changing the design concepts. SOA is built on Web services and loose coupling of software components. The asynchronous messaging method of integration of SOA is a vital aspect for developing Web-based applications [3].

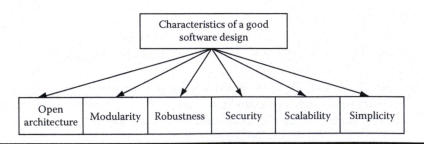

Figure 11.1   Characteristics of a good software design.

11.2.1 Design Types

Software design on any project may consist of many work products, which together can be termed the software design for the software product that will be built during the software project. Some examples include prototypes, structural models, object-oriented design, systems analysis, and entity relationship models.

11.2.2 Design Standards

If design standards [4] are implemented on a project, then it will help in streamlining activities that are involved during the software design phase. Some industry standards for software design include operator interface standards, test scenarios, safety standards, design constraints, and design tolerances.

11.2.3 Design Activities

Software design activities produce many intermediate documents and work products [5]. These include product architecture description, allocated requirements, product component descriptions, product-related life-cycle process descriptions, key product characteristic descriptions, required physical characteristics and constraints, interface requirements, verification criteria used to ensure that requirements have been achieved, operating environments, modes and states for operations, support, training, manufacturing, disposal, and verifications throughout the life of the product.

11.3 Software Design Methods

There are two methods for designing software products or components, the bottom-up and top-down approach.

11.3.1 Top Down

In the top-down approach [6], the top structure of the product is conceived and designed first. Once the structure is perfected, components that will make the product are designed. Once the major components are designed, the features that make the component are designed (Figure 11.2).

Apart from the functional consideration for making the structure, nonfunctional considerations are also considered from the top level for example, how the security, performance, usability, aspects will be provided in the product.

There are many benefits to the top-down approach. Nonfunctional aspects are taken care of at the beginning of design, and hence they are an integral part of the product and not an afterthought. This makes a secure, robust, and usable product. A top-down approach also helps in creating reusable components and hence increases productivity as well as maintainability. This approach also promotes integrity, as the whole product is designed inside a single framework. So a fragmented and dissimilar approach for designing different parts of the product is avoided.

The drawback of the top-down approach is that it is a risky model. The whole design has to be made in one go instead of making attempts to incrementally building the design, which is relatively a safer option. Generally, the top-down design approach is adopted on waterfall model-based projects.

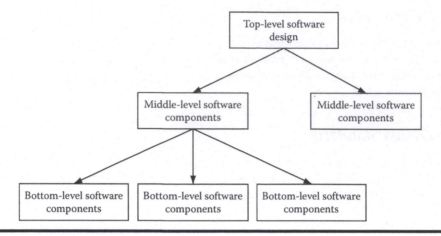

Figure 11.2   Top-down software design.

11.3.2 Bottom Up

In the bottom-up approach [7], first, the minute functions of the software product are structured and designed. Then, the middle-level components are designed, and, finally, the top-level structure is designed. Once some components are designed, they can be shown to the customer, and a buy in can be made for the project.

There are some benefits to the bottom-up approach. It leads to incremental building of design that ensures that any missing information can be accommodated later in the design (Figure 11.3).

With increasing use of incremental and iterative development methodologies, the bottom-up design approach is becoming more popular than the top-down approach. In fact, nowadays, agile models do not go for elaborate and complete software design from the beginning of the project. In each iteration, a design is thought of for the requirements that are taken during the iteration. To compensate for a sturdy and elaborate design upfront, the project team engages in refactoring (discussed later in the chapter) the design to make sure that it does not become bulgy and unmanageable in later iterations.

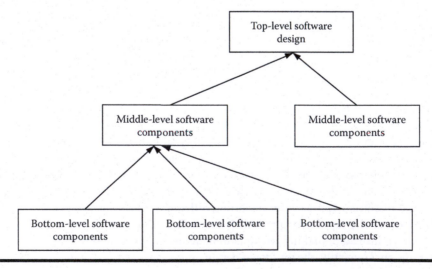

Figure 11.3   Bottom-up software design.

11.4 Design Version Control

In product development for a software vendor, many versions of the same product have to be developed for fulfilling different customers. With changes in requirements whenever they occur, software design also changes accordingly. These factors call for many versions of design of the product. When we have many versions of the design, then we need to have a dependable mechanism to control and manage all these versions of the designs of the same product [8].

At the top level of the hierarchy of files on the configuration and version control tool, the directory name should be the project/product name. This main directory should branch out with one branch for each version of the product. Inside each branch, all design files should be kept inside one subdirectory named something like "design documents." This way, each distinct design version should be completely separate from design documents of other versions of the product.

11.4.1 Subversions

During the software development life cycle, the design changes with changes in requirement specifications or when it is felt to change design as it no longer supports additional requirements. In such cases, the main design is changed to meet new conditions. However, the main design version is also kept. The new design is saved as a separate file. So we have two design documents now. Whenever the design has to be changed, a new file should be created from the old one and saved as a new file. All of these new files become subversions of the old files. This process is known as subversioning.

11.5 Design Characteristics

When we create software designs, we need to make sure that the design not only fulfills requirement specification needs but also ensures that the design is robust, versatile, and defect free. So the design needs to have some characteristics that make it useful. Here, we discuss some design characteristics [9].

Modular: The design should be modular, so that construction can be done in modules, and thus construction tasks can be divided and done in parallel to each other. This helps in reducing the project schedule and makes a better-managed software product even during maintenance. The biggest advantage of modular design is that complexity can be reduced by means of breaking software features into smaller software parts. Complexity in any software product is the biggest enemy, which creates problems like high-defect injection rates, difficult coding, difficult maintenance, and many other related difficulties.

Simple: The design should be simple, so that it will be easier to understand by developers and other project team members. This will make sure that the construction work can be carried out without many problems that are associated with difficult or complex designs.

Maintainable: To reduce maintenance costs, the design should be such that when any maintenance is needed, it can be performed without much overhead work. Some of the requirements of a software design to be maintainable are that the modules are well formed, reference to calls are well documented, modules are self-contained, and not many calls are made for other modules. If the software design is well structured, then maintaining it will be much easier.

Verifiable: The software design should be verifiable, so that it can be easily verified as to whether it suits the needs of the construction work that follows the design.

Portable: The design should have portability built into it, so that the same design can be used for writing source code for different hardware/software platforms.

Reliable: The software design should be reliable, so that it does not introduce software defects when source code is written based on the design. Generally, when a software design is complex, large, or difficult to understand, then probability of defect injection during software construction is higher. Thus, a reliable software design should not be complex or large or difficult. Larger software designs should be modularized.

Secure: The software design should take into consideration the security needs of the users for whom the software product is being made. This is especially true for software products, which are meant to be deployed outside of the firewall of any organization (accessible from the Internet).

Scalable: The software design should be scalable, so that when the smaller software product is scaled up, no design changes should be required. Even if some design changes are required, then it should not lead to rewriting of parts of the source code. For example, the design should be such that when additional features are to be added to the existing software product then the external interfaces of software design parts should not to be changed in order to add those additional features and only internal structures may need to be changed. This strategy will make sure that even if some parts of the software construction need to be rewritten, it will not affect other parts of the software product.

11.6 Software Design Techniques

Software design is the phase when a short sighted or myopic vision can turn the software product development into a nightmarish affair for downstream phases. A good software design not only ensures a smooth transition to the development phase but also ensures that the software product has a good shelf life during operation. So what are the keys to a good design? A good design should start from the most possible abstract architecture of the software product often termed as "high level design" [10]. Subsequent transition of the abstract design should lead to platform-specific design often termed as "low level design" [11]. The platform-specific design or low level design will be in terms of a good database model and a good application model (Figure 11.4).

Over the years, many software design techniques have evolved with the evolution of different programming paradigms. Starting with the early procedural programming paradigms, programming has evolved into present day "service-oriented architecture." Software design has kept the pace with these evolving paradigms, and thus it has also been evolving. So, we have early structural design paradigms to modern day SOA designs. Let us discuss some of these design techniques.

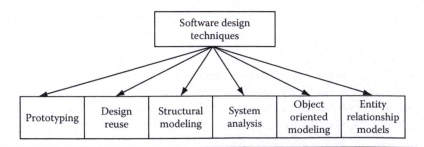

Figure 11.4 Software design techniques.

11.6.1 Prototypes

What better way to establish a good rapport with the end users than to sketch out a prototype of an application after you have all the customer requirements? Prototyping is cheap and fast. It also gets a buy in from customer at an early stage of the project. If not a full prototype of the application, a partial prototype can help you win over your customer. There are many automatic code generation tools that allow you to drag and drop some components on screens, and the tool generates the code and makes a working prototype of the application that you can demonstrate to your customer. An miscommunication or misunderstanding between the customer and the project team gets cleared once the differences of opinion are sorted out early on during the prototype demonstration sessions. This greatly helps in reducing the risks of not meeting customer expectations. In any case, customers do not care about internal workings of the application. They are always concerned about what the application screens look like and how the application behaves with different kind of inputs and events.

The downside about prototypes is that many customers assume the prototype is the fully functional application and later on wonder why the application is taking so much time in development when they saw the working demonstration so early in the project. Customer expectations become difficult to manage in such instances. Prototypes can only show the user interface screens. When complex logic is involved in developing applications, that logic cannot be depicted in prototypes, as program logic is mostly not visible and cannot be developed in prototypes.

11.6.2 Structural Models

Most software applications are built using components. At the bottom are the smallest units of functions and procedures in a software application. These functions are contained within classes or packages depending on the programming language used. Many classes together build a component. Components in turn make modules. Modules in turn make the complete application. For ease of working, maintenance, and breaking development tasks to allocate to group of developers, it is essential that an application is broken down into manageable parts. Breaking into parts for an application can best be done using a structural analysis.

From requirement specifications, a feature set is made to decide what features will be in the application. This feature set is analyzed and broken down into smaller sets of features, which will go into different modules. This is represented in a structural model of the application.

11.6.3 Object-Oriented Design

It has always been difficult to represent business entities and business information flow in a software model. With object-oriented design, this problem was solved. Business entities are represented as objects in the object-oriented software design. Properties of these objects are made in such a way that they are similar to the properties of the business entities. These objects are instantiated from classes in the form of child classes. These child classes inherit all the properties of their parent class, and they can have some more properties of their own in addition. So if we have a group of similar objects with somewhat different properties, then we can implement classes in such a way that a base parent class has child classes with different properties. This concept aligns very much to the real-world scenarios.

Object-oriented design takes input from use cases, activity diagrams, user interfaces etc.

11.6.4 Systems Analysis

System analysis is the process of finding solutions in the form of a system designed from the inputs coming from business needs. The fundamental question addressed in system analysis is whether a business scenario can be converted into a software application, so that the user can use the software application to do his routine business tasks. For instance, a person may want to access his bank account using an Internet connection to the online Web site of the bank. This scenario calls for many things that are involved in the whole chain of objects and events. The system analysis will be concerned with user activities, what objects on the Web site act with user activities, how these objects interact with the underlying software system of the bank, and how connections are made between the user and the Web site and between the Web site and the bank system. System analysis will analyze all these things. Based on the analysis, a system model can be made that will be used in developing the application.

11.6.5 Entity Relationship Models

Entity relationship models are one of the ways to represent business entities and their relationships to each other through diagrams. These diagrams are used for creating databases and database tables. How many tables are needed to fulfill the needs of the software product, how these tables are related to each other, and in what form data are to be kept inside these tables, etc. are decided through these diagrams.

With object-oriented modeling, it is possible to correlate each object with a corresponding database object. This kind of representation helps to make a clean database design.

11.6.6 Design Reuse

For large software products, the design can be broken into many design parts representing each module of the product. Each of these design modules contain a lot of design information that can be represented as design components. Many details inside these design components can be repeated inside different components. If we can use a standard method of representing the same information for these components, then it is possible to use these pieces of information in many components by reusing them. It will reduce effort in designing the product. This method of design reuse is known as internal design reuse.

A more potent design reuse is becoming available after the advent of the open source paradigm and SOA. In the case of open source, the design reuse is in fact a case of copying existing design and then using it exactly as it is or modifying it to suit your needs. But in the case of SOA, you are not copying or modifying a software design. You are using the existing design as it is. You are also not buying the application/component whose design you want. You are simply buying a service from the owner of the application/component and using that service in building your application. The owner of that application/component publishes full details as to how to integrate your application with his application/component. The full interface details are provided by the owner. Using this information, you design your own application. You assume as if the application/component provided as a service is available with you, and your application uses this application/component.

SOA is indeed leading to a reuse model that is going to transform the world of computing and our lives in years to come.

11.7 Software Design for Internet

Given the fact that the majority of software development these days is for the Internet, it is important to recognize how Internet applications are different from traditional software products and what design considerations are involved in developing them. In these days, even if some application being developed is meant to be running inside a company firewall, it makes sense to structure it like an Internet application for future use as well as for maintenance needs (Figure 11.5).

Internet applications are inherently different. Thus, their design is also different from legacy client/server applications. Some of the characteristics that impact their design include:

- They are used by a large number of people. So they need to have good performance built into design.
- Many of these users are novice when it comes to using computers and software applications. So the design should be such that the application does not break down easily even when the user keeps clicking on wrong places in the application.
- They are information providers with lots of content.
- They are asynchronous.
- The front end is a browser with all the processing is done at the back end.
- They are stateless.

Due to these unique features of Internet applications, they need a different kind of design. For instance, since they are used by a large number of users concurrently, the design should incorporate provision for light features, which will not fail even during peak loads on the application servers. Similarly, an asynchronous connection facility can be provided by designing loosely coupled components. All transactions should be made stateless, so that if any transaction is in progress and the connection between server and user machine breaks, the transaction is reverted back.

11.8 Software Design Quality

Quality in the design of the software application can be built by adhering to best practices (software engineering principles) in processes adopted for the design as well as making sure that requirements have been converted into good design. After the design is complete, design work products (design documents) should be reviewed, and the project should only be allowed to proceed further if the design documents pass the quality criteria. If any defect is found during review, then it should be rectified.

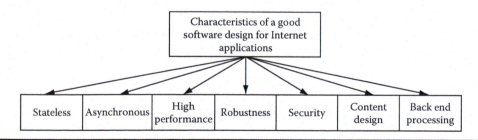

Figure 11.5 Characteristics of a good software design for Internet applications.

From the qualitative point of view, the software design should adhere to attributes like reliability, usability, and simplicity. The design should avoid complexity, inconsistency, and inefficiency. Complexity issues should be addressed by thinking about coupling and cohesion issues related to relation of code units, modules, function, etc. to each other. Inefficiency issues should be addressed from user perspective as to how much time and effort they may need to take to perform a transaction using the application. Inconsistency issues can be addressed by having a solid architecture on which units and other program units should be based.

From quantitative perspective, good software design can be thought of in terms of how many procedure calls may be involved in a transaction, how many steps need to be taken to perform a transaction, etc.

Quality control for software designs can be done by checking the design after it is built for defects. Removing these defects will ensure better quality of the software design and hence the software product. Quality assurance for software designs can be done by ensuring that there is a well thought out process exist for the entire design exercise, so that defect injection in the design can be prevented.

11.9 Concurrent Engineering in Software Design

Concurrent engineering deals with taking advance information from an earlier stage for a later stage in project, so that both the stages can be performed simultaneously. Though project activities are planned ahead in time, most often there are dependencies between a previous task and the next task in line. So, the latter task cannot start until the previous task finishes. That is why you cannot start developing an application until its design is complete. Moreover, the development will depend on the design. Until all details about design are made, you cannot start development. So, the development team cannot start their job until they have a software design in their hands.

Still some aspects about latter tasks can be done in advance. For instance, what development language will be used and how the application can be partitioned for development work can be decided at the design stage itself. Similarly, how maintenance and support functions will be done for the application can be determined at the design stage itself. Knowing in advance helps in taking care of issues that may arise in later stages.

11.10 Design Life-Cycle Management

Software requirements go through design process steps to become a full-fledged software design. At the high level, system analysis is performed. System analysis includes a study of requirements and finding feasibility of converting them into software design. Once the feasibility is done, then the actual software design is made. The software design is in the form of activity diagrams, use cases, prototypes, etc. Once the design process is complete, these design documents are verified and validated through design reviews. Once the design is reviewed and approved, then the design phase is over (Figure 11.6).

11.11 Module Division (Refactoring)

Whenever a software product is designed, it is done with good intentions. Care is taken to ensure that the design is extensible, so that when customer needs increase over time, the product can be extended to take care of those increased needs. Unfortunately, even this foresight is not enough,

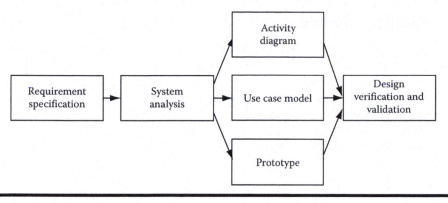

Figure 11.6   Software design life cycle.

and it becomes difficult to extend the product functionality further. In such cases, it becomes necessary to change the internal structure of software code without changing external behavior of the software product. To do this, one technique is employed, which is known as refactoring. Using refactoring, the internal design of a piece of software code is improved by decreasing coupling among classes of objects and increasing cohesion among classes. Refactoring is very similar to the concept of normalization in relational databases (Figure 11.7).

Some of the indications of code analysis that may suggest that the code needs refactoring include duplicate code at many places, using long methods, a large class with many concepts, the need to pass a large number of parameters, too much communication between classes resulting from a large number of calls for methods in code, and message chaining by calling one method which in turn calls another method. When software code starts having these characteristics, then it is better to go for code cleaning or refactoring. Going for refactoring will be justified by savings in time due to better code reuse and make it easier to maintain code and scale up the product.

Refactoring can be achieved by dividing cumbersome classes into smaller classes that can be managed and used in a better way. In the new code, the functions will be the same, but many of the functions will be moved now into new classes.

On agile projects, the project team builds the software product without making an elaborate design from start. One product module is built after another in the subsequent project iterations. This fact makes it necessary to adjust the software design as the product evolves in this fashion. The adjustment in the software design in such cases is done using refactoring.

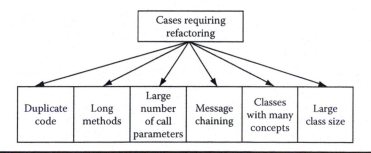

Figure 11.7   Characteristics of a software product code that requires refactoring.

11.12 Module Coupling

One area similar to refactoring is coupling between modules. As products mature and more and more lines of code are added to the existing product, coupling between modules tends to increase. This has a profound impact when any changes in code are required. Changes in code result in more than normal occurrence of defects as dependency between modules keeps increasing with increase in the size of the product.

To reduce the chances of product defects, it is necessary to reduce the number of calls among different modules and classes. SOA architecture provides great help here. SOA architecture essentially promotes loose coupling, and this implies more or less self-contained classes having less dependency on other classes.

Increasing module coupling with increase in size of software product is always a concern. Frequent refactoring can help in reducing module coupling among classes.

11.13 Case Study

In the previous chapter, we have seen how requirements for the project were made. Now we will see how the software design was made for appointment scheduling component. The complete design consisted of user interface decision flow diagrams, activity diagrams, use cases, and entity relationship diagrams. We will see the logic implemented in the activity diagram for loading/unloading calculations for trucks in this chapter.

11.13.1 Software Design for Loading Calculation

The logic for the loading calculation can be represented by a piece of pseudo-logic. It is presented here.

```
If variable load time then
        If calculated load time > Max reservation time then
             load time = max reservation time
        elseif calculated load time < Min reservation time then
             load time = min reservation time
        else load time = calculated load time
   else load time = fixed load time
end if
elseIf default receiving load time is true then
   if default receiving load time = fixed load time then
        load time = fixed default receiving load time
   elseif default receiving load time = variable load time then
        If calculated load time > Max reservation time then
             load time = max reservation time
        elseif calculated load time < Min reservation time then
             load time = min reservation time
        else load time = calculated load time
        end if
   end if
else load time = default reservation time
endif
```

In this pseudo-logic, some specialized terms are used related to the domain for which the application was made. Those terms are explained here.

Variable load time = If the loading/receiving time for a truck varies with some factors like goods to be loaded/received and truck types, then loading/receiving time will be variable and needs to be calculated.

Fixed load time = If the loading/receiving time for a truck does vary irrespective of factors like goods to be loaded/received and truck type, then the load time is fixed, and it is always stated.

Max reservation time = reservation time on a dock door is given as minimum or maximum reservation time. Max reservation time is the upper limit of this timeframe.

Min reservation time = opposite of Max reservation time (lower limit of timeframe).

Default receiving load time = each dock door or a group of dock doors is given an option of what could be the loading/receiving time. The options are fixed or variable load time.

The activity diagram for the loading/receiving load time calculation is given in Figures 11.8 and 11.9. Please note that the calculation for both loading and receiving is exactly the same.

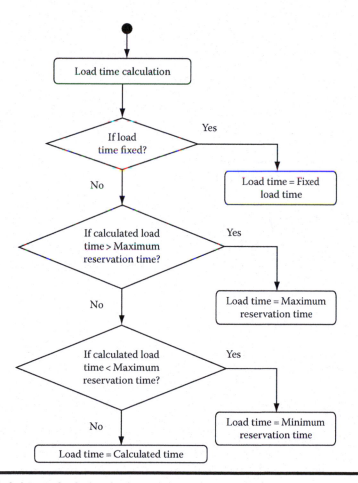

Figure 11.8   Load time calculation logic.

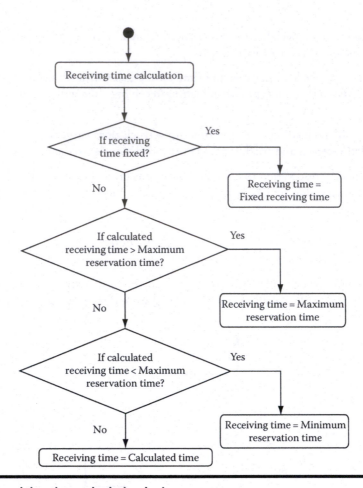

Figure 11.9 Receiving time calculation logic.

11.13.2 Quality Assurance

The completed software design is reviewed for flaws, maintainability, implementability, and testability. If a design is not implementable into source code, then it must be modified to make it implementable.

11.14 Chapter Summary

Software design is carried out in two parts. First, a high level design is made. At this stage, a high level representation of the software product to be made is carried out. The high level design contains the macrostructure of the product, including division of the product into modules, relation between these modules for the software internal structure. Moreover, at this stage, decisions about the data layer, application layer, and presentation layer are made.

Once we have the high level design, then the finer level of details about the software product is done during low level design. At this stage, decisions about how much abstraction and encapsulation will be made at the class level, and how functionality can be achieved by class instantiation if object-oriented design is chosen.

For quality assurance at the design level, a design review should be conducted to check if the software design has any defects. The defects could be anything from outright design flaw to missing of any requirement specifications in the design or not representing the requirement specification in a proper way. A design defect could also be in terms of how the design is not testable or maintainable. If any defects are found, then they should be rectified.

Review Questions

11.1 What is a software design?

11.2 What constraints are considered while making the software design?

11.3 What techniques can be used for making a software design?

11.4 How can quality of a software design be ensured?

11.5 What is a design life cycle?

11.6 What are the design methods?

Recommended Readings

1. H. Zhu (2005) *Software Design Methodology*, Butterworth-Heinemann, New York.
2. R. Mall (2005) *Fundamentals of Software Engineering*, Prentice Hall Learning India, New Delhi, India.
3. M. Rosen, B. Lublinsky, K. T. Smith, M. J. Balcer (2008) *Applied SOA: Service-Oriented Architecture and Design Strategies*, Wiley, New York.
4. R. T. Futrell, D. F. Shafer, L. Shafer (2002) *Quality Software Project Management*, Prentice Hall PTR, Upper Saddle River, NJ.
5. H. Fujita, D. M. Pisanelli (2007) *New Trends in Software Methodologies, Tools and Techniques*, IOS Press, Amsterdam, the Netherlands.
6. D. M. Buede (2009) *The Engineering Design of Systems: Models and Methods*, Wiley, Hoboken, NJ.
7. G. A. Lancaster (2001) *Software Design and Development*, Pascal Press, New South Wales, Australia.
8. V. Grimm, S. F. Railsback (2005) *Individual-Based Modeling and Ecology*, Preinceton University Press, Princeton, NJ.
9. S. L. Pfleeger, J. M. Atlee (2006) *Software Engineering: Theory and Practice*, Prentice Hall, Upper Saddle River, NJ.
10. A. J. Lattanze (2008) *Architecting Software Intensive Systems: A Practitioners Guide*, CRC Press, Boca Raton, FL.
11. D. Phillips (2004) *The Software Project Manager's Handbook: Principles That Work at Work*, Wiley, New York.

Chapter 12

Software Construction

In the previous chapter, we learned

- What is software design?
- What are the considerations for constructing sound software?
- What techniques are used to design software?
- How is quality assurance done during software design?

In this chapter, we will learn

- What is software construction?
- What are the considerations for sound software construction?
- What techniques are used to construct software?
- How is quality assurance done during software construction?

12.1 Introduction

A layman believes that software construction is the entire software development process. But, in fact, it is just one of the crucial tasks in software development; software requirement management, software design, software testing, and software deployment are all equally crucial tasks. Furthermore, the process of software construction itself consists of many tasks; it not only includes software coding, but also unit testing, integration testing, reviews, and analysis.

Construction is one of the most labor intensive phases in the software development life cycle. It comprises 30% or more of the total effort in software development. What a user sees as the product at the end of the software development life cycle is merely the result of the software code that was written during software construction.

175

Due to the labor intensive nature of the software construction phase, the work is divided not only among developers, but also small teams are formed to work on parts of the software build. In fact, to shrink the construction time, many distributed teams, either internal or through contractors, are deployed. The advantage to this is that these project teams do the software coding and other construction work in parallel with each other and thus the construction phase can be collapsed. This parallel development is known as concurrent engineering, which is discussed in Chapter 9.

Constructing an industry strength software product of a large size requires stringent coding standards [1]. The whole process of construction should follow a proven process so that the produced code is maintainable, testable, and reliable. The process itself should be efficient so that resource utilization can be optimized and thus cost of construction can be kept at a minimum.

12.2 Coding Standards

Developers are given software design specifications in the form of use cases, flow diagrams, UI mock ups, etc., and they are supposed to write a code so that the built software matches these specifications. Converting the specifications into software code is totally dependent on the construction team. How well they do it depends on their experience, skills, and the process they follow to do their job. Apart from these facilities, they also need some standards in their coding so that the work is fast as well as has other benefits like maintainability, readability, and reusability (Figure 12.1).

At any time, a code written by a developer will always be different from that written by any other developer. This poses a challenge in terms of comprehending the code while reusing the code, maintaining it, or simply reviewing it. A uniform coding standard across all construction teams working on the same project will make sure that these issues can be minimized if not eliminated (Figure 12.2).

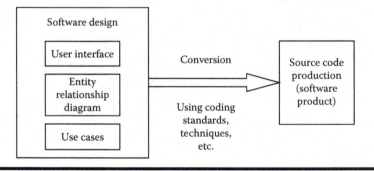

Figure 12.1   Source code production (conversion) from software design.

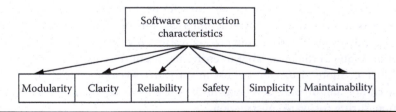

Figure 12.2   Software construction characteristics.

Some of the coding standards include standards for code modularity, clarity, simplicity, reliability, safety, and maintainability.

12.2.1 Modularity

The produced software code should be modular in nature [2]. Each major function should be contained inside a software code module. The module should contain not only structure, but it should also process data. Each time a particular functionality is needed in the software construction, it can be implemented using that particular module of software code. This increases software code reuse and thus enhances productivity of developers and code readability.

12.2.2 Clarity

The produced code should be clear for any person who would read the source code [3]. Standard naming conventions should be used so that the code has ample clarity. There should be sufficient documentation inside the code block, so that anybody reading the code could understand what a piece of code is supposed to do. There should also be ample white spaces in the code blocks, so that no piece of code should look crammed. White spaces enhance readability of written code.

12.2.3 Simplicity

The source code should have simplicity and no unnecessary complex logic; improvisation should be involved, if the same functionality can be achieved by a simpler piece of source code [4]. Simplicity makes the code readable, and will help in removing any defects found in the source code.

Simplicity of written code can be enhanced by adopting best practices for many programming paradigms. For instance, in the case of object-oriented programming, abstraction and information hiding add a great degree of simplicity. Similarly, breaking the product to be developed into meaningful pieces that mimic real life parts makes the software product simple.

12.2.4 Reliability

Reliability is one of the most important aspects of industry strength software products [5]. If the software product is not reliable and contains critical defects, then it will not be of much use for end users. Reliability of source code can be increased by sticking to the standard processes for software construction. During reviews, if any defects are found, they can be fixed easily if the source code is neat, simple, and clear.

Reliable source code can be achieved by first designing the software product with future enhancement in consideration as well as by having a solid structure on which the software product is to be built. When writing pieces of source code based on this structure, there will be little chance of defects entering into the source code. Generally during enhancements, the existing structure is not able to take load of additional source code and thus the structure becomes shaky. If the development team feels that this is the case, then it is far better to restructure the software design and then write a code based on the new structure than to add a spaghetti code on top of a crumbling structure.

12.2.5 Safety

Safety is important, considering that software products are used by many industries where human lives are concerned, and that human lives could be in danger because of faulty machine operation or exposure to a harmful environment [5]. In these industries, the software product must be ensured to operate correctly and chances of error are less than 0.00001%. Industries like medicine and healthcare, road safety, hazardous material handling need foolproof software products to ensure that either human lives are saved (in case of medicine and healthcare) or human lives are not in danger. Here the software code must have inbuilt safety harnesses.

12.2.6 Maintainability

As has been pointed out after several studies, maintenance costs are more than 70% of all costs including software development, implementation, and maintenance [6]. To make sure that maintenance costs are under limit during software construction, it should be made sure that the source code is maintainable. It will be easy to change the source code for fixing defects during maintenance.

12.3 Coding Framework

Like most construction work, you need to set up an infrastructure based on which construction can take place. For software construction, you need to have a coding framework that will ensure a consistent coding production with standard code that will be easy to debug and test [7]. In object oriented programming, what base classes are to be made, which will be used throughout construction, is a subject that is part of the coding framework. In general, coding frameworks allow construction of the common infrastructure of basic functionality which can be extended later by the developers. This way of working increases productivity and allows for a robust and well structured software product. It is similar in approach to house building where a structure is built based on a solid foundation.

12.4 Reviews (Quality Control)

It is estimated that almost 70% of software defects arise from faulty software code. To compound this problem, software construction is the most labor intensive phase in software development. Any construction rework means wasting a lot of effort already put in. Moreover, it is also a fact that it is cheaper to fix any defects found during construction at the phase level itself. If those defects are allowed to go in software testing (which is the next phase), then fixing those defects will become costlier [8]. That is why review of the software code and fixing defects is very important. There are some techniques available like deskchecks [9], walkthroughs [10], code reviews, inspections, etc. that ensure quality of the written code (Figure 12.3).

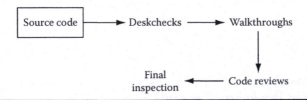

Figure 12.3   Source code review methods and their operation sequence.

These different kinds of reviews are done at different stages in software code writing. They also serve different purposes. While inspections provide the final go/no go decision for approval of a piece of code, other methods are less formal and are meant for removing defects instead of deciding whether a piece of code is good enough or not.

12.4.1 Deskchecks (Peer Reviews)

Deskchecks are employed when a complete review of the source code is not important. Here, the developer sends his piece of code to the designated team members. These team members review the code and send feedback and comments to the developer as suggestions for improvement in the code. The developer reads those feedbacks and may decide to incorporate or to discard those suggestions. So this form of review is totally voluntary. Still, it is a powerful tool to eliminate defects or improve software code.

12.4.2 Walkthroughs

Walkthroughs are formal code reviews initiated by the developer. The developer sends an invitation for walkthrough to team members. At the meeting, the developer presents his method of coding and walks through his piece of code. The team members then make suggestions for improvement, if any. The developer then can decide to incorporate those suggestions or discard them.

12.4.3 Code Reviews

Code reviews are one of the most formal methods of reviews. The project manager calls for a meeting for code review of a developer. At the meeting, team members review the code and point out any code errors, defects, or improper code logic for likely defects. An error log is also generated and is reviewed by the entire team.

12.4.4 Inspections

Code inspections are final reviews of software code in which it is decided whether to pass a piece of code for inclusion into the main software build.

12.5 Coding Methods

Converting design into optimal software construction is a very serious topic that has generated tremendous interest over the years. Many programming and coding methods were devised and evolved as a result. As is well known in the industry, the early software products were of small size due to limited hardware capacity. With increasing hardware capacity, the size of software products has been increasing. Software product size affects the methods that can be used to construct specific sized software products. Advancement in the field of computer science also allows discovery of better construction methods. To address needs of different sized software products in tandem with advancement in computer science, different programming techniques evolved. These include structured programming, object-oriented programming, automatic code generation, test-driven development, pair programming, etc.

12.5.1 Structured Programming

Structured programming evolved after mainframe computers became popular [11]. Mainframe computers offered vast availability of computing power compared to primitive computers that existed before. Using structured programming, large programs could be constructed that could be used for making large commercial and business applications. Structured programming enabled programmers to store large pieces of code inside procedures and functions. These pieces of code could be called by any other procedures or functions. This enabled programmers to structure their code in an efficient way. Code stored inside procedures could be reused anywhere in the application by calling it.

12.5.2 Object-Oriented Programming

In structured programming, data and structured code are separate and accordingly are modeled separately. This is an unnatural way of converting real life objects into software code because objects contain both data and structure. Widely used as an example in object-oriented programming books, a car consists of a chassis, an engine, four wheels, body, and transmission. Each of these objects has some specific properties and has specific functions. When a software system is modeled to represent real-world objects, both data and structure are taken care of in object-oriented programming. From outside of a class that is made to represent an object, only the behavior of the object is visible or perceived. Unnecessary details about the object are hidden, and in fact are not available from outside. This kind of representation of objects makes them robust, and a system built on using them has relatively few problems [12].

12.5.3 Automatic Code Generation

Constructing and generating software code is very labor intensive work. So there has always been fascination about automatic generation of software code. Unfortunately, this is still a dream. Some CASE and modeling tools are available that generate software code. But they are not sophisticated. They are also not complete. Then there are business analyst platforms developed by many ERP software vendors that generate code automatically when analysts configure the product. These analyst platforms are first built using any of the software product development methodologies. The generated code is specific to the platform and runs on the device (hardware and software environment) for which the code is generated.

Generally, any code consists of many construction unit types. Some of these code types include control statements such as loop statements, if statements, etc., and database access, etc. Generating all of the software code required to build a software application is still difficult. But some companies like Sun Microsystems are working to develop such a system.

12.5.4 Software Code Reuse

Many techniques have evolved to reduce the labor intensive nature of writing source code. Software code reuse is one such technique. Making a block of source code to create a functionality or general utility library and using it at all places in the source code wherever this kind of functionality or utility is required is an example of code reuse. Code reuse in procedural programming techniques is achieved by creating special functions and utility libraries and using them in the source code. In object-oriented programming, code reuse is done at a more advanced level. The classes

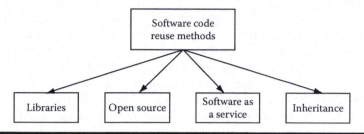

Figure 12.4   Code reuse methods.

containing functions and data themselves can not only be reused in the same way as functions and libraries, but the classes can also be modified by way of creating child classes and using them in the source code (Figure 12.4).

Apart from creating and using libraries and general purpose classes for code reuse, a more potent code reuse source has evolved recently. It is known as "service oriented architecture" (SOA). More about SOA can be found in Chapter 25.

12.5.5 Test-Driven Development

This concept is used with iteration-based projects especially with eXtreme Programming technique. Before developers start writing source code, they create test cases and run the tests to see if they run properly and their logic is working. Once it is proved that their logic is perfect, only then they write the source code. So here, tests drive software development, and hence it is appropriately named test-driven development.

12.5.6 Pair Programming

Pair programming is a quality driven development technique employed in the eXtreme Programming development model. Here, each development task is assigned to two developers. While one developer writes the code, the other developer sits behind him and guides him through the requirements (functional, nonfunctional). When it is the turn of the other developer to write the code, the first developer sits behind him and guides him on the requirements. So developers take turns for the coding and coaching work. This makes sure that each developer understands the big picture and helps them to write better code with lesser defects.

12.6 Configuration Management

Configuration management plays an important role in the construction phase. Due to changes in requirements and design, an already developed source code needs to be changed. So it happens that the development team ends up with many versions of a source code during the project. If the version control management is not handled properly, then many developers may start working on a wrong version of source code, and thus a lot of rework may be needed in the end. There is one more dimension to configuration management for the construction phase. During construction, many software builds are maintained for different versions of the product being developed. These builds can break if a bad piece of code is checked into the build by any developer. When the build is broken, then no other developer can check in his code. Thus, development is halted until the build is rebuilt with the correct code. Imagine what may happen in the case of distributed teams located at far-flung locations with different time zones and a central build is being maintained. It will be difficult to communicate and manage the build process in such a scenario. In such scenarios, smoke test application can be deployed, which can run whenever a new code is checked-in in the build. If the smoke test fails, that means the build has failed and thus the automated system can e-mail the build information to concerned people. If the build fails, then the developer who had checked-in in the code gets the message and immediately tries to fix the build. Once the build is fixed, then other developers can check-in their code.

Thus, configuration management plays an important role in construction phase.

12.7 Unit Testing

Whenever a developer writes a piece of code, he feels confident that he has written a clean code and that it does not need testing. But most of the time he is wrong. It is because no source code is perfect, especially the first time. Only after some rounds of review it becomes perfect. At the same time, it is very difficult to review one's own code. That is why a quality control measure is taken in form of unit testing to ensure that developers test their codes themselves and only then can submit their code if the code passes the unit tests (Figure 12.5).

For unit testing, generally developers are comfortable as long as there are no changes required (due to change in design or requirements) in their code. But once some change takes place in the code somewhere, other things change. What would be the impact of that change on other parts of the software product under development? Similarly what impact will it have on their own code if changes take place in other modules being written by other people? Generally, it is one of the most challenging situations in software construction to find the impact of change on other parts of the product under development. Such situations call for unit testing of the written code, and no piece of code should go to build without doing this. A formal and rigid adherence to unit tests should be a must for all source codes being written and no liberty should be allowed.

12.8 Integration Testing

Most software development is done after partitioning the software application under development first and then allocating it to distributed teams. Generally, modules of code are developed first. Later, they need to be integrated with each other to make a complete software application. Modules are integrated with each other through open interfaces. Whether or not the integration

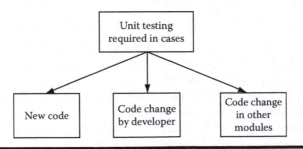

Figure 12.5 Scenarios when unit testing must be done.

is working fine, it must be tested to ensure integration has been achieved. This kind of testing is known as integration testing.

Integration testing has been becoming more and more important, as most software being developed is modular in nature. With the advent of SOA, which is all about loosely coupled software components, integration testing has become even more important.

12.9 Software Construction Artifacts

The software construction phase is one of the most labor intensive phases in software development cycle. This phase generates the complete source code of the application. Apart from source code, documentation is also made so that when any maintenance is required on the built application, the source code could be well understood, and changing any source code will be easy. Review reports are also generated after reviews are conducted.

12.10 Software Construction in Iterative Model

Iteration-based development for any project signifies a lesser extent of risk and perfection in craft. Iterative development is definitely a good approach, as it provides an opportunity to spread the risk over many iterations and thus helps in stopping any catastrophe to occur. Since software design will be based on just a handful of requirements, it helps to avoid complexity in the construction work. The main bug bear of software construction is complexity. Sans complexity, development work would be more productive and will have a lower number of defects (Figure 12.6).

Using techniques like pair programming, test-driven development, continuous integration, formal reviews, etc., ensures that good quality is achieved from the very beginning of construction and keep the same level of quality throughout the development process.

12.11 Case Study

In the construction management part of our continuing case study, we will see how the software product source code was being written as well other activities performed.

Here are some key statistics about the project:

Number of developers: 21
Average speed of writing source code (developer productivity): 2000 SLOC per month, per
 developer

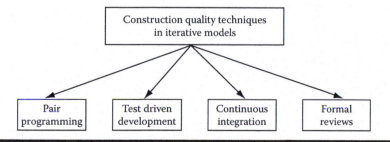

Figure 12.6 Quality-driven construction in iterative development.

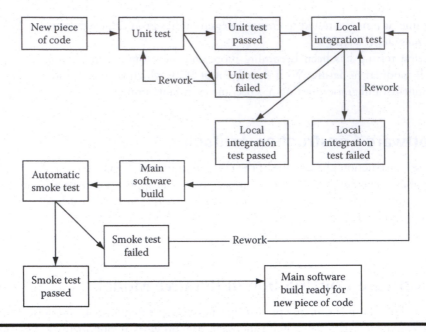

Figure 12.7   Software continuous build and integration life-cycle management.

Total source code written in one iteration: 126,090 SLOC
Total source code written in the whole project: 475,901 SLOC
Number of defects fixed in one iteration: 121
Number of defects fixed in the project: 434

12.11.1 Continuous Integration

Continuous integration of source code is an important aspect of all software development work at the SaaS vendor. The central source code build is continuously integrated from the source code developed by all development teams. Once any developer checks and tests his own code for unit and integration on his own local build of the software product, he checks in his code on the central build. This exercise is depicted in Figure 12.7.

Some other highlights of the product development effort for release 6.0 included having quality assurance and quality control measures built into the development life cycle. The developers used to do unit and integration testing for their own written source code, while the development team also used to do code walkthroughs and code inspections.

12.12 Chapter Summary

Software construction is the phase in which the actual software product is built. On all other development phases of the software project, some work products are built that help in building the actual product. However, from the user perspective, construction is where their actual product gets developed. Software construction is labor intensive and thus it consumes a big chunk of the project schedule. To reduce the schedule for construction work, concurrent engineering techniques are employed. In applying concurrent engineering, software design is made in such a way that construction work can be easily divided among several teams, so that they can work parallel to each other and thus complete the construction work in less time. To make the software source code maintainable and reliable, a host of techniques are used including a standard coding framework, standard coding conventions, etc. To ensure code quality, unit testing and integration testing are done whenever a source code unit is completed or integrated with the main software build. At the completion of major construction work, code inspections and other methods of reviews are done to ensure defects are discovered and removed. To increase productivity, several techniques are used like pair programming, code reuse, etc.

Finally, the source code should be checked for defects. This can be done by using static methods and dynamic methods. The static methods are code inspections, code analysis, code walkthroughs, deskchecks, and peer reviews. The dynamic methods are unit and integration testing.

Review Questions

12.1 What are the common activities conducted during construction phase in the software development life cycle?

12.2 What quality control measures are taken during construction phase?

12.3 What is done to construct a software application at faster speed?

12.4 Define pair programming.

12.5 What coding standards should be followed during source code writing?

12.6 Describe different kinds of reviews performed during software construction.

Recommended Readings

1. B. Hook (2005) *Write Portable Code: An Introduction to Developing Software for Multiple Platforms*, No Starch Press, San Francisco, CA.

2. R. Garud, A. Kumaraswamy, R. N. Langlois (2003) *Managing in the Modular Age: Architectures, Networks, and Organizations*, Wiley, New York.

3. M. Fomitechev (2006) *Enterprise Application Development with Visual C++ 2005*, Wiley India Pvt. Ltd., New Delhi, India.

4. D. Pilone, R. Miles (2007) *Head First Software Development*, O'Reilly, Sebastopol, CA.

5. M. Pecht (2009) *Product Reliability, Maintainability, and Supportability Handbook*, 2nd edn., CRC Press, Boca Raton, FL.

6. R. O. Lewis (1992) *Independent Verification and Validation: A Life Cycle Engineering Process*, Wiley, New York.

7. S. McConnell (2004) *Professional Software Development: Shorter Schedules, Higher Quality Products, More Successful Projects, Enhanced Careers*, Addison-Wesley, Reading, MA.

8. C. Jones (2007) *Estimating Software Costs: Bringing Realism to Estimating*, McGraw-Hill Osborne Media, New York.

9. J. Tian (2006) *Software Quality Engineering: Testing, Quality Assurance and Quantifiable Measurements*, Wiley India Pvt. Ltd., New Delhi, India.

10. J. McManus (2004) *Risk Management in Software Development Projects*, Butterworth-Heinemann, Oxford, U.K.

11. E. E. Brent, R. E. Anderson (1990) *Computer Applications in the Social Sciences*, Temple University Press, Philadelphia, PA.

12. M. E. Henderson, S. L. Lyons (1999) Object oriented methods for interoperable scientific and engineering computing, *Proceedings in Applied Mathematics, 99*, Society for Industrial & Applied Mathematics.

Chapter 13

Software Testing

In the previous chapter, we learned

- What is software construction?
- What are the considerations for making software construction?
- What techniques are used to construct software?
- How is quality assurance done during software construction?

In this chapter, we will learn

- What is software testing?
- What is verification and validation?
- What techniques are used for testing software?
- How does software testing help in increasing quality of a software product?

13.1 Introduction

It is a fact that the exact number of defects in a software product is difficult to find. At best it can be predicted using some defect estimation tools. It is also impossible to detect all defects in a software product. Nevertheless, finding and fixing critical bugs up to an acceptable limit as per expectations is important. If there are more defects in the product after the product enters production, then the project team will be in big trouble. The support costs for a bug ridden product will be too high. So, less than required testing is a certain call for rebuke from stakeholders.

Testing more than required will increase project costs unnecessarily [1]. When the project starts, the customer specifies what level of quality for the product is expected. The project manager needs to first make sure that the processes to be followed for building the product are at least so good that the produced product will have a certain level of quality with a certain level of defects. Then, he should have a test plan such that the product defects are further reduced by finding defects and fixing them. So the testing phase must be well planned with required budget, schedule, and testing processes that will ensure that a certain number of critical defects are caught and fixed (Figure 13.1).

13.2 Problems with Traditional Development Model

Traditionally, software testing was done only after software was constructed. This used to limit the scope of software testing in the development life cycle (see Figure 13.2).

This practice led to a situation that was too little and too late. By the time software was constructed, already faulty requirement specifications and faulty software design had resulted in defect ridden software. Removing all the defects originating from different phases of the project

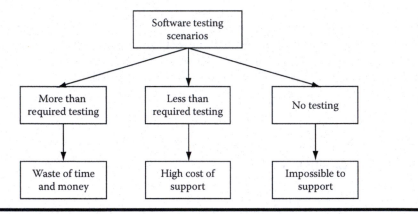

Figure 13.1   Software testing scenarios.

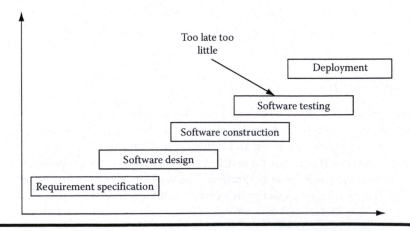

Figure 13.2   Traditional software development model (too little, too late testing).

in one go is a huge challenge. That is why this approach always used to result in defect ridden software products. Even if there was an attempt to remove defects so late in the life cycle, it would be exorbitantly costly to do so in one go and it would also mean devoting a considerable amount of time in detecting and fixing all those defects. This would likely be infeasible.

Definitely a better approach was needed to make better quality software products.

13.3 Verification and Validation

The problems encountered in the traditional approach to software testing led to the practice of verification and validation.

In most quality standards documents, software testing is divided into two parts: "validation" and "verification." While verification implies that the developed software is working as intended by checking the requirement specifications, design, source code, etc., in static mode, validation implies that the software has been validated to be working after running it and checking whether all functionality meets the requirements [2].

Verification techniques are also known as static testing, since the source code is not run to do testing. Figure 13.3 shows that each work product including requirement specifications, design, and source code during software development is tested using static methods. The requirement specifications are reviewed for completeness, clarity, design ability, testability, etc. The software design is reviewed for robustness, security, implementability, scalability, complexity, etc. The source code is reviewed for dead code, unused variables, faulty logic, constructs, etc.

Once the source code is ready to be run as a system, validation testing can be started. Validation testing is also known as dynamic testing as, in this case, the source code is actually run to determine that it is running per specifications. During validation, unit, integration, system, and finally user acceptance testing are performed. Unit testing is done to ensure each unit piece of source code is free from defects. Once unit testing is done, then this piece of code is integrated with the main source code build. But before integrating to the main build, it is strongly advisable to do local integration testing on the developer's own computer. Only when the source code runs smoothly and all integration tests pass, the source code should be integrated with the main build. When all

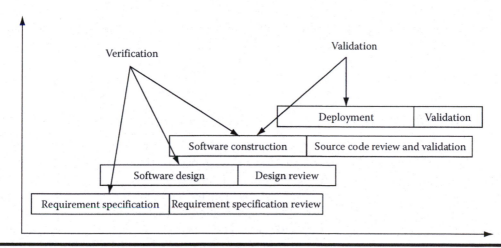

Figure 13.3 Software verification and validation.

source code is thus integrated, the main build is ready for system testing. All system tests are then performed and defects are fixed. When the system testing is over, and in fact the software product is shipped to customers, they do user acceptance testing.

13.4 Test Strategy and Planning

Software testing is a vast field in itself, and so the common practice is to consider it as a separate project. In those cases, it is known as an independent verification and validation project. As such, a separate project plan is made for that project and is linked to the parent software development project.

There are many techniques available to execute software test projects. It depends on the kind of test project. However, most test projects must have a test plan and a test strategy before the project can be ready for execution.

Often due to time constraints, testing cycles are cut short by project managers [3]. This leads to a half-tested product that is pushed out the door. In such cases, a large number of product defects are left undetected. Ultimately, end users discover these defects. Fixing these defects at this stage is costly. Moreover, they cannot be fixed one at a time. They are to be taken in batches and are incorporated in maintenance project plans. This leads to excessive costs in maintaining the software. It is lot cheaper to trap those bugs during the testing cycle and fix them. It is appropriately said that "testing costs money but not testing costs more!"

Test strategies should include things like test prioritization, automation strategy, risk analysis, etc. Test planning should include a work breakdown structure, requirement review, resource allocation, effort estimation, tools selection, setting up communication channels, etc.

13.4.1 Test Prioritization

Even before the test effort actually starts, it is of utmost importance that the test prioritization should be made. First of all, all parts of the software product will not be used by end users with the same intensity. Some parts of the product are used by end users extensively, while other parts are seldom used. So the extensively used parts of the product should not have any defects at all and thus they need to be tested thoroughly.

For making such a strategy, you must prioritize your testing. Put a high priority on tests which are to be done for these critical parts of the software product and put a low priority on uncritical parts. Then test the high priority areas first. Once testing is thoroughly done for these parts, then you should start testing low priority areas.

13.4.2 Risk Management

The test manager should also do plan for all known risks that could impact the test project. If proper risk mitigation planning is not done, and a mishap occurs, then the test project schedule could be jeopardized, costs could escalate, and/or quality could go down.

Some of the risks that can have severe, adverse impact on a test project include an unrealistic schedule, resource unavailability, skill unavailability, frequent requirement changes, etc. Requirement changes pose a serious threat to testing effort, because for each requirement change, the whole test plan gets changed. The test team has to revise its schedule for additional work as well as to assess impact of the change on the test cases they have to recreate. Some enthusiastic test engineers estimate much less effort than it actually should be. In that case, the test manager would be in trouble trying to explain why testing is taking more than the scheduled time schedule. In such cases, even after loading testing engineers more than 150%, the testing cycle get delayed. This is a very common situation on most of the test projects. This also happens because the marketing team agrees on unrealistic schedules with the customer, in order to bag the project. Even the test manager at that time feels that somehow he will manage it, but later on it proves impossible to achieve. Other test engineers unnecessarily pad their estimate, and later on, when the customer detects it, the test manager finds himself in a spot. When the software development market, along with the software testing market, is hot (this is the case most of the time, as businesses need to implement software systems more and more and so software professionals are in great demand), software professionals have many job offers in hand. They leave the project at short notice and the test manager has to find a replacement fast. Sometimes, a project may have some kind of testing for which skilled test professionals are hard to find. In both situations, the test manager may not be able to start those tasks in need of adequate resources.

For test professional resources, a good alternative resource planning is required. The test manager should, in consultation with human resource manager, keep a line of test professionals who may join in case one is needed on his project.

For scheduling problems, the test manager has to ensure in advance that schedules do not get affected. He has to keep a buffer in the schedule for any eventuality.

To keep a tab on the project budget, the test manager has to ensure that the schedule is not unrealistic and also has to load his test engineers appropriately. If some test engineers are not loaded adequately, then project costs may go higher. For this reason, if any test professionals do not have enough assignments on one project, they should be assigned work from other projects.

13.4.3 Effort Estimation

For making scheduling, resource planning, and budget for a test project, the test manager should make a good effort estimate [4]. Effort estimate should include information such as project size, productivity, and test strategy. While project size and test strategy information comes after consultation with the customer, the productivity figure comes from experience and knowledge of the team members of the project team.

The wideband Delphi technique uses brainstorming sessions to arrive at effort estimate figures after discussing the project details with the project team. This is a good technique because the people who will be assigned the project work will know their own productivity levels and can figure out the size of their assigned project tasks from their own experience. Initial estimates from each team member are then discussed with other team members in an open environment. Each person has his own estimate. These estimates are then unanimously condensed into final estimate figures for each project task.

In an experience-based technique, instead of group sessions, the test manager meets each team member and asks him his estimate for the project work he has been assigned. This technique works best when team members are well aware, particularly, of their prior experience of similar project tasks.

Effort estimation is one area where no test manager can have a good grasp, at the initial stages of the project. This is because not many details are clear about the project. As the project unfolds, after executing some of its related tasks, things become clearer. At that stage, any test manager can comfortably give an effort estimate for the remaining project tasks. But that is too late.

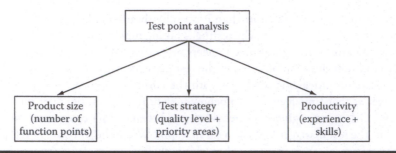

Figure 13.4 Test point analysis components.

Project stakeholders want to know, at the very beginning of the project, what would be the cost estimates and when the project would be delivered. These two questions are very important for project stakeholders and it is on top of their mind. Unfortunately, test managers are not equipped to provide accurate an schedule and costs for the project at those initial stages, because of unclear project scope, size, etc. Nevertheless, it is one of their critical tasks that they have to finish and provide the requested information. The best solution is to find a relatively objective method of effort estimation and provide the requested information.

13.4.3.1 Test Point Analysis

There are many methods available for effort estimation for test projects. Some of them include test point analysis [5], the wideband Delphi technique [6], experience-based estimation [7], etc. In the test point analysis technique, three inputs required are project size, test strategy, and productivity. Project size is determined by calculating the number of test points in the software application which is being developed. Test points, in turn, are calculated from function points. The number of function points is calculated from the number of functions and function complexity. If the number of function points in the application has been calculated by the development team, then test points are calculated from the available function point information. Otherwise rough function point data can be used (Figure 13.4).

A test strategy is derived from two pieces of information from the customer, what will be the quality level for the application, and which features of the application will be used most frequently. Productivity is derived from knowledge and experience of the test team members. While productivity can be calculated objectively without taking reference from any statistical data, it makes sense to use past productivity data from previously executed projects to make productivity figures more realistic.

In case of iterative development, testing cycles will be short and iterative in nature. The test manager should make the test effort calculations accordingly.

13.5 Test Automation

Most testing tasks are done manually, as they are still difficult to automate. Wherever automation is possible, it can be evaluated. Care should also be taken not to do automation blindly [8]. This is because the initial effort for automation is more than manual testing.

Testing tasks include requirements and design document review, test case scenario creation, test case creation, test case execution, test case management, and defect tracking. Out of these tasks, test case execution and test case management are the only tasks for which good automation tools are available.

13.5.1 Test Case Execution Automation

If a test case has to be executed only a few times, then automating that test case will be more expensive compared to manually running it, the reason being that automation effort for a test case is more than manually executing the test case. Usually, the efforts break even when a test case is executed around 13 times [9]. So, only if it has to be executed at least 13 times, it makes sense to automate it. But first of all, why does a test case have to be executed more than once at all? Because, in software product development, new versions of the software keep getting developed to cater to the needs of the market. The newer versions may contain old features as well as new features. The older version of the software was tested using existing or newly created test cases, at that time. With addition of new features, it is important to retest the old features to make sure they still work. So old functional tests now become regression test cases. The suite of regression test cases keeps increasing with newer releases of the software [10]. At some point, the regression test suite becomes so large that manually executing tests becomes a liability. Nobody wants to keep executing those large numbers of test cases again and again. Keep in mind most software vendors have minor releases of their product each quarter. So an ever increasing suite of regression test cases has to be run each quarter. It takes a considerable period of time to execute them. As the software has to be released fast, the project manager cannot wait just because regression test cases are still being implemented. Thus, in this case, automating the whole suite of regression test cases is going to be profitable.

The current trend for automation is to create a keyword framework [11] as follows: For each major function create a keyword. Write the automation script for that function and then save the function with same name as the keyword. After all the required functions are created, relate these functions with the test cases that would have been already created before automation scripts were written. Now when you run the scripts, it will cover all the test cases and it will be same as executing the test cases, manually. This way of inducing automation is known as keyword driven automation framework. The benefit of such a strategy is that it allows for reuse of script and makes automation creation modular. This also makes maintenance of scripts easier. If any test case gets changed, the whole script does not have to be changed. Only the script for which the keyword was affected due to a change in test case has to be changed.

13.5.2 Test Case Management Automation

Test case management is also a good candidate for automation. There are some good tools that facilitate it. They allow keeping many versions of test cases and a repository of automation scripts, which allows teams located at many sites to work more effectively.

13.6 Test Project Monitoring and Control

Test projects involve a large variety of activities including test case design, test case management, test case automation, test execution, defect tracking, verifying, and validating the application under test, etc. [12] (Figure 13.5).

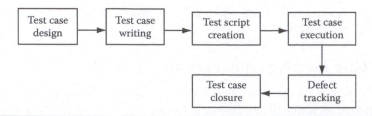

Figure 13.5 Test life cycle.

13.6.1 Test Case Design

A proper test case design plan goes a long way in ensuring that test cases are designed properly. The test manager has to ensure which kind of tests are to be designed, how many test cases have to be written for particular modules, and which test areas are priority areas.

13.6.1.1 Test Types

An application may have to be tested for functionality, performance, usability, compatibility, and many other kinds of things, to make sure it is really useful for end users. For each kind of testing, a set of test cases has to be written and executed and, finally, the system should be verified and validated. For applications that have many versions, regression tests also have to be performed. Managing all these kinds of testing is a big task for the test manager. A good test manager will first divide the testing tasks on the basis of test types. Then tasks can be further divided by modules. After that, he can allocate testing tasks to test engineers appropriately.

There is one more way of segregating tests. Depending on the project phase, we need to perform system testing, integration testing, or user acceptance testing. Usually when the application is built after the construction phase, it has to be tested and verified whether it is functioning per requirements. Integration testing is performed when the application needs to be integrated with any other external application to ensure that integration is proper. User acceptance testing is done by end users. If any defect is found during these tests, they are fixed so that the application goes into production with as few defects as possible.

13.6.2 Test Case Management

There could be existing test cases as well as new test cases that also need to be created. Test case management involves managing different versions of test cases, keeping track of changes in them, keeping a separate repository of test cases based on type of tests, as well as creating and managing automation scripts.

13.6.3 Test Bed Preparation

Test bed preparation involves installing the application on a machine that is accessible to all test teams [5]. Care is taken to ensure that this machine is free of any interference from unauthorized access. Test data is populated in the application. Care should also be taken to ensure that the test bed resembles the production environment as closely as possible, including all software and hardware configurations.

For all types of testing, it is very important that the "application under test" (UAT) should be tested under an environment that is as close to the environment under which the proposed application will be deployed for production. That is why test bed preparation is very important. The application should be installed on a dedicated server that has the same configuration as the proposed production environment. This server should not be used for any other purpose except for testing. It should be installed centrally, so that even distributed teams, contractors, or service providers can easily access it using remote desktop sharing or any peer to peer networking protocol over the Internet. If the application can be directly accessed over the Internet, then it is even better.

There should not be any testing done on applications that are deployed on the local test engineer's machine. To gain familiarity with the application and preliminary testing, it is acceptable to have a local copy of the application, but never for testing when defects are to be logged and verified by many people. It is because it is very important to reproduce the defect when the developer or any concerned person asks for it. In case of disputes, if a defect cannot be reproduced, then it becomes difficult for the test team to justify why a defect has been logged when others cannot reproduce it. That is the reason for which the test bed should be prepared very carefully and kept as isolated from any other environment as much as possible to preserve its integrity.

The test data preparation is also a very tricky affair. The test data should closely resemble what the end users use in their daily transactions. For this, the test team can get some business data already used by the end users. The test bed should be populated with a similar kind of data.

13.6.4 Test Case Execution

Test case execution involves executing prepared test cases manually or using automation tools to execute them. For regression tests, automated test execution is a preferred method. After each test case is executed, it may pass or fail. If it fails then defects have to be logged.

Exit criteria for test case execution cycle are generally defined in advance. Generally, when a certain level of quality of the application is reached, then test execution stops.

13.6.5 Defect Tracking

Defect tracking is one of the most important activities in a test project [13]. During defect tracking it is ensured that defects are logged and get fixed. All defects and their fixing are tracked carefully (Figure 13.6).

Defect count per hour per day is a common way of measuring performance of a test team. If the testing is done for an in-house software product, traditionally, it used to not be a performance evaluation measurement. What really counted was the number of defects found in production when the software product was deployed and used by end users. But it is too late a performance measurement. What if many of the test team members left before the product was deployed? In fact this is a

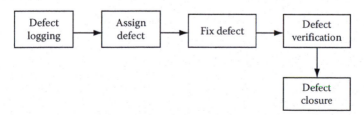

Figure 13.6   Defect life cycle.

reality, given the high attrition rate (as much as 20% at many corporations) of software professionals. Once they are gone, there is no point in measuring the performance. Thus, a better measurement would allow for more immediate results. This is achieved by measuring the defect count per hour per day. Then there is the case of outsourced test projects. If the contract is only for testing up to deployment and not afterward, then measurement does not make sense after the contract has ended.

A good defect tracking application should be deployed on a central server that is accessible to all test and development teams. Each defect should be logged in such a way that it could be understood by both development and testing teams. Generally, the defects should be reproducible, but in many instances, this is difficult. In such instances, a good resolution should be made by the test and development managers.

13.7 Test Reporting

During the execution of a test project, many initial and final reports are made. But status reports also need to be made. Test reports include test planning reports, test strategy reports, requirement document review comments, number of test cases created, automation scripts created, test execution cycle reports, defect tracking reports, etc. Some other reports include traceability matrix reports, defect density, test execution rate, test creation rate, test automation script writing rate, etc.

13.8 Test Artifacts

Software testing involves making a test strategy, test project plan, resource requirements, test case repository creation, running test cycles, defect tracking, bug verification and validation and, finally, certifying the developed product. So the test artifacts include test plan document, test strategy document, test cases, test cycle logs, defect list, verification and validation reports, and product certification.

13.8.1 Management Artifacts

Customers are concerned not only with project cost and schedule, but they are also concerned with critical defects, which the test team has either detected or not. So the management artifacts (metrics) include project cost compliance, project schedule compliance, and quality (number of critical defects caught versus number of critical defects which went into production).

Some other management artifacts include traceability matrix, defect density rate, resource loading, etc.

13.9 Practical Considerations

The most important consideration for any test project is whether the testing was effective for the time and money spent for the whole testing effort. Effectiveness is measured in terms of how many critical defects have been caught by the test team and how many critical defects have escaped into the product and caught by end users. All other considerations about the project could only be circumferential. If the test team has done a lot of work but has failed to catch enough critical defects, then the whole effort is a failure.

That is why the test manager has to show that the test effort was worth spending the money and time by showing number of critical defects caught.

13.10 Software Testing in Iterative Model

In an iterative model, each iteration is a short cycle. So the amount of testing in each iteration is also small. Thus, unlike in waterfall model, software testing has a lesser role in the iterative development life cycle.

Generally, software defects tend to increase with the size of software products. Since in iteration mode the software product is small, there will be fewer defects in the product. Although in reality, as the software product grows in size over many iterations, the number of defects per line of software code is bound to increase. In iterative development, regression testing is also a big issue. In each iteration, there will be a large number of regression test cases to run. As the product size increases with iterations, the set of regression test cases also increases. It becomes a liability after a while. Manually running all those regression tests takes a lot of time, which becomes a hindrance for the release schedule. In such cases, the best option is to go for automation of these regression test cases. Automated test cases take much less time (sometimes if the manual running of test cases was taking 5 days, after automation it took only 5 h) to run.

13.11 Case Study

We continue our case study with our SaaS software vendor. Whenever they started any project whether a customer specific or new product release, the software testing team was taken onboard early on the project. After the test manager received the software requirement specification document (SRS), he would go through it. He would make a test strategy and decide which testing team out of two teams (both outsourced and offshored) would be involved with the project. Then, he would make a test strategy and do some rough estimates for effort required, managing risks, automation required, types of tests required, etc. When the software design documents (in the form of mock-ups and flowcharts) are received, the test team starts writing test cases. It also determines how many test cases are to be automated, and hence how many test scripts are to be written. Then, how many existing test scripts are to be changed to make them work with the change in software design is also determined. A final effort estimate for writing test cases and test scripts is based on all these factors. An effort estimate is also made for running test cases and then completing the defect life cycle. Effort estimation for defect life cycle is a bit difficult, as nobody knows just how many defects will crop up in the defect cycle. But from historical figures using SPC methods, an estimate is made that is close to reality.

Effort estimation differs depending on whether a new version or a customer version is to be developed. For a new version release, the release date is fixed in advance. So time duration for the project is fixed along with the volume of work (number of features to be developed). The effort in such a case is calculated and accordingly the project team size is determined. However, in case of our SaaS software vendor, there is not much effort estimation difference between development for a customer version and development for a new version of the software product. The reason is that they sign a contract with customers on fixed price/fixed schedule basis. It is because they study customer requirements and the contract is signed only after this study. So the customer study is, in fact, done for free and they charge only for the implementation. Thus, at the onset of the project itself, there is always a fixed due date. Functional black box testing is the most prevalent kind of testing done. Then come regression tests, which are all automated. Apart from functional testing, integration testing, usability testing, security testing, etc., are also done. Some of their application runs on hand held devices. So mobile testing is also done using emulators. They also have software parts that integrate with hardware devices like printers (for printing RFID tags, for instance). Testing of these components is also done.

For automation, a keyword driven framework is used. Thus, when the test cases are written, care is taken so that the test cases can be used by the scripting for automation. Each time in a test case, a set of steps is to be executed in sequence, it is captured as a keyword and a specific keyword is assigned for it. Each test case containing these keywords must be identified to have the specific keyword. For instance, a keyword named "Login" can have fixed steps of going to the URL of the website, key in username, password, and then clicking on the OK button. Instead of recording activities in each test case where it is required, the script will store all the steps for these activities and assign them to the keyword "Login," and thus these steps will be recorded only once. This saves a lot of future maintenance effort. All automation tests follow this convention.

Since the SaaS software vendor is also supposed to maintain the production instances of the software product for its customers as well as its own versions, there is a maintenance and support group which looks after these operations. The center, which keeps all the hardware including servers, back up servers, routers, etc., and from where all production instances are hosted, is known as the network operations center. The testing team also plays an important role in support function by running sanity tests daily on all production instances of the application. If any problems are encountered, they are reported to the support team and they fix it immediately.

13.12 Chapter Summary

Software testing is one of the most important activities carried out in software projects. It is here that the software product developed is verified and validated. If the product contains a large number of defects that could not be fixed before the release due date, then the product cannot be shipped by the shipping date. A software product containing too many defects is extremely costly in terms of providing support. It is most important to detect and remove most critical defects before shipping the product. Software testing helps in achieving these goals.

To make sure that the software product being made is of good quality, the work products from a very early stage (project initiation) should be tested. In fact, there should be a comprehensive quality assurance plan so that each and every work product is tested for defects that should be removed at the point of origin itself. For this, a verification and validation approach should be employed.

Review Questions

13.1 What is independent verification and validation?
13.2 Why is software testing necessary?
13.3 What are testing types?
13.4 What activities are done in a software testing phase/project?
13.5 What are the benefits of test automation?
13.6 Describe the defect life cycle.

Recommended Readings

1. K. M. Gardner, A. R. Rush (1998) *Cognitive Patterns: Problem-Solving Frameworks for Object Technology*, Cambridge University Press, New York.
2. E. Dustin, J. Rashka, J. Paul (1999) *Automated Software Testing: Introduction, Management, and Performance*, Addison-Wesley, Boston, MA.
3. S. De Cesare, M. Lycett, R. Macredie (2005) *Development of Component-Based Information Systems*, M. E. Sharpe, Armonk, NY.
4. E. Dustin (2002) *Effective Software Testing: 50 Specific Ways to Improve Your Testing*, Addison-Wesley, Boston, MA.
5. A. Ahmed (2009) *Software Testing as a Service*, CRC Press, Boca Raton, FL.
6. D. Huizinga, A. Kolawa (2007) *Automated Defect Prevention: Best Practices in Software Management*, Wiley, Hoboken, NJ.
7. W. E. Perry (2006) *Effective Methods for Software Testing*, 3rd edn., Wiley, New York.
8. K. Li, M. Wu (2004) *Effective Software Test Automation: Developing an Automated Software Testing Tool*, Sybex, Alameda, CA.
9. C. Kaner, J. Bach, B. Pettichord (2006) *Lessons Learned in Software Testing*, Wiley, New York.
10. P. Jorgensen (2002) *Software Testing: A Craftsman's Approach*, CRC Press, New York.
11. B. A. Posey (2002) *Just Enough Software Test Automation*, Prentice Hall PTR, Upper Saddle River, NJ.
12. W. E. Lewis, G. Veerapillai (2005) *Software Testing and Continuous Quality Improvement*, CRC Press, Boca Raton, FL.
13. R. D. Craig, S. P. Jaskiel (2002) *Systematic Software Testing*, Artech House, Norwood, MA.

Chapter 14

Product Release
and Maintenance

In the previous chapter, we learned

- What is software testing?
- What is verification and validation?
- What techniques are used for testing software?
- How does software testing help in increasing quality of a software product?

In this chapter, we will learn

- What is software release?
- What is software maintenance?
- What activities are performed in software release?
- What activities are performed in software maintenance?

14.1 Introduction

The software product which you have been building for so long is now complete. You need to take it to the customer's site and get it implemented so that the end users can start using it. However, do not run fast in anticipation of wrapping things as early as possible. After all this is your magnum opus and you need to be careful. You need to make sure that all your tasks are completed, for example, product support cost estimate, walk around for known bugs, which version of the software product to be released, if release should be an alpha, beta, or normal release, training needs fulfilled, and customer support strategy (Figure 14.1).

14.2 Product Release Management

Project teams working for software product vendors struggle to keep pace with release of the software product. There is pressure from the market to launch new versions by certain dates. New features are to be added, porting the product to new platforms, old features are to be enhanced, existing bugs are to be removed, and yet it has to meet the deadline. It is a constant struggle that calls for good product release strategies. Depending on the situation, the project manager may need to convince the management to cut short some of the product features to meet the deadline as well as meet quality standards. A half-baked product will never have any takers; instead the project manager may be blamed for its poor quality issues. Bargaining also has to be done for other requirements of bug fixes, feature enhancements, etc. If quality concerns are paramount, then moving some of the tasks of new features to a future release may be the best solution for meeting quality standards. If the software vendor is not too sure about product quality, then he may opt for an alpha or beta release of the product. In that case, the product will be released only among a few selected groups and not in the market as a whole. The controlled product release is the best option in these conditions [1] (Figure 14.2).

In fact, product release management is such a dynamic environment that if proper planning is not done at a minute level and constant vigilance is not applied over project activities, then a huge mess can be created and there will be no time to clear it. So the project manager must be vigilant all the time (Figure 14.2).

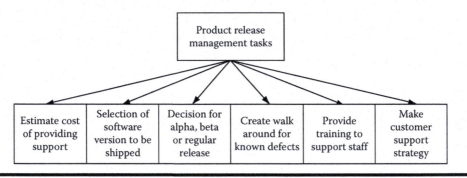

Figure 14.1   Task list for software product release.

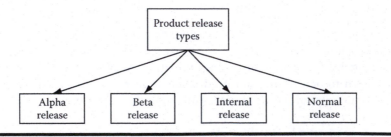

Figure 14.2   Software product release types.

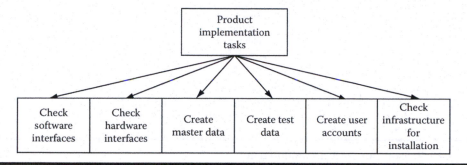

Figure 14.3   Task list for software product implementation.

Finally, for the product's scheduled release, how the customer support will be provided should be chalked out. Walk arounds for known issues, estimated number of critical bugs still remaining in the product, training for the support staff, etc., should be done. The cost of support, depending on the number of estimated users, walk arounds, and remaining bugs should be figured out. These measures will ensure that the product is transitioned into market without facing major difficulties.

14.3 Product Implementation

The product that has been developed and thoroughly tested now needs to be implemented at a customer site. You need to prepare all master data and test transaction data for testing the implemented product. You need to get all required hardware and software that need to be there for installing your software product. You need to make sure that you have developed and tested all the hardware and software interfaces for integrating your product, with existing legacy systems and infrastructure. You also need to make sure that your product will run smoothly on customer premises without any interference with their existing applications [2] (Figure 14.3).

Often project teams run into problems during implementation, due to unforeseen circumstances or negligence on part of the production team or customer's team. Therefore, prepare a list of your own requirements and hand it over to your customer's support team so that they are prepared when you arrive for implementation.

14.4 User Training

Make sure that the user manual prepared by your team is up to date and in synch with the version of your software product, which you will implement at the customer site. It is not possible to provide training to all users. So prepare a list of roles that are needed to operate the product. Give this list to the end users and ask them to select one user per role who will receive the training. Apart from the user manual, you also need to prepare a tutorial to include probable scenarios that may arise during operation of the product. The tutorial will provide a step-by-step guide for using the product under those scenarios. This will be a very important step in training, because if users do not learn it during training, then they will contact you later after implementation and ask you to provide information as to how to use the product in those circumstances [3]. This will lead to a waste of your support team's time. It is lot better to train them now, during user training, rather than face user requests later.

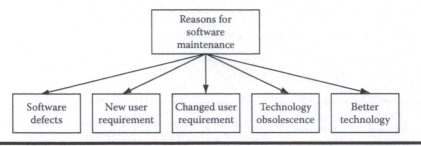

Figure 14.4   Reasons for software maintenance.

14.5 Maintenance Introduction

Software products do not age or wear out like physical products. Then why is there a need to have maintenance of software products? Well, there are some factors which make it absolutely necessary. Here are some of the reasons:

1. *Technology obsolescence* [4]: The software platform (operating system, medium of user, interface) or the hardware platform on which the software product runs gets obsolete.
2. *Software defects*: There are major software defects in the product and it is difficult to operate. For this reason, a software patch may be needed to be applied so that these defects are removed.
3. *Change in user requirements*: The business organization that was using the software product has seen a change in business transactions or business workflows that are not supported by the software product (Figure 14.4).

It is estimated that more than 70% of all costs associated with software product development, implementation, and support and maintenance is consumed in the activities of supporting and maintaining software products [5]. Why is it so? What can be done to change this situation, so that support and maintenance costs get minimized as compared to development and implementation costs?

These kinds of queries have always puzzled the business community. This recognition has resulted in an awareness of the importance of finding ways to build such a software product. This situation has led to including maintainability characteristics during the entire product development cycle. Yet, a lot of work remains to be done during the maintenance phase of any software product. How to manage these activities so that costs can be minimized is an area of concern yet to be resolved.

14.6 Maintenance Types

Software maintenance is of four types: corrective, adaptive, preventive, and perfective maintenance [5]. If the software has some defects, then it will take a corrective maintenance to rectify it. If there are some changes in the operating environment of the software product, then the product can be made useful by doing adaptive maintenance. If there is an insecurity that although the product is running fine in future we may have difficulty in using it, then preventive maintenance is employed. If there are some deficiencies in the product that must be rectified, then perfective maintenance will fit the bill (Figure 14.5).

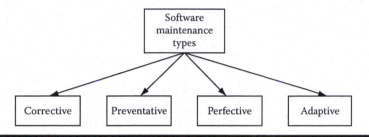

Figure 14.5   Software maintenance types.

14.6.1 Corrective

Even after thorough reviews and testing, the software product contains many defects when it goes into production. These defects are uncovered as users start using the application. They are logged with the support staff and after a sizable number of errors are detected, the software vendor instructs his maintenance team to create a patch to rectify them. The maintenance team then makes a plan and fixes those defects. After application of the patch containing the fixes, the software starts running without these defects [6].

14.6.2 Adaptive

The operating environment in which a software product runs in operation includes the hardware and software platform as well as the interfaces for human and other machine interactions. If any of these change over time, it becomes difficult to run the software product. In such cases, it becomes necessary to do adaptive maintenance so that the software product becomes reusable. This kind of maintenance may involve changing the interface or porting the application to another hardware/ software platform [7].

14.6.3 Perfective

This kind of maintenance is needed when there is a change in the business environment, and thereby users need additional/modified functionality in the software product to do their tasks. A business workflow may have changed, a business transaction may have changed, or an altogether new business transaction was represented in the software product. For all these kinds of requirements, a perfective maintenance may be needed [8].

14.6.4 Preventive

Generally after a lapse of time, there are likely changes in business or operative environment, or there may be changes in hardware/software environment. These changes are bound to occur and they affect the way the software product operates. Many of these changes can be perceived in advance. In such cases, preventive maintenance on the software product can make sure that the product will be useful even after these environmental changes occur [9].

14.7 Maintenance Cost

A software product is generally very valuable to an organization if it is used for doing a large portion of their daily business. If for some reason the software product has become unusable, then the organization in fact will be making losses on their revenue. Moreover, large enterprise software

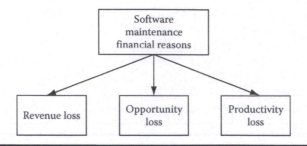

Figure 14.6 Financial reasons for software maintenance.

products are that much crucial! When the organization faces such a case, it is left with no alternative but to either get an entirely different software product that will replace the existing one or do maintenance of an existing product to make it usable.

Following are some financial reasons for which a maintenance may be needed:

1. *Loss in business revenue*: It may happen that business transactions are faulty and thus the business may lose revenue.
2. *Opportunity loss*: Sometimes there could be some business opportunity in the marketplace, but due to some software problems it could not be availed.
3. *Productivity loss*: If the software product becomes difficult to operate due to many walk arounds or lengthy processing then productivity will become lower for business personnel (Figure 14.6).

Maintenance of an existing software product has its own share of problems. The maintenance will incur costs. A profit/loss analysis can be done, to see if it is more profitable to conduct a maintenance program on the software or keep using it as it is. The losses due to problems with the software can be compared to probable cost of maintenance and an ROI (return on investment) can be done. If we get a desirable ROI then it is better to go for maintenance.

14.8 Maintenance Process

For any work, it is always better to have a process model instead of doing things on an ad hoc basis. When it comes to software maintenance, some process models have been defined. Some of the popular ones include the quick fix model, Boehm's model, Osborne's model, iterative enhancement model, and reuse oriented model (Figure 14.7).

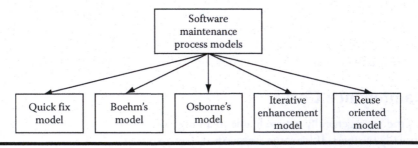

Figure 14.7 Software maintenance models.

Quick fix model: This is the simplest of maintenance models; whenever any defects with the software products are found they are immediately fixed. There is no planning involved in the whole process and it is mostly an ad hoc approach.

Boehm's model: Boehm's model is based on economic models and often involves calculating ROI, for any planned maintenance. If ROI turns out to be good, then it is carried out or else it is dropped.

Osborne's model: Osborne realized that difficulties in carrying out maintenance work are due to gaps in communication. He proposed four steps to prevent this situation. He stated that a maintenance plan should include all change requests in the form of maintenance requirements. A quality assurance plan should accompany the maintenance plan. Metrics should be developed to measure and assess quality of work carried out during maintenance. Finally, reviews should be held after maintenance work to assess quality of work done.

Iterative enhancement model: This model is based on the similar concept of iterative software development. All software defects and change requests are logged and then a small set from this list is taken for making fixes. This set is prepared based on the priority of changes required. High priority fixes are done before low priority fixes.

Reuse oriented model: This type of process is adopted for component-based software products. For fixing any defects, existing components are analyzed and then the appropriate changes are made.

14.9 Maintenance Life Cycle

Like the software development, software maintenance also has a life cycle. Requirements for software maintenance come from the list of defects that have been logged. Either the list of defects can be taken as a whole or a subset of defects from this list can be taken for a fixing plan. It makes a lot of sense to go for an iterative approach. This approach is similar to the concept of iterative software development. This way it can be ensured that highly visible, important, and priority defects are fixed first and other defects which do not make much impact on operations of the product are tackled later (Figure 14.8).

In the software maintenance life cycle, testing is a crucial phase. This phase also consumes a lot of time and effort. But the value addition in all this effort and time spent helps in reducing defects, which in the long run is a much cheaper alternative compared to no testing/cursory testing and later spending money in providing support.

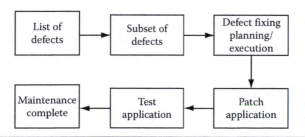

Figure 14.8   Maintenance life cycle.

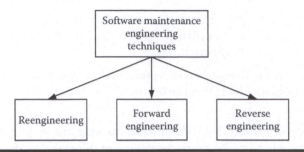

Figure 14.9   Software maintenance engineering techniques.

14.10 Maintenance Techniques

Maintenance of software products sometimes becomes a tough proposition. There is no proper documentation that can be used for understanding how the product is designed and constructed. Sometimes there is no documentation at all. Even if documentation is there, it is not up to date. This out-of-date documentation is not of much use for any maintenance work (Figure 14.9).

Sometimes even if the documentation is up to date, the maintenance work is difficult due to dirty design or construction work.

All these situations call for some specific techniques for maintenance work depending on the situation. Some of the common maintenance techniques include reengineering, reverse engineering, and forward engineering.

14.10.1 Reengineering

Reengineering is also known as reuse engineering. This technique is a standard method for maintenance work for component-based software products. Details about all components in the software products are well known. When any maintenance work is needed, from the list of defects, each defect is specifically analyzed to find out the root cause of the defect. Once this analysis is successful, then fixing that defect becomes easy.

14.10.2 Reverse Engineering

Reverse engineering technique is most useful when nonexistent or sketchy documentation is available for the software product. Due to unavailability of documentation, there is no information as to what the design is and how the product is constructed. In such a situation, it is almost impossible to do any modification in the source code for any maintenance work.

In such cases, the reverse engineering technique is adopted. Using this technique, similar components or product parts are constructed as compared to existing product components/parts. This way the software product functionality is changed as the new constructed parts will have the desired functionality.

14.10.3 Forward Engineering

Forward engineering is just the opposite of reverse engineering. In this situation, we have ample documentation about the existing product. Due to new customer needs, the existing product needs to be extended so that the new needs can be fulfilled. All new extended development is based on the existing design and construction methods and will be made for the same hardware/software platform.

14.11 Case Study

In our series of case studies, here is the piece related to software release and maintenance.

14.11.1 Software Release

Our SaaS vendor releases minor versions of its product on a quarterly basis and major versions on a yearly basis. For each minor release, new features to be added are carefully planned. The product manager makes sure that the release plan for a minor release will be on time by assigning priority to each new feature. The high priority features will be definitely added and the low priority features for that iteration will be added if any time remains in the iteration.

Our SaaS vendor does not release alpha or beta releases of its product as they do not serve mass markets. Their product is an enterprise computing product and is used by large retailers, government offices, logistics providers, manufacturers, and distributors. They always release new versions of their product to their existing customers. Since they do not do alpha or beta releases, they make sure that their new version is tested thoroughly by their testing team, and no major defects are passed in the production instances. Since there are no immediate customers who will be available for doing user acceptance testing, the internal testing team does the user acceptance testing as well.

14.11.2 Software Maintenance

The software vendor keeps all of the production instances of its software product at its data center (also known as operations center). All previous versions of the software as well as the current working version of the software product run at this center as production instances of different versions of their software product. The maintenance team makes sure that all versions of the product are available for users. They run sanity test scripts daily on all instances. If any problems are found, they is immediately resolved. These scripts are run at night. If any problems are found then, it is made sure that they are rectified before office hours start and people start using the application.

In packaged software or custom built software that are not used in an SaaS environment, this kind of quick fix is not possible. So in those cases, a maintenance plan is made to fix all or most defects found by users during a time span of 3 months or more. But with SaaS environments, this kind of maintenance is not needed at all. All defects are quickly and easily fixed, without hampering work of end users.

14.12 Chapter Summary

Software product release is a messy affair for most project teams. Even when a project team is working with the most pessimistic schedule estimates, things get delayed and create problems in completing tasks on time. It is human nature that they tend to relax at the beginning of an assigned task, and thus when the schedule deadline approaches a large part of the task is not complete. This puts pressure on the individual as well as the project team. This is precisely what happens around the product release dates most of the time. So apart from what the project team will be exactly doing at the time of software release (product implementation and user training), the team ends up doing some backlog work as well. For user training, appropriate users should be identified out of the pool of probable users. These users who will get the training should be excellent students (and teachers) who will later train other users.

When first implementing a product, the right version of the software should be identified, as the project team usually has a number of release candidates. The required infrastructure, data preparation, hardware configuration, etc., should be chalked out and people responsible for this work should be informed in advance, before the implementation team actually visits the implementation site. If the software product is distributed via the web, then it should be made sure that the link to download the software works fine. Mirroring sites should also be made available so that users will be able to download the software even during peak load hours. Customers of the software should be clearly identified and targeted. For instance, depending on whether the software product is an alpha, beta, or regular release, the customers will be different.

Software development may involve developing a software product spanning from a few months to a few years. But the product will be used anywhere from 5 years to more than 10 years. Many software applications are in fact used even after their expected service life has expired. During this whole time span, the software needs to be supported and maintained. Support and maintenance involve costs. Due to this large time span, in fact the support and maintenance costs are more than development costs. Sometimes it can be as high as 1500% of the development costs. To minimize support and maintenance cost, it has to be ensured during development that the software can be easily maintained.

Review Questions

14.1 Why is maintenance needed for software products?

14.2 What techniques are employed for software maintenance projects?

14.3 What is the life cycle of a maintenance project?

14.4 Define maintainability. How can a software product be made maintainable?

14.5 List common maintenance processes.

14.6 What activities are involved in software release?

Recommended Readings

1. D. J. Anderson (2004) *Agile Management for Software Engineering: Applying the Theory of Constraints for Business Results*, Prentice Hall PTR, Upper Saddle River, NJ.
2. K. Bittner, I. Spence (2007) *Managing Iterative Software Development Projects*, Addison-Wesley, Boston, MA.
3. N. D. Birrell, M. A. Ould (1988) *A Practical Handbook for Software Development*, Cambridge University Press, Cambridge, U.K.
4. G. Ramesh (2005) *Managing Global Software Projects*, Tata McGraw-Hill, New Delhi, India.
5. C. Jones (2007) *Estimating Software Costs*, Tata McGraw-Hill, New Delhi, India.
6. P. Grubb, A. A. Takang (2003) *Software Maintenance: Concepts and Practice*, World Scientific Publishing Company, River Edge, NJ.
7. S. Fishman (2007) *Legal Guide to Web and Software Development*, Nolo, Berkeley, CA.
8. C. B. Tayntor (2003) *Six Sigma Software Development*, Auerbach, New York.
9. S. Beydeda, M. Book, V. Gruhn (2005) *Model-Driven Software Development*, Springer, New York.

SOFTWARE ENGINEERING MANAGEMENT

Chapter 15

Process Standards Introduction

In Part III, we will learn

- What is software process improvement?
- How can process selection be made for a software project?
- What are the benefits and drawbacks of the waterfall model of software development?
- What are the benefits and drawbacks of the agile model of software development?

In this chapter, we will learn

- What is software engineering management?
- How are statistical process control techniques useful for software projects?
- What are the benefits of the standard process model implemented across the organization?

15.1 Introduction

The quality of any product/service is one of the most important factors for its success in the market. A shoddy quality product/service is simply not acceptable. Consumers will reject such a product.

Therefore, a good quality product/service is a must. But how do consumers know whether a product/service is of good quality? By getting its quality certified by some certifying agency. These certifying agencies use some standards to measure physical, aesthetic, chemical, or any other aspect of the product/service to know if it meets those exacting standards. If it does, then they certify it; if not, they do not. Consumers see this certificate and know that the product/service is of good quality and, only then, they buy it.

The manufacturer/service provider uses standard methods to manufacture/devise any product/service of good quality. Without standard methods a good quality product/service is possible, but it cannot be repeated. So once in a while the product/service will be of good quality, but most of the time it will not be good. Nevertheless, if a good standard method is employed, then, most of the time, quality of the product/service will be good. This is why a good quality method or process is very important, as it enables to produce good quality product/service consistently and repeatedly.

When it comes to software development projects, a good quality process becomes even more important because software products or applications are very complex and difficult to produce. Even when the product specifications devised during system design are good, there is no guarantee that the software produced will be of good quality because the coding may be of shoddy quality.

15.2 Root Cause of Problems in Software Projects

Software development projects are plagued by many problems. The most important problems include lack of visibility, variability in quality, cost and schedule escalation, etc. [1]. Lack of visibility in software projects can be attributed to unclear software requirement specifications and frequent change in requirement specifications. Due to these two factors, downstream activities in the software development cycle get affected and thus it becomes difficult to schedule these activities with good accuracy. Variability in quality, cost, and schedule from one project to another results from nonstandard methods employed to execute projects (Figure 15.1).

Apart from nonstandard methods, lack of clear specifications of work products also plays a major role in variability from one project to another [2]. Suppose the requirement says the application should have a search facility for available flights for a certain city on a given date and time. This problem can be modeled in many different ways. Again, how this functionality is going to be implemented may not be clear to the software architect initially. So in the initial estimate, he can give a rough figure. Only when the design is actually to be made, the actual implementation becomes clear and the software architect can provide an accurate estimate. Similarly, integration of different modules is a tricky affair. Estimation for effort required for integration is mostly a guess. Many issues arise when integration is actually done. Effort estimation techniques like function point analysis (FPA), wideband Delphi technique (WBD), COCOMO, etc., try to provide effort estimation but none of them have good accuracy. At most, they help in making a rough estimate.

Many details at the beginning of the project are not clear. They become clear only after a few iterations over specific project tasks. The requirements themselves start changing over the project execution and they make the baseline project plan totally irrelevant. The project manager has to

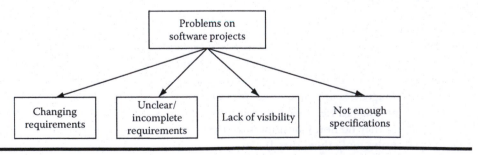

Figure 15.1   Problems on software projects.

incorporate necessary changes in project tasks due to these changes in requirements and adjust his project plan accordingly [3].

It is not obvious how to design from given requirements even if they are written in the best way. Even if the design is good, it is not obvious how to construct the application. Due to lack of clarity, the development team resorts to iterations. Iterations make the project plan vulnerable and the initial project plan becomes invalid, and the project manager has to make adjustments in project plan to accommodate these iterations.

15.3 Solutions for Problems in Software Projects

To make software projects more amenable to predictable results and better control, the most potent tool is to use software engineering methods on the project as much as possible. Consistent process modeling across varied projects will ensure consistency in quality, cost, and schedule. A well-defined process model will ensure good visibility in the entire life cycle of product development. Quality assurance methods built into the process model will ensure that both process and work products can be measured at frequent intervals during the entire project execution cycle. Once you can measure process and work products accurately, you will be able to manage them better.

When you want to make a product feature, characteristics of the feature should be well known. Suppose you are making a warehouse application. In reality, physical warehouses are of different sizes, used for different purposes, are located at different distances from certain places, and have many other specific characteristics. When a warehouse is represented in a software application, the size of the software product should be well known from exact requirement specifications given by the customer. This will freeze the volume of work to be done. This product part can be made in a certain number of ways. Specific programming language, specific platform, and specific architecture can be employed to make this product. Again this will give an accurate volume of work to be performed. The people who will be doing this work have a certain level of experience and skills. So the productivity factor can be determined from this fact. Productivity and size can provide an accurate estimate for total effort required for the project. In such a scenario, everything in the project is measurable and so can be managed with ease.

This kind of standardization on projects is possible in the future, and can totally eliminate uncertainty from the project. This is where software engineering comes in. Software engineering ensures that software projects and the tasks associated with them can be accurately scheduled. Thus, a perfect project plan can be accurately made and executed. Currently, however, it is a bit difficult as standardization of software development processes is still in its infancy. However, definitely it is evolving fast and in the not so distant future, it will become a reality.

As can be imagined, software projects have three components to be managed: quality, schedule, and budget. The major components of costs in software development projects are the human resources. This cost component can be controlled and reduced by efficient utilization of time of the involved team members. Once project size and project team productivity are measured and can be treated, almost fixed, once the team is formed, the schedule will be very well known. Before the project team is formed, it can be tweaked by selecting a balanced team for the project. Tasks that are critical and impact the project the most should be manned by experienced and higher paid professionals. Tasks that are not so critical should be manned by people with lower experience and lower salary. These same factors will also influence budget for the project.

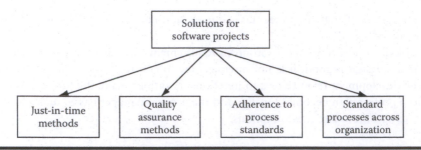

Figure 15.2   Solutions for problems on software projects.

The third dimension in software projects is quality. Software engineering helps here as well. When standard processes are strictly followed and all possible causes of errors are eliminated or reduced, software product quality will improve (Figure 15.2).

One more solution for software projects is to go the lean way. In other industries, lean and just-in-time concepts helped to overcome many problems including quality, inventory, costs, etc. On software projects, if we do not try to take the entire requirements and instead try to build the software product incrementally by taking a few requirements at a time, then the same benefits of just-in-time methods can be reaped here. More about these concepts are presented in the iterative and agile model of software development elsewhere in this book.

15.4 Standard Process for Software Projects

Any standard process can be applied to produce similar sized products/services that have similar characteristics. Let us suppose we have one software development project formed to make a software product having 100 KLOC (kilo lines of code), and we have another software development project formed to make a software product having 10,000 KLOC. Can the same standard process be applied for both projects?

The answer is yes and no.

The real answer lies in the details.

The waterfall model establishes a process framework of having firm phases in the development life cycle for software products. The phases include requirements, design, build, test, and release. This top level of process framework can be applied to all software development projects. What about other kinds of projects? In a typical maintenance project, the product life cycle could be reported as bug analysis, bug fixing, testing, bug closure, release, etc.

Similarly, the process for product development is different from that of application development. This is because software products are inherently different from software applications. Software products are characterized by frequent releases of the product at short intervals. Most software vendors have a minor release of their software every quarter and a major release on a yearly basis. In such an environment, iterative and incremental development model is far more suitable than a traditional waterfall model.

Due to these differences in processes, different process models were developed by standards creation organizations like SEI (Software Engineering Institute) at Carnegie Mellon University, ISO, IEEE, etc. On the other hand, for iterative and incremental development models like eXtreme Programming, Scrum, and cleanroom engineering were developed [4].

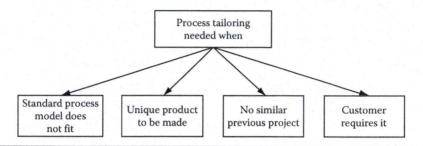

Figure 15.3   Process tailoring for software projects.

Given that project resources are limited, the project manager has to deliver the project within those limited resources. He has limited time, project team size, and budget. He has to optimize his resources to produce the best results from his project. Using standard processes may seem to increase his work. Although he may resist using those standard processes, it nevertheless ensures better quality.

15.4.1 Process Tailoring

Standard SDLC processes need not fit requirements of any specific project [5]. For instance, the project needs to be delivered over many iterations. These iterations are complete right from software requirements to software testing. This process is different from standard process of delivering the entire project, without any iterations involved and in a sequential manner. So how can a process model like CMMI be applied for this project? Clearly in this case, an iterative development model would be more appropriate. Now suppose we need to develop a software product for a customer where we strongly feel that instead of developing the software from scratch, we should take an existing open source software product and customize it per customer requirements. This kind of project definitely will not fit any of the standard development models. So how can we choose a model for this project? (Figure 15.3). By tailoring the process! More information about process tailoring can be found in Chapter 16.

15.5 Standard Process across Software Projects

For most organizations, each software project is a stand-alone affair. There is no connection between one project and the other even if the two projects are executed one after another by the same project team, and that the two projects are almost identical. This was the scenario up to the 1990s. Many practitioners had observed that each project team was reinventing the wheel in executing these stand-alone projects. So, even though reusable components were on one hand, being developed based on these projects to prevent reinventing the wheel in building a software system, the project management practice on the other hand was never benefiting from the lessons learned from previously executed projects.

This scenario is still true for many in-house projects, and even on a few outsourced ones. But some people started seeing the light at the end of the tunnel and realized that if lessons learned from previously executed projects can be applied to new projects, a large improvement is possible on these new projects in terms of gains in productivity.

For small projects consisting of a few people and lasting for a few months, informal project management without a process model, is fine. Since complexity is low and not many people are

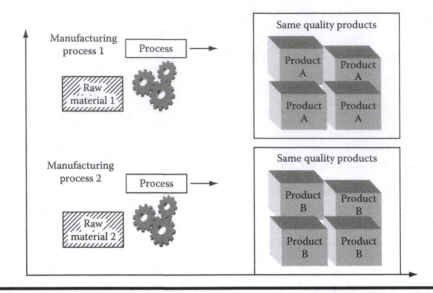

Figure 15.4 **Manufacturing processes and products with same quality from same process.**

involved in such projects, error due to communication gaps is not there. But on large modern day projects, complexity and size is considerable. Many people will be involved and will work on the project for several months, if not several years. Management of such projects will also have many layers. At such engagements, error due to communication gaps is inevitable. If informal methods for doing work are employed, chances of error are even higher.

Apart from errors there is one more dimension to project management. How does one ensure that a software product being produced out of these projects has the same consistent quality project after project? Due to differences in management styles, knowledge and experience of team members, environment factors, etc., quality of one project is very different from the other [6].

Let us take an example from manufacturing and compare it with software projects.

In manufacturing, when raw material is processed in sequence (e.g., assembly line), we get products with the same quality. Similarly, from another assembly line, different kinds of products of the same quality are produced. Coming to software projects, a service provider can set up many software development models and process software projects. In our example (see Figure 15.4), we have two process models, CMMI and rational unified process (RUP). All projects that are processed using CMMI will produce software products with the same quality. Similarly, all projects which are processed using RUP will produce software products of similar quality to each other (Figure 15.5). This is how consistent quality across all projects is achieved.

Some of the benefits of using standard processes across projects are

1. Better quality
2. Opportunity to use metrics data from previously executed projects
3. Same quality across projects
4. Opportunity to use shared resources
5. Less effort as learning from one project can be applied to other projects
6. Making software project management more science than art

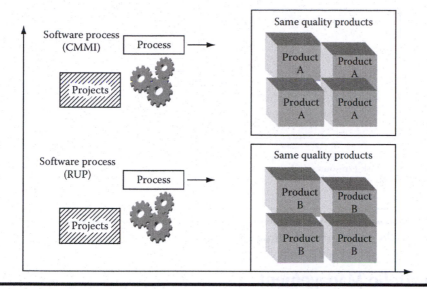

Figure 15.5 Software development processes and products of the same quality from the same process for many projects.

15.6 Program Management

Program management deals with managing a group of projects at a higher level and using shared resources and common management practices so that all the projects under the same program management can be managed effectively with fewer resources, and lower costs. At the same time, program management also helps in meeting some set objectives for an organization.

How does program management fit into the overall organizational objectives?

One of the problems in a project-based organization is that resource utilization cannot be achieved 100%. In environments such as manufacturing where the process is continuous, resources (like machines, man power, etc.) are used 100% without any problems. But projects are not necessarily continuous. A project is started, executed, and finally closed. When a project starts, it needs resources until it gets finished. The moment it gets finished, all the resources it was using need to be released. Now resources are of two types. One is consumable and another is fixed. Fixed resources include machinery and human resources. So when a project completes, human resources and machinery become idle. They must be utilized on another project or the organization that owns them or they will lose their capital (in terms of salary for human resources, depreciation for machinery), since these resources will not be doing any productive work which can bring revenues. At the same time, on one project, not all resources are employed for the entire duration of the project. They may be assigned to tasks, and when that task gets completed then they are no longer needed on that project (see Figure 15.6).

These resources must be assigned to other projects so that they do not sit idle. One of the topmost objectives of any program management is to strive to achieve resource utilization close to 100%.

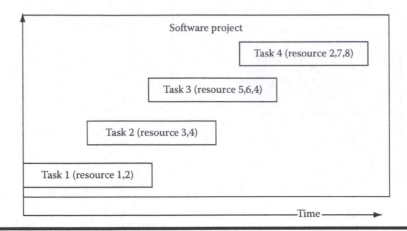

Figure 15.6   Tasks and associated resources on a project.

15.7 Portfolio Management

Portfolio management concerns itself with the objective of maximizing returns from the collection of projects, in a portfolio. They work in the same way as mutual fund portfolios. A mutual fund invests money into many stocks and bonds in such a way that the return on the invested money is the maximum possible, and at the same time as it is looking to minimize the risks. Some of the stocks and bonds have high return potential with higher risks, whereas some other stocks and bonds have a much lower return potential but have a very low risk as well. Based on research, the portfolio manager decides how much of the money from the mutual fund should be invested in high risk–high growth potential stocks and how much in low risk–low return potential stocks. This balanced approach ensures a good return on money invested with much lower risks (Figure 15.7).

On similar terms, a project portfolio determines how to make an approach so that from a portfolio of projects, maximum returns can be achieved with the lowest possible risks. A portfolio of projects may contain some low risk–low return projects, some medium risk–medium return projects, and some high risk–high return projects. An organization should create a strategy by which it can decide how many low risk–low return, medium risk–medium return, and high risk–high return projects should be taken in the portfolio, so that the objective of maximum returns can be achieved with minimum risks.

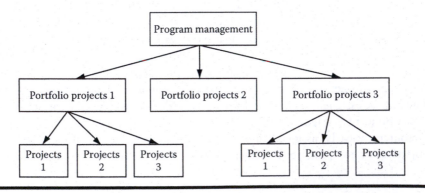

Figure 15.7   Portfolio management.

15.8 Statistical Process Control on Software Projects

Sometime back, in a paper titled "Is Statistical Process Control Applicable to Software Development Processes?" [7] Bob Raczynski had argued that measuring software development processes and using statistical process control (SPC) is not useful. Bob argued that since software development processes involve intellectual but prone to error inputs, in the form of coding done by human beings, SPC processes cannot be applied. SPC processes are better suited for mass manufacturing, where the same process steps can be repeated again and again with the same inputs. In such cases, if any variation occurs in quality of output, then the root cause of the quality problem can be immediately traced using SPC.

I beg to differ with Bob. I have accepted that software development is a labor intensive activity, and any human activity is prone to errors. I have also accepted that in such environments, it is difficult to implement SPC methods. Still, the fact remains that human activity can be measured and compared in a controlled environment. That is why we have different hourly pay rates for different people. Highly skilled people get higher hourly rates and low skilled people get lower hourly rates. Definitely, higher paid people have better output than lower paid people. So a person's quality of output is measurable. Similarly when a task is assigned to a person with his known ability, the quality of output can be anticipated in advance. This is especially true in environments where process standards are implemented successfully and people work in a predictable environment.

As mentioned in Section 15.3, through software engineering techniques it is possible to reasonably quantify project tasks. Project size can be measured and estimated, and productivity can also be found out. Although some elements of subjectivity may still persist in these estimates, SPC helps in making better estimates for size and productivity as it further eliminates subjective elements. Using project data from previously executed projects, estimates can be improved.

SPC data is also useful for quality control. How many defects were found in a similar sized project and how much effort was required in finding and fixing those bugs, gives a good idea for the coming project to estimate time and resources required for achieving a certain quality level.

It is also a fact that software development activities are creative activities. When creativity is involved, it is difficult to apply a standard process framework. Measured output is also difficult. On the other hand, providing a totally free-for-all environment results in unpredictable output. The goal of any project is to provide a measurable output during and after project execution. Using a standard process can ensure that a measurable and predictable output can be achieved and ensures starting, progress, and closure of any activity in a controlled manner.

Once we start thinking in terms of measurable output on projects, we are getting closer to comparing project activities to manufacturing activities. And when we are dealing with thousands of projects going on at a development center of outsourcing companies, we start treating projects on a mass scale. When that happens, uniqueness of projects starts fading and a mass projects environment starts taking shape. See what is happening to other services. Take for example, a call center. Using shared resources and standard processes and methods, it is possible to provide good call center services to customers at very low prices, and yet with much better quality. When software development projects are executed at such a mass scale, we see the possibility of introducing "mass servicing" concepts for these projects. It provides benefits like shared resources, high level of productivity, provisions to access highly skilled resources, expert services, etc., at one place.

So, we are observing that software projects are no longer viewed as projects in the traditional sense. They are evolving more like mass services. This trend is helping customers to reduce software development projects costs, substantially. The more that software development projects become similar to mass services, the more they will become cheaper. It is exactly what happened when manufacturing turned into mass manufacturing, a long time ago.

15.9 Cost of Nonstandard Processes

Many project managers and team members resist in complying with standard processes [8]. They feel it makes them work more and they try to adopt shortcuts. By doing so, are they doing any good? Suppose a customer requirement change has arrived. Without consulting all people down the line, the architect makes changes in the design. The project manager makes no further effort to properly document the changes made by the architect. So now, the architect is working on a different version of the requirement and the coding team is working on a different one (because they have a copy of the design that was made for the earlier version). Somehow the coding team gets to know that they are working on a wrong requirement version. By the time they realize this, they have already lost a good number of man hours working on the wrong version.

Consider another example. A requirement change comes and the project manager thinks changing the design may increase the work to be done. He decides a quick fix in coding can do the job. So he gets this quick fix done by the coding staff. Of course he and his team purposefully forget to document this change (documenting may have added a few extra hours). Now, when a new requirement change request comes, nobody knows exactly what changes were done in the previous build of the software. After incorporation of this changed requirement, the team inadvertently will be introducing defects in the software.

Again suppose the project manager decides to take a shortcut by not going through design, and incorporates new requirement changes directly into the code. The changed features are not reflected in the design documents but are there in codes. Similarly, due to a time crunch, the project manager cuts short testing of the application and ships it without proper testing.

As long as there are not many changes in the project plan, noncompliance with standard processes is manageable. But the moment there are changes everywhere, the downstream processes get affected. Without proper documentation and absence of process for change control, chances of error increase. The larger the project, the greater is the risk of defects entering into the product. They are one of the biggest risks any project can face. Given the nature of software projects, requirements get changed often, especially with iterations. So it is very important that proper documentation and process are followed.

15.10 Organization Training

The software industry is always in flux; it is always changing. Furthermore, the rate of change is increasing. What used to be a cutting-edge technology just yesterday is today obsolete. What is considered today as advanced technology will become stale tomorrow. Fifty years ago, if somebody learned a trade, it would help him to earn livelihood for life. Today, if a software professional learns a programming tool, he will have to relearn a new programming tool tomorrow, as the old one becomes obsolete. This constantly changing technology has necessitated retraining for new tools and technologies so that all professionals' skills are current.

In this scenario, any software development/maintenance organization must keep retraining its staff so that they have current skills and thus can work on software projects without any problems [9].

15.11 Software Project Abandonment

Sometimes due to various reasons, a software development project may not be completed and may have to be abandoned. Reasons for such decisions could be many, but the most important reasons include cost overrun, schedule overrun, lack of technological expertise, change in need of the organization, organization closure, etc. Some external factors could be a change in political circumstances, war, civil unrest, natural calamity, etc.

In some other instances, the project could be completed, but the project may have failed on many counts. The project could have a schedule overrun, cost overrun, less than expected number of features, poor quality, etc. In fact it is estimated that more than 70% of all software projects fail on some account or an other [10].

Nevertheless, the success rate of software projects is improving. The biggest factor contributing to this fact is the increase in maturity level of software development/maintenance processes. Increase in maturity level of software engineering and software project management is definitely a factor which will help in keeping up the increasing success rate of software projects. Mature software development processes help in reducing risks of schedule, cost overrun, and poor product quality.

15.12 Defect Prevention

During software testing many software defects can be detected and subsequently rectified [11]. What is the cost of defect removal in software testing? Is there any alternative way to produce quality software products with an acceptable number of defects at a lesser cost?

Research has shown that defect prevention during design and coding is cheaper than defect detection and removal during software testing. Why is it so? How can any software development organization take advantage of the information stated previously?

Let us study it. Suppose, during design some defects were introduced in the software design due to faulty blueprint. This faulty design was used and coding was done. Since the design was faulty, naturally the coding will also have faults. This scenario will be similar to the process depicted in Figure 15.8 where an already defective part is being further processed to produce a defective part.

For instance, suppose we have a module for tax calculation that has two components. One component calculates federal government tax and another component calculates tax for the state. Depending on the state, the tax rate is different from that of another state. In the design, this fact was not taken into account, even by mistake. Now coding was done with this faulty design. So coding also has the defect that a flat state tax is being calculated for all states. Due to faulty coding, the rounding of decimal places was wrong. The end result is that the application has some defects. How many defects do we have now?

This information can now be found either during testing or when the application is deployed and used by end users. But first of all, let us see how many defects were introduced in the application. Suppose the state tax calculation is used at 100 places in the application. So we have 100

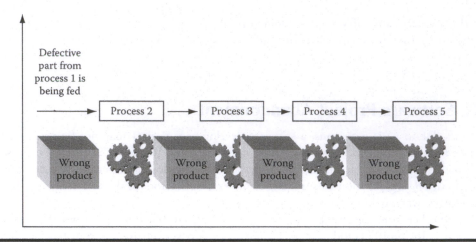

Figure 15.8 Input defective part is being processed to produce a defective part.

defects from the faulty design. Now suppose the decimal rounding is used at 200 places in the application including doing the sum of taxes (federal and state). In total we have 300 defects in the application.

Now let us analyze the cost impact in different scenarios (Table 15.1).

There are two scenarios when we consider the defect at the design stage. In first case, the design defect is caught during design review stage and is fixed there so that this defect does not enter the coding stage. In another scenario, the design defect is not caught and the entire coding is done based on a faulty design. The defect was caught in testing and so now not only design is to be changed but the coding is also to be changed. So the coding hours are also lost. In design review the defect could have been caught within 2 h. But instead the design defect entered into coding and so depending on the language and code reuse, a certain amount of coding hours are lost. If the tax calculation component was developed using any object oriented language and the code was reused throughout the application then may be 20 h of coding hours are lost. But if code reuse was not implemented or any procedural language used, then chances are that all of 200 h of coding are lost (100 defects to be fixed at 2 h per defect fixing). Coming to the coding defect, since the defect is at 200 places and it takes 3 h to fix each defect, it will require 600 h to fix all these coding defects. Compared to these costly scenarios, if the defects were caught at the point

Table 15.1 Defect Cost Analysis

Stage	No. of Defects	Defect Multiplication	Time Required for Fixing (h)	Hourly Billing Rate	Cost of Fixing ($)
Design defects	1		2	100	200
Coding defects due to design defects	100	100	200	60	12,000
Coding defects	1		3	60	180
Coding defects into testing	200	200	600	60	36,000

of origin of the defects, the fixing could have been achieved at a fraction of these costs. Even if it would have taken some extra hours in conducting inspections, then those few hours could have been spent well, in view of saving time and costs at downstream activities.

The moral of the story is that defect prevention is the best policy in software development projects. The earlier the defect is caught in the development life cycle, the better.

That is why defect prevention is an integral part of software development projects. Defect prevention is implemented using software engineering techniques.

15.13 Software Project without Process

In software industry parlance, there is a term called "jumping to the code". On many software development projects, the project teams start coding the moment they get the requirements. The management at these places also thinks that making a project and process plan is a waste of time. Steve McConnell, of Construx Software and the author of such books as *Code Complete* and *Rapid Development: Taming Wild Software Schedules* argues that on many projects, jumping to the code creates more rework and quality issues than it lets the project team do some productive work. On many such projects, the actual schedule overruns by as much as 1500% with associated cost overruns. These kinds of projects are characterized by more firefighting than anything else.

Here is a case study which shows how the lack of a well-defined process standard can severely affect software projects.

Suppose a company realized that it was losing market share due to its obsolete technology infrastructure. The root cause was that the order fulfillment cycle was taking more than 2 days compared to the average of 1 day for the competitors. It was due to the fact that arranging trucks and loading them from their warehouses was taking more than 10 h on average compared to an average of 3 h for the competitors. This was happening because the warehouse application was not integrated with their transportation management system. A team was formed to study and present recommendations for improving the situation. After their study, the team suggested that the two applications should be integrated seamlessly so that information from the transportation system would be available to the warehousing system whereby the warehouses would have advance information about available trucks and what kind of content can be loaded on these trucks. Using this information, they can plan for truck loading and intimate the same to logistics service providers who supply trucks.

A software development team was formed with the task of integrating these applications. They analyzed the interfaces of the two applications and started work on integration. After 2 months of the start of their work, the MIS manager asked the project manager to submit a status report on the project. The project manager submitted a report saying that the project would be completed 1 month late because of difficulty faced by the team in understanding the interfaces for integration. The MIS manager, in turn, called for a status review meeting and asked the project team to discuss the issues on the project. In the meeting, the MIS manager realized that the project will not be completed even within 1 month of delay as the team still lacked understanding of the tasks involved. Next day after the meeting, the MIS manager met the CIO of the company and informed him about the situation. The CIO then decided to scrap the project and decided to hire a specialist service provider that was a expert on integration work. Later, the service provider team was able to do integration within 3 weeks.

During his study on why the project failed in the first place, the CIO found that his MIS team failed because they were not following a standard process. Everything done by the team was on ad hoc basis. The team lacked skills on specialized tasks like integration, and so a plan should have been made first to train the team for the associated skills. Only then they should have started working on their tasks. He also found out that the project manager had not included a quality review process in his project plan. Without sticking to quality control at each stage of the project, it is impossible to achieve worthwhile quality at the end of the project.

The CIO published his findings on the company intranet and later set up a process control group at the MIS level whose task was to ensure each project would incorporate quality control as well as adherence to standard processes.

So we see that if any project is executed without a standard process then there are risks of project failures in terms of quality, costs, and schedules.

15.14 Process Improvement

One of the goals of CMMI standards is to select and deploy incremental, innovative improvements that measurably improve the organization's processes and technologies [12]. How an organization is currently using processes to execute projects and how performance on these projects can be improved further is a continuous process that needs to be measured, analyzed, and corrective actions taken. This will help in improving productivity and quality further, which in turn will result in increased customer satisfaction and reduced costs of operations.

Some techniques that can provide substantial gains include peer reviews, code inspections, automation, and standard templates (Figure 15.9).

Process improvement is the most important aspect of implementing software process models. The CMM model has a maturity level of 5 when companies reach optimization level. At this level, companies have a separate software engineering process group (SEPG) that not only oversees implementation and observation of follow-up of process standards on projects, but also keeps looking for opportunities to improve processes further. Whenever they find that some process can be improved, it makes a plan of implementing an improved process on projects. It develops the new process model and then chooses an appropriate project to pilot it. The project is then executed with this new process model. Results of that project are analyzed and assessed to determine if the project benefited from the new improved process model. If it does then this new process model is applied to all projects that get executed with the same base model.

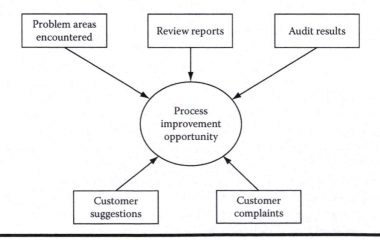

Figure 15.9   Process improvement opportunities.

15.15 Final Word

Any person or organization can learn a new thing in two ways. It can either do trial and error or use past experience (both success and failure) to learn. If the person or organization is always resorting to trial and error, then it can be said that it is not learning from past experience. Most people learn through experience. As they age, they have ample experience to cope with even difficult situations in life. This is because they apply the learning they have gained in the past to deal with the current situation. Sadly in context of organizations, past experience is often not applied to deal with new challenges. In software services companies, they may have executed hundreds of projects in the past but when a new project arrives, they reinvent the wheel in planning and executing this project (not using the experience of past projects). They simply do not apply the past learning. In effect, they resort to trial and error for dealing with a new situation.

If these companies want to improve, then repeatable process techniques (in form of software development process standards) is extremely useful. For using statistical methods, data from past projects is saved in a repository. When a new project arrives, past data can be retrieved and put to use. For instance, effort and cost estimates for a new project can be calculated using the data from similar past projects.

This is true for most activities that are similar to past projects. If some task that is totally different from past projects arrives, in those cases, statistical methods will not work. In such cases, the project is to be treated like a research and development project and should be executed accordingly.

Review Questions

15.1 Discuss if quality processes alone can produce a quality product.
15.2 What is the difference between process quality and product quality?
15.3 Name some of the standards for software development projects.
15.4 What are the costs of nonstandard processes in software development projects?
15.5 What kinds of processes are involved in any software development project?
15.6 What factors contribute to software development/maintenance project abandonment?
15.7 What can be done to avoid project abandonment?

Recommended Readings

1. K. Ewusi-Mensah (2003) *Software Development Failures: Anatomy of Abandoned Projects*, MIT Press, Cambridge, MA.
2. H. Fujita, M. Mejri (2005) *New Trends in Software Methodologies*, IOS, Amsterdam, The Netherlands.
3. M. Wiener (2006) *Critical Success Factors of Offshore Software Development Projects*, Springer, London, U.K.
4. T. Li (2008) *An Approach to Modelling Software Evolution Processes*, Springer, Berlin, Germany.
5. R. Conradi (2006) *Software Process Improvement: Results and Experience from the Field*, Springer, Berlin, Germany.
6. J. T. Marchewka (2006) *Information Technology Project Management*, Wiley, New York.
7. S. H. Kan (2003) *Metrics and Models in Software Quality Engineering*, Addison-Wesley, Boston, MA.
8. B. Meyer, M. Joseph (2007) *Software Engineering Approaches for Offshore and Outsourced Development Projects*, Springer, Berlin, Germany.

9. S. Datta (2007) *Metric-Driven Enterprise Software Development: Effectively Meeting Evolving Needs*, J. Ross Publishing, Fort Lauderdale, FL.

10. J. McManus (2004) *Risk Management in Software Development Projects*, Butterworth-Heinemann, Oxford, U.K.

11. D. Huizinga, A. Kolawa (2007) *Automated Defect Prevention: Best Practices in Software Management*, Wiley, Hoboken, NJ.

12. E. McGuire (1999) *Software Process Improvement: Concepts and Practices*, Idea Group Inc, Hershey, PA.

Chapter 16

Software Process Standards and Process Improvement

In the previous chapter, we learned

- What is software engineering management?
- How are statistical process control techniques useful for software projects?
- What are the benefits of the standard process model implemented across the organization?

In this chapter, we will learn

- What are the major process standard models for software development?
- What are the major process improvement models?
- What is a process improvement life cycle?
- How does process improvement help on software projects?

16.1 Introduction

Software product development for large software products, especially belonging to governments or global corporations, needs highly structured project management methodologies. The size of these projects is in excess of 1 million lines of code. They require software development teams in excess of 50 or more professionals. Sometimes the team size could be in excess of 500 professionals. In fact, to manage such large numbers, the product itself is broken down into many product components and the project team is divided into many smaller project teams; each team is responsible for the development of one product component.

An informal and unstructured approach to manage such large teams is impossible. To manage such large sized teams, a structured and well-defined process and project management is a must [1]. The entire process should also be very formal. A formal, rigid, and structured approach prevents chances of miscommunication and errors.

To facilitate such structures, organizations like the ISO, IEEE, and Software Engineering Institute at Carnegie Mellon University developed many process standards. These process standards define what process steps must be followed during planning and execution of projects. They also define how to keep improving the process so that better product quality and process productivity can be achieved continuously.

On the other hand, on many projects, agility is required to take care of changing business requirements so that the software product being built takes these changes into its design instantly, and fulfills the purpose for which it is being built. This concept is in direct contrast to the formal and rigid approach of plan driven methodology.

Any software project has to adjust itself between these two extremes. Depending on the requirements, it can be a purely plan driven project, a rather agile one, or something in between.

16.2 CMMI Standards

The Software Engineering Institute (SEI) at Carnegie Mellon University has been engaged in doing pioneering work related to software engineering for more than two decades. It has been developing standards for software engineering. These standards have been helping software services and products companies to develop, maintain, and operate software systems in an economical manner. But their more important objective is to help companies in producing software products and applications with extremely high quality.

Over the years, they have developed many standards. Some of their popular standards include the CMM (Capability Maturity Model), PCMM (People Capability Maturity Model), SECM (Systems Engineering Capability Model), etc. With the passage of time, these standards were modified or discontinued as market conditions changed as well as due to increasing maturity of developing and maintaining software products and systems; processes of doing these activities also changed.

Creation of separate process models for different aspects of product development or maintenance resulted in some problems for companies adopting these standards. For instance, when a software product was being developed, a CMM was used. When the product was released and went into production, SECM was followed. So the software vendor had to keep developing and maintaining two separate models for its processes.

Adopting, refining, and maturing any single process model is a Herculean task. It not only involves hiring experts and outside consultants for benchmarking and then certifying processes, but it also involves management commitment and demands a deep involvement of all employees of the organization. It requires everybody to change the way they do their jobs. Change management is one of the most difficult tasks in any organization.

One more consideration that goes against having more than one process is that of keeping two teams for doing similar work. When any bug fixes are required in the maintenance of a software product, a separate development team will do the fixing. Keeping two teams doing almost the same job is costly. On the other hand, if only one team is doing both development and maintenance, then the team will have to follow two processes, which is very difficult. It may lead to quality and productivity issues.

To overcome these things, a single process definition was conceptualized which can be applied across all processes of software development, maintenance, and integration. SEI released CMMI (Capability Maturity Model Integration) to provide a single platform of processes for all kinds of activities related to software development, integration, and maintenance [2].

In this book we will follow conventions as stipulated in CMMI standards.

16.2.1 CMMI Standards in a Nutshell

The CMMI process model is divided into two parts: CMMI-DEV and CMMI-ACQ. CMMI-DEV is for organizations that either develop and maintain their own software products or applications or outsource it to service providers. CMMI-ACQ is for service providers. Both parts have the same high-level process model so that they are compatible with each other. SEI is also developing a version of CMMI for services (CMMI-Services).

Each of these parts is divided into the main process area categories of process management, project management, support, and acquisition. The process-management process provides details as to how any organization can refine and improve its processes within the organization that will be doing the outsourced project. This aspect of CMMI standards differs from standards developed by other agencies like ISO or IEEE. These agencies develop standards that are more at project level and not at organization level.

Process areas inside the project management category include project planning (PP), project monitoring and control (PPC), integrated project management (IPM), requirements management (REQM), and risk management (RSKM).

Process areas inside the acquisition category include solicitation and supplier agreement development (SSAD), agreement management (AM), acquisition requirements development (ARD), acquisition technical management (ATM), acquisition verification (AVER), and acquisition validation (AVAL).

Process areas inside the support category include configuration management (CM), decision analysis and resolution (DAR), measurement and analysis (MA), and process and product quality assurance (PPQA).

These categories of processes in CMMI are divided horizontally. CMMI is also divided vertically in the form of maturity or capability levels. Any company looking to certify its processes needs to certify certain processes in a phased manner, over time. In staged implementation, certification is done for a single maturity level instead of multiple maturity levels. They should get to level 1 from level 0 by certifying processes so that many of its processes can be performed using some ad hoc measures. If any company wants to improve its processes from level 1 to level 2 then it should be able to demonstrate that its processes can be managed. At level 3, it should have its processes well-defined. At level 4, its processes should be improved using statistical processes' methods. At level 4, its processes should also be repeatable. At level 5, its processes should be optimized.

At level 2, "requirement management," "project planning," "project monitoring and control," "supplier agreement management," "measurement analysis," "process and product quality assurance," and "configuration management" processes should be certified. At level 3, "requirements development," "technical solution," "product integration," "verification," "validation," "organization process focus," "organization process definition + IPPD," "organization training," "integrated

Table 16.1 CMMI Standards in a Nutshell

Process Area	SDLC Phase	Management Area	Features
Organizational innovation and deployment	All	Organization management	Project process change
Organizational process definition + IPPD	All	Organization management	Project process definitions
Organizational process focus	All	Organization management	Identify key process areas at project level to modify
Organization process performance	All	Organization management	Evaluate changed project process areas for performance
Organization training	All	Organization management	Identify key process areas for training staff
Project monitoring and control	All	Project management	Monitor and control project to keep project on track
Project planning	All	Project management	Make sound project plan
Process and product quality assurance	All	Project management	Use SPC methods and process compliance for both process and product quality
Quantitative project management	All	Project management	Use SPC methods to monitor and control project
Risk management	All	Project management	Define and mitigate risks on projects
Supplier agreement management	Any	Project management	Manage suppliers effectively
Causal analysis and resolution	Any	Project management	Risk and issue mitigation and project control
Integrated project management + IPPD	All	Project management	Collaboration of all disciplines
Measurement analysis	Any	Project management	Taking process and product measurements
Configuration management	All	Project management	Change management
Decision analysis and resolution	Any	Project management	Project control
Requirements development	Software requirements	Product life-cycle management	Use standard defined processes for requirement development

project management + IPPD," "risk management," and "decision analysis and resolution" areas need to be certified. At level 4, "organization process performance," and "quantitative project management" areas need to be certified. At level 5, "organization innovation and deployment," and "causal analysis and resolution" areas need to be certified.

In Table 16.1 we can see that out of 21 process areas, 5 areas are defined for a software development life cycle, 11 areas for project management, and 5 areas for organization processes. So clearly there is a strong process focus on improving organizational processes that help in delivering consistent product quality across projects.

16.3 ISO Standards

ISO (International Organization for Standards) develops standards for certifying business processes [3]. This approach is a fundamental shift from the traditional approach of certifying only end products or services for quality. In fact, ISO standards do not make any standards for certifying end products or services at all. They believe if any product or service is produced/delivered using a standard process, then quality of that product/service will be high. On the contrary, if no process or bad process is applied to produce/deliver any product/service, then quality of the produced/delivered product/service will be most likely bad.

ISO standards are very abstract because the top-level standards are meant to be applied to just any kind of organization engaged in manufacturing or providing services or any kind of business. At a very detailed level, these standards are branched out. So specific detailed standards apply to organizations operating in specific industries. For each standard there are specific requirements. When any organization applies for certifications, they are audited first for top-level requirements and then for specific detail level requirements.

For organizations involved in providing software related services, the detail level requirements relate to the way software services are performed.

16.3.1 ISO Standards in a Nutshell

If you study ISO standards, you will see that most emphasis is given on project management. The other emphasis is given on process quality. It is believed that by achieving process quality we can automatically achieve product quality. Though this is debatable, it is quite clear that without process quality, product quality cannot be achieved (Table 16.2).

16.4 IEEE Standards

IEEE is a global organization developing, maintaining, and publishing standards for many areas related to software development, maintenance, and operation. They also have the goal to make computer science and computer engineering recognized disciplines, similar to the status enjoyed by other science and engineering disciplines, like electrical engineering, mechanical engineering, physics, etc. They believe computer science and computer engineering currently are in a prescience and preengineering stage, and will evolve to become fully legitimate disciplines in the near future. They have also advocated that computer science and computer engineering are two separate disciplines and should be separate from each other to help them evolve.

Table 16.2   ISO Standards in a Nutshell

Section	Process Area	SDLC/Project Area	Features
Section 1	Introduction	Project management	General usage guidelines
Section 2	Implementation approach	Project management	Approach for implementation
Section 3	Definitions	Project management	Definitions of terms used in the guide
Section 4	Systemic and resource requirements	Project management	Resource requirements planning for software and hardware resources
Section 5	Quality planning and control	Project management	Quality planning and control
Section 6	Resource requirements for quality control	Project management	Resource requirements planning for quality control
Section 7	Software life-cycle processes		
Section 7.1	Product realization	Product planning	Product planning
Section 7.2	Customer priorities	Software requirements	Software requirements
Section 7.3		Software design, construction testing	Software design, construction and testing
Section 7.4		Supplier management	Supplier management
Section 7.5		Software build and release	Software build and release
Section 7.6		Project monitoring	Project monitoring
Section 8	Remedial measures	Project control	Project control

To make these disciplines fully legitimate disciplines and professions the IEEE Computer Society has formed joint committees with organizations such as ACM and the Open Group. They have taken following initiatives to achieve their goal:

1. Help, advocate, and initiate start of professional education system.
2. Help in accreditation of professional education programs.
3. Help in skills development mechanisms for professionals entering the practice.
4. Help in creation of certification for professionals administered by the profession.
5. Advocate licensing of professionals administered by government authorities.

6. Help in creation of professional development programs to maintain currency of knowledge and skills.
7. Help in creation of code of ethics.
8. Help in creation of professional societies.

The IEEE Computer Society is also developing a body of knowledge for the computer engineering profession. It is known as SWEBOK (Software Engineering Body of Knowledge).

16.4.1 IEEE Standards in a Nutshell

IEEE standards are focused toward using standard processes and tools to achieve project excellence and make software projects successful. Apart from guidelines for process compliance, IEEE also addresses key issues and practical considerations which arise on software projects. Apart from process definitions for SLDC phases, it also provides guidelines for supporting processes like configuration management; software engineering (project planning/control); process and product quality; methods and tools; and related disciplines like mathematics, computer science, etc., which are needed to execute software projects (Table 16.3).

16.5 Rational Unified Process

When things do not work at extremes, then a middle ground is sought. This is how you can describe Rational Unified Process (RUP). RUP has a linear structure like waterfall models as well as iterative steps like those in agile methods. When Grady Booch, James Rumbaugh, and Ivar Jacobson worked together and merged their own theories to form a unified process model at Rational Corporation (later IBM Corporation), they had one thing in mind: remove the bottlenecks from the waterfall model and make a framework that will allow smooth software development, even if uncertainties exist in the development process. The model allowed linear progression for straightforward tasks that are crystal clear. For not so clear tasks, the model advocated iterations so that clarity can be achieved and tasks can be completed over many iterations. The model is a matrix, where project phases of inception, elaboration, construction, and deployment are pitted against the disciplines of business modeling, requirements, analysis and design, implementation, and test and deployment. There are three supporting engineering disciplines of configuration management, project management, and environment management. Later the RUP model was modified to include production maintenance.

16.5.1 RUP in a Nutshell

Table 16.4 depicts the important aspects of RUP.

16.6 Agile Methodologies

You can easily discern the difference between manufacturing and engineering if you can visualize a car assembly line and a sea bridge. Agile methodologies in manufacturing and in software development are entirely different concepts. Whereas in manufacturing, agile methods were introduced to reduce inventory costs and to improve product quality. In the software industry,

Table 16.3 IEEE Standards in a Nutshell

Process Area	SDLC Phase	Management Area	Features
Software requirements	Software requirements	Project management	Requirement elicitation, development, validation, management
Software design	Software design	Project management	Key issues, structure and architecture
Software construction	Software construction	Project management	Managing activities, practical considerations
Software testing	Software testing	Project management	Test levels, test strategy, verification, validation, practical considerations
Software maintenance	Software maintenance	Project management	Maintenance method, cost economics, practical considerations
Software configuration management		Project management	
Software engineering management		Project management/ organizational management	Project planning and control, review and evaluation
Software engineering process		Project management/ organization management	Process change management, process assessment, measurement
Software engineering tools and methods		Project management	Tools for requirements, design, construction, testing, maintenance, methods for all SDLC processes
Software quality		Project management/ organization management	Quality management, practical considerations
Knowledge areas of the related		Project management	

Table 16.4   RUP in a Nutshell

Process Area (Workflow)	SDLC Phase (RUP Phase)	Management Area	Features (Artifacts, etc.)
Business modeling	Inception	Project management	
Requirements	Inception	Project management	Requirement specification document
Analysis and design	Elaboration	Project management	Use cases, activity diagrams
Implementation	Construction	Project management	Source code, source code documentation
Test	Transition and all other phases	Project management	Test strategy, defect log
Deployment	Transition and all other phases	Project management	User and system manuals, user training
Operations and support	Production and all other phases	Program management	Maintenance plans, bug list
Configuration and change control	All phases	Project management	Artifact versions, software code versions
Management environment	All phases	Program management	Process improvement documents, project support tools and methods
Project management	All phases	Project management	Project plans, status reports
Infrastructure management	All phases	Program management	Process improvement documents for operations, project support tools and methods for operations

agile methods were introduced to deal with uncertainties and subsequent change requests in software requirements. One point is common in the agile concept at both places. While agile methods in manufacturing ensure smooth operations by controlling inventory intake, agile methods in software development ensure smooth project progress by controlling requirement intake. That is the crux of the existence of agile models for software development.

Extreme programming is the perfect example of extreme agility. It only takes a handful of requirements at a time and delivers a fully functional product by developing the product only for these requirements. When an iteration is complete, another batch of requirements is taken in the next iteration. Extreme programming introduced some noticeable concepts in software development like test-driven development, pair programming, story boards, etc. The Scrum model is similar to extreme programming in that only a handful of requirements are taken to develop a fully functional product to meet these requirements. Scrum introduced concepts like requirement log, scrum master, product owner, etc.

16.6.1 Extreme Programming in a Nutshell (Table 16.5)

Table 16.5   Extreme Programming in a Nutshell

Process Area	SDLC Phase	Management Area	Features (Artifacts, etc.)
Pair programming	Construction	Project management	
Planning game	All	Project management	Release planning, iteration planning
Test driven development	Construction, test	Project management	Unit tests, source code
Whole team concept	All	Project management	Customer is a team member
Continuous integration refactoring	Construction	Project management	Central and single code repository
	Design	Project management	Improving design
Small releases	All	Project management	Lower risk
Coding standards	Construction	Project management	Maintainable code
Collective code ownership	Construction	Project management	Anybody can change code
Simple design	Design	Project management	Maintainable design
System metaphor	Requirements	Project management	One requirement at a time
Sustainable pace	All	Project management	Avoid overloading resources

16.7 Test Process Improvement Techniques

All the major software process standards are meant to help software projects in all aspects of the project. They provide a process model so that a specific software development life cycle can be established. They provide a mechanism so that software development process can be improved (for increasing productivity and quality).

There are also some process improvement models which have been devised exclusively to improve the testing part of the software projects. Some of the techniques that have been devised over the years include Test Maturity Model (TMM), Critical Test Process (CTP), Test Process Improvement (TPI), and Systematic Test and Evaluation Process (STEP).

There have also been efforts made by people and organizations to devise mechanisms for process improvement that are not specific to the software industry, but in fact they are generic in approach and thus can be applied to any industry. One of the most famous of these techniques is Deming's PDCA approach.

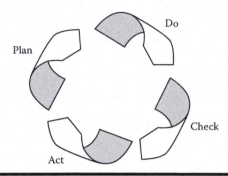

Figure 16.1   Deming's PDCA process improvement cycle.

16.7.1 Deming's PDCA Technique

The earliest process improvement concept can be traced back to Deming's Plan, Do, Check and Act (PDCA) model, which was a general purpose method. It can be applied by anybody who wants to improve his or the organization's processes. It is cyclical in nature, and so its scope is continuous.

The quality of a software product can be achieved either by doing quality control of the product (by means of thorough testing the product for quality), or by observing development processes rigorously as well as improving them so that quality of the software product is improved. In other words, instead of keeping focus on the quality of the product, improving the process that creates the software product will improve quality of the software product. The ISO standard model for software development is based solely on this assumption. Other process models also stress this fact (Figure 16.1).

16.7.2 Test Maturity Model

SEI-CMU has a CMM process model for software development. Test Maturity Model (TMM) was developed to complement CMM as it lacked a maturity model for software testing. TMM has a five level process for improving testing processes that correspond to the five levels of CMM (Figure 16.2).

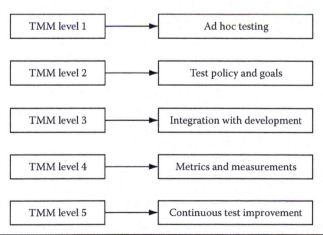

Figure 16.2   TMM levels and process definition.

16.7.2.1 Level 1: Initial Level

An organization can be placed at level 1 if its testing functions are immature. Testing function is considered to be secondary to software development and testing is carried out after the software is developed. There is no planning for testing and all testing on the project is done on an ad hoc basis.

16.7.2.2 Level 2: Definition

An organization can reach level 2 in the TMM when the testing function can be organized by means of setting of a testing policy and a goal. The company is also able to make a testing plan and can employ basic testing techniques and methods.

16.7.2.3 Level 3: Integration

An organization reaches level 3 when it can create a distinct testing function on a software development project. At this level, an organization is able to integrate this distinct testing function with the development function. The testing life cycle will include a testing function complete with its own methods, processes, and standards.

16.7.2.4 Level 4: Management and Measurement

At level 4, an organization can effectively measure all testing processes and methods. Managing anything requires that it should be measured first. If measurement is not possible, then it cannot be managed. Thus, when any organization reaches level 4 in TMM, its testing processes can be effectively measured and thus managed.

16.7.2.5 Level 5: Optimize

At level 5, an organization will be able to improve its processes to cut costs and improve quality by evolving its processes beyond the current status. At this stage, an organization will be able to reduce defects in the software product by implementing a comprehensive quality assurance policy during the entire software development life cycle.

16.7.2.6 Further Developments in TMM

In the TMM, goals and subgoals are defined for each level of maturity. An organization must be able to achieve these goals to reach to that level. The goals are allocated to roles of manager, developer/tester, and customer/user. People assigned to these roles must achieve their own set of goals as defined in the TMM level for a particular level.

After the advent of CMMI (Capability Maturity Model Integration) by SEI-CMU, the TMMi (Test Maturity Model integration) model was developed, which replaced the TMM. The TMM was meant only for software development projects and not for software maintenance projects. TMMi is aimed to work both for software development as well as for software maintenance projects.

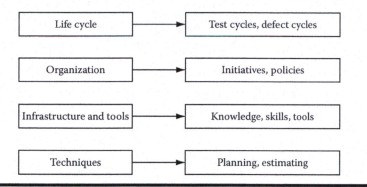

Figure 16.3   TPI process definition—key areas, subareas, and associated cornerstones.

16.7.3 Test Process Improvement

TMM is essentially a staged model. The maturity of an organization is improved through stages that correspond to levels of the model. The TPI (Test Process Improvement) model is, in contrast, a continuous model where the test function is improved not through stages or levels but rather through a continuous approach (Figure 16.3).

TPI has a set of four key areas, and a successful implementation of this model is achieved when the corresponding cornerstones are achieved. These key areas and their associated cornerstones include life cycle, organization, infrastructure and tools, and techniques. When an evaluation of an organization is done for implementing the TPI process model, each of these key areas are assessed on a scale of A–D, A being the lowest rank. If any key area is not mature enough to be given even a low value of A, then that key area is not given any marks at all. Again, not all areas can be given the full rating of D or even a C. They may be restricted to be given marks only up to B. Some such areas include estimating and planning (under techniques key area).

When scoring is done for each key area and its subareas, the scores should also be linked to each other. So if one area is related to another, a high score in the former and a low score in the latter cannot be done. It is because performance in one area will be directly or indirectly influenced or related to the performance in the other area.

In a nutshell, TPI is a process reference model. Once a process model is assessed then it can be classified on a scale of controlled, efficient, or optimizing rating. The optimizing rating means the most mature process model, and controlled rating means the process model that can be managed and process measurements can be taken. An efficient rating lies between these two ratings.

16.7.4 Critical Testing Process

Critical Testing Process (CTP) assumes that only some, not all, activities on a test function are critical. If these critical activities can be measured, controlled, and managed, then the entire testing function can be managed well. This concept is very different from other process models in that other process models stress managing the entire test function. This process model works on the same concept as defined by the Pareto method, which says 20% of the software product parts contain 80% of defects and doing exhaustive testing of this 20% area will improve software quality tremendously.

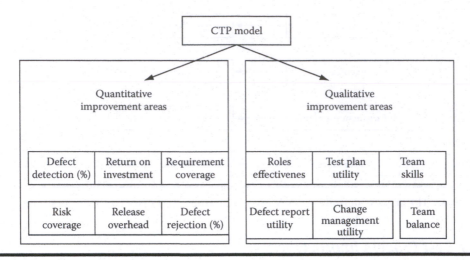

Figure 16.4   CTP process model.

The CTP model is a content reference model. A context specific tailoring of the process model is needed to make any improvement in the existing model. The tailoring consists of identification of any challenges, recognition of attributes of any good processes, and selection of the order and importance of implementation of process improvements. During process assessment, strong and weak process areas are identified. Based on the assessment, a list of process areas to be improved is prepared and prioritized. The priority areas are marked per organization needs. During the CTP assessment, some typical quantitative areas examined include defect detection percent, return on investment on testing function, requirement coverage, risk coverage, test release overhead, and defect report rejection rate. Some qualitative areas include test team role and effectiveness, test plan utility, test team skills (in testing, domain knowledge, technology), defect report utility, test result report utility, change management utility, and balance (Figure 16.4).

A plan is prepared to improve all the weak areas identified in the assessment. The CTP itself makes generic suggestions for improvements in those areas. But to make the implementation effective, the implementation team should better tailor the suggested recommendation to suit the needs of the organization.

16.7.5 Systematic Test and Evaluation Process

STEP (Systematic Test and Evaluation Process) is similar in its approach to that of CTP; STEP is a content reference model and not a process reference model. The implementation team can implement the process improvement project in any order or priority of process areas. This concept is different from the TMM model where the organization seeking TMM implementation must implement it in process areas in the order specified by the TMM model.

This model recommends that a testing process should have certain specific characteristics. These characteristics include a requirement based testing strategy. Testing should start at the beginning of the software development life cycle. Test cases are used as requirements and usage models. Testware design is the basis for software design. Defects are detected at their origin and should be removed at that point. Defects are systematically analyzed, testers and developers work together on defects.

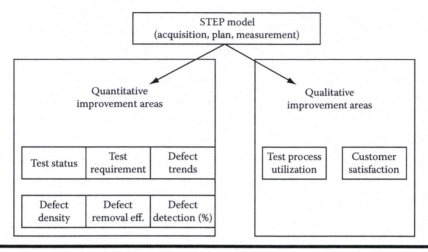

Figure 16.5 STEP process model.

The STEP model is a complementary process that works with agile methodologies of software development like Scrum and eXtreme Programming. The software development life cycle starts by making test cases that form the basis for requirements. The source code development starts with writing code to validate these test cases. This approach is known as test-driven development (Figure 16.5).

In the STEP model, three areas of testing are focused for improvement: planning, acquisition, and measurement. An interview across the organization is arranged to assess qualitative improvement, and quantitative improvement is sought from measured metrics. The quantitative metrics include test status over time, test requirements, defect trends including detection, severity and clustering, defect density, defect removal effectiveness, defect detection percentage, defect life cycle, and cost of testing. Qualitative metrics include defined test process utilization, and customer satisfaction.

16.7.6 Process Improvement Life Cycle

When we strive for process improvement, we need to start with a launching pad. Process standard models provide this launching pad. Process improvements cannot be done in a big bang approach. Every new approach should be first tested on a pilot basis, and when the results are found satisfactory, then the new approach can be applied across the board on all projects.

Any process improvement strategy can be implemented using some basic steps (Figure 16.6).

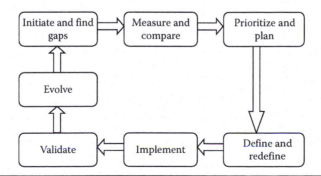

Figure 16.6 Steps for implementing process improvement.

The entire exercise is taken as a project. At the beginning of the project, the initiative is taken to start the process improvement project. The stakeholders make their commitment for the project and a team is formed of outside consultants and process champions sourced from the organization. First, they compare the existing process model with the standard model and find and record all deviations (and gaps) that exist. The project team then starts making stocks and measurements of attributes of existing processes. Once measurements are taken, they are compared with the standard values for attributes of processes as defined in the standard process model that is being implemented. At the end of this exercise, the project team is able to make a list of process areas that need improvement and new process areas that are to be introduced. The project team then finds which of the areas (that need improvement) has more importance compared to others and assigns higher priority to these high importance areas. Then it can make a project plan to implement the changes in the process model based on these priorities. It will define process design for the new process areas to be introduced and redefine design for process areas that need to be improved. This exercise will create a roadmap for implementing the improved process model. Once this roadmap of implementation is ready, it can be implemented on a pilot basis. Results from this pilot study can be validated. If the results are good, then the process model can be implemented organization wide.

This exercise of process improvement is in general a continuous approach. Once a new and improved process model is working fine, this model can be further improved by evolving it. The same cycle of process improvement done previously can be repeated to get more benefits from further process improvements.

16.8 Process Standard Certifications

If an organization certifies its processes with any of the major certification organizations like IEEE, ISO, SEI-CMU, etc., then they get various kinds of benefits, some of them obvious and some of them not so obvious. Let us see some of the benefits here.

16.8.1 Benefits of Certification

All of the major certifications provide a framework and a systematic approach to managing business processes to produce a product/service that conforms to customer expectations [4]. If a supplier (software services provider) has certified its processes to any of these standards, then its customers can be assured that the products or services shipped by them will have a certain level of quality. This creates a comfort level for customers in doing business with its supplier.

There are many benefits to these certifications:

- These certifications help in improving business processes and thus savings in operation costs.
- These certifications help in improving business processes waste/scrap reducing, and improving product quality.
- These certifications are used by many corporations as a marketing tool, as they help to bag projects from customers. Many customers make it mandatory for its suppliers to have this certification.
- Many countries impose certification on exporters so that their product/services have a certain level of quality.

16.8.2 How to Apply for a Certification

To become certified, a business must develop a quality system that meets the requirements specified by the standard for which it has approached, for certification in the area and product for which the kind of products or services the organization produces/delivers [5]. Once the organization quality system has been documented and implemented, the organization must invite an accredited external auditor to evaluate the effectiveness of their system. If the auditor determines that the quality system meets all certification requirements, they will certify the system.

16.8.2.1 Certification Requirements

1. A supported language for documenting quality practices
2. A system to track and manage evidence that these practices are being followed in the organization
3. An independent audit to assess and certify compliance

16.8.2.2 Time and Cost of Certification

There are many advantages to these certifications, but certification process is time consuming and costly. It can take anywhere from 6 to 18 months to document business operations. Then it may take another 1–3 months to verify actual operations. So in total, it can take from 7 to 21 months for the certification process, depending on the size of the organization and complexity of the business processes.

The certification process may cost anywhere from $10,000 to $20,000 in the form of consultant fees and fees for certification registration. Apart from fees, additional costs include the time that has to be spent by the employees in the whole process.

16.8.3 Future of Certifications

Most certification agencies work with governments to help them adopt standards so that products/services produced/delivered by government bodies have good quality. These agencies keep developing new standards for software development, software services, software products. Most of the time they are developing hardware/software interface standards for many new devices as well as their delivery.

Review Questions

16.1 Do CMMI standards support iterative software development?

16.2 How are SDLC processes supported in CMMI?

16.3 How are ISO standards different compared to other standards like CMM or IEEE?

16.4 Do IEEE standards support iterative software development?

16.5 Describe the STEP process. What are the main components of this process?

16.6 What are the major areas of Deming's PDCA process?

16.7 Describe the TMM process.

Recommended Readings

1. P. Rook (1990) *Software Reliability Handbook*, Springer, New York.
2. M. B. Chrissis, M. Konrad, S. Shrum (2003) *CMMI: Guidelines for Process Integration and Product Improvement*, Addison-Wesley, Reading, MA.
3. R. W. Miller (2004) *Managing Software for Growth: Without Fear, Control, and the Manufacturing Mindset*, Addison-Wesley, Reading, MA.
4. D. F. Rico (2004) *ROI of Software Process Improvement: Metrics for Project Managers*, J. Ross Publishing, Boca Raton, FL
5. L. Batten (2008) *CMMI 100 Success Secrets*, Emereo Pty. Ltd., Singapore.

Chapter 17

Process Selection

In the previous chapter, we learned

- What are the major process standard models for software development?
- What are the major process improvement models?
- What is a process improvement life cycle?

In this chapter, we will learn

- What are the differences between plan driven and agile software development?
- What are the strengths and weaknesses of plan-driven software development?
- What are the strengths and weaknesses of agile software development?
- What are the best practices for a software life cycle?
- How is the best model for software development chosen?

17.1 Introduction

The traditional waterfall model (also known as plan driven), as a software development life cycle, has been criticized for issues like high risk, long time in delivery, heavy upfront commitment, and inflexiblity [1]. Although the waterfall model has positive attributes and is extremely useful for large projects, organizations and individuals have been in search of alternative approaches for software development that can help in mitigating the negative aspects. Rational Corporation introduced such an alternative with its Unified Process Model for software development projects. Similarly, other popular approaches like Scrum [2], eXtreme Programming [3], Cleanroom

Software Engineering [4], Microsoft Solutions Framework, Oracle Unified Method, etc., have offered different life-cycle models to overcome the shortcomings of the waterfall model.

Today agile and waterfall model camps both claim they are better than the other. Who is right and who is wrong?

17.2 History of Plan-Driven Model

Any work undertaken as a project must have some purpose, stated or otherwise. The work must have a start date and an end date. If not a firm end date then a probable one may do. How much it will cost (probable cost) should also be known at the beginning. What exactly will be the result of this work should also be stated. The stakeholders, ensure these things are known in advance. They also should know status of goings on during execution of the software project at regular intervals so that they know that things are going smoothly or not (Figure 17.1).

When the size of a software project is large and may consume a considerable amount of time and money, the stakeholders will have to pay considerable attention to most details about the project. If this project is failing in any of the parameters mentioned so far (start date, end date, project cost, project reports, project results, etc.) then the stakeholders will be in trouble as they have large stakes in the success of the project. For this reason, the stakeholders evaluate the project carefully before sanctioning it to make sure that the risk to start the project is worthwhile. In the early days of computers and software, hardware used to cost many times more than the software. So stakeholders paid more attention to hardware purchases and little attention to software. So software projects were easily sanctioned, even when the software project team's credentials were not convincing enough. So in those days, software projects used to get delayed, or cost more than planned, etc., due to little attention from stakeholders. Slowly, due to advancement in technology, the computer hardware started becoming cheaper while software costs remained the same. Thus, while the cost of hardware to software in early days was in the ratio of 100:1, now it has completely reversed, it is now 1:100. So stakeholders today pay a lot of attention to software costs and do not think twice about hardware costs.

Now, the software project teams have to continuously provide justification for every dollar spent to the stakeholders showing their worth. Moreover, they have no option but to increase their productivity and quality of work, consistently, to keep their jobs. Stakeholders also started demanding visibility in the project so that they can know what is going on at any given time, so that they may monitor progress. They started demanding a complete picture of the project including a firm end date, cost, and product quality before sanctioning the project. The software industry responded by implementing process standards, which could help in answering

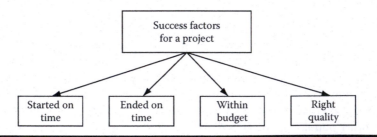

Figure 17.1 Success factors for a project.

the questions of the stakeholders. The earliest models were the pure waterfall models. The waterfall model had some shortcomings and so some refined waterfall models were developed in later years.

When the stakeholders started having business models that were changing frequently, they started asking the software industry to shrink the project duration, even if it meant higher costs. The software industry in response came up with concurrent and parallel engineering methods of software development so that the schedules could be collapsed and development cycles could be reduced.

After analysis of hundreds of projects, many standards development organizations came up with process standards. Some of them include CMM, CMMI, ISO, IEEE-SWEBOK, etc. These standards come with a promise that if they are implemented, the software development processes will be repeatable, predictable, matured, and will have the ability to improve processes continuously, so that product quality and process productivity can be improved.

17.3 Strengths of Plan-Driven Model

Plan-driven or waterfall models have many strengths [5]. The entire software project can be planned before work is even started on the project. Each phase of the project is well-defined and all processes involved have firm start date and end dates. Each process also has well-defined relationship with other processes (Figure 17.2).

This allows for a preview of the entire project. The effort and cost estimate is provided at the beginning of the project so that the stakeholders can decide if they want to proceed or not, depending on the kind of expected project budget.

17.4 Limitations of Plan-Driven Model

In the plan-driven model, a working software product is available only after the complete development life cycle is executed. That means if a project for building a software product is of 1 year duration, the software product is available only after one year. For the entire year, the stakeholders have no idea if the software product is being built correctly or not. Suppose the project took a year for completion. After one year, the stakeholders see the software product and find that it is not suitable for them, then the entire effort wasted along with the money spent on the project. This is the single major risk in waterfall models (Figure 17.3).

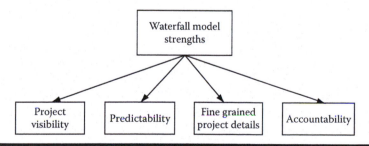

Figure 17.2   Strengths of waterfall model.

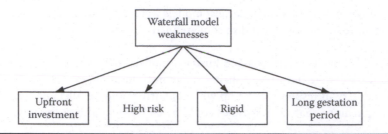

Figure 17.3   Weaknesses of waterfall model.

The second weakness of the waterfall model is that once the project plan is fixed, no changes are allowed. This means that the software requirements cannot be changed. But, in practice, due to various reasons, software requirements need to be changed many times during project execution. If the software requirements are permitted to be changed, then the issue of rework arises. Many parts of the already made software design and construction may need to be changed and thus a lot of rework emerges. Rework causes project schedule and budget to increase from planned figures. The escalated project schedule and budget then becomes a nightmare for stakeholders.

17.5 History of Agile Methods

During the 1990s, Grady Booch, James Rumbaugh, and Ivar Jacobson had separately developed some models for managing different parts of software life cycle [6]. Rational Corporation (IBM) invited them to work on a project to make a complete model for managing the entire software life cycle. This life cycle tried to eliminate all the problems associated with waterfall models. It contained provisions for iterations, for tasks which are not very clear and need revision more than once. This is the first time that concept of iterations for project tasks was conceived. Later, many agile models were put forth by people and organizations who tried to solve some problems related to software development models and came with good solutions in the end. Some of these models include Scrum, eXtreme Programming, Oracle AIM, etc.

The crux of all these agile models is the concept that software development is a complex undertaking and it can be best achieved using iterations. In the initial iteration, only the tasks which are well-defined and well understood are taken in the project, and undefined or not so well defined tasks are left for subsequent iterations. Over time, when these tasks are well understood, they are taken in an iteration and worked on.

17.6 Strengths of Agile Methods

For most of the software development industry in the early days, projects never had any formal methods to develop software products [7]. Everything was done on an ad hoc basis. This resulted in schedule and cost creep and bad product quality. Then after the famous software crisis of the 1970s, the waterfall software development model was evolved. This model was further refined and some variants were developed. Unfortunately, these rigid formal models also did not have much success. Then came agile methods. Agile methods introduced some formal methods that ensured the software projects could be handled and managed so that these problems could be resolved.

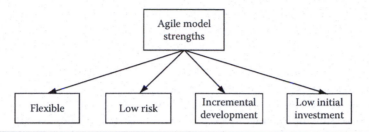

Figure 17.4   Strengths of agile model.

A basic cause of problems associated with software projects is unclear or changed requirements or unclear software design. In such situations, a very formal and rigid method is not successful for project management. Agile methods tackle this problem, by allowing the project to begin with only a small set of requirements. Whenever changes in requirements are needed, the project allows incorporating those changes. Thus, the fundamental flaw in software project management is removed with agile methods (Figure 17.4).

Agile methods are really great for one more very important aspect about software products. They allow for incrementally building software products. Instead of going for a big bang approach, software vendors can develop their products incrementally. In fact, since 2000 onward, most software vendors have taken this approach, as it provides flexibility and risk mitigation. They keep doing market surveys to know which kinds of features customers are looking for. Based on the results of these surveys, they decide to develop and then add the features that are in demand. This approach saves them a lot of money by not investing it in developing and adding product features which are not in demand.

17.7 Limitations of Agile Methods

Agile methods are great for time- and material-based projects as well as for incrementally developed products [8]. However, here is a list of their shortcomings (Figure 17.5).

Size: It is difficult to increase team size beyond 20 people or so, if the situation warrants. It is because agile methodology demands that the communication among team members should be a face to face affair rather than through the written word. This obviously constrains the team size.

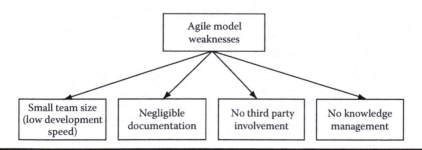

Figure 17.5   Limitations of agile model.

Offshoring: Mode of communication again constrains options of availing benefits of offshoring. Offshoring requires an elaborate framework of communication so that onshore and offshore teams can communicate effectively. But agile methods do not permit such a mode of communication.

Documentation: Projects based on agile methods produce bare minimum documentation. For scenarios where contracts need to have transactions documented, lack of documentation creates a problem. In any case, good documentation provides a means to audit a project. If documentation is missing then it is difficult to audit a project. This means that if failure occurs, it is difficult to trace the root cause of the problem. Similarly, if any project is a success, it is difficult to find the success factors in the absence of documentation.

Third party involvement: A third party can never get involved on a project if there is not enough documentation. Third parties can get involved on projects for many reasons. The most obvious reason is that a project is done not by just one project team. In most cases, a bigger project is split into many smaller projects and each of these is done by a different project team. In many industries, this is how projects are done. Then why should it be different for software projects?

Close ended: Everything on a project is done by a small cohesive and tightly integrated team in agile projects. This makes it impossible to contract a part of the project work to a third party service provider.

Knowledge management: All the lessons learned and knowledge gained on a project is left only in the brains of the team members. There is no way this information can be shared outside the project team. When a person leaves the organization, there is no way the knowledge gained by him can be retailed in the organization.

17.8 Once and for All

From all the discussion, one thing is final: One size does not fit all! While some process methods may suit a particular kind of project, some other process method may suit other kinds of projects. Even the so-called no process methodology may suit some kind of project, as evidenced by small projects, where trying to force a formal process method is no doubt a suicide attempt. If there are only one or two brains working, then there is simply no point in having an arrangement for well-defined documentation, quality process, etc.

For projects where 4–20 people are needed to be working on the project, agile methods fit the bill. Here some documentation and formal methods are adopted but they are not excessive. They work for projects where the amount of effort required is to produce a million lines of code per year, or less. They can employ anywhere from 5 to 20 people on the project. With some amount of process customization it is possible to scale them up. Even though they suit colocated project team environment, with process customization, they have also been successfully offshored. Agile (or iterative) methods suit well for projects where the software product does not need to be developed at an extremely fast pace (e.g., employing more than 50 people to complete it faster than say employing only 20 people). Using any of the agile methods, the maximum size of the product that can be developed over a period of 1 year is 500,000 SLOC (source lines of code). For larger products, the development effort can span several years (Table 17.1).

For even larger projects where 20–100 people need to work on a project, Rational Unified Process model, Unified Process model, Oracle Process model, or some other well known process model can

Table 17.1 Software Development Process Selection Decision Chart

Requirements	Appropriate Methodology
Large project size	Waterfall
Unclear requirements	Iterative/agile
Rapid development projects	Waterfall with concurrent engineering
Outsourced projects	Waterfall/modified agile
COTS implementation projects	Waterfall/agile (depending on size and speed)
SaaS implementation projects	Waterfall/agile (depending on size and speed)
Open source projects	Waterfall/agile (depending on size and speed)
Mid sized projects	Rational unified process
Knowledge management requirements	Waterfall model
Process improvement requirements	Waterfall/modified angle
Same process across organization	Waterfall/modified angle
Statistical process control requirement	Waterfall/modified angle

be used. These projects can run from a few months to few years. They typically produce software products ranging from 500,000 to 2,000,000 SLOC per year. In an open source or SOA environment, the product size could be even bigger and the project can run longer. Sometimes these projects run for more than 10 years.

Apart from size and speed of development considerations, one more factor is vital in appropriate process selection. It deals with the fact that not all of the project information is available at the beginning of the project. For instance, if in a project the features of the product to be made are largely unknown, then it is extremely difficult to gauge the size of the project. In such a situation, the project team will be in a fix to find out the appropriate process, team size, and project duration and cost. In such a situation, it will be best to take a slow and cautionary approach instead of a big bang approach. Agile methods are the best when it comes to taking a cautionary approach. The waterfall model and its variants fit right at the other end, where a big bang approach is needed. In the middle of the road are the processes that provide take best of both worlds. They have iterations, but they can also take all of the requirements at one go and make a complete product instead of making small pieces of the product in successive iterations. The iterations used here are for refinement, and they are different from those found in extreme agile methods. In extreme agile methods, the iterations are complete. Each iteration runs from requirements to release cycle. In contrast, in the middle of the road approach, iterations run only to remove defects that were injected in the previous iteration. So we can have two iterations for the requirements phase, three iterations for the design phase, and so on.

When we speak of software engineering at the process level (and not at the project level), we are usually concerned with things like process improvement, increasing productivity, and increasing quality. At the same time we also imply decreasing variability, increasing visibility, and collapsing project schedules. When we analyze the way we do things under an agile methodology, we realize that there are not many of these aims built in the agile methodology. In contrast, plan-driven methodologies always strive to have these goals. So from this perspective, plan-driven methodologies outscore agile methodologies.

The bottom line is that the best approach, when it comes to process selection for any project, depends on many factors. Of course there is one more dimension to process selection for software projects. All these goals of process improvement, productivity improvement, quality improvement, etc., work only in environments where we have a pool of many projects. And these pools are available mostly with large service providers. Internal IT departments and small service providers mostly execute a small number of projects at any given time. In these environments, it is difficult to implement these strategies due to their small size operations. Thus, agile methods suit them better.

An incremental software development model suits software vendors that make software products in anticipation of market demand. The market demand dictates which software features they should develop so that they will be able to add them in their core software product. Here the agile methodology comes to the rescue, as it allows the software vendor to build and then add the required software features instead of wasting time and resources on developing something that is not wanted by the markets.

17.9 Best Practices for Process Selection

Most people in the software industry know that contracts for software development projects are of two types: fixed cost/fixed schedule and time and material based [9]. If both the customer and the software developer know exactly what software is to be developed with a clear project scope (i.e., complete knowledge of requirements) at the beginning of the project, then a fixed cost/fixed schedule contract can be made. But if many project details are not clear at the outset, then time- and material-based contracts are most suitable. Thus a plan-driven project methodology is best suited for fixed cost/fixed schedule contracts and agile methodology is best suited for time- and material-based contracts. From this perspective, selection of a process model based on size of the product does not arise. A decision is best made from the perspective of clarity of scope of the project.

Agile methods are good when project clarity can be at best described as subdued and not crystal clear. Due to their nature of working, these agile methods are not suitable for product development where the product is supposed to be large and where a large team needs to be deployed to it so it can be developed fast. Parallel and concurrent development is needed in such cases. On the other hand,

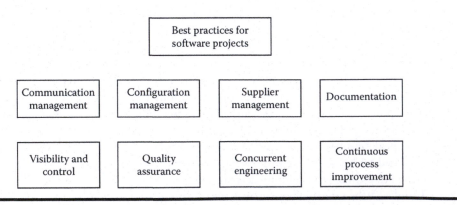

Figure 17.6 Best practices for software projects.

projects adopting methodologies like CMMI, ISO, or IEEE tend to be highly so structured that sometimes the heavy structure stifles product development (Figure 17.6).

There could be a middle road somewhere that can permit a plan-driven approach with the flexibility of agile methods, and where the best of both worlds can be taken and limitations from either approach (plan driven vs. agile) can be avoided. Such approaches are now possible. Many software vendors now customize agile methods and insert planning components in their customized models to make a hybrid model. On the other extreme, a waterfall model is customized to put iterations over tasks which need elaboration over many iterations due to lack of clarity.

It cannot be overemphasized if we say that there are some considerations to be thought of when selecting a process. We need to find out some of the best ways of doing things so that we come up with the best process for our needs. Regardless of the software development model chosen, here are some best practices available for many components of the project:

Communication: Communication is the most vital component of any large software project. If there are many teams located at many sites, then a good and effective medium of communication is a must so that each team can communicate with other team effectively and effortlessly. As Internet use has become widespread and offices are equipped with high bandwidth connections, using Internet-based communication media makes available to the project teams easy, affordable, and effective communication. Some of the communication media available currently include modern instant messengers and e-mails along with video conferencing, desktop sharing, virtual whiteboards, and some other media. All of these media can be easily used if teams are located at many different geographies.

Configuration management: A Web-based central configuration management system is the best option for distributed teams. It can enable storing and accessing of all documents, artifacts, code builds, and project documents to all distributed teams. Modern configuration management systems are highly secure and reliable. Having a centralized configuration management system for all teams makes sure that there is just one current version of each document, code build, and other project artifacts to deal with. In short, there should be only one version of the truth for the entire project.

Third party involvement: From cost and time to market and quality aspects, it is important that if any opportunity exists for availing services of third party service providers, the opportunity should be tapped instantly, even if it means hiring a service provider who is located at a different geographical location. A central configuration management along with modern communication channels will ensure that services of third parties can be obtained without many problems.

Documentation: A good approach to documentation must be provided so that different teams working on the same project will not have any difficulty in communicating and working with each other. Furthermore, it will also ensure that maintenance work after implementation of the software product can be done without much difficulty.

Predictability and visibility: A project plan will be made with most of known project details and some assumptions, wherever project details are not known. The project plan will be updated whenever project details for which assumptions were made become known. The assumptions will be replaced by the known details. This practice will ensure good predictability and visibility into the project.

Quality control: Quality control checks, in the form of reviews and inspections, should be inserted in each phase of the project to ensure only checked work products pass through to the next phase in the project. For each project phase, there should always be entry and exit criteria to ensure good quality of the work products.

Concurrent engineering: For large sized projects, if a short timeframe is desired (which is often the case), then concurrent engineering principles can be applied for project work so that many large teams can be deployed to do the project work, so that they can work simultaneously to collapse the project schedule.

Process improvement: Process improvement is vital from a business point of view. If at any organization, there is no process improvement program in place, after some time they will not be able to compete in the market as their costs will be high and quality will be low compared to their competition. For process improvement, a separate Software Quality Assurance (SQA) department should be in place to keep an eye to see if any existing project processes can be improved.

17.10 Converting Traditional to Agile Model

Suppose you are given a software development project and asked to use an agile model for development, instead of a traditional model. How can you do it?

Suppose you have broken down the application functionality into a set of three features. The corresponding work products in this case will be as follows:

Feature 1: requirement specification 1 → design specification 1 → construction model 1
Feature 2: requirement specification 2 → design specification 2 → construction model 2
Feature 3: requirement specification 3 → design specification 3 → construction model 3

In the traditional waterfall model, the development phases may resemble those depicted in Figure 17.7:

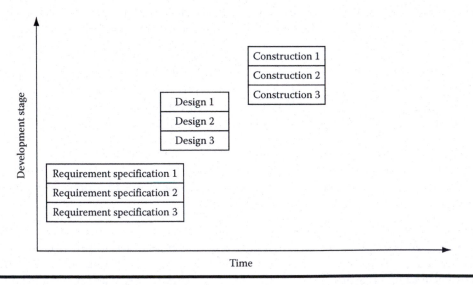

Figure 17.7 Development life cycle in waterfall model.

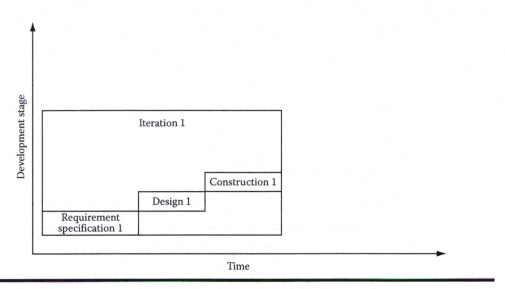

Figure 17.8   Development life cycle in agile model for iteration 1.

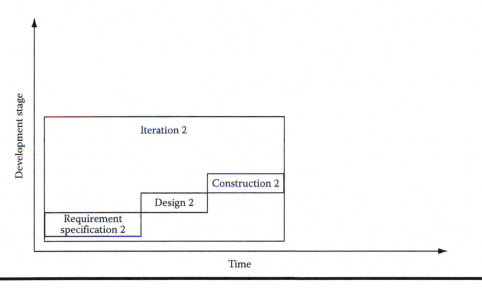

Figure 17.9   Development life cycle in agile model for iteration 2.

In this waterfall model, all features are taken at once and development means writing requirement specifications for all three features at the same time. Then design is also made for all three requirement specifications. Similarly, construction also begins simultaneously for all three features.

To convert the development to an agile model, however, we should take one feature at a time for development. In one full iteration, we will make requirement specification, design, and

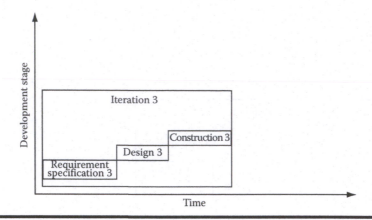

Figure 17.10   Development life cycle in agile model for iteration 3.

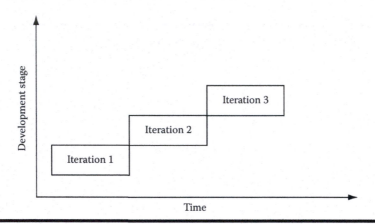

Figure 17.11   Development life cycle in agile model for complete product development.

construction for that feature. Once we finish the iteration, we can move onto the next iteration by taking the next feature. Finally, when all the features are developed, the project is complete (Figures 17.8 through 17.11).

Of course, only the development activities on the project are shown. There will be regular verification and validation activities during the development life cycle for quality assurance purposes.

17.11 Case Study

Here is a case study taken from a real example to show how an appropriate process selection can be made based on the business requirements.

When our SaaS software developer/service vendor decided to find the best process to develop its product, way back in 2003, there were many factors to be considered. Some of the major factors for consideration included

■ Tap benefits of offshoring (talent and lower costs of development)
■ Go for product development in such a way that it can win some customers even when the product is still being developed

- Fully functional product at early stage even with fewer features
- Flexible product development road map so that product features can be preponed/postponed as per market conditions
- Software development at a speed of 1,000,000 SLOC per annum

These were some of the requirements, which the vendor wanted to consider for an appropriate software development process selection. Agile methods (including Scrum, eXtreme Programming, etc.) are great for product development. But they could not be selected because of the need to engage offshore teams and speed of development (at best with an agile method, a speed of 50,000 SLOC could be achieved per annum). From a documentation point of view, agile methods were again not suitable as the vendor wanted to have good documentation for its products. Any variant of the waterfall model was out of question, because the vendor wanted to develop the product incrementally. They were using the Eclipse platform for software development. Luckily they had a solution available with the Eclipse platform itself. Eclipse has introduced a software development process model called Unified Process Model which is refined from the Rational Unified Process. This process model meets most of the requirements of the vendor. So they chose this as their software development process model.

Exercise

17.1 Discuss the rationale for selecting the development life cycle on any software project.

Review Questions

17.1 For a small project of size 2000 SLOC, which process model may suit the best and why?
17.2 What factors determine selection of a process model?
17.3 What are the benefits of a plan-driven (waterfall) model?
17.4 What are the benefits of an agile model?
17.5 What are the drawbacks of a plan-driven (waterfall) model?
17.6 What are the drawbacks of an agile model?

Recommended Readings

1. D. B. Yoffie (1997) *Competing in the Age of Digital Convergence*, Harward Business Press, Boston, MA.
2. G. Lenz, T. Moeller (2003) *NET: A Complete Development Cycle*, Addison-Wesley, Boston, MA.
3. K. Beck (2000) *Extreme Programming Explained: Embrace Change*, Addison-Wesley, Reading, MA.
4. J. F. Peters, W. Pedrycz (2003) *Software Engineering: An Engineering Approach*, Wiley, New York.
5. A. Jaaksi (1999) *Tried & True Object Development: Practical Approaches with UML*, Cambridge University Press, Cambridge, U.K.
6. J. Hunt (2006) *Agile Software Construction*, Springer, London, U.K.
7. M. Cohn (2004) *User Stories Applied: For Agile Software Development*, Addison-Wesley, Boston, MA.
8. D. J. Anderson (2004) *Agile Management for Software Engineering: Applying the Theory of Constraints*, Prentice Hall PTR, Upper Saddle River, NJ.
9. R. T. Futrell, D. F. Shafer, L. Shafer (2002) *Quality Software Project Management*, Prentice Hall PTR, Upper Saddle River, NJ.

PEOPLE MANAGEMENT

Chapter 18

Introduction to People Management

In Part IV, we will learn

- What is people management on software projects?
- How can team performance be improved on software projects?
- How should supplier management be done on software projects?
- How can customer expectation be effectively managed on software projects?

In this chapter, we will learn

- What is people management on software projects?
- What characteristics are required for successful software project management?
- How can software project managers effectively manage teams, suppliers, and customers?

18.1 Introduction

Projects, after all, are all about people. This is especially true in the case of software projects. More than 90% of software costs can be attributed to labor costs. Hardware and infrastructure costs pale in comparison to costs associated with salaries of software professionals.

Software development is a creative activity. Without creative inputs from project team members, no software system can be developed. Software skills are not easy to learn and practice.

At the same time, managing a software project is not easy. A typical software project manager needs many qualities that will enable him to manage the project. In this chapter, we discuss various qualities needed to become a successful project manager.

18.2 People Management

The internal project teams need to be constantly in touch with the business end users and understand their needs. They need to find ways so that the existing software systems used by them can be made more user friendly and thus increase productivity of end users with these systems. Whenever new projects come, they will be able to deliver it since they know the needs of the business end users. They also have to be constantly in touch with suppliers so that the suppliers understand the exact needs of end users and thus provide the right functionality in the software systems they are building. In a nutshell, the internal project team needs to have both technical expertise and good knowledge of business so that the software systems they build satisfy the needs of businesspeople.

On software projects, there are customers, suppliers, and project teams. People involved on software projects from each of these groups have to play different roles.

Suppliers (software service providers) are given service level agreements (SLAs). They need to stick closely to these SLAs. Successful suppliers not only deliver services based on these SLAs but in fact provide more value to their customers through the experience they have accumulated from executing past projects and delivering unmatched quality services. They continuously refine their processes and thus are able to cut delivery costs and schedules. They also certify their processes with CMMI, ISO, or IEEE certifications so that new customers have confidence in their delivery competence.

Customers need to specify exactly what they want from the software system. They need to arrange for the budget, steer the project in the right direction, and allocate people who will be end users of the proposed system to provide inputs for the requirements on which the software system will be built (Figure 18.1).

18.3 Team Management

How can you make sure that your team is performing well? Are you getting the right performance from your team? What should you do to better the performance of your team? These are questions that any project manager is always concerned with. After all it is his team that has to deliver the goods. They are the most important resources that he has at his disposal.

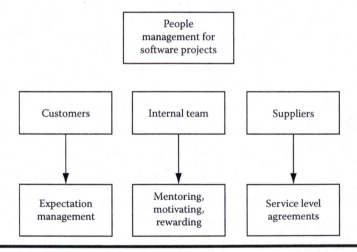

Figure 18.1 People management on software projects.

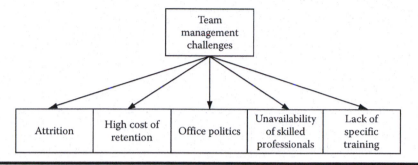

Figure 18.2 Team management challenges.

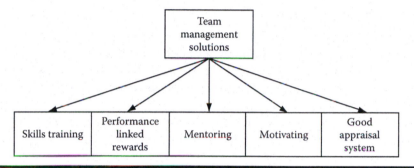

Figure 18.3 Solutions for team management challenges.

Good project managers recognize these aspects well. They constantly strive to improve team performance. They use modern management techniques, best practices that are available with process standards like ISO, CMMI, IEEE, etc., and the knowledge gained by their organization in executing past projects for constantly improving team performance. Some specific techniques for doing this include skills training, performance-linked rewards, and team mentoring (Figure 18.3).

Some of the biggest challenges faced by project managers are attrition, unavailability of IT professionals with the right skill set, and lack of training (Figure 18.2).

Team management is discussed in detail in Chapter 19.

18.4 Supplier Management

Software service suppliers have grown to become truly global players. Their success stems from the increasing need of software services by customers the world over. These software service suppliers have accurately recognized the needs of their customers and have come up with fitting solutions to fulfill these needs with innovative delivery models and by making constant efforts to improve their services (Figure 18.4).

Customers, on the other hand, have developed good mechanisms to effectively deal with their suppliers to get more and more value for the money spent. In Chapter 21, we will discuss organization structures, contract agreement methods, supplier communication management, and account management.

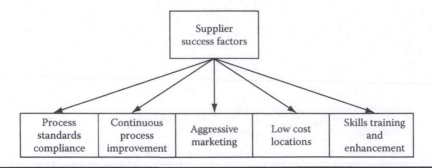

Figure 18.4   Success factors for software services suppliers.

18.5 Customer Management

How does one deal effectively with an internal or external customer? Different organizations have different software product needs. IT organizations must fulfill these needs; otherwise, their existence is at stake. They need to effectively meet customer expectations. If these expectations are based on some wrong notions, the project manager must convince the customer about the infeasibility of such a solution (Figure 18.5).

If the project manager comes to a point where he needs to bargain about something on the project with the customer, he must present his case convincingly. He also needs to present good status reports to the customer so that the customer sees good value in the project. If some issues arise on the project, the project manager must resolve them amicably with the customer (Figure 18.6).

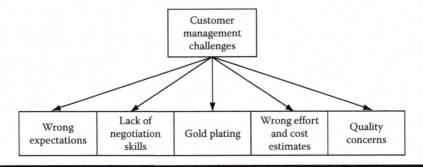

Figure 18.5   Customer management challenges.

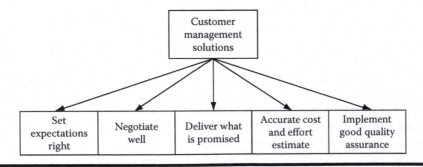

Figure 18.6   Solutions for customer management challenges.

18.6 Communication Management

Communication management is one of the most important facets of any project. If communication is not effective, the customer or the supplier or the team members may misunderstand that piece of information and the project will be botched. What communication methods should be deployed on the project? It is important to take into consideration the effectiveness of communication methods as well as the ease of understanding. The project manager must ensure smooth and effective communication across customers, suppliers, and internal team members.

Review Questions

18.1   What are the typical challenges on software projects related to managing people?

18.2   What are the typical challenges on software projects related to managing the project team?

18.3   What are the typical challenges on software projects related to managing the customer?

18.4   What are the typical challenges on software projects related to managing suppliers?

Chapter 19

Team Management

In the previous chapter, we learned

- What is people management in software projects?
- What characteristics are required for a successful software project management?
- How can software project managers effectively manage teams, suppliers, and customers?

In this chapter, we will learn

- What is team management in software projects?
- How does one motivate the team?
- What are various organization structures for software projects?
- How does one foster good communication within the project?
- How might one plan for good knowledge management?

19.1 Introduction

In any project team, there are many kinds of people with different personalities, attitudes, learning abilities, skills, and experiences. Efficiently managing the resources is vital for the success of a project.

There are people who vouch that other things do not matter on the project. What really matters is people. But not all people are the same. Some are good performers while others may have difficulty with their assignments. People with difficulty with their assignments cause the productivity of the team to go down. The project manager must identify the performers and nonperformers and deal with each of them accordingly [1]. But how do you rate people? After all, you need your team members to perform in the project. The people who are real performers in the project should be acknowledged for their contributions. Other not-so-good performers should be periodically interviewed and apprised about the expectations the management has from them. So there should be good tools to assess the performance of each project team member. If performance is good, they should be rewarded, and if not, measures should be taken to see if performance can be improved.

Sometimes team members have attitude problems. They think they are the best and they are above the system. This kind of situation is aggravated when the project manager also feels the same way. So these people who consider themselves as some sort of a tsar are left to do things in their own way. If these kinds of things happen, then it destroys the team's discipline. It also demoralizes other team members. This in turn severely affects the performance of the entire project team. So the project manager should never allow this kind of thing to happen. Everybody must work according to the conventions of the system. If somebody is good at some work, he can do that work better than others. But it does not mean that he is entitled to violate the system's protocol [2].

Project managers should be adept at handling different kinds of people. It is the best policy to stick to a defined process to carry out any kind of work. No shortcuts should be ever allowed. Shortcuts are always detrimental in the long run and especially in large complex projects, they make the job even more difficult. A project manager must be aware of what is going on. If he finds any noncompliance in the process, he should immediately cut it short [3].

The best-managed projects are the one where a project manager does not stick his nose into every activity of the project. Rather, he should keep an eye as to what is going in the right direction and what is going in the wrong direction. For things going wrong, he should take immediate action to rectify the errors. He should also be a good mentor, coach, and leader for the entire project team [4]. For junior members of the team, he should have a good policy in place so that they are mentored properly and are able to deliver their assignments as quickly as possible. If a team member needs training, the project manager should ensure that proper training is arranged.

Also, motivation and lack of it affects productivity. In a highly structured and process-oriented environment, chances of putting individual creativity to solve work-related problems are limited. Most work becomes monotonous and people working in such environments develop a feeling that they are human machines. They start losing motivation to continue working in such environments. This results in high attrition rates. On the other hand, less structured and less process-oriented work environments encourage people to apply their creativity in their work. Here people are indeed happy to continue doing their work and have a high motivation level. The attrition rate is thus far less compared to the other workplace where work is monotonous. This discussion is important because software service organizations deal with these issues and find it difficult to handle many issues related to this subject. On one hand, process-oriented environments are more productive and outcome of the work done by people here is very much predictable. Customers like to place their work with such companies. But service providers find it difficult to deal with their attrition rates, which are very high. On the other hand, in less-structured environments, creativity is high but productivity is low and outcome of the work done by people working is less predictable. This kind of environment exists in captive units of software vendors or large global companies who develop their own software products for their own use. In the current business scenario, they cope with lower productivity and thus face a dent in their business margins, but days are not far when this situation will change. They will have to succumb to the pressure from software service companies that enjoy higher productivity levels [5].

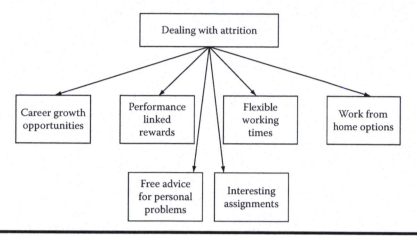

Figure 19.1   Strategies to deal with attrition.

To deal with the problem of attrition, service companies employ some management techniques (Figure 19.1). They provide very good work environments for their employees and encourage them to further their studies or adopt hobbies or causes so that employees find something worthwhile to keep working with them [6].

Project managers should recognize these deep and far-reaching issues and find ways to keep work assignments of their team members interesting. Further, they not only have to fulfill the objectives of the project but also have to realize the objectives of the organization and find ways to fulfill both.

19.2 Organization Structure and Policies

People who work in organizations follow the policies laid down by the organization [7]. Within this framework they try to do their assigned work. There is a always mixed population of efficient and not-so-efficient employees in any organization. Generally the collective outcome of their work is what can be seen at the organization level. As a rule of thumb, 80% of people do their work satisfactorily. That means if a project is executed in normal conditions, more or less the performance results should not be far away from the expectations of the customer.

Let us look at a case study in an organization with regard to its performance. An organization is facing problems continuously about its performance in its projects. They tried many times to find out a solution for this perennial problem but nothing seemed to work. Initially they blamed some of their staff for poor performance and fired some of them. But the problem still persisted. Finally after all attempts to rectify things failed, they called in a renowned consultant. The consultant studied how the people were doing things. After deep study he prepared a report and called for a meeting of top executives of the company to present his findings (Figure 19.2).

After going through the findings; the management was in for a shock. The report said that the organization did not have a defined process model. Each project was being managed with ad hoc measures. So even when the staff on these projects was working overtime and putting in more hours of work, the performance on projects was poor. The consultant suggested that the company must adopt a standardized process model. Adopting the model means changing the organization structure as well. The model will help in setting a structured approach to everything done in the

Figure 19.2 Organization problems.

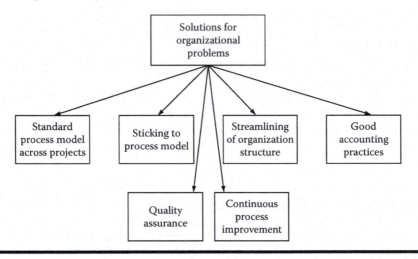

Figure 19.3 Solutions for organizational problems.

organization, including project management. The model will help in streamlining each organization process. This will result in reduced rework. This means better resource utilization and saving of costs. The model will help in keeping the quality of work consistent throughout the organization and project after project. A central process improvement unit also needed to be set up so that further improvement in the process model would also be possible over time by refining and fine tuning the process model (Figure 19.3).

This case study shows the importance of having good organization policies. Even a good project team may fail to deliver if the organization for which it is working has bad policies. So organization policies play the most important role in the success of any project.

19.2.1 Project Organization

There could be many forms of project organization structures depending on the type of project and the methodology chosen to execute it [8]. In the case of making a custom software application, a type of waterfall methodology is chosen with a linear project structure. Different kinds of work in

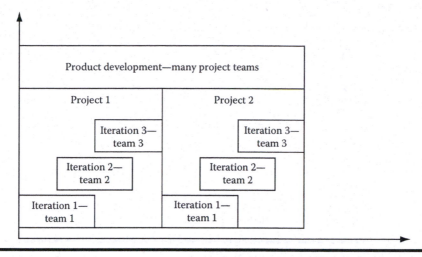

Figure 19.4   Time-boxed product development and software team deployment.

the project will be done by people with the right skills. Once their assignment is over, they are no longer in the project team and will move to some other project. For instance, a design engineer will do the software design, and once the design is completed, he is taken off of the project.

In the case of software product development, the best way is to do it in iterations. Align each iteration with a minor release of the product. For every two to four minor releases, there will be a major release of the product. Align the major release with one cycle of the project. The iterations can be time boxed. In such an arrangement, there will be more than one iteration executed at any given time. There will also be more than one team working. Each team will be working with its own iteration. Figure 19.4 depicts three teams that are working with three iterations. The project manager should always make project plans ahead of execution of these iterations. At the top of the hierarchy is the complete project development roadmap, which may contain more than one project.

In such environments, the phases of the project are very much blurred. So we have software design, software requirement, software construction, and software testing going almost together. So people with different roles (software designing, software construction, and software testing) keep working on the project all the time. Each iteration is of short duration and by the time the tasks on the present iteration finishes, it is time to start working on the next iteration. So all project team members with different roles keep working on the same project (consisting of these iterations) all the time and thus do not need to move on to another project.

19.2.2 Line of Business Organization

Software projects that require a large number of functional inputs may contain functional experts who are from different departments and have been sourced to work on the project. The project manager may not be able to evaluate the work done by these functional experts. In such cases, these experts may report both to the project manager and to their line managers. The project manager may assign tasks to them but the completed tasks will be evaluated by the line managers who understand and can rate the work done by these functional experts. So we end up with a matrix structure for the project where team members may be reporting to more than one manager [9] (Figure 19.5).

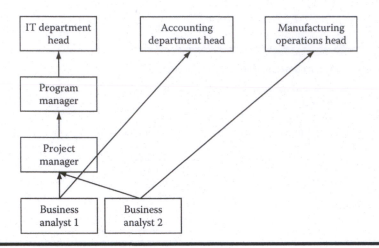

Figure 19.5   Example of a matrix organization.

19.2.3 Program Management Organization

In-house IT organizations have a single program management office. This office takes care of all software projects running or in the pipeline. So in general, the program management office and the IT organization are the same thing. Software service companies, on the other hand, have a very complex organization structure into which the program management fits (Figure 19.6). More details about organization structures at service companies are discussed in Chapter 21 [10].

A large business organization needs a large number of software systems. Some are needed at the department level while others are needed at the business unit level. Then some software systems belong to the enterprise class while others are used for personal productivity enhancement

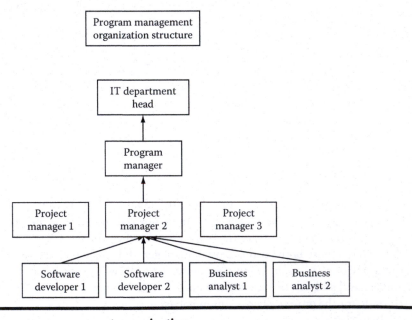

Figure 19.6   Program management organization.

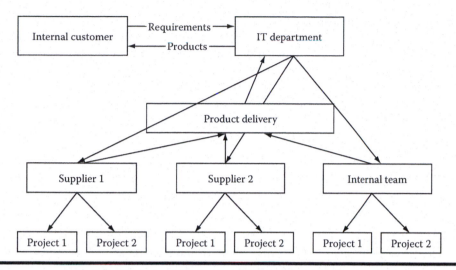

Figure 19.7   Organization structure for internal IT department with outsourced part of project while another part of the project is done by internal team.

reasons. So different kinds of software are either acquired (purchased) by the organization or developed in-house. The IT organization not only needs to deal with new software but also needs to provide support for existing software that is in operation.

So an in-house IT organization has a myriad of projects to look after and should utilize its resources thoughtfully to fulfill the needs of its internal customer.

19.2.4 Internal IT Organization Structure

The IT department of a business unit has its own internal team that develops software products to fulfill the needs of the business. It also procures IT systems from suppliers whenever it is not viable for an internal team to develop the product in-house. Sometimes the IT systems from suppliers are prebuilt and they only have to be implemented at the business site. At other times, the software needs to be developed by the supplier. So essentially the suppliers are of two types: software product vendors and software service companies who build software products on requests from its customers (Figure 19.7).

19.3 Motivating the Team

Salary is the most important motivating factor for any employee. But it is not the only motivating factor. The monetary benefits, that is, salary and other incentives fulfill the needs his or her of food, shelter, medicine, entertainment, and retirement security. These are basic needs of a human being. But meeting these needs alone cannot satisfy a human being. He looks for something more. Once the basic needs are fulfilled, he is driven by a higher level of need. And this need has to do with recognition in society. In the software industry, salaries of professionals are very high. So they can easily fulfill their basic needs from the high salary they get from their organizations. It is observed that attrition rates at software service companies are much higher than that at product development companies. At software service companies, professionals are forced to do monotonous tasks compared to the tasks at product development companies where any professional's job content requires more creativity. Professionals at these organizations feel a sense of fulfillment because they are allowed to use their creativity. In turn, the organization recognizes this fact and appreciates their efforts. In comparing salaries at these two places, there is no difference. So it is not the salary that determines attrition rates.

Project managers must understand the needs of the professionals working on their project teams and find ways to fulfill them. Only then they will be able to motivate their team members [11].

19.4 Team Effectiveness

When people work in a team environment, it becomes difficult to assess who has done good work and who has not. After all, based on the performance of individual team members, their career growth can be determined. They also need to be rewarded for their work based on their performance. If the performance of a team member is not satisfactory, he needs to be counseled to determine what has caused his poor performance and how the performance can be improved in future projects.

Project managers use tools and techniques for determining the performance of their team members. Analyzing performance data also helps to create strategies to improve team effectiveness and thus increase productivity and customer satisfaction [12].

19.4.1 Appraisals

Conducting appraisals is an integral procedure used to evaluate the performance of individual team members. Appraisals can be done through self-assessment, management assessment, or both. In self-assessment, a blank appraisal form is given to each team member and he is asked to complete and return it to the manager. The form contains many objective and subjective questions and the team member uses his own conscience to answer these questions. Some of these questions are about the work he has done for the assessment period (usually yearly or half yearly). He is supposed to write about his achievements and failures. In other part of the form, there are questions regarding his views about the team members, the manager, and the organization environment that affect his productivity. There may be some other sections in the appraisal form as well. Once the manager receives the completed form, he assesses it and later calls each member to discuss what he has written. He also compares his own assessment about the team member. Finally, he rates the performance of the team members based on these assessments. This form of performance assessment is a good technique as the team members feel that they are involved in the whole process and it is fair to them.

The management appraisal assessment process is more autocratic in nature as the team member does not have any say in the whole process. This appraisal assessment process is slowly falling out of favor and is being replaced with the self-assessment method.

19.4.2 Performance Measurement

For measuring performance, a good time-tested mechanism should used to easily identify top, average, and poor performers. The poor performers should be interviewed to identify what has caused their poor performance. After this interview, they should be given a trial period to improve their performance. After the trial period, they should be again evaluated. If they perform well, they can continue as a valuable resource for the organization. If they do not improve their performance, they should be placed in the list of people who should undergo a check as to whether they should continue with the organization or given a pink slip.

Generally, immediately firing employees from their job is not the right solution. They should be given an opportunity to improve their performance. For some personal or organizational issues, they might not have performed well in the first instance. So in the second instance, they should be provided with an environment devoid of factors that might have caused the poor performance. The employee himself should be given an opportunity to list these factors.

19.4.3 Job Allocation

In manufacturing, production targets are set months in advance [14,15]. Production schedules are chalked out monthly or weekly. Each processing center is allotted a target production. Employees work toward achieving these targets. Some incentives in the form of bonuses are given on achieving these targets. Employees also receive their salaries and other benefits. Most of the people working in these manufacturing environments are not ambitious. They are content with their jobs and lives. Most of them work with the same employer for their entire career. In such environments, most of the things are pretty stable. The only thing that is dynamic is a continuous improvement in productivity and product quality. Improvement in productivity is achieved by introducing automation, reduction in production cycle times, etc.

However, the software industry boldly contrasts with the scenario found in the manufacturing industry. Here, people are highly skilled and are in high demand in the market for their skills. If they are not satisfied with their assignments, they do not think twice to quit their job and accept an offer from another company. So software project managers are always under pressure to appease their staff with their demands whether reasonable or not.

To diffuse this kind of situation, project managers try to find ways to keep the software professionals in their teams satisfied. One of the good measures to do that is to provide them with some challenging assignments. Similarly job rotation also helps especially when it comes to onsite assignments.

So while doing job allocation, the project manager should keep these things in mind.

19.5 Training

The software industry is characterized by a constantly changing technology. Change in technology calls for new technical skills. Software professionals need to keep learning new skills. Otherwise they will be in danger of possessing obsolete skills, which may no longer be useful for any projects. Whenever a need or an opportunity arises for training, the project manager should tap it and send his team members for the training. He also needs to assessment which team member needs training based on their assignments. He should make a training schedule accordingly [15].

19.6 Nurturing

Any project team consists of experienced as well as inexperienced team members [16]. Inexperienced team members need to be nurtured so that they become productive and do their assignments. The project manager plays a vital role in nurturing the potential talent in his staff. He should involve senior team members in this effort. The project manager should assign small project tasks to these inexperienced team members and ask senior team members to help them complete the assignments. With the help of experienced team members, the juniors learn how to do these assignments in the right way.

In offshore projects, junior team members need to learn to work with people from different cultures. They need to learn how to communicate effectively with these people. For this, the project manager should give them training for learning effective communication methods.

19.7 Conflict Management

Sometimes, some team members indulge in office politics or try to offload their assignment on others or find ways to avoid or delay their assignments. Sometimes due to some personal reasons, two or more team members may develop some conflict with each other. All these scenarios affect the project badly, and in the best interest of the project, the project manager should recognize the early signs of trouble and take some proactive action. If that action does not help and the conflict does not get resolved, the project will be in deep trouble. The project manager must have good conflict resolution skills. He should consult the parties involved in the conflict and try to find out the cause of it. Once the cause is identified correctly, then a proper solution should be found that will be acceptable to both parties [17].

19.8 Knowledge Management

I have worked with a textile company that developed its own in-house ERP system. The company had its own IT department and a development team. The in-house-built ERP system was being used by all departments, marketing, sales, production, finance, and accounting. It was working fine for them over the years. The development team was maintaining the operations of the deployed ERP system as well. They also kept modifying this system and adding new functionality as per end-user requests. But slowly team members from the development team started leaving the organization. All of them were finding lucrative job offers from fast-expanding software service companies. The textile company paid very low salaries to their IT staff and the management was not willing to increase their salary on a par with software service companies. They feared that this would cause an imbalance in salary between IT staff and people in other departments. The result was that most of the original members of development team who had built the system left the organization. This created a big vacuum in the IT department. The IT department was no longer able to support the ERP system as the creators of the system had left and with them the knowledge about the system was also gone. Ultimately the company decided to scrap this legacy system and implement a standard ERP system from a software vendor.

As the aforementioned case shows, knowledge acquired over the years is very important for any organization. But when people leave the organization, all the acquired knowledge goes out of the organization with them. How can such incidents be prevented? One good solution is to keep a knowledge repository where all lessons learned in the projects, documents about products being used, processes being followed, issues resolved, project specific information, etc., should be kept. But the most important consideration here is that old and not updated information is of no use.

All information in the repository must be updated. Whenever a product is updated with a new version or patch, documents about that product should also be updated. Process changes must be documented immediately in the repository. It is the best policy to keep all information updated with clear history of changes reflected.

With a good and well-maintained knowledge repository in place, the company no longer needs to worry if any key staff decide to leave the organization. The knowledge gained during their tenure with the company is safely kept in the knowledge repository. Now the company is no longer dependent on star performers of the company, or at least for the knowledge they have acquired while working for the company. However, it should be kept in mind that all knowledge is not only in written form. A large percentage of knowledge still resides in the minds of the people, but at least keeping a knowledge repository ensures that all is not lost when somebody leaves.

A knowledge repository also helps when statistical process control techniques or historical data–based decisions are used. For instance, effort estimation for a project is a very difficult task. But if you have information about past projects in the repository, then effort estimates for new projects become easy using the information from old projects.

In a nutshell, we can say that knowledge comes from people working in the organization, and storing and keeping this valuable information in a repository in turn becomes extremely important for the organization [18]. Any organization should develop its knowledge management in such a way to ensure that it is not dependent on people so that when anybody leaves the organization, it does not affect the organization much.

19.9 Communication Management

Proper communication in software projects is one of the most important factors that cannot be ignored [19]. If the communication is unstructured and on an ad hoc basis, it will lead to chaos. What are the customer requirements? Where are they kept? What is meant by a specific requirement? The same requirement stated in one document may mean different things to different project team members. Specifications mentioned in the same design document may mean different things to different developers. The scale of chaos will be exacerbated further if many distributed teams located at geographically distant places work on the project. Due to the differences in culture and language, they will assume different meanings for things mentioned in project documents. In fact, it may become a free for all environments where no productive work may be possible.

So it is very important that all project team members speak the same project language, which means that all project-related communication is done in a language that is understood by all the team members of the project. The responsibility for setting the common project language rests with the project manager. All specification documents, including requirement specifications, design specifications, coding standard specifications, test case creation specifications, etc., should be written in such a way that they follow a specific language pattern including a common naming convention, standard document templates, etc.

Experienced software professionals get used to most of the naming conventions and meaning of specifications after working on software projects. But inexperienced team members may find it a bit difficult. It is the responsibility of the project manager to quickly educate new staff in project language skills. These fresh team members should be constantly helped by senior staff. After working on two to three projects, the inexperienced professionals will get used to the project language used.

19.10 Case Study

In our continuing case study, in this chapter, we will see how people management is exercised at our SaaS vendor. The in-house team of the software vendor does product management, requirement gathering, requirement analysis, software design, software development, software testing, and software maintenance. There are three database administrators (DBAs) who look after development, testing, and production databases. One of the DBAs is an in-house team member and the other two are from the partner teams. There is a product manager who is responsible for all the product development/maintenance activities and who reports to the chief technology officer of the company. Then there is a global project manager who is responsible for all the development projects whether customer specific or new product version development. The global project manager is also responsible for coordination work between the in-house team and the outsourced teams. Each project manager reports to the global project manager. There is a technical support manager who looks after both software testing and technical support. Under his control, there is a technical support lead and a test lead. The test lead does not have any in-house test teams, but he manages test teams located at two offshore locations. The technical support lead has three members on his in-house team and rest of the team is located at the two offshore locations. There are five business analysts who travel to customer sites to gather their requirements. These requirements are then developed into software specifications and put in a software requirement specification document (SRS). These business analysts also work with the marketing team and help in demonstrating the software product to potential customers. Whenever a project team is formed, the project manager decides which business analyst will work on the project after a consultation with the global project manager. The project manager also selects software architects for the project. The test manager assigns testing jobs to software testers after a consultation with the project manager. Once a product version is implemented and goes into production, end users start using it. If any defects are found by the end users, it will be fixed. The testing team also runs sanity test scripts daily on all production instances of the application. The problems found are reported to the support team. The support team immediately fixes them.

As things stand, all four teams (two in-house teams located at two sites and two outsourced teams located at offshore locations) are working seamlessly. They heavily use Internet-based communication tools like instant messengers, e-mail, virtual whiteboards, desktop sharing, voice over IP (VOIP), etc., for fast communication. Team members also travel from one location to another once in a while. This makes for a good camaraderie among different teams.

Review Questions

19.1 Define software project team management in your own words.
19.2 What motivation techniques are available to motivate the project team?
19.3 Explain in brief what you understand by knowledge management.
19.4 Explain in brief what you understand by communication management.
19.5 Briefly describe a software project organization structure.
19.6 How can you evaluate performance of project team members effectively?

Recommended Readings

1. M. Sliger, S. Broderick (2008) *The Software Project Manager's Bridge to Agility*, Addison-Wesley, Upper Saddle River, NJ.
2. I. Evans (2004) *Achieving Software Quality through Teamwork*, Artech House, Norwood, MA.

3. C. Ravindranath Pandian (2004) *Applied Software Risk Management: A Guide for Software Project Managers*, CRC Press, Boca Raton, FL.
4. M. D. Lewin (2004) *Better Software Project Management: A Primer for Success*, Wiley, New York.
5. R. Fincham (1994) *Expertise and Innovation: Information Technology Strategies in the Financial Software Sector*, Oxford University Press, Oxford, U.K.
6. S. Sahay, B. Nicholson, S. Krishna (2003) *Global IT Outsourcing: Software Development across Borders*, Cambridge University Press, Cambridge, U.K.
7. C. G. O'Regan (2002) *A Practical Approach to Software Quality*, Springer, Berlin, Germany.
8. P. Morris, J. K. Pinto (2007) *The Wiley Guide to Project Organization and Project Management Competencies*, Wiley, New York.
9. M. van Genuchten (1992) *Towards a Software Factory*, Springer, Berlin, Germany.
10. E. Verzuh (2003) *The Portable MBA in Project Management*, Wiley, New York.
11. R. E. Fairley (2009) *Managing and Leading Software Projects*, Wiley, New York.
12. S. L. Mcshane (2008) *Organizational Behavior*, McGraw-Hill Education (India) Pvt Ltd., New Delhi, India.
13. K. Heldman, C. M. Baca, P. M. Jansen (2007) *PMP Project Management Professional Exam Study Guide*, Wiley, Hoboken, NJ.
14. J. E. Tomayko, O. Hazzan (2004) *Human Aspects of Software Engineering*, Firewall Media, New Delhi, India.
15. M. V. Zelkowitz (1995) *Advances in Computers*, Academic Press, New York.
16. L. Bass, P. Clements, R. Kazman (2003) *Software Architecture in Practice*, Addison-Wesley, Boston, MA.
17. E. G. Carayannis, Y.-H. Kwak, F. T. Anbari (2005) *The Story of Managing Projects: An Interdisciplinary Approach*, Praeger Publishers, Westport, CT.
18. S. Debowski (2007) *Knowledge Management*, Wiley, New York.
19. J. Phillips (2003) *PMP Project Management Professional Study Guide*, McGraw-Hill Professional, New York.

Chapter 20

Customer Management

In the previous chapter, we learned

- What is team management on software projects?
- How does one motivate the team?
- What are the various organization structures for software projects?
- How does one foster good communication planning within the project?
- How might one plan for good knowledge management?

In this chapter, we will learn

- What is customer management on software projects?
- What are typical customer expectations from software projects?
- How can a good rapport be established with customers?
- Why should one avoid temptations for gold plating on software projects?
- How can one negotiate well with customers on software projects?

20.1 Introduction

Unlike in other industries, close contact with the customer in the software industry is very important. In other industries, the specifications for the project supplied by the customer are more often than not very specific and do not need much clarification or elaboration. It is not so with software projects. Software requirement specifications are never specific or elaborate [1] (Figures 20.1 and 20.2).

That is why the project team needs to work closely with the customer, whether external or internal, to get their software requirements right. Getting the requirements right is very crucial

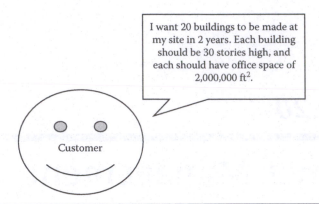

Figure 20.1   Customer requirements in a construction industry.

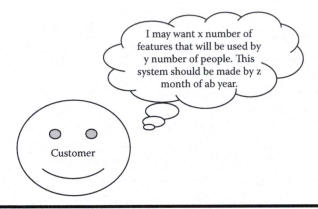

Figure 20.2   Customer requirements in a software industry.

to building the software, which will serve the customer and fulfill their needs. One of the biggest causes of most of the failed projects is not understanding customer requirements properly. On the extreme end, even after spending a lot of time with the customer, the customer is not able to communicate their true requirements to the project team. The basic reason lies with the miscommunication between the two parties. End users understand the business aspect while the software development project team understands technology. So there is no common ground between the two sides. To overcome this situation, project teams should hire good functional consultants who understand the business aspects and how software can meet those business requirements. These functional consultants are people who have worked in the same industry as a line manager for which the software is to be developed. They should also have undergone training on software systems that are used to solve business needs of that particular industry to understand both sides of the coin.

Still customer management is an area that needs a lot of effort from the project team to ensure that they are able to satisfy the customer. One major area where the project team needs to do a lot of rework is the requirement change request that the customer places with the project team. The project team needs to incorporate these changes in their software design so that the software meets customer expectations. There are also issues related to wrong or misplaced expectations of the customer regarding what the software can do or cannot do. Similarly, customers sometimes falsely expect to get the software quicker than agreed by the project team. They wonder why developing that particular software is taking so much time.

The bottom line is that the customers (stakeholders) are spending money and time for the project. This investment must be justified; otherwise there is no point in continuing with the project [2].

20.2 Customer Expectation Management

Software development is a costly and time-consuming task [3]. It uses costly resources (software professionals are highly paid because of the high demand of software skills in the market) and is often a laborious task. Software development is not just software coding (as is imagined by many novice customers). It involves developing and managing requirements, making sound software design, analyzing the design, writing source code, testing, and making user manuals and other documents. On top of these activities, the work products are to be verified and validated at each step to ensure that the software product does not contain many defects. If it takes one full workday to write software code, it takes four more days to do all these other activities. If these activities are not performed well while developing the software product, the software product may not be of much use (due to bad quality). It will not possess reliability, security, usability, maintainability and other characteristics which are so essential for the software product to be used effectively.

If the software product does not possess these qualities, we will end with a software product that

- Will be very difficult to use as it may crash, or a defect may surface most of the time, preventing the end user from using it in his day-to-day business work
- Will be prone to hacks and loss/theft of critical business data
- Will be very time consuming, as doing even a small task may require a long navigation through the software product
- Will be very difficult to work with when a new business need arises and is to be incorporated in the product
- May need a high level of costly support from the support team for operating it

For all of these reasons, it makes sense to make a sound software product instead of dishing out a half-baked one.

One more aspect about customer expectations is about delivering goods with something extra for free. Many project managers believe in the saying "commit less and deliver more!" Is this saying true? Let us discuss this. If you have delivered extras apart from what you had committed to the customer, the following things may happen:

- The customer may believe that what he expected could have been delivered for less money.
- The customer may believe that what he expected could have been delivered in less time.
- The customer may believe that the number of errors in the software product could have been less if the time spent on creating those extra features could have been utilized in testing instead.
- You believe the extras are good for the customer, but the customer may think otherwise.
- The next time you send an estimate for the next project, the customer may think it is overestimated because the estimate may include time you will spend on working on those extras (Figure 20.3).

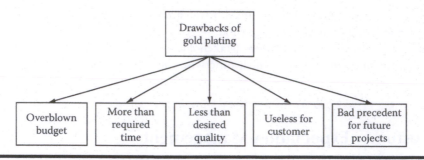

Figure 20.3 Drawbacks of gold plating.

If you complete the project before the due date and deliver it to the customer (whether due to overestimate or overtime or for some other reason), then

■ You may antagonize other project managers working on other projects because they are strapped of cash, whereas you are wasting cash and may have to return unused budget to the customer.
■ Next time you send an estimate for the next project, the customer may think it is overestimated even if that is not the case.

So it makes sense to deliver only what has been committed and to stick to the due date.

20.3 Negotiation Management

During project execution, many situations arise when the project manager has to choose among many less-than-desired choices. Sometimes, due to a lot of rework, the project schedule gets delayed and the project manager is forced to discuss options with the customer. At some other times, some technology issue arises, which forces the project manager to make some alternative choices. In all of those situations, the project manager needs to explain convincingly to the customer what the choices are and the benefits and drawbacks of opting for those choices. If the project manager is convinced about a particular choice, he should try to make the best bargain with the customer [4].

Sometimes, the customer may have a false notion about a particular feature and be bent on getting it implemented. But the project manager knows that it is not appropriate for the software and that it is not feasible in the given budget and time frame. In such a case, he should be able to convince the customer why such an idea is not feasible. Similarly, when forced to cut some features short because of schedule constraints, the project manager should be able to convince the customer.

Sometimes, during the course of the project, the project manager may see the requirement of incorporating a feature that was originally not planned. In such a situation, the project manager can do some hard bargaining with the customer to get that feature incorporated in the project plan (Figure 20.4).

In product development for a software vendor, the project team often works with a top-down project plan. They have a deadline ahead of the project and they need to develop new features. In such cases, the project manager needs to do a lot of hard talking in order to convince the top management to drop features from the project plan that are not feasible in the given time frame.

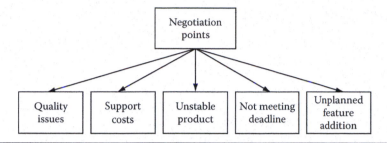

Figure 20.4   Negotiating factors in top-down software product development projects.

He needs to convince the top management about quality issues if the project team is not given adequate testing time on the project.

In short, the project manager has to do much negotiation during the project with the customer and so needs good negotiation skills to be successful.

20.4 Rapport Building Management

No matter how hard the project team has worked, customers may not be impressed if this fact is not communicated to them in a proper manner [5]. If the project manager is of the type who does not indulge in rapport building, the project team may lose an important leveraging handle—that of building a good rapport with the customer! Every human being expects some appreciation for his honest and hard work. Appreciation also happens to be one of the best motivating factors. If the appreciation comes from the customer, there is no match for it. It is one of the best rewards any project team can get.

From the onset, the project manager must start gelling with the members of the customer team. He should share light moments with them. He should share his honest concerns about the project and some of the hardships his team may face given the budget, costs, quality expectation, and the technical and functional difficulties that may arise on the project. Good rapport will also help the project team get more information from the customer about the project than what is mentioned in the contract and the project documents. This will help them in delivering the goods with more customer satisfaction than what could be possible with just those documents.

20.5 Reporting Management

Customers are always looking for timely status reports. In these reports, they look for performance indicators and see if all things are going in the right direction [6]. If something in the report looks to be going in the wrong direction, a customer will look for further details as to what is the root cause for this problem. The project manager should also attach explanation for any deviations and should indicate the course of action to rectify the deviation. The customer will be more than happy to see this proactive approach.

Project managers use project reporting tools to create good project status reports. Some of the reporting techniques include Gantt charts, earned value management, etc. They also incorporate proper milestones in their project planning so that status reports can be sent whenever these milestones are achieved.

20.6 Return on Investment

When any project is proposed, the stakeholders try to find out how it will benefit their organization and what will be the costs incurred [7]. From these figures, they try to find out what will be the return they will get on the investment they will make in terms of expenses they will incur on the project. For instance, a large law firm may decide to have a software product that will manage their customer appointments and billing. Currently, these functions are done manually. Suppose due to manual appointments, the law firm has estimated that they are losing approximately 500 h of time of their lawyers in the form of waiting for appointments, unutilized time, or due to wrong appointments per month. If, on average, each lawyer bills $200 per hour, the law firm stands to lose $100,000 per month. The law firm may thus decide to reduce this wastage of waiting time and to find a software solution. They invited some software vendors and software services vendors to find out an appropriate solution for their problem. Quotations of appointment and billing software systems from software vendors were estimated to be in the range of $200,000–$300,000. The implementation time (including customization and development of new interfaces) was quoted in the range of 1–3 months. The law firm would thus hire a consultant to compare, evaluate, and finally suggest the best solution among those presented (Figure 20.5).

The consultant would study all the solutions and make a report. He would then present the report to the law firm pointing out the costs, time, feature benefits, and other considerations to the management. After much deliberation, the law firm may decide to choose a solution that would cost them $350,000 (including software licenses, implementation, and customization) and that would be implemented in 3 months time. The most important consideration for the management would be to see how much time could be saved from being wasted. They find that this solution would reduce wastage of time to the tune of 50 h per month from the current 500 h. So, per calculations the ROI came at good 300% per annum (per month saving of $100,000 – $200 × 50 = $90,000. Per annum saving of 12 × 90,000 = $1,080,000. Expenses = $350,000. ROI = $1,090,000 × 100/$350,000 = 308%).

20.7 Bottom Line

Value proposition for the project is the bottom line on which any customer sanctions the project. If the customer does not see a good value proposition, he will not sanction the project in the first place. If the project is sanctioned and work is started on the project but priorities change midway,

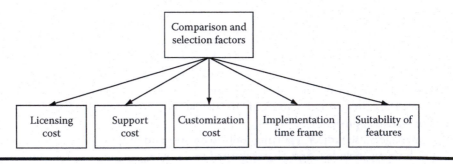

Figure 20.5 Software solution comparison and selection factors.

the project may be abandoned. The project can also be abandoned if the project team fails to deliver the values that the customer is looking for. If the project costs rise more than anticipated by the customer, the project will be in danger of getting scrapped. Similar is the case with project delays. The project manager must stand on his toes to do everything to save the project if these things occur. No matter what kinds of maladies are being faced by the project manager on the project, the top priority for him should always be to make the customer happy.

20.8 Case Study

We continue our case study about the mid-market software vendor here. The vendor has some of the largest retailers, manufacturers, and distributors in the United States, the United Kingdom, Western Europe, and Russia as its customers. They also have some large customers in the government sector. They partner with logistics service providers to create hubs and infrastructure through which they service their customers. This strategy pays off well for them. While logistics service providers provide physical infrastructure to move goods for the customers, the vendor provides its cutting-edge software solution to help provide visibility into movement of goods from one warehouse to another. This visibility is very crucial for customers as they plan to replenish their warehouses and stores using this information. All the partners in the supply chain (manufacturers, distributors, logistics service providers, and retailers) will get to know in advance when a replenishment will be fulfilled, when a truck will be needed at a warehouse for loading/unloading, what merchandize will be sought by customers, the status of a truck in transit, the freight charges for goods movements, etc. Indeed without all this information, the customers will find it difficult to do their everyday business.

When a new customer signs for implementation of the system, a project team is formed. The business analyst visits the customer site and gathers customer requirements. He makes the customer requirement specifications and puts them in the SRS document. Generally, the implementation cycle is 2–4 months long. Most of the features sought by the customer are already present in the software product. Some minor customization may be needed in these features per requirements. Sometimes, the customer requirement may also turn out to be a new feature that is not present in the existing product. In such cases, this feature is to be made for the customer. Once all these issues have been chalked out, the software architect designs the software. The development team then makes the required new features or customizes the existing features. All along, the testing team reviews the design, SRS, and construction for defects. Any defects found are fixed. Finally, the system is implemented. Once the system goes up, the end users start using the application. Any defects found are fixed easily and quickly or a walk around is provided to users for those defects in cases when fixing those defects is not possible.

The vendor finds one area of concern from customers. It deals with concern of security of business transaction data. Since the application is a SaaS application, the vendor hosts the application for the customer. Thus, the vendor has access to business transaction data of its customers. Customers thus fear that their data can be stolen or misused by the software vendor or its employees. To mitigate this concern, the vendor signs a confidentiality agreement with its customers. The terms of the contract are such that if any loss or theft of data happens, the vendor is fully responsible for it and the customer can sue the vendor for breach of trust. This is the single-most concern almost all new customers face.

Review Questions

20.1 How can you ensure that customer expectations are met by your project team?

20.2 Why should the project manager have good negotiation skills?

20.3 What should a project manager do in case there are deviations in project execution?

20.4 Why is rapport building with the customer important?

Recommended Readings

1. D. Leffingwell, D. Widrig (2003) *Managing Software Requirements: A Use Case Approach*, Addison Wesley, Boston, MA.
2. K. F. Cross, J. J. Feather, R. L. Lynch (1994) *Corporate Renaissance: The Art of Reengineering*, Wiley, New York.
3. B. Barkley, J. H. Saylor (2001) *Customer-Driven Project Management: Building Quality into Project Process*, McGraw-Hill Professional, New York.
4. G. Pitagorsky (2007) *The Zen Approach to Project Management*, International Institute of Learning, New York.
5. R. Lethbridge (2004) *Object-Oriented Software Engineering*, Tata McGraw-Hill, New Delhi, India.
6. R. K. Wysocki (2006) *Effective Software Project Management*, Wiley, New York.
7. K. El Emam (2005) *The ROI from Software Quality*, CRC Press, Boca Raton, FL.

Chapter 21

Supplier Management

In the previous chapter, we learned

- What is customer management on software projects?
- What are typical customer expectations from software projects?
- How can a good rapport be established with customers?
- Why should one avoid temptations for gold plating on software projects?
- How can one negotiate well with customers on software projects?

In this chapter, we will learn

- What is supplier management on software projects?
- What are the typical outsourcing arrangements made for software projects?
- How should one manage suppliers on software projects?
- What are some of the organization structures of large software service suppliers?
- How can suppliers effectively manage contracts?

21.1 Introduction

Software projects are characterized by labor-intensive processes like software construction, software maintenance, and software testing. They are also characterized by high levels of software skills. Due to the high level of skills required, software professionals are costly. For any organization, keeping these highly costly resources idle after completion of a project is not a viable option. This has led to the proliferation of contracting companies that keep software professionals on their payroll and contract them to customers whenever they have any software project coming up. Thus, a large number of software professionals have become contractors who work with different

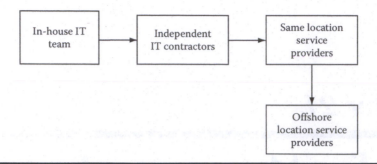

Figure 21.1   Evolution of IT service providers.

customers on different projects depending on the availability of work. This arrangement worked fine until some smart entrepreneurs discovered the benefits of outsourcing software projects to low-cost countries like India. Thus, a new form of outsourcing emerged, which is known as offshore outsourcing. Some of the large software service companies bagged projects from customers and began to execute them using their development centers in low-cost countries, thus reducing the development costs. This phenomenon also came in handy because customers could hire large teams and execute the projects faster, thus collapsing the project schedule. This helped them to go to market fast and tap the market opportunity quickly, providing them with a distinct market edge [1] (Figure 21.1).

This kind of new arrangement necessitated good strategy to control these offshore service providers. Over a period of time, supplier management techniques matured and customers started using them effectively.

There are indeed various challenges when software services of offshore suppliers are obtained. Nevertheless, the benefits far exceed these challenges and hence this model has become a huge success. To avail the benefits, however, one must understand the process of evaluating, selecting, and working with suppliers.

21.2 Supplier Search Management

Software service suppliers come in many shapes and sizes [2]. There are some large service providers who operate successfully in many verticals. On the other hand, there are many small service providers who work in niche market segments. As a customer, you should be able to know if a particular service provider will be able to do your work. You should know about the services offered and about the provider's track record. Thorough research will help you find a list of reliable and potential service providers who can do your work.

21.2.1 RFP and RFI

A request for proposal (RFP) and a request for information (RFI) are great tools to evaluate and compare suppliers [3]. An RFI is usually a pre-RFP stage where the customer asks potential suppliers to send information about what they do, how they do it, and if given a chance to work on a specific project, how they will go about it. An RFI is not a formal invitation by a customer to the supplier to bid on a project. RFPs, on the other hand, are part of a bidding process for a project. Thus, RFIs play a role in evaluating a supplier, whereas RFPs are used for selecting suppliers (Figure 21.2).

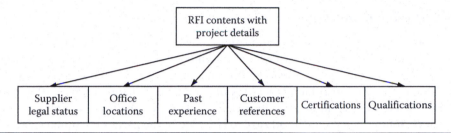

Figure 21.2   Contents of an RFI.

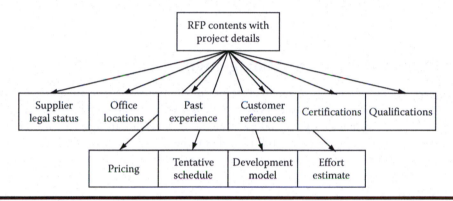

Figure 21.3   Contents of an RFP.

An RFI can contain a lot of information, but a basic minimal RFI contains information about the supplier's legal status, supplier's service office locations, past experience on projects, customer references, supplier's qualifications and certifications, etc. Project-specific details are also included but are not required or not expected to be provided in detail (Figure 21.3).

An RFP, on the other hand, must contain details about the supplier as well as all details about the proposed project. Project-specific details may include pricing, tentative schedule, and project methodologies adopted. The customer sends the RFP questionnaire to all potential suppliers. Once the customer receives these filled-in RFP responses, each response is evaluated. The ones which do not meet the customer selection criteria are rejected. The selected responses are compared to each other and finally the best RFP response is selected.

21.2.2 Supplier Qualifications

Supplier qualifications should be evaluated thoroughly [4]. It is necessary to ascertain (a) whether the supplier has any quality standards certifications like CMMI, ISO, etc.; (b) whether the supplier has industry certifications, like the ones provided by Microsoft, Sun Microsystems, and Oracle, etc. for the company; (c) whether the supplier's employees have these industry certifications; and (d) whether the supplier workforce is equipped with basic undergraduate- or graduate-level qualifications, including technical degrees.

21.2.3 Supplier Experience

Even if a supplier has all the requisite qualifications, one may not be sure if they can deliver what one is looking for [5]. The supplier's past experience and customer references are good measures to know if they can deliver the goods or not. For instance, suppose you want to build a supply-chain planning solution for your distribution network of a food retail chain with over 10,000 stores in the network. What you should look for in such an instance is whether the service provider has built a software solution for a similar industry to take care of the needs of a similar-sized business. If the supplier insists on having done it before and you have doubts about his customer references then you should plan on a site visit of those customers and cross-check the supplier's claims. If the claims are true then you can go ahead in the negotiation for the contract with the supplier. Otherwise, it is better to look further and find another supplier.

21.3 Supplier Agreement Management

If the supplier has never worked with the customer in the past, then the customer is not aware of how good the supplier is. Even though the supplier's qualifications, certifications, and experience help, still the customer should not take any chances. An elaborate agreement must be made with the supplier that will be legally binding and commercially viable for both parties [6]. The agreement should take into account service-level agreements, penalties for poor performance, rewards for excellent performance, and need for revising the contract in future depending on changed needs.

21.3.1 Short-Term Agreements

Short-term agreements are made for small jobs that are mostly one-time affairs [7]. In such cases, the customer is not looking for a long-term relationship with the supplier. The customer's intentions will be to find a supplier who can do the job cheaply. To protect customer interest, a clause may be included to receive support from the supplier in future if any problems are faced with the product.

Generally, there are freelancers in the market who undertake these short-term contracts. They take the contract, do it quickly, and move on to their next assignment.

21.3.2 Long-Term Agreements

Large software services engagements are characterized by long-term agreements [8]. This is where most of the software services providers operate. Some of the large engagements are multi-year and multibillion dollar agreements. No customer can sign a deal of such magnitude without being fully satisfied with the supplier's ability and past experience. These agreements have elaborate details as to how the work will be performed, how many people will be engaged, detailed scope definition of the assignment, and legal clauses for any lapses from either party when contract agreements are not fulfilled. Generally, the customer opts for a review at the end of each year and revision of the contract, based on any changes in his needs.

These contracts are written or reviewed by lawyers and are signed by legal counsel from each party as there is a big risk involved. The supplier prepares detailed project plan and shares it with the customer. Top managers from suppliers are involved in such contracts apart from the project manager who will oversee the project for the contract.

If elaborate details about the project are not clear then a time-and-material-based contract is signed. The project team from the supplier bills the customer for the amount of time spent by the team on the project, generally on a monthly basis. Once all details about the project are clear, the project can be converted into a fixed-cost/fixed-budget project.

21.4 Supplier Communication Management

Communication with the supplier is very important [9]. Right from contract terms to actual work on the project, communication needs to be precise and unambiguous. The customer must ensure that the supplier team understands what is to be done. The supplier needs to provide all deliverables with proper documentation so that their work is understood well by the customer. This two-way communication with complete details about work to be done and work that has been done increases the amount of documentation. The positive side of higher amount of documentation is that there is complete reference of all work done. Any third party will be able to understand what was required to be done and what actually has been delivered. This helps when any dispute arises between the customer and the supplier. The documentation also serves as a reference material for the product made. So when the software product has to be supported, the reference manuals become extremely useful.

When the supplier team is from a different culture another country then communication needs are increased manifold. All instruction for the work to be done should be in fair detail so that it is understood by the supplier team. Description about what is to be made and how to make it is provided with all the details. The supplier team reads these instructions and works accordingly. Chances of error thus get eliminated.

The downside of the need to provide too much detail is that the project schedule gets prolonged. After all, preparing these details requires much of time. But doing it reduces risk of miscommunication and chances of making errors. In real life, a balance needs to be established between providing too much detail or not providing any details at all. If the customer and supplier teams have been working for sometime then a rapport is built between these two teams. Consequently, even a small amount of detail is sufficient for doing any contract work. Although in the beginning, the amount of detail required may be high, it gets reduced once a good rapport is built between the two teams.

21.5 Organization Structure

Software services providers have grown to become large global companies. Most software professionals from countries like India are employed in these organizations. Therefore, it is important to understand the organizational structures of these companies.

With increase in size, companies found it difficult to manage their businesses. Though at the top functional level, organization structure remained the same—vice presidents for marketing and sales, finance, human resources, etc.—things started changing at the middle level. Under marketing and sales they now have heads that look after services for different verticals. These verticals are divided into banking, finance, securities and insurance services (BFSI), supply chain management services, and other miscellaneous services. Each vertical is further divided into business consulting services, software development services, and miscellaneous services. Each of these service groups is again divided into account management where each account represents a customer with all ongoing projects for that customer. At the bottom of the hierarchy are the projects.

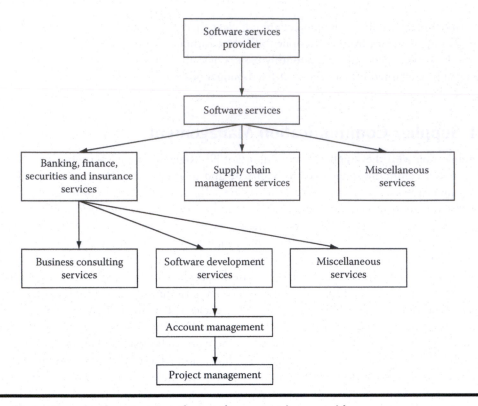

Figure 21.4 Organization structure for a software services provider.

This kind of arrangement evolved as these service providers increasingly refined their offerings with concomitant increase in their organization size, to offer better services to customers [10] (Figure 21.4).

21.6 Account Management

Each customer is very important for software services companies. To keep customer satisfaction at maximum, these companies do everything. They appoint an account manager who looks after all ongoing projects [11]. These account managers may have one or more customers assigned to them. They not only ensure smooth functioning of the projects, they also ensure that the relationship with the customer is a long-lasting one. They regularly visit customer sites and try to ensure that all issues with the customers are resolved satisfactorily. They keep satisfying all needs of the customer so that the customer is willing to give more business.

21.7 Project Offshore Transition

When an in-house project is outsourced, some changes are needed on the project so that it can be carried out by an external team [12]. The foremost change is establishing a service-level agreement with the contractor or service provider so that they will deliver their services, based on the requirements of the customer who has outsourced the project to them. This is followed by knowledge transfer about what the requirements are, what the customer wants from the project, and what work has already been done by the internal team. Only then does the external team take over the project.

When dealing with offshoring a project then some new issues arise. The external team now belongs to a country having altogether a different culture and work ethic. The team members may not have good English-language writing and speaking skills. They will be working in a time zone which may make virtual meetings impossible. Productivity of these team members will be different. Government regulations about labor laws, taxes, etc. will be different. So unlike in same-shore outsourcing (where the outsourcer is located in the same country) offshore outsourcing is a different ball game altogether.

Thus when a project goes offshore, many things need to be checked. The most important check is about the people who will execute the project.

For project transitioning, a well-defined approach is needed. It will help if the outsourcing company has any recognized process standards certification. A pilot project to start with will be the best approach. A few people from the offshore team should be sent to the customer site to get first-hand information about the project. This team should be briefed about the project by the internal team that has been downsized. Once this part of the external team receives knowledge transfer from the onshore team, they will come back to their offshore location. They will now transfer the knowledge acquired about the project to the rest of the team. Now the full team will start working on the project. Whenever any major or minor milestones are met, a report is sent to the customer. Whenever any issues arise, they are resolved and work continues. When the pilot project completes satisfactorily, the customer can decide to opt for full-fledged offshoring of its projects.

21.8 Case Study

We continue our case study about the mid-market software vendor here. The vendor has outsourced a large part of its software development to two outsourcing service providers who are located at offshore locations.

The vendor has done this outsourcing deal to take advantage of cost reduction and tap global talent for its product development. They have outsourced many parts of software testing, software development, and some software design. They have also outsourced some part of software maintenance. The cost arbitrage through outsourcing has come to 3:1. That means the outsourced staff costs just one-third of the cost of onshore staff. Productivity of the outsourced staff is the same as that of their own staff. If the entire staff would have been onshore then their total annual development cost would have been $50,000,000. But thanks to outsourcing, the total costs are $30,000,000 (onshore costs $20,000,000 and offshore costs $10,000,000. A staff of 20 people is working at the onsite location and a total of 30 people are working at two offshore locations). In effect they are saving $20 million per annum on their software development costs.

The customer ensured that the productivity level of people at the offshore location would be the same as its own staff. So even though it had no influence in the selection of people by its outsourcing partner, it had made sure that the final selection of each team member working at its partner site would be made by the customer. The customer would provide the partner with a list of positions to be filled on the project. The partner would then shortlist a number of candidates and would provide this list to the customer. The customer would then interview these candidates and select the right candidates for the job. One of the most important objectives during candidate selection is to make sure that the candidate has prior experience and exposure to tools, technologies, methodologies, and working on similar outsourced projects. This will make sure that the candidate will be productive sooner after a short training period.

Review Questions

21.1 Define supplier management in your own words.

21.2 What are the key components of a supplier agreement?

21.3 What are the tools used for supplier evaluation and selection?

21.4 What do customers consider for supplier selection?

21.5 How can you transition a project to an offshore location?

Recommended Readings

1. M. F. Corbett (2004) *The Outsourcing Revolution: Why It Makes Sense and How to Do It Right*, Kaplan Publishing, New York.
2. J. L. Bossert (2004) *The Supplier Management Handbook*, ASQ Quality Press, Milwaukee, WI.
3. M. Wiener (2006) *Critical Success Factors of Offshore Software Development Projects*, DUV, Wiesbaden, Germany.
4. Q. Wang, D. M. Raffo (2008) *Making Globally Distributed Software Development: A Success Story*, Springer, New York.
5. T. Kendrick (2003) *Identifying and Managing Project Risk*, American Management Association, New York.
6. F. Alan Goodman (2005) *Defining and Deploying Software Processes*, CRC Press, Boca Raton, FL.
7. J. T. Marchewka (2006) *Information Technology Project Management*, Wiley, New York.
8. G. Walker (2003) *Modern Competitive Strategy*, McGraw-Hill/Irwin, New York.
9. J. McManus (2004) *Risk Management in Software Development Projects*, Butterworth-Heinemann, Oxford, U.K.
10. R. Sangwan, N. Mullick, M. Bass, D. J. Paulish (2006) *Global Software Development Handbook*, CRC Press, Boca Raton, FL.
11. T. Davis, R. Pharro (2003) *The Relationship Manager: The Next Generation of Project Management*, Gower Publishing Ltd., Hampshire, U.K.
12. K. Berkling, M. Joseph, B. Meyer, M. Nordio (2009) *Software Engineering Approaches for Offshore and Outsourced Development*, Springer, Berlin, Germany.

TOOLS AND TECHNIQUES

Chapter 22

Software Project Management Tools Introduction

In Part V, we will learn

- What is technology management on software projects?
- How can team performance be improved on software projects by use of tools?
- What are some of the common tools and techniques that are used on software projects?
- What tools and techniques will be available in the future for software projects?

In this chapter, we will learn

- What is tools and techniques management for software projects?
- What characteristics of tools are required for a software project?
- How is tool selection done?

22.1 Introduction

Every business move is all about either increasing market share or improving productivity. Increase in market share brings more revenue, and increase in productivity reduces costs. Both of these factors are eternal business considerations no matter what is the status of economy or industry or the business unit itself. If it has to survive, it has to battle on both of these fronts all the time. Depending on the situation, the degree of emphasis on either of the two may vary; nevertheless, their presence will never go away. Top level growth of any organization is determined by its

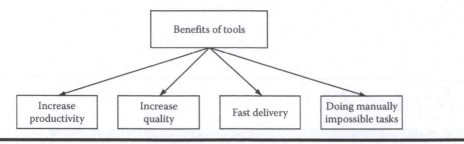

Figure 22.1   Benefits of tools.

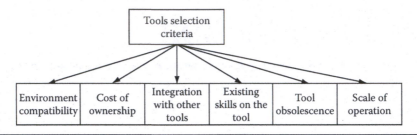

Figure 22.2   Tool selection considerations.

ability to innovate its products and services and enhance quality. Bottom level cost improvement is achieved by continuously increasing productivity. There are many ways in which this bottom line productivity can be improved.

Tools, in any form, are used by human beings to increase their productivity. For instance, a software developer can write his code on a plain text editor. When he has to compile or debug his code, he will have to run the code against the compiler. His productivity can be increased if the text editor integrates with the compiler as he will now have a single interface to work with instead of two interfaces on two separate applications. If he is provided with a smart debugging facility that can provide detailed information about why and where his code is failing, he can quickly fix his code. This will save a lot of time in debugging and thus increase his productivity (Figure 22.2).

Modern software projects use a lot of tools in all areas of the project, including project management, product life-cycle management, etc. In software projects, tools are not only used for increasing productivity but they are also used for improving product quality (Figure 22.1).

However, when choosing tools for software development projects, one should not only consider how much productivity each tool will provide but also how the tool will fit into the overall environment of the project and the project team (Figure 22.2). Let us consider many of these aspects in this chapter.

22.2 Compatibility with Environment

A project manager always keeps looking for the best tools that will help improve the productivity of his team. Therefore, most project managers and their teams keep evaluating the latest tools in the market that promise to increase productivity. Nevertheless, if a tool, however good it may be, does not fit properly in the environment in which it has to be used, it is of no use to the project team. They will not be able to use it effectively. For instance, a remarkably good

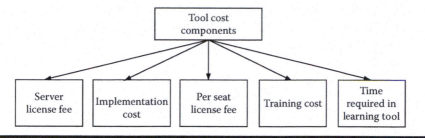

Figure 22.3   Tool cost components.

database access management tool may not serve much purpose if the team has only limited work to do with databases. Instead, the team should invest in tools that will be used extensively on the project.

22.3 Cost of Tool

Some tools may be too expensive to afford. But if its cost of use per seat is good compared to some other tools, it can be a viable option. For instance, there are two tools in the market that seem to be equally good. The price of one tool is $400 (server license) plus $15 per seat. The price of the other tool is $1000 (server license) plus $10 per seat. Suppose you have team of 100 people and all of them will be using this tool. In this situation, your price for the first tool will be $1900 and that for the second tool $2000 (Figure 22.3).

The price difference, thus, is just $100 even though the second tool seemed to be more expensive than the first one. If you feel that the second tool is more compatible to your needs, buying it would be a better decision than buying the first one.

22.4 Data Integration among Tools

Suppose a project team uses 10 tools and none of these tools can be integrated with each other. In this scenario, data generated from each tool will have its own version of truth. For example, the static analyzer tool may report that the total number of software defects is 25 but the configuration management system may report the static defects in the source code as 36. Which version is true? Similarly, the test management system may report the total number of defects in the system testing as 140 but the configuration management system may report the system defects as 360. Again which version is true? (Figure 22.4).

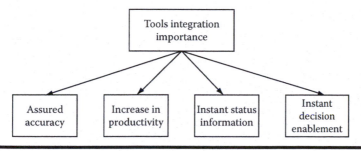

Figure 22.4   Importance of tool integration to each other/project environment.

When you decide to buy a tool, remember your existing configuration and find out if the new tool can be integrated with your existing tools. If the new tool cannot be integrated, or it is too difficult to integrate it with the existing tools, it is simply not worth it. Seamless integration of new tools with existing tools is a must.

22.5 Existing Skills on Tools

Providing training to the project team on a new tool is expensive. It is not only the price of training but also the time invested on the training instead of getting any productive work done. No doubt training is important and essential; nevertheless, if it is not required or if it can be avoided then it is better. If many team members already have good skills on a particular tool, that tool should be used on the project even if the tool is costlier than other tools. In this way, the cost of training on learning new tools can be saved.

22.6 Tool Obsolescence

Like many commodities, tools also have a shelf life. They start their journey with their birth, they mature, and finally they die when they become irrelevant in the market. If you are going to buy a tool, make sure that it is mature and it is not at a stage in its life when it may see its demise soon. Check with the tool vendors how they provide support for their discontinued products. Some vendors provide support for their obsolete products for a long time. Some others do not. If that is the case, what options does the vendor provide to its customers when it decides to discontinue its support for the tool? Do they provide free training and licenses for their newer tools? If not, what kind of discount do they provide to their existing customers?

22.7 Scale of Operation

Some projects are long term in nature. Sometimes they also grow in size over time. So it can happen that a project has 10 people at the start of the project grows to more than hundred 3 years down the line. It is very much possible that if a tool had been bought for a project that was supporting 10 people, it could no longer be used as it does not support more people to work with that tool. When you invest in a tool, ensure that it can support your team even if the team size grows.

Review Questions

22.1 Why should a new tool be integrated with existing tools? Explain the benefits of integration of tools.

22.2 What steps can you take if a tool becomes obsolete? What steps should you take to make sure that you are not buying a tool that is already obsolete or will become obsolete soon?

22.3 What cost factors are considered when a new tool is evaluated?

22.4 Why is it required that the tool can be used even when the scale of your project goes up?

Chapter 23

Project Management and Software Life-Cycle Tools

In the previous chapter, we learned

- What is tools and techniques management on software projects?
- What characteristics of tools are required for a software project?
- How is tool selection done?

In this chapter, we will learn

- What are the common tools and techniques available on software projects?
- What are the tools available for software life-cycle management?
- What are the tools available for software project management?

23.1 Introduction

It is very true that software development projects are all about people. But imagine you have a fabulous team and you start on your project without any tools at your disposal. No integrated development environment (IDE) tools, no modeling tools, no testing tools, etc. Can you imagine your life and that of your team? We take it for granted that we have these tools at our disposal. We do not realize how useful these tools are for our work and that without them our work would be crippled [1].

In this chapter, we will study tools that are used in different software development project life-cycle phases.

23.2 Requirement Management Tools

During requirement development and management, we use many tools [2], listed as follows:

- *Requirement elicitation tools*: User questionnaires, database reports from a customer management system to get customer suggestions/complaints, voice recorder, taking minutes of the meeting
- *Requirement development tools*: Data normalization and structuring tools (Figure 23.1)

During requirement elicitation, requirements are gathered using questionnaires, meetings, etc. Indirect requirements are gathered from customer feedbacks/complaints, etc. The project team can give a demo of the product and during question hour, customers can ask questions about certain features of the software product. These can form a basis for developing requirements. The project team can also visit work locations of customer sites and interact with people who can provide inputs, which again can be the basis for requirements (Figures 23.2 through 23.4).

Once we have gathered all the requirements, we need to develop them. First of all we need to normalize all the data from different sources. We also need to structure these requirement data so that all data are in one form and can be taken on one document or database. We also need to find dependency between these requirements. For all of these activities, we need tools. If not advanced tools, then basic tools like word processors, Excel sheets, etc., can be used.

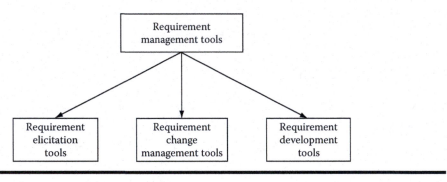

Figure 23.1   Requirement management tools.

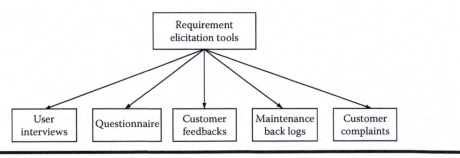

Figure 23.2   Requirement elicitation tools.

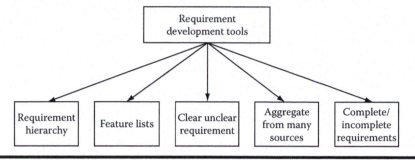

Figure 23.3 Requirement development tools.

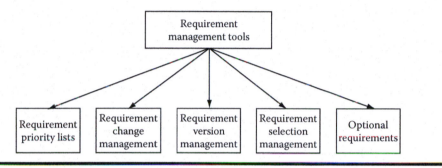

Figure 23.4 Requirement management tools.

23.3 Software Design Management Tools

During software design, many models are made, including entity relationship diagrams, use case models, data flow diagrams, and UI navigation charts [3]. Based on these design specifications, software construction is done by writing source code manually. For some time, efforts have been made so that source code can be generated automatically when the software design is made. Though automatic generation of complete source code has still not become a reality, many tools generate skeletons of source code and some amount of rudimentary code along with some documentation. This is useful as a basic structure is made on which source code writing can be based (Figure 23.5).

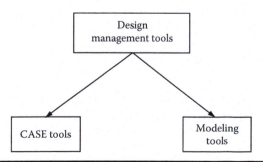

Figure 23.5 Design management tools.

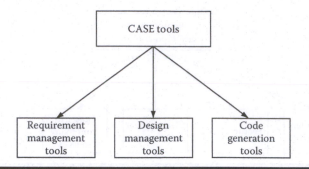

Figure 23.6 CASE tools.

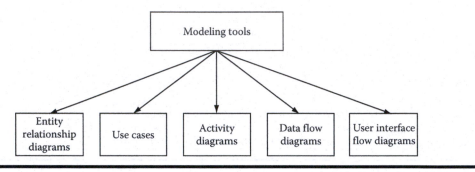

Figure 23.7 Modeling tools.

23.3.1 CASE Tools

Computer-aided software engineering (CASE) tools try to integrate software design with software construction in one phase [4]. When software is designed, the source code is automatically generated. Users can also select the programming language in which the source code needs to be generated. CASE tools include tools for creating entity relationship diagrams, data flow diagrams, use cases, activity diagrams, etc. Examples of some of the CASE tools include ERWIN, Rational Unified Processing Model, etc. (Figure 23.6).

23.3.2 Modeling Tools

Software design mostly involves modeling different parts of the software using standard notations [5]. Both physical and logical models are available. The most commonly accepted notation language is Unified Modeling Language (UML). The system is designed using tools like Microsoft Word, Visio, rational tools, etc. (Figure 23.7).

23.4 Software Build Management Tools

When we have software design ready, we start writing the source code. Much source code must be written before a software system actually takes shape. Due to the large volume and labor-intensive nature of the work, it takes a lot of time to write source code. Various tools and techniques

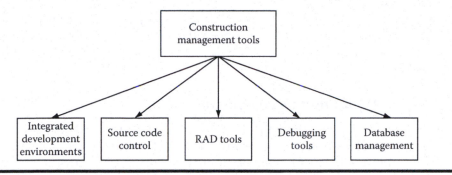

Figure 23.8 Software construction management tools.

have been developed over the years to enable developers to write source code faster. Some other tools also help developers to write better source code so that it may be free of defects (Figure 23.8).

23.4.1 Integrated Development Environment Tools

IDEs are the most popular programming tools used by almost all developers [6]. An IDE is an integrated set of tools that has text editors, compilers, debuggers, and many other tools built in. Some IDEs are so advanced that developers do not need any external tool when they are writing, debugging, integrating, or doing any work related to software construction. Microsoft has Visual Studio IDE, which has a text editor, compiler, debugger, etc. Connection to version control tool, database, etc., is easy. It supports writing source code in Visual Basic, C#, and some other Microsoft programming languages. Similarly, many other vendors have created good IDEs for Java (Figure 23.9).

23.4.2 Source Code Control Tools

When many developers concurrently work on building a software product, they write their code in their IDEs on their local machines [7]. They test the code on their local machine. Finally, they check in their source code at the central server. This server maintains a clean build of the software product being developed. If for any reason this build breaks, no developer will be able to check in their source code on this server. This hampers the work of other developers. It is, therefore, very important that the build on the central server should always be clean and it should never be allowed to break. A software product under development breaks when you try to run it, and it throws an exception and the run interrupts. This happens to programming errors. When a

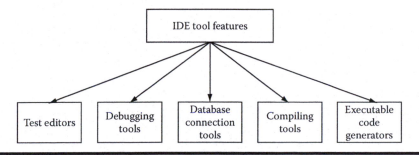

Figure 23.9 Integrated development environment tool features.

software build is broken, if somebody checks in his code on top of the broken build, nobody will know if this fresh code is clean or if it would break the build. Most version control tools, therefore, have a mechanism that does not allow check-in of a new code if the build is already broken. Chapter 5 provides a more detailed discussion on version control tools.

23.4.3 Rapid Application Development

Rapid application development (RAD) tools have been used in the software industry since the 1990s to increase productivity of software construction activity, that is, in writing source code [8]. RAD tools are similar to IDEs with additional features to enhance productivity. They have many features in their environment that make the developer's work easier and more productive.

The original RAD tools were used for prototyping. Subsequently, they became part of regular source code writing tasks.

23.5 Software Testing Management Tools

Software testing is also a resource-intensive phase in the software development life cycle like software construction. Software testing involves tasks like test case creation, test case execution, test case automation, defect reporting, defect tracking, test case management, etc. For most of these tasks, some sort of tools are available, and these are being used by project teams (Figure 23.10).

23.5.1 Test Management

When test cases are created, the local copy of the test case is with the test engineers. One copy of the test case should also be kept at a central repository. When new versions of the software need to be tested, the old test cases become handy for regression testing. If domain experts are working on the test team and if automation of test cases is also to be done, a central repository becomes very useful. Both test cases and test scripts can be stored in the repository. Thus, manual testers, domain experts, and automation engineers can all work simultaneously. A good test management software tool should be used that will integrate with automation tools so that automation scripts stored on the test management tool can be run from within the tool. Similarly, defect-tracking tools can also be integrated with the test management tool. In this way, all the testing activities can be centralized, which will provide an excellent platform for clear visibility and task tracking and will definitely increase productivity [9].

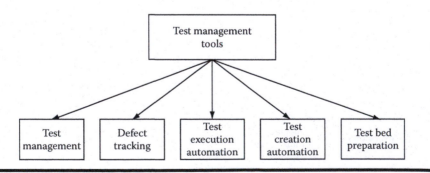

Figure 23.10   Test management tools.

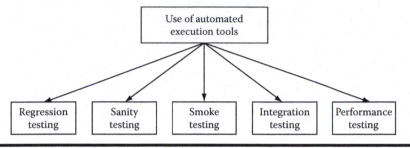

Figure 23.11   Use of test execution automation tools.

23.5.2 Defect Tracking

When test cases are run against the software Application under Test (AUT), the result can be either pass or fail. When a test case passes, this means that the application is working fine and vice versa. When a test case fails, this means that the application has a defect. This defect is logged using a defect-tracking tool. The defect information passes on to the developer. The developer fixes the defect on the AUT. The tester tests to know if the defect has been fixed properly. If it is fixed properly, he will close the defect. If not, he will reopen the defect. This continues until the defect is fixed.

There are good defect-tracking tools from both open source as well as traditional software vendors in the market. Some of them include BugZilla from Mozilla, Test Track Pro from Seapine Software, etc.

23.5.3 Automation Tools

Regression, performance, sanity, and other kinds of test cases are automated using automation tools. For test case automation, some tools only involve record and play kind of automation. Some tools support more features like manually enhancing the test script, allowing integration with the AUT (vendor dependent), etc. To reduce maintenance efforts, some automation framework is also used along with automation (Figure 23.11).

23.6 Project Management Tools

Software project management involves preparing and maintaining several documents. These documents contain a lot of project data. These data are measured and recorded and then analyzed in comparison to results achieved with best practices.

For carrying out these measurements, the project manager and the project team need good tools and techniques, which should be selected based on the specific needs of the project. It will be a waste of time and resources if inappropriate and irrelevant measurements are taken and maintained.

In this chapter, let us look at some of the tools and techniques that are used for project planning, monitoring, and control.

The project plan consists of documents like WBS, resource allocation, risk planning, communication planning, and configuration management.

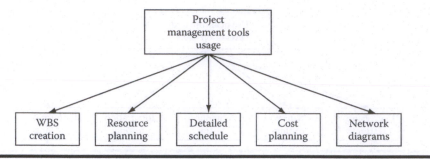

Figure 23.12   Project management tools usage.

23.6.1 Project Planning Tools

Project planning tools will provide WBS structure, resource planning, schedule, and cost, and will provide the platform to monitor and control the project. Some of the tools available for project management include MS Project and Primavera. Many other tools that can be used for this purpose are also available in the market (Figure 23.12).

23.6.1.1 Configuration Management Tools

Configuration management tools not only provide configuration and version control for source code and project documents but also provide facilities for controlling software evolution, maintaining product integrity, changing control and version control, and other tasks. Popular configuration management tools include Visual Source Safe and Perforce (Figure 23.13).

23.6.1.2 Communication Management Tools

On software projects, much communication goes on among team members, customers, and suppliers. Communication includes sharing project documents, task status information, meetings, reviews, issues, status reports, etc. These documents and tasks are done using methods like meetings, virtual meetings, instant messengers, Web demonstration tools, e-mails, whiteboards, remote desktop connections, etc. (Figures 23.14 and 23.15).

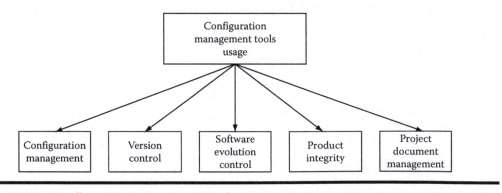

Figure 23.13   Configuration management tools usage.

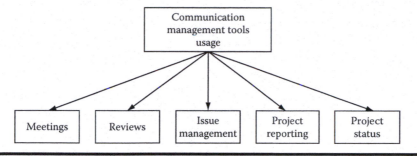

Figure 23.14   Communication management tools usage.

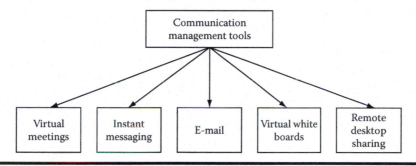

Figure 23.15   Communication management tools.

Review Questions

23.1   Why are integrated development environments used?

23.2   What does a defect-tracking tool do?

23.3   Explain what is meant by CASE tools.

24.4   What kinds of tools are used in requirement management?

Recommended Readings

1. V. Sikka (2004) *Maximizing ROI on Software Development*, CRC Press, Boca Raton, FL.
2. C. T. Leondes (2001) *Computer-Aided Design, Engineering, and Manufacturing*, CRC Press, Boca Raton, FL.
3. N. F. Kock (2006) *Systems Analysis and Design Fundamentals*, Sage, London, U.K.
4. A. W. Brown, D. J. Carney (1994) *Principles of CASE Tool Integration*, Oxford University Press, Oxford, U.K.
5. L. C. Briand, C. Williams (2005) *Model Driven Engineering Languages and Systems*, Springer, Berlin, Germany.
6. J. McGovern, S. W. Ambler (2003) *A Practical Guide to Enterprise Architecture*, Prentice Hall PTR, Upper Saddle River, NJ.
7. R. J. Muller (1998) *Productive Objects: An Applied Software Project Management Framework*, Morgan Kaufmann, San Francisco, CA.
8. J. W. Rittinghouse (2003) *Managing Software Deliverables: A Software Development Management Methodology*, Digital Press, Clifton, NJ.
9. D. Graham, E. Van Veenendaal, I. Evans, R. Black (2008) *Foundations of Software Testing: ISTQB Certification*, Cengage Learning, Independence, KY.

Chapter 24

Software Project Templates

In the previous chapter, we learned

- What common tools and techniques are available in software projects?
- What tools are available for software life-cycle management?
- What tools are available for software project management?

In this chapter, we will learn

- What common templates are available in software projects?
- Why should templates used in software projects?
- What common attributes are there for various kinds of templates which are used in software projects?

24.1 Introduction

Templates and common shared libraries provide two things. They ensure that a common platform is used for documentation and project communications. So we have uniformity in project communications for all parts of the project. This makes it easier for all project stakeholders and team members to understand all the communication, and the chances of miscommunication get reduced. It also ensures that the productivity of communication gets increased. After reading any communication, understanding the message does not take much time contrary to a situation where disparate kinds of documents with no uniformity across each other are communicated and thus understanding them becomes difficult [1].

The other benefit of using standard templates is that people will not miss any project work due to forgetfulness. Suppose task A is a part of the project and it consists of six steps of work to finish.

Suppose a person working on it finishes five steps and forgets to finish the sixth step and checks in his work. Other people are not aware of it and in fact the project is proclaimed to be complete after all others are finished. The unfinished product is now being used by users. When using it, users report some defects in the product. The support analyst analyzes the defect and then the defect is passed on to the support team to fix. When a postmortem of the project is done, it is discovered that the defect originates from the missing step in Task A. When people use standard templates, the person who owns a particular project template never fails to document any task or task step or requirements to check before finishing a task. In essence, these filled templates become checklists for the team members.

But the most important benefit of using templates is that project and development data can later be sent to databases and thus this information can be stored permanently. At the basic level, templates provide a mechanism to put data into good structures. When data are stored this way, they can be extracted easily and can be stored in database repositories. In contrast, unstructured data (e.g., in form of e-mails, chat sessions on instant messengers, and data in unformatted documents) is difficult to get extracted. These unstructured data are, thus, not of much use. Knowledge management systems are in fact built from data extracted from structured project templates [2].

In this chapter, we will study what essential ingredients go in different types of project templates used in software projects.

24.2 Software Life-Cycle Template Guidelines

Software life-cycle templates are used during the entire period when software work products are being made. In the requirement management phase, requirements are gathered, developed, and managed. A good template with required steps will ensure that these activities are performed correctly, and no vital steps go missing. Similar templates are used for other development phases in the project.

24.2.1 Software Requirement Template Guidelines

The requirement management template contains information about functional and nonfunctional requirements that need to be gathered, analyzed, and developed [3]. Nonfunctional requirements include requirements for performance, security, quality level, usage intensity, and safety. The proposed solution should be able to meet levels and criteria prescribed by the customer, and these pieces of information should be recorded in the template. Functional requirements should contain information about system features, external interfaces, user interfaces, hardware interfaces, software interfaces, communication interfaces, etc.

Here is the list of parts of requirements:

Functional requirements

- System features
- External interface requirements
- User interfaces
- Hardware interfaces
- Software interfaces
- Communication interfaces

Nonfunctional requirements

- Performance requirements
- Safety requirements
- Security requirements
- Software quality level requirements
- Usage intensity

Inputs for the requirement management process:

- High-level requirements
- System operation concepts
- Customer needs

Outputs from the requirement management process:

- Baselined, validated requirements
- Interface documents
- Reuse plans
- Traceability matrices
- Operational scenarios
- Historical records

Major tasks in requirement management (Table 24.1)

Table 24.1   Major Requirement Management Task List

Analyze high-level requirements
a. Examine, discuss, and understand the high-level requirements and operation concepts
b. Identify the scope of the requirements and the purpose of the software, and analyze any constraints affecting the software requirements from the perspective of cost, schedule, technology, or quality
c. Limit requirements scope within technology constraints
d. Develop operational scenarios
e. Perform make/buy/reuse (Reuse/COTS) study and document the results
f. Document major assumptions made in conducting the analysis
Define detailed requirements and specifications
a. Refine operation concepts and operational scenarios to ensure that all functionality is documented
b. Expand the high-level requirements to detailed requirements
c. Define external interface requirements
d. Allocate the detailed requirements and specifications to subsystems or major components

(continued)

Table 24.1 (continued)   Major Requirement Management Task List

e. Analyze detailed requirements to make sure that they are within technology constraints
f. Trace detailed requirements to high-level requirements and subsystems, find verification methods for each of the detailed requirements, and prepare a matrix that contains all the relationships among verification methods and detailed requirements
g. Document the detailed requirements and specifications developed
Verify requirements and specifications
a. Conduct requirement peer reviews to ensure agreement regarding the intent and purpose of each requirement and the reason for limits, tolerance, and margin in each specification
b. Clarify ambiguous requirements
c. Determine the technical feasibility of each requirement and any risks inherent in candidate approaches
d. Verify consistency, necessity, and completeness both internal to the requirements and against driving documents
e. Model performance or prototype as needed
Validate requirements and specifications
a. Determine and document the method of validation to be used for each requirement

Requirement review checklist (Table 24.2)

Table 24.2   Requirement Review Check List

a. Compliance with standards—Does the requirement specification comply with standard software process model or tailored branch/project-level standards and naming conventions?
b. Completeness of specifications—Does the requirement specification document address all known requirements? Have "TBD" requirements been kept to a minimum or eliminated entirely?
c. Clarity—Are the requirements clear enough to be turned over to an independent group for implementation?
d. Consistency—Are the specifications consistent in notation, terminology, and level of functionality? Are any required algorithms mutually compatible?
e. External interfaces—Have external interfaces been adequately defined?
f. Testability—Are the requirements testable? Will the testers be able to determine whether each requirement has been satisfied?
g. Design-neutrality—Does the requirement specification state what actions are to be performed, rather than how the sections will be performed?
h. Readability—Does the requirement specification use the language of the intended testers and users of the system, not software jargon?

Table 24.2 (continued)   Requirement Review Check List

i.	Level of detail—Are the requirements at a fairly consistent level of detail? Should any particular requirement be specified in more detail? In less detail?
j.	Requirements singularity—Does each requirement address a single concept, topic, element, or value?
k.	Definition of inputs and outputs—Have the internal interfaces, that is, the required inputs to and outputs from the software system, been fully defined? Have the required data transformations been adequately specified?
l.	Scope—Does the requirement specification adequately define boundaries for the scope of the target software system? Are any essential requirements missing?
m.	Design constraints—Are all stated design and performance constraints realistic and justifiable?
n.	Traceability—Has a bidirectional traceability matrix been provided?

24.2.2 Software Design Template Guidelines

A software design template enables the project team to capture and record modeling tools to be used, architecture details, model details (activity diagrams/use cases/work flow diagrams, etc.), module details, component details, etc. [4]. It should also contain information on what design metrics will be used in the project.

Inputs required for software design process:

■ Preliminary software design (if available)
■ Validated and project-approved requirements
■ Operation scenarios
■ Interface documents
■ Reuse plans
■ Test plan
■ Requirement traceability matrix
■ Requirement inspection documents from reviews

Outputs from software design process:

■ Design documentation
■ Requirement change requests
■ Software design document presentation materials
■ Updated requirement traceability matrix
■ Lessons learned
■ Suggested refined estimates of system size, effort, and schedule
■ Requirement inspection documents from reviews collected and placed under appropriate configuration control for tracking to closure

Major tasks in software design process (Table 24.3)

Table 24.3   Major Design Management Task List

Expand and refine architecture
a. Define functions—In conjunction with the operating system requirements for the structure of application programs and communication between application programs. Decompose the designated processing into lower-level component processing
b. Identify lower-level reusable software from prior efforts—Identify any reusable components that can be incorporated into the design according to the reuse strategy specified in the project plan
c. Identify software units—Identify the software unit names. Follow the naming conventions defined for the project
d. Identify software unit interactions/interfaces—Define the software unit interface requirements for all software units in the system
e. Select IT security components if applicable—Identify components of the system that could be vulnerable to a breach of system security. Develop a security assurance strategy to ensure that the design for the identified software components minimizes or eliminates the potential for breaches of system security
f. Establish failure detection and correction—Identify the components of the system that could fail. Develop a correction/recovery strategy to ensure that the design for the identified software minimizes or eliminates the potential for failures of the system

Design software units
a. Establish I/O for each unit—Generate and coordinate data and control definitions for the software unit inputs and outputs
b. Select algorithms—For each software unit (or operation on each class), select algorithms to accomplish the required function. Develop this internal logic in accordance with the standards specified in the project plan
c. Select data structures—For each software unit (or operation on each class), select appropriate data structures to accomplish the required function
d. Define unit-level data requirements/communication protocols—Define unit-level data requirements and communication protocols and formats between each software unit in the functional group
e. Determine reusability requirements for each unit—When future reuse is an objective of the software being developed, determine applicable design requirements to facilitate reuse
f. Develop software unit design for each unit
g. Finalize user interface(s)
h. Estimate utilization and size of each component of the system or unit as appropriate— Estimate resource utilization for the component of software being designed. Include CPU throughput, memory utilization, and I/O channel usage
i. Conduct one or more design walkthrough/inspections so that each unit is inspected

Prepare material
a. Critical design review presentation materials
b. Traceability matrix updates
c. Planning refinements/updates
d. Lessons learned

Design review task checklist (Table 24.4)

Table 24.4   Design Review Check List

1. Completeness
a. Review requirement traceability matrix to ensure the coverage of all requirements
b. Ensure the coverage of real-time requirements, performance issues (memory and timing), spare capacity (CPU and memory), maintainability, understandability, database requirements, loading and initialization, error handling and recovery, user interface issues, software upgrades, software reuse and modifications, and all inputs and outputs
c. Clearly and correctly identify interfaces
d. All functions clearly and accurately described in sufficient detail
e. All interfaces clearly and (appropriately) precisely defined
f. Adequate data structures defined
g. All error codes documented
2. Suitability
a. Deviations from the requirements are documented and approved
b. Assumptions are documented
c. Major design decisions are documented
d. The design is expressed in precise unambiguous terms
e. Dependencies on other functions, operating system, hardware, etc., are documented
f. The design follows notational conventions

24.2.3 Software Build Template Guidelines

Software build management is concerned with what programming language can be used, how integration with various internal and external interfaces can be achieved, which team will develop what, how unit and integration testing will be performed, etc. [5]. These pieces of information are to be covered in the build template. It should also contain information as to which build metrics will be used.

Inputs required for software construction process:

- Software design
- Validated and project-approved requirements
- Operation scenarios
- Interface documents
- Reuse plans
- Test plan
- Requirement traceability matrix
- Requirement inspection documents from reviews

Outputs from software construction process:

- Software source code
- User manual
- Software coding documentation
- Updated requirement traceability matrix
- Lessons learned
- Requirement inspection documents from reviews collected and placed under appropriate configuration control for tracking to closure

Major tasks in software construction process (Table 24.5)

Table 24.5 Major Construction Management Task List

Build preparation
a. Decompose function—In conjunction with the operating system requirements for structure of application programs and communication between application programs. Decompose the designated processing into lower-level component processing
b. Identify lower-level reusable software from prior efforts—Identify any reusable components that can be incorporated into the construction according to the reuse strategy specified in the project plan
c. Identify software units—Identify the software unit names. Follow the naming conventions defined for the project
d. Identify software unit interactions/interfaces—Define the software unit interface requirements for all software units in the systems
e. Select IT security components (if applicable)—Identify components of the system that could be vulnerable to a breach of system security. Develop a security assurance strategy to ensure that the design for the identified software components minimizes or eliminates the potential for breaches of system security
f. Establish failure detection and correction—Identify components of the system that could fail. Develop a correction/recovery strategy to ensure that the construction for the identified software minimizes or eliminates the potential for failures of the system
Construct software units
a. Establish I/O for each unit—Generate and coordinate data and control definitions for the software unit inputs and outputs
b. Select algorithms—For each software unit (or operation on each class), select algorithms to accomplish the require function. Develop this internal logic in accordance with the standards specified in the project plan
c. Select data structures—For each software unit (or operation on each class), select appropriate data structures to accomplish the required function
d. Define unit-level data requirements/communication protocol—Define unit-level data requirements and communication protocol and formats between each software unit in the functional group

Table 24.5 (continued)   Major Construction Management Task List

e. Determine reusability requirements each unit—When future reuse is an objective of the software being developed, determine applicable design requirements to facilitate reuse
f. Develop software unit construction for each unit
g. Build user interface(s)
h. Estimate utilization and size of each component of the system or unit as appropriate
i. Conduct one or more construction walkthrough/inspections so that each unit is inspected
Prepare material
a. Critical construction review presentation materials
b. Traceability matrix updates
c. Planning refinements/updates

Construction review task checklist (Table 24.6)

Table 24.6   Major Construction Review Check List

1. Completeness
a. Review requirement traceability matrix to ensure the coverage of all requirements
b. Ensure the coverage of real-time requirements, performance issues (memory and timing), spare capacity (CPU and memory), maintainability, understandability, database requirements, loading and initialization, error handling and recovery, user interface issues, software upgrades, software reuse and modifications, and all inputs and outputs
c. Clearly and correctly identify interfaces
d. All functions clearly and accurately described in sufficient detail
e. All interfaces clearly and (appropriately) precisely defined
f. Adequate data structures defined
g. All error codes documented
2. Suitability
a. Deviations from the requirements are documented and approved
b. Assumptions are documented
c. Major construction decisions are documented
d. Dependencies on other functions, operating system, hardware, etc., are documented
3. Correctness
a. The logic is correct

24.2.4 Software Testing Template Guidelines

A set of software testing templates include templates for test strategy document, test plan document, test metrics document, resource plan document, etc. [6].

Software testing task checklist (Table 24.7)

Table 24.7   Major Testing Task List

The objectives of the testing have been clearly defined and documented, and all of the test plans/procedures, environment, and configuration of the test item(s) support those objectives
Configuration of the system under test has been defined/agreed to
All interfaces have been placed under configuration management or have been defined in accordance with an agreed-upon plan. A version description document has been made available to test team prior to the review
All applicable functional, unit-level, subsystem system, and qualification testing has been conducted successfully
All test-specific materials, such as test plans/test cases/procedures, have been made available to all team members prior to conducting the review
All known system discrepancies have been identified and disposed in accordance with an agreed-upon plan
All required test resource people, facilities, test articles, test instrumentation, and other test-enabling products have been identified and are available to support required tests
Roles/responsibilities of all test participants are defined and agreed to
Test contingency planning has been accomplished, and all personnel have been trained

Test effort success criteria
The criteria for deeming a test effort successful are as follows (Table 24.8):

Table 24.8   Test Effort Success Criteria List

Adequate test plans are completed and approved for the system under test
Adequate identification and coordination of required test resources are completed
Previous component, subsystem, and system test result form a satisfactory basis for proceeding into planned tests
Risk level is identified and accepted by program/competency leadership as required
Plans to capture any lessons learned from the test program are documented
The objectives of the testing have been clearly defined and documented; and the review of all the test plans, as well as the procedures, environment, and configuration of the test item, provides a reasonable expectation that the objectives will be met
The test cases have been reviewed and analyzed for expected results, and consistent with the test plans and objectives
Test personnel have received appropriate training in test operation and safety procedures

24.3 Project Management Template Guidelines

24.3.1 Work Breakdown Structure (WBS) Template Guidelines

Guidelines for creating and maintaining WBS structure for the project plan (Table 24.9) [7]:

Table 24.9 Work Breakdown Task List

1. A project WBS may be tailored and constructed to reflect unique characteristics of the product effort as appropriate

2. The WBS is a tree-structured, activity-oriented list of all work needed to meet the requirements of the project
 	
  a. The WBS is organized by product or service such that activities for a product (or subproduct or service) are normally grouped within a section of the WBS
 	
  b. The WBS provides a mechanism for the collection of cost and schedule data on a product-by-product (or service) basis, as well as for the project overall
 	
  c. It provides a framework for identifying material, services, schedules, staffing, and cost associated with each work element of the project
 	
  d. It addresses all work required, including organizing, planning, monitoring, controlling, and reporting the status of all work elements across the project
 	
  e. The WBS is used as the set of activities to be scheduled for the project. Estimation of resources required is also frequently based on the work defined in the WBS. If there is work you must do that is not reflected in your WBS, it is likely to have no schedule or resources. It will probably result in a schedule and/or cost variance
 	
  f. The checklist provides a list of most high-level activities that a project may have to perform. It includes a WBS dictionary to assist in selecting the appropriate items. Use the example of a project WBS in Figure 6.6 (Chapter 6) as a guide in creating, formatting, and documenting your WBS. Your WBS will have many different WBS items but will need many of the same items as in the example.

3. Although the WBS is product or service based, remember to include management and process activities (e.g., reporting, integration, training, requirements management) that must be accomplished to meet the project requirements. These must be included as WBS elements or they will not be scheduled and they will have no resources allocated to them. Some of the management processes that must be covered are planning, monitoring and control, measurement and analysis, requirements management, acquisition management, and risk management

4. Organize the specific work elements that must be accomplished into successively smaller work elements such that
 	
  a. The subdivisions (or decomposition) of work elements are referenced in terms of levels
 	
  b. The highest levels usually reflect the major deliverable work areas or milestones

24.3.2 *Project Planning Guidelines*

Inputs to project planning process are as follows [8]:

- Requirement document(s) or statement of customer needs or replanning criteria (change in requirements or constraints, or significant variance from the original plan)

The outputs of project planning process are as follows:

- The baselined project plan and its subsidiary plans
- The plan for tracking the progress and cost of work elements

Major tasks (Table 24.10)

Table 24.10   Project Planning Task List

a. Identify (or update) software deliverables and external dependencies
b. Identify (or update) the development and/or acquisition strategy
c. Define (or update) the management and technical approaches to completing the work
d. Develop (or update) the work breakdown structure
e. Develop (or update) the schedule
f. Estimate (or update) product size and project effort and cost
g. Define (or update) the organization and resources needed
h. Develop and document (or update) strategies for data management, risk management, stakeholder management, and measurement and analysis
i. Write and baseline the project plan
j. Maintain the project plan as needed

24.3.3 *Project Monitoring and Control Guidelines*

Inputs for project monitoring and control [9]:

- Baselined software project plan and subsidiary plans
- Established development environment
- Initial progress tracking worksheet
- Project status information
- Technical review materials
  Review packages
  Change requests
  Requests for action (RFAs)
  Review item dispositions (RIDs)
  Impact analysis (for requirements changes), etc.

Outputs from project monitoring and control:

- Project status reports
- Issues
- Lessons learned
- Risk information
- RFAs
- RIDs

Major tasks (Table 24.11)

**Table 24.11   Project Monitoring
and Control Task List**

1. Monitor project activities and resources
2. Monitor work products and project data
3. Monitor software acquisition
4. Monitor commitments
5. Manage corrective actions
6. Generate reports and review progress
7. Conduct milestone reviews
8. Document lessons learned

Recommended Readings

1. K. Elleithy (2007) *Advances and Innovations in Systems, Computing Sciences and Software Engineering*, Springer, Berlin, Germany.
2. E. McGuire (1999) *Software Process Improvement: Concepts and Practices*, Idea Group Inc., Hershey, PA.
3. R. F. Goldsmith (2004) *Discovering Real Business Requirements for Software Project Success*, Artech House, Boston, MA.
4. J. Highsmith, J. A. Highsmith (2002) *Agile Software Development Ecosystems*, Addison Wesley, Boston, MA.
5. B. W. Boehm, V. R. Basili, H. D. Rombach, M. V. Zelkowitz (2005) *Foundations of Empirical Software Engineering: The Legacy of Victor R. Basili*, Springer, New York.
6. G. D. Everett, R. McLeod (2007) *Software Testing: Testing across the Entire Software Development Life Cycle*, Wiley, Hoboken, NJ.
7. D. Milošević (2003) *Project Management Toolbox*, Wiley, Hoboken, NJ.
8. R. E. Fairley (2009) *Managing and Leading Software Projects*, Wiley, Hoboken, NJ.
9. J. P. Lewis (2004) *Project Planning, Scheduling, and Control*, Tata McGraw-Hill, New Delhi, India.

Chapter 25

Future Tools and Techniques

In the previous chapter, we learned

- What common templates are available in software projects?
- Why should templates be used in software projects?
- What common attributes are there for various kinds of templates that are used in software projects?

In this chapter, we will learn

- What future tools and techniques will be available in software projects?
- What tools will be available for software life-cycle management?
- What tools will be available for software project management?

25.1 Introduction

In a very good article about the future of programming, it was said that limitations in advancement of any technology is not the limitation of the technology but of the human brain. We created robots but then suppose androids came. Is it possible that these androids would become smarter than human beings anytime in the future? As far as physical capacities are concerned, there doesn't seem to be any constraints. Androids can have massive memory and storage power, which may make them superior than human beings in the future. They could also have lightning speed processing power in the future. Would these factors make androids have superior intelligence compared to human beings? It is most unlikely, because whatever intelligence is being provided to androids is being supplied by human beings. The way human beings think and the way human beings memorize is what will go into these androids. It is simply impossible that what human beings do not know can go to androids. After all human beings can teach only up to what they know and not more. So limitations of intelligence of the ultimate androids will be same as that of human beings. With conscious effort, human beings would always create robots and androids who will obey the commands of human beings, and under no circumstances, would they will disobey any command given by a human. So after all, human beings would be safe from androids and robots.

This discussion is interesting. But now let us come to our main topic. What holds for the future of programming, programming tools, techniques, and software development in general?

There is one caveat here though. We all hear about computer science, computer engineering, and software engineering, but has any of us heard about software science? Computer engineering goes with computer science, but what goes with software engineering? Why is there no such thing as software science? Probably because computer science has usurped all areas that could have gone under software science if it ever existed!

25.2 Software Industry Trends

There is no denying that there has been tremendous progress in all areas covering computer science, software engineering, hardware engineering, artificial intelligence, and many areas related to or dealing with computers and software after the advent of computers and their software [1]. Indeed the efforts of millions of people over these years have really paid off. The software industry is one of the fastest growing and changing fields in the history of human kind (Figures 25.1 and 25.2).

Here let us find out what the latest trends are in the software industry today.

25.2.1 Open Source

Today, open source has become an established force in the software industry [2]. The open source community voluntarily develops software products or components and makes then available to the entire world with the source code for free or for a small fee. Since the source code is available, other developers can see it, evaluate it, and can make changes in the source code. They in turn can publish it to the wide and vast community of open source people. This is a very strong business model.

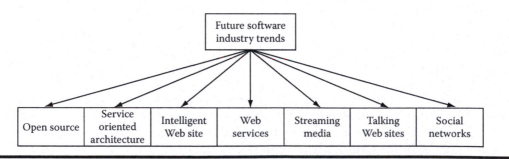

Figure 25.1   Future software industry trends.

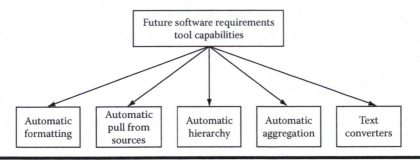

Figure 25.2   Future capabilities of management tools for software requirements.

In stark contrast, for any proprietary software product, development is constrained by the amount of time and money a software vendor can afford. So there is a limit up to how much the product can be tested or further developed. This constraint does not apply to the open source community. Each developer involved in open source development works on his own and can contribute as much as he wants. And since it is open to anybody in the world, a large number of developers can contribute to the same product.

Currently open source is a big success story. It is suitable for developing small neatly built software products to some of the large products like Linux, MySQL, etc. It is going to expand further in the future and will remain a strong force in the software development community.

25.2.2 Application Service Provider

The application service provider (ASP) model is based on the idea of providing access to software product via subscription instead of the traditional model where you must purchase the license of a product to install and use it [3]. Users pay subscription fees at regular time intervals much like cable TV. If any user fails to pay, his access to the application is denied. It is a very good model because users do not need to pay the hefty price usually associated with a software product. Here they pay only a small subscription fee. ASP is still around but has not gained much ground due to low awareness, data theft worries, partial but not full control of the application, etc.

The term, "ASP," originated in the 1990s. Now it is known as software as a service (SaaS) [4].

25.2.3 Software as a Service

SaaS can be a complete application per se, but it can also be a service that can provide valuable information or service in conjunction with another application. Some of the SaaS applications that work with other applications include live feeds (news, broadcasts, etc., services), live services (airline fares, online tickets, etc.), Internet searches (for goods or services), software applications, etc. When SaaS is a complete application, it can provide its services on its own and may not need services from any other SaaS service (www.salesforce.com and www.onenetwork.com).

SaaS has a great future. With evolution of the Internet and usage of the Internet becoming even more widespread, SaaS will have expanded market and will grow more.

25.2.4 Service-Oriented Architecture

Service-oriented architecture (SOA) was invented for SaaS products [5]. Traditional software products were not made for mass markets. Rather they were made for use by limited groups (offices, organizations, etc.). SaaS has changed all that. Now software products are made for mass markets. It has fundamentally changed the architecture of software products to suit the needs of providing access to mass markets. As software products are now being marketed more as a service, these products should have facilities that can effectively make it work as service rather than as a product. All of these are taken care of by adopting SOA architecture. As SaaS grows, so will SOA.

The most important aspect of SOA applications is their ability to integrate with other applications. But before integration, they also should have some properties that will make them searchable so that people looking for an appropriate SaaS service can easily find them. For this, the service providers register themselves in searchable directories at appropriate places so that their service can be easily found. Once somebody finds a suitable service, they can register themselves for this service. Here comes the role of integration. The integration is done using Web Services (WSs). WSs integrate with other applications using what is known as loose coupling. When two or more SaaS applications get integrated, there is never a permanent integration among these applications. They integrate only for the time they need to integrate. For instance, a user's computer may integrate with one SaaS application if he has registered for it. Later, the user finds a better SaaS application for his needs and decides to register for it. The moment he registers for it, there is a new integration between the user computer and the new SaaS application. The old integration between the user computer and the old SaaS application vanishes without a trace.

25.2.5 Intelligent Web Sites

What can you expect in the future from the current trend of sophisticated Web sites? In fact, what we are seeing today can still be considered as a nascent stage in the development of the Internet. In the future, we can have Web sites that can store a profile of a user's habits and preferences and will present content based on the specific user's requirements. This kind of Web site will be intelligent in a true sense.

25.2.6 Web Services

With SOA, we have a great technology that defines new trends in software industry. But without WSs, this technology will not be able to tap the promise it invokes. WSs allow asynchronous and on-demand integration between two SOA-based applications. It is this capability that will transform the way any software application will be used. Without WSs, SOA architecture is like a great innovation sitting on a shelf which is just a showpiece.

25.2.7 Streaming Media

We already have some great Web sites with streaming media (e.g., YouTube). We are actually experiencing just the beginning of a revolution. All kinds of media will become available on the Internet in the future. Currently, bandwidth is a constraint in the choice of richness of streaming media to be deployed. With increase in bandwidth in the future, a great number of rich media can be deployed. So the true functionality of television, radio, and other media will be fully available on the Internet.

25.2.8 Social Networks

Google is a phenomenon that has changed the Internet forever. In fact, it has made an impact on other kinds of businesses as well. The advertising network of Web sites has changed the way the advertising is done. Now even costly products and services can be offered for free by generating revenue not from sale of products and services but from advertising.

Social networks are an offshoot of this phenomenon. In social networks, the user of a Web site is not open to anyone who is surfing the Internet but only to those whom the user has given access. Orkut, Twitter, Facebook are some of the most popular social network.

25.2.9 Influence of New Trends on Software Industry

Innovation in technology opens new ways of doing business and new ways for fulfilling personal goals. At the same time, new trends and innovations in our business and personal life result in the creation of new technology to fulfill those needs. So this works both ways. The new trends in technology that we are observing have not started on its own. Some of them have started to fulfill the existing needs, and the remaining part has been conceived by brilliant people and organizations who created these innovations that are driving creation of new needs.

25.3 Software Requirement Management Tools

There are not many specialty tools that are currently used for requirement management [6]. Most people do their gathering of requirements and management jobs with word processors and simple databases. Some tools, however, let users analyze the requirements that they have gathered and allow them to be stored in specific ways so that users can manage their requirements better. The malady with requirements is that they come from many sources in many formats (like e-mails, questionnaire responses, interviews, old archived requirements, etc.). Formatting these requirements and then putting them in the right perspective is still a daunting task.

In the near future, however, there will be specialty tools to help people do the tasks associated with requirement management. There will be data retrieving and data cleansing programs to get requirements from customer complaints/suggestions and other sources. The voice into text converters will become usable so that programs can convert spoken voice during user interviews into text and store them. There will be efficient tools that will convert unformatted requirements from many sources into uniform requirements.

25.4 Software Design Management Tools

Computer-aided software engineering (CASE) tools ably handle such tasks as configuration management, data modeling, model transformation, source code generation, and the creation of many kinds of diagrams. Most of these tasks are related to software design. Currently there are CASE tools on the market that produce the skeletal framework of source code when the software design is to be made by software architects manually. There are many kinds of documents needed as part of software design to construct the software product (Figure 25.3).

Some common types of documents made include entity relationship diagrams, use cases, activity diagrams, workflow diagrams, etc. All of these different types of documents are made manually.

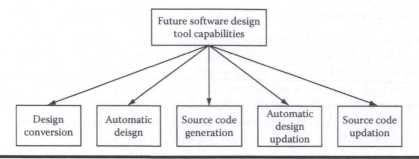

Figure 25.3   Future capabilities of software design tools.

It will become possible in the future to create one type of design document manually and other types automatically. When the original manual document is changed, automatically created documents will also change without the need to change them manually. The software source code generated by these tools will also become more usable.

25.5 Software Build Management Tools

Software construction is the most labor-intensive phase in software development life cycle. So although software design is ready, it takes a lot of time before the software product actually gets into shape and users can see it. Naturally increasing productivity for software construction activities will shrink the time required to build any product. Much work has been done by many vendors to bring tools for this purpose (Figure 25.4).

Right from automatic code generators to IDEs to CASE tools, much work has been done to increase source code generation speed. Some tools are successful while others could not do much. Let us see some of these efforts.

25.5.1 Automatic Code Generator

Automatic code generators have not succeeded so far, but they will become a reality in the future [7]. To build functionality to provide automatic building capability of all kinds of widgets with all possible properties is a gargantuan task. It is like building an industrial robot that can build a complete car from scratch. It is possible to build such a generator in the future but it may take some time.

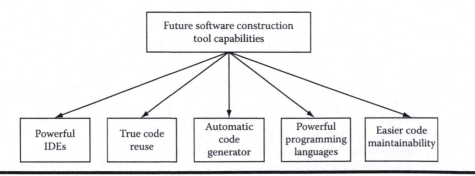

Figure 25.4   Future capabilities of software construction tools.

25.5.2 *Integrated Development Environment Tools*

Currently some IDEs are on the market that allow developers to carry out all kinds of programming tasks visually, but functionality is still not complete [8]. They can have a database.

25.5.3 *Programming Language*

Currently Java is the most popular programming language because of its rich library and functionality [9]. Ruby is becoming popular these days because of its easy language structure. In the future, some newly introduced programming languages may become popular. But their success will depend on how easy they are to use, how good their libraries are, how productive they will be, and how much support they will provide to different platforms.

25.6 Software Testing Management Tools

Software testing will become, moreover, a verification and validation service for the complete product development life cycle. This is in line with the software engineering approach to reduce defects in the work products instead of finding defects and then fixing them after the software is constructed. So the role of software testing will increase along with that of software engineering (Figure 25.5).

25.6.1 *Test Management*

Test management will be completely involved with all work product reviews starting from requirement reviews to design reviews to build review to final inspection of the software product [10]. The tools used for managing test projects will incorporate these changes in the future so that they will be able to support the changing role of software testing.

25.6.2 *Defect Tracking*

Defect tracking tools will no longer be stand-alone tools. They will be part of an integrated test management suite. This will not only help to keep track of all defects in the software product, but these defects will be visible and can be tracked easily. Defect tracking will also become an integral part of evaluating the performance of the test team.

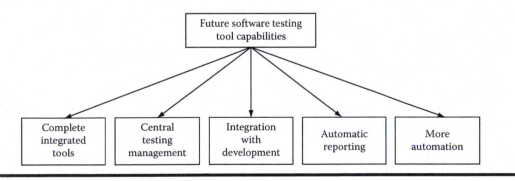

Figure 25.5   Future capabilities of software testing tools.

25.6.3 Automation Tools

Automation tools play an important role in increasing the productivity of a test effort. These tools are used in recoding test scripts based on test cases, and when we want to test the application, we run these scripts. Currently, they are used for automating performance and functional test cases. In the future, these tools will be able to support more environments, recognize new kinds of user interface components, and support many types of testing.

25.6.4 Test Creation Tools

Some tools on the market unsuccessfully try to automate test creation. Test creation is still not within the reach of software tools. It requires smarter tools that can think like human beings. It will take quite a long time to have a good test creation tool.

25.6.5 Test Coverage Tools

There are two types of test coverage tools. One kind inserts software test code in the source code of the application for finding test coverage. The other type of tool generates test codes inside the tool itself and runs this code against the application to find out test coverage.

25.7 Software Project Management Tools

Software project management uses tools and techniques similar to those used in project management in other industries apart from software project specific tools [11]. Most of them are well established and time tested. For project planning, we have tools for making project and schedule plans, resource plans, earned value management, risk plans, effort estimation, cost estimation, quality plans, communication plans, configuration plans, etc.

Traditional planning techniques like Gantt charts, EVM, PERT/CPM charts, etc., are still good and being used. Software tools like Project, Primavera, and others are good for making and tracking these plans. They are also used for making resource plans, project tracking, etc. These and similar other tools are going to be used widely in future. Software vendors will mostly keep enhancing the existing features though some more features may be added from time to time. Already there are many good project management tools on the market that do their work online. Using such tools, project teams update their reports on these tools so that project managers and other managers responsible for evaluating their work can get the reports online. The online tools are really useful as there is no discrepancy due to inundated data or report not sent in time or similar excuses. Online tools also enable managers to get reports even when they are traveling (Figure 25.6).

The most popular effort estimation techniques used currently are function point analysis, wide band Delphi, COCOMO, and some others. For effort estimation, the currently used techniques will also be used in future.

With the advent of distributed teams working on the same project, the need for good communication tools, such as virtual meetings, instant messaging, virtual white boards, and voice over IP, arises; teams located at geographically far distances could communicate effectively and in real time without the need to travel. It is one area that has seen tremendous progress in the past decade. Without these tools, it is almost impossible for distributed teams to work on projects. In the future more and more new kinds of tools will be developed. Existing tools will definitely be enhanced.

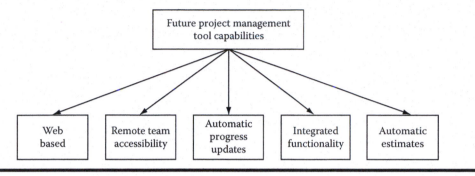

Figure 25.6   Future capabilities of software project management tools.

Configuration and version control tools also have witnessed a lot of progress to be in synch with trends in software development methodologies. For distributed teams, centralized configuration management tools like Perforce, Visual Source Safe, etc. provide a lot of features. These systems provide totally secure access, accurate version control, ability to integrate with other systems easily, and ability to configure them as per user requirements. In future, existing features will be enhanced and some more new features will be added.

Recommended Readings

1. H. Fujita, I. Zualkernan (2008) *New Trends in Software Methodologies, Tools and Techniques*, IOS Press, Amsterdam, the Netherlands.
2. J. Feller (2005) *Perspectives on Free and Open Source Software*, MIT Press, Cambridge, MA.
3. S. M. Levy (2002) *Project Management in Construction*, McGraw-Hill Professional, New York.
4. G. Blokdijk (2008) *SaaS 100 Success Secrets—How Companies Successfully Buy, Manage, Host and Deliver Software as a Service (SaaS)*, Emereo Pty Ltd., Queensland, Australia.
5. D. Krafzig, K. Banke, D. Slama (2005) *Enterprise SOA: Service-Oriented Architecture Best Practices*, Prentice Hall PTR, Upper Saddle River, NJ.
6. M. Khosrow-Pour (2006) *Emerging Trends and Challenges in Information Technology Management*, Idea Group Inc., Hershey, PA.
7. J. Carne (2007) *Challenging the Boundaries of Symbolic Computation*, Imperial College Press, London, U.K.
8. J. A. Jacko (2009) *Human–Computer Interaction. New Trends*, Springer, Berlin, Germany.
9. H. Fujita, D. M. Pisanelli (2007) *New Trends in Software Methodologies, Tools and Techniques*, IOS Press, Amsterdam, the Netherlands.
10. H.-J. Bullinger (2009) *Technology Guide: Principles, Applications, Trends*, Springer, Berlin, Germany.
11. M. Rao (2007) *Knowledge Management Tools and Techniques*, Butterworth-Heinemann, Oxford, U.K.

Appendix A: CMMI Process Standards

CMMI process standards are the most recent set of standards for software projects and their organizations, devised by Software Engineering Institute at Carnegie Mellon University. They are divided into organization level, project level, and development life-cycle level process standards.

A.1 Organizational Level Process Standards

CMMI has one of the most elaborate definitions for organization level processes. Any organization following CMMI standards for its software development processes will benefit immensely in terms of consistent project delivery with a certain level of quality. Costs will also get reduced as productivity will increase. Using a set of five process areas at the organization level, CMMI puts emphasis on creating and implementing process improvements across the entire organization, which results in better productivity and quality. Better productivity, in turn, translates to lesser costs and time in executing and delivering projects. Better quality, in turn, translates to customer satisfaction, which in turn translates into more business.

A.1.1 Organization Innovation and Deployment

The purpose of organizational innovation and deployment is to select and deploy incremental and innovative improvements that measurably improve the organization's processes and technologies. The improvements support the organization's quality and process performance objectives as derived from the organization's business objectives.

The biggest challenge in any organization is change. Changing any process that may affect any person's work always faces resistance. But improvement is not possible without change. Using an elaborate framework for change will allow dissipating the resistance as this framework will be pervasive throughout the organization and there will be management control in implementing it. So its success rate will be high.

A.1.2 Organization Process Definition + IPPD

The purpose of organizational process definition (OPD) is to establish and maintain a usable set of organizational process assets and work environment standards. Integrated product and process definition (IPPD) helps in defining an integrated approach for product development with the goal of improving product attribute quality along with the process quality improvements using collaboration among various disciplines.

OPD helps in creating and maintaining a set of organizational processes that are common across all divisions of the organization. When integrated teams are involved (such as development and maintenance teams), a process definition that covers such teams will govern the processes. Whenever a new project is to be started, it will tailor (modify) these processes according to the requirements of the project.

IPPD includes application of defined processes on the projects.

A.1.3 Organization Process Focus

The purpose of organizational process focus is to plan, implement, and deploy organizational process improvements based on a thorough understanding of the current strengths and weaknesses of the organization's processes and process assets.

This process area involves assessing current practices and processes and comparing them with best practices and benchmarks. Thus, this process area involves gathering process data from all areas of the organization. These data are then properly formatted and refined.

A.1.4 Organization Process Performance

The purpose of organization process performance (OPP) is to establish and maintain a quantitative understanding of the performance of the organization's set of standard processes in support of quality and process-performance objectives, and to provide the process performance data, baselines, and models to quantitatively manage the organization's projects.

Organization process performance is gauged by measuring data from processes and comparing them with a set of desired performance indicators. Tailoring of processes for different projects results in different kinds of data from each project. Therefore, organizations should not allow too much of tailoring of processes for projects. If significant tailoring happens across projects, project data should be grouped separately for similar projects. Some of the data that is collected include schedule and cost, reliability, defect identification and removal data, defect removal effectiveness, latent defect estimation, response time, project progress, and a combination of these areas.

A.1.5 Organization Training

The purpose of organizational training is to develop the skills and knowledge of people so they can perform their roles effectively and efficiently.

Training can be imparted for any area that is common to organizations. Specific training can be imparted when required by a project team. The objectives of any training should be to increase effectiveness of business processes and meet business objectives.

A.2 Project Management Processes

CMMI has ten process areas that support software project management processes. CMMI supports all kinds of project management methodologies and using CMMI ensures that project management is done in an effective way. All project management processes are tailored from organization level standards so that consistent quality, schedule, and cost are maintained across all projects for any organization.

A.2.1 Causal Analysis and Resolution

The purpose of causal analysis and resolution is to identify causes of defects and other problems and take action to prevent them from occurring in the future. It makes more sense to prevent defects entering into software products than to detect defects and remove them. This is more cost effective. That is why finding out what is going wrong in the development process and eliminating the cause of the problem helps in reducing defects entering into the product. Using statistical process control techniques, data from previous projects about common causes of defects are analyzed, and then this knowledge is applied to the current project. Apart from causes of defects, other factors such as productivity, quality, cycle time, etc., are also analyzed from previous project data and are applied to the current project to improve the project.

A.2.2 Configuration Management

The purpose of configuration management (CM) is to establish and maintain the integrity of work products using configuration identification, configuration control, configuration status accounting, and configuration audits.

Indeed, there are many versions of software parts, documents, and project artifacts in the same project. If a proper version of these parts is not maintained, team members may be working on wrong versions of documents and software parts.

A.2.3 Decision Analysis and Resolution

The purpose of decision analysis and resolution (DAR) is to analyze possible decisions using a formal evaluation process that evaluates identified alternatives against established criteria.

Issues arise due to many reasons. All issues are not of the same importance. Some issues are critical while others are not so critical. Resolving critical issues immediately is a prime concern for any project manager so that its adverse effect on the project can be minimized. Identifying, prioritizing, establishing a proper channel for resolution, and determining the required action are some of the areas that are decided using DAR.

A.2.4 Integrated Project Management + IPPD

The purpose of integrated project management (IPM) is to establish and manage the project and the involvement of the relevant stakeholders according to an integrated and defined process that is tailored from the organization's set of standard processes. When integrated teams are involved on a project, IPPD also applies.

This is also known as tailoring of processes to suit the needs of a specific project. When there is no set of established processes at any organization, each project will have its own set of processes decided by the project manager. This leads to substantial differences in quality, productivity, and schedule among projects. A better way to reduce variability among projects is to take established processes at the organization and tailor (modify) them to suit specific needs of the project. This is what is achieved using IPM processes. Basically four groups of processes are tailored here: development activities, service activities, acquisition activities, and support activities.

A.2.5 Measurement and Analysis

The purpose of measurement and analysis (MA) is to develop and sustain a measurement capability that is used to support management information needs.

It is a fact that you cannot manage anything if you cannot measure it. All processes involved in planning, executing, and controlling any project should be measurable; only then can a project manager manage it. So measuring project processes and then analyzing them against best practices or benchmarks empowers a project manager to take appropriate actions.

A.2.6 Project Monitoring and Control

The purpose of project monitoring and control (PMC) is to provide an understanding of the project's progress so that appropriate corrective actions can be taken when the project's performance deviates significantly from the plan.

This is one of the most important process areas related to projects. Work breakdown structure, project baseline information, CM, and many support areas are linked to this process. Using this process, a project manager can keep his project on track using various control measures.

A.2.7 Project Planning

The purpose of project planning (PP) is to establish and maintain plans that define project activities. PP is done by tailoring organizational processes to suit the specific needs of the project. Whenever there is a change in plan, it is to be updated accordingly. PP is related to the technical solution, risk management, and requirement management process areas. It needs an estimation for effort and a workable schedule taking into account the productivity and risks involved.

A.2.8 Quantitative Project Management

The purpose of quantitative project management is to quantitatively manage the project's defined process to achieve the established quality and process-performance objectives.

Using statistical process control methods ensures that all processes are repeatable and deviations are minimized. This ensures consistent quality of a process, which results in consistent quality of products being developed. All processes related to PMC, MA, OPP, IPM, etc., are followed per organizational objectives. Project attributes that are monitored here include defect density, cycle time, and test coverage. Some of the subprocesses measured for improvement include requirement volatility; project size, schedule, and cost planned versus actual values; peer review coverage; test coverage; training effectiveness; reliability; number of defects found in each project phase; etc.

A.2.9 Risk Management

The purpose of risk management is to identify potential problems before they occur so that risk-handling activities can be planned and invoked as needed across the life of the product or project to mitigate adverse impacts on achieving objectives.

To determine risks for a project, sources of risk are identified. A risk management strategy is then defined based on analysis of risk and its projected impact. The strategy is then implemented to mitigate those risks. Work products for risk management include risk source lists and risk category lists. Some of the causes of risk include uncertain requirements; estimates not available as similar projects were not executed previously; infeasible design; unavailable technology; unrealistic schedule; inadequate staffing; incapable subcontractor; inadequate communication; and disruption to operations due to natural, political, business, or any other cause.

A.2.10 Supplier Agreement Management

The purpose of supplier agreement management is to manage the acquisition of products from suppliers.

This process area includes supplier selection, supplier relationship management, contract and agreement creation and execution, product and services acquisition, etc.

A.3 Software Development Life-Cycle Processes

CMMI has elaborate supporting processes for all phases of the software development life cycle. In fact, right from requirements, it supports maintenance and retirement of software products.

A.3.1 Requirements Management

In any business, demand from consumers is fulfilled by appropriate supply. In the case of software development, demand from customers comes through software requirements. The software development organization, whether internal or external, fulfills this demand by developing the required software and delivering it to the customer.

In most industries, the demand is precise, concrete, and measurable. But in the software development industry, the demand is not clear even after the software is delivered. That is why most software development projects fail on some account or another. Due to lack of clear requirements at the very beginning of the project, requests for change in requirements keep coming in throughout the entire software development life cycle. As discussed throughout this book, this creates many kinds of problems in software development.

It is a fact of life that requirements keep changing or that additional requirements keep coming. A software development project manager, therefore, has to devise a way so that his project can accommodate this aberration. One good way to handle this is to choose and use a standard process for requirements management that suits your needs.

Even if you have an umbrella process model that covers every aspect of work getting done in your organization, for example, the CMMI model, the model itself has many alternative components for doing individual tasks. So there could be many alternative standard ways for managing requirements. Some of the standard methods for managing requirements include using a standard template for gathering requirements, using version control to manage requirement changes, using an iterative model for managing requirements, etc.

A.3.1.1 Requirements Development

This process area describes three types of requirements: customer requirements, product requirements, and product component requirements. Taken together, these requirements address the needs of relevant stakeholders, including those pertinent to various product life-cycle phases (e.g., acceptance testing criteria) and product attributes (e.g., safety, reliability, and maintainability). Requirements also address constraints caused by the selection of design solutions (e.g., integration of commercial off-the-shelf products).

Requirement development is very important because the whole software project depends on it. If requirements are not defined properly or are ambiguous, the software design and construction will be faulty. Requirements should be gathered and developed with utmost care.

A.3.1.2 Requirement Management

Requirements are managed and inconsistencies with project plans and work products are identified. Whenever any doubts about any requirement arise, a clarification is sought from the concerned stakeholder and the changes made are then incorporated. It is also part of requirement management to obtain commitment to the requirements from the project participants. Changes to the requirements are also managed as they evolve during the project. Bidirectional traceability among the requirements and work products is also maintained. Inconsistencies between the project plans and work products and the requirements are also identified. Configuration and version control for all changed requirements are also part of requirement management.

A.3.2 Design and Construction (Technical Solution)

The technical solution process area is applicable at any level of the product architecture and to every product, product component, and product-related life-cycle process. Throughout the process areas, where we use the terms product and product component, their intended meanings also encompass services and their components.

The design process should ensure that all the requirements and changed requirements are incorporated in the correct version of the software design. It should also be ensured that due to any changes in requirements, defects should not be introduced into the design.

The construction process produces all the software code in large volume. Each developer is assigned a piece of the software design. So after developing the pieces, these source code pieces need to be integrated so that the application built from those pieces works as intended and envisaged in requirement documents. That is why unit and integration testing should be carefully done at each iteration of development.

A.3.3 Validation

The purpose of validation is to demonstrate that a product or product component fulfills its intended use when placed in its intended environment.

Validation ensures that the produced product works as intended. Typical work products include validation deficiency reports, validation criteria, validation procedures, etc.

Validation is done for requirements and design, product and product components, user interfaces, user manuals, training materials, and process documentation.

A.3.4 Verification

The purpose of verification is to ensure that selected work products meet their specified requirements.

For verification, a proper software testing plan and execution is needed. A separate test plan is recommended. The test plan should incorporate all functional and nonfunctional requirements.

A.3.5 Product Integration

The purpose of product integration (PI) is to assemble the product from the product components, ensure that the product, as integrated, functions properly, and deliver the product.

There should be defined processes for PI so that incremental or one-stage integration between software products or software components can be achieved. Most of the technical solution process areas are covered when PI is done.

A.3.6 Process and Product Quality Assurance

The purpose of process and product quality assurance is to provide staff and management with objective insight into processes and associated work products.

The objective at the organization level should be to align and refine processes so that the high quality of project processes is maintained. Whenever noncompliance is found, it is to be rectified. Evaluation of the processes followed is done periodically and it is assessed for any noncompliance.

Appendix B: ISO Standards

The International Standards Organization (ISO) is an independent body that devises different sets of standards for products, services, and processes. These standards are used by private and government organizations to trade with each other. For instance, a manufacturer makes power generation equipment in Germany and wants to sell it to some customers in South Africa. If the manufacturer's power generation equipments are certified by ISO standards, the South African customer will know that the equipments will be of a specific quality and thus will not have to worry about the quality aspect. If the price is right, he may like to buy this merchandise. Similarly, when a service provider's processes are certified by ISO, the buyer will know that he can rely on the services, which will convince him buy those services.

ISO has developed an elaborate set of standards for processes involved in developing software products. Software service providers can get their processes certified by an assessor for ISO standards so that their potential customers can be confident about their quality of work.

B.1 Requirements

ISO itself does not audit and certify any organization for ISO standards. It only does research, develops ISO standards, and publishes those standards. Business process verification and certification for ISO standards is done by consulting companies authorized by ISO. There are many consulting companies authorized by ISO that audit and certify the business processes of organizations to assess if these organizations can be certified with ISO standards.

Before they audit and assess business processes, they first observe if the organization that has applied for ISO certification meets the requirements for certification.

1. An applicant organization is required to develop a set of procedures that covers all key processes in the business
2. An applicant organization is required to monitor processes to ensure they are effective
3. An applicant organization is required to keep adequate records
4. An applicant organization is required to check output for defects, with appropriate and corrective action where necessary
5. An applicant organization is required to review individual processes regularly and the quality system itself for effectiveness, facilitating continual improvement

B.2 ISO Family of Standards

Over the years, ISO has been developing many standards for the certification needs of many kinds of organizations. Over time, some standards have become obsolete due to the dynamic nature of markets and changes in business processes due to these changes in market conditions. In those cases, ISO discontinues obsolete standards and develops new ones. These new standards then replace old ones. Some of the standards that were developed for software-related services are described next.

The ISO 9000 family of standards includes the following standards:

1. *ISO 9000:2000 Quality management systems—Fundamentals and vocabulary*: This set of standards covers the basics of what a quality management system is and contains the core language of the ISO 9000 series of standards. These documents are used only for guidance purposes and not for certification purposes. However, these documents provide important reference material to understand terms and vocabulary related to quality management systems. ISO revised this standard to ISO 9000:2005 in 2005.

2. *ISO 9001:2000 Quality management systems—Requirements*: This set of standards is intended for use in any organization that designs, develops, manufactures, installs, and/or services any product or provides any form of service. It provides a number of requirements that an organization needs to fulfill if it is to achieve customer satisfaction through consistent products and services that meet customer expectations. It includes a requirement for the continual (i.e., planned) improvement of the quality management system for which ISO 9004:2000 provides many hints.

   This is the only implementation for which third-party auditors may grant certification. It should be noted that certification is not described as any of the "needs" of an organization as a driver for using ISO 9001, but does recognize that it may be used for such a purpose.

3. *ISO 9004:2000 Quality management systems—Guidelines for performance improvements*: This set of standards covers continual improvement. It gives you advice on what you could do to enhance a mature system. This standard very specifically states that it is not intended as a guide to implementation.

   There are many more standards in the ISO 9001 family, many of them not even carrying "ISO 900x" numbers. For example, some standards in the 10,000 range are considered part of the 9000 family: *ISO 10007:1995* discusses configuration management, which for most organizations is just one element of a complete management system. ISO notes: "The emphasis on certification tends to overshadow the fact that there is an entire family of ISO 9000 standards… Organizations stand to obtain the greatest value when the standards in the new core series are used in an integrated manner, both with each other and with the other standards making up the ISO 9000 family as a whole."

   Note that the previous members of the ISO 9000 family, 9001, 9002, and 9003, have all been integrated into 9001. In most cases, an organization claiming to be "ISO 9000 registered" refers to ISO 9001.

B.3 Salient Features of ISO 9001 (ISO IEC 90003)

ISO has merged discontinued series of standards 9001, 9002, and 9003 into a single standard which is referred to as ISO 9001. The latest version is ISO IEC 90003 for software-related services. ISO IEC 90003 is a quality management standard for computer software and related services. It replaces the old ISO 9000-3 1997 software standard. ISO IEC 90003 explains how ISO 9001 2000 can be applied to software and related services.

ISO standards are divided into sections at the top level. ISO presents quality management *requirements* and *guidelines* in sections 4–8 of ISO 90003. Sections 1–3 cover technical topics that are introductory in nature. Section 1 is the description for the set of standards as well as requirements to implement this certification. Section 2 provides information for the approach to be taken to implement this certification. Section 3 contains a description of all the definitions used in this certification. Sections 4–8 provide guidelines that actually describe what this version of ISO standard is all about.

Here are the salient features of this set of standards (sections 4–8).

Section 4: Systemic Requirements and Guidelines

Section 4.1: Establish a Quality Management System for Software Products

Here major process areas include developing a quality system for software products and software services. To achieve these goals, suitable processes are identified for building the quality system, including software development, software development planning, software quality planning, software operation, and software maintenance. The sequencing of the process steps and their interaction with each other are described. The implementation of quality management systems, their effectiveness, and the support for these processes are documented. How improvement will be done in the quality management system using effectiveness monitoring, measuring effectiveness, improving effectiveness is determined.

Section 4.2: Document Your Software-Oriented Quality System

Section 4.2.1: Developing Quality Management System Documents

This section deals with taking care of documentation for quality system, software processes, and life-cycle models.

Section 4.2.2: Preparing a Quality Management System Manual

This section deals with preparing user manuals for processes, process interactions, process scope, and procedure to increase or decrease scope.

Section 4.2.3: Control Quality Management System Documents

This section deals with version control of documents and handling issues like obsolescence and usability of documents.

Section 4.2.4: Maintain Quality Management System Records

This section deals with issues regarding record retention, record keeping management system, and how records are used.

Section 5: Management Requirements and Guidelines

Section 5.1: Support Quality

This section deals with the role of management in influencing the organization toward adhering to quality processes in fulfilling customer and product requirements. It also involves creating a management system that helps in setting and achieving quality norms. It specifies the need to have adequate resources that will help in implementing the quality management system. Once implemented, measures are to be taken so that the system is used by people. After-implementation effort also involves improving the quality management system by doing periodic reviews and assigning resources for quality system improvement efforts.

Section 5.2: Focus on Your Customers

This section deals with identifying customer requirements accurately and then meeting them through the fulfillment cycle. Customer satisfaction should be the hallmark of service. Effort should be made to enhance customer experience.

Section 5.3: Establish a Quality Policy

If you want to be a quality-conscious organization, you need to define your quality policy, which will serve your organization's purpose, meet your requirements, and ensure that your quality objectives are met through policy adherence. To ensure that everybody adheres to the quality policy, the policy needs to be communicated properly so that it reaches everybody. Review of policy implementation should be done at regular intervals so that changes required in the policy can be done per the current business environment.

Section 5.4: Perform Quality Planning

Once you have defined your quality objectives for functional areas at all organizational levels, you can start planning on how to implement them. They should include quality management for software products and a mechanism for quality improvement of the process.

Section 5.5: Control Your Quality System

You need to find a mechanism to control and manage your quality system. For this, assign people with proper authority and responsibility and communicate this change within the entire organization. A person from top management should be appointed to oversee work. Assess the effectiveness of the quality system and get status reports at regular intervals. Whenever required, include a provision so that the quality system maintenance can be done for effecting required changes in the system. Communication on all things regarding the system should be done in such a way that it reaches all employees in the organization.

Section 5.6: Perform Management Reviews

A procedure for management reviews of status reports should be made. This should include mechanisms for doing regular reviews, effectiveness evaluation of the quality program, and maintenance of status reports. Proper examination of the audit (review) results should be done so that opportunities for improvements can be identified, customer feedback can be examined and incorporated in the quality system, produced software product quality data can be examined and process performance information, effectiveness of corrective and preventive actions, and finally overall management review reports can be provided. The review reports should be used to make improvements in the quality system to make it more effective, improve software product quality, and also address current and future manpower needs of the organization.

Section 6: Resource Requirements and Guidelines

Section 6.1: Provide Quality Resources

This area covers the needs to address resource requirements for meeting customer requirements, regulatory requirements, and the supporting quality system. Resources needed for the quality system can be categorized as resources for support, resources for implementation, resources for quality system improvement, resources for meeting customer requirements, and resources for meeting regulatory requirements.

Section 6.2: Provide Quality Personnel

The employees selected for the quality department should have appropriate experience, education, training, and skills to do their job effectively. Proper training programs should be arranged for software development staff and software project management staff, and regular status checks should be done to know if these programs are effective.

Section 6.3: Provide Quality Infrastructure

For implementing a quality system you need to set up an infrastructure on which the system can be built. The infrastructure needs should be identified first based on hardware, software, and physical facilities needed for software development. Tools that will facilitate software development and that will support, protect, and control these activities should be identified. Tools will also be needed to manage these activities. Proper guidelines should be drawn to maintain this entire infrastructure so that these activities do not get hampered in need of maintenance.

Section 6.4: Provide Quality Environment

The work environment for the people in the organization should help in facilitating productivity. A suitable work environment should be identified, and this should be implemented and managed.

Section 7: Realization Requirements and Guidelines

Section 7.1: Control Software Product Realization Planning

Here, processes that help in setting quality objectives for software products as well as risk mitigation strategies are identified. Once a realization process is identified, these processes should be developed. The software production life-cycle model should be identified and all project activities associated with that model should be chosen. All software projects should be planned and executed according to the chosen model. Correlation between the life-cycle model and quality management system should also be made.

Section 7.2: Control Customer Processes

Software requirements from customers should be identified clearly. Parameters that affect the use of the software product should be identified. Compliance to regulations imposed by the government and other agencies in operation of the software product should also be ensured. To get customer requirements, tools and methods appropriate for the occasion should be employed. Once requirements are gathered, they should be analyzed. Analysis should be done in view of contract, software engineering, software maintenance, and software quality requirements. If there are any concerns regarding supporting information from the customer, concerns from design and development points of view, etc., should be clarified. Before making a commitment, evaluate your own capabilities, weaknesses, profitability, etc. Also evaluate the capability of your suppliers. Appoint a senior level executive as account manager for fulfilling customer requirements and communicating with customers. Create a communication channel for consistent and regular communication with your customer. Also ensure that regular reviews and assessments are conducted for the project work being done. Establish problem resolution mechanisms so that whenever any issues arise, they are resolved satisfactorily.

Section 7.3: Control Software Design and Development

Once the requirements are analyzed and the project team is ready to go ahead, they will start doing software design and development. To facilitate this process, they should first have information about the stages involved in these activities. They should also have controlling procedures for these activities lest something goes wrong. The project team should have a clear organizational structure and every member's responsibilities should be clearly defined. Clear communication channels need to be established for interaction among the design and development teams. Whenever changes occur, all team members should be informed. The project plan should be updated accordingly as well. Each and every activity should be clearly defined in the project plan so that people know the activities that are to be performed and the activities are in the pipeline. Outputs from each activity should be documented. Management activities should also be clearly defined. The support that will be needed for these activities should be stated. The training requirements should also be specified. Verification and validation needs should be identified as should the rules, tools, techniques, and conventions that will be needed for the design and development. Elaborate plan for verification and validation activities should be specified for development, maintenance, and operation. Service level agreements should be the guiding principles for all these activities.

What input, input definitions, and their evaluation for fitness will be needed for design and development? Use inputs only after reviewing them. These inputs must come from functional, performance, quality, security, and any other requirements from the customer. The possible outputs from software product design and development should be determined. Based on the output, control activities related to design and development. Keep a record of what outputs were produced. Once design and development are ready, review them before moving forward in the project. During reviews, establish procedures for problem resolutions. Keep a record of how a problem was fixed for future reference. Also keep records of nonconformities, errors, and defects in the product encountered during reviews.

After reviews, perform verification of design and development of the software product. Keep a record of activities and outputs performed during verification. After verification, perform validation of design and development to know if the product conforms to the specifications outlined in the requirements. Conduct software testing activities and fix errors.

Once testing is complete, incorporate any change request in the design and development. Repeat verification, validation, and testing after making changes. After finding that the software product meets the specifications of the customer, hand over the product to the customer.

Section 7.4: Control Your Purchasing Function

Here, you manage your suppliers, contractors, and subcontractors. Establish procedures to ensure that products and services supplied by your suppliers meet your requirements. Establish procedures to control your purchases of services, products, and outsourced activities. Also ensure procedures for purchases of parts and components including software components.

Establish mechanisms to ensure that parts, components, products, and services are delivered with proper documentation. Establish procedures for inspection and verification of purchased goods and services.

Section 7.5: Manage Production and Service Provision

After the software product has been installed and used by the customer, it needs to be maintained, and timely updates for defects found by end users need to be made. All the activities here are related to making the software product usable. Thus, apart from user training and guidance, a good service mechanism also needs to be established so that end users' problems can be logged and a satisfactory solution can be provided so that work does not get hampered.

During the software project, many artifacts and their different versions are developed. It is very important that all of them are maintained and tracked during the life cycle of the project. Establish a mechanism that will ensure that all artifacts can be safely and accurately archived and easily retrieved whenever required. The software built during development also needs to be kept in such a way that incremental development can be done.

Section 7.6: Control Monitoring Devices

A large number of devices are used for project control and monitoring. This section identifies monitoring and measuring devices depending on the needs of the project. First, needs for monitoring and measuring are identified and then suitable devices are described. Here, calibration needs of these devices are also identified and measures for calibration are adopted. Monitoring and measuring devices also need proper protection against unauthorized use, damage, deterioration, and obsolescence. From time to time, these devices also need to be validated so that their measuring ability is intact and that they measure correctly. It is also important that the users of these devices be trained in the correct use of the devices. Therefore, proper documentation, guidelines, and training should be provided to those doing the measurement using these devices.

Section 8: Remedial Requirements and Guidelines

Section 8.1: Carry Out Remedial Processes

Whenever deviations in execution of a project are found, they have to be corrected. To find these deviations, you need to plan for remedial processes. But first you need to monitor, measure, and analyze project processes to know whether they conform to the project plan. Embedded in the project plan is the quality plan. By monitoring, measuring, and analyzing project processes you continuously evaluate your project processes. You can in fact plan your quality plan so that it will help in improving effectiveness of the quality management system itself.

Section 8.2: Monitor and Measure Quality

Once your quality management system is set up and used in projects, you are ready to monitor and measure your quality metrics. You can use many methods to do this, as described in your quality management system. Some of the metrics include customer satisfaction through data from helpdesk calls, direct and indirect customer feedback, internal and external audits, etc.

Section 8.3: Control Your Nonconforming Software Products

This area discusses software products you have made that do not conform to the quality norms as set in the requirements document. You need to identify which of your software products are not conforming by measuring their quality attributes and comparing them with the quality norms. Once identified, take appropriate measures to control software products so that they conform to the norms. This can be done by planning for devising work-arounds or applying patches that will remove the defects in the production instance. Sometimes due to faulty documentation or improper training, users may be using the products wrongly. These instances should also be identified and corrected. Once these nonconformities are removed, the product should be demonstrated to the customer and these issues should be closed.

Section 8.4: Analyze Quality Information

The quality management system should have all the relevant metrics—monitoring, measuring, and analyzing capability—otherwise it will not be effective. The first thing in this regard should be to identify what kind of metrics information is needed for your project. Once these metrics are identified, information required for these metrics needs to be gathered from your project data. The data can be collected from your internal systems, customers, suppliers, products, processes, etc. Once you have metrics data, you can easily analyze it.

Section 8.5: Take Required Remedial Actions

Once you have vital project metrics data, you can take remedial action to rectify the nonconforming process areas as well as improve effectiveness of your quality management system. The data available from the audits done with your process will help in improving the effectiveness of the quality management system. Management reviews will also help to increase effectiveness of the quality management system. Any nonconformity whenever found should be strictly dealt with; otherwise, it will promote wrong practices with project teams. If any data show that nonconformity may likely occur in future, process areas where these observations are found need to be reviewed and necessary actions should be taken to prevent future nonconformities.

Appendix C: IEEE Standards

C.1 IEEE Standards Organization

The IEEE standard has defined major phases of software product life cycle as Software Requirements, Software Design, Software Construction, Software Testing, and Software Maintenance. These are known as Knowledge Areas (KAs). They are further divided into subareas. Then, there are support processes like Software Configuration Management, Software Engineering Management, Software Engineering Tools and Methods, Software Quality, and Knowledge Areas of the Related Disciplines. They are further divided into subareas.

IEEE standards are presented in a manner that is very close to how a software project is planned and executed in the real world. Unlike other standards, IEEE standards do not appear to be imposed from outside on any typical software projects. They look more like a model on which any software project can be modeled, instead of just as a guide. Implementing these standards on any large-sized software projects is easy.

C.2 IEEE Standards Knowledge Areas

IEEE standards are first divided into primary and supporting knowledge areas. These knowledge areas are then divided into subknowledge areas. Each of these subareas then has major tasks. These tasks then may contain subtasks.

Software Requirements: Software requirements knowledge area is divided into many subareas as follows.

Software requirements fundamentals: Provides definition of software requirements and how they are distinct from system requirements.

Requirements process: Defines the process involved in gathering and managing software requirements.

Requirements elicitations: Provides methods of gathering software requirements including interviews, meetings, and questionnaire.

Requirements analysis: Provides methods as to how to analyze software requirements.

Requirements specifications: Provides information as to how to make specifications, so that software requirements are understood by any project stakeholders or project team members without requiring further reference.

Requirements validations: Provides information as to how to validate any software requirement whether the requirement is not ambiguous or incomplete.

Practical considerations: When software requirements are being elicited they are in crude form. Only after many iterations, these requirements become clear. Then, requirement changes are order of the day. Over the project duration, many versions of requirements are formed. Managing these versions and relating them with the correct version of software being developed is a complex and difficult task. These practical considerations are discussed in this standard.

Software Design: The subareas of Software Design are as follows.

Software design fundamentals: This area provides information for different aspects of activities that are performed in software design.

Key issues in software design: This area discusses issues that arise due to either difficulty in converting requirement into a software equivalent or sometimes difficulty in meeting any requirements due to any reason except technical issues.

Software structure and architecture: What will be the architecture of the product and how will it be structured?

Software design, quality analysis and evaluation: How will software be designed? How will quality be taken care of in design?

Software design notations: This area provides information about how to present the architecture and structure in an acceptable form, so that it may be understood by project team members easily.

Software design strategies and methods: What strategy will be taken for software design? What method will be adopted for the design?

Software Construction: The subareas of Software Construction are as follows.

Software construction fundamentals: General description of construction methodology.

Managing construction: How will the construction process be managed?

Practical considerations: What practical limits, constraints, and trade offs will be adopted for constructing the product?

Software Testing: The subareas of Software Testing are as follows.

Software testing fundamentals: General description of testing methodology.

Test levels: Will unit testing, integration testing, and system testing be done?

Test techniques: What test techniques (code based/simulation based/UI based, etc.) will be employed during testing phase?

Test-related measures: What metrics will be used for measuring effectiveness of testing?

Test process: What processes (performance, functional, usability, automation, etc.) will be employed for testing?

Software Maintenance: The subareas of Software Maintenance are as follows.

Software maintenance fundamentals: General description of software maintenance process areas that will be followed.

Key issues in software maintenance: Documentation of issues faced during maintenance.

Software maintenance process: Description of processes adopted for software maintenance.

Techniques for software maintenance: Techniques adopted for software maintenance (reengineering/reverse engineering, etc.).

C.3 IEEE Supporting Knowledge Areas

Software Configuration Management: The subareas of Software Configuration Management are as follows.

Management of the SCM process
Software configuration identification
Software configuration control
Software configuration status accounting
Software configuration auditing
Software release management and delivery

Software Engineering Management: The subareas of Software Engineering Management are as follows.

Initiation and scope definition
Software project planning
Software project enactment
Review and evaluation
Closure
Software engineering measurement

Software Engineering Process: The subareas of Software Engineering Process are as follows.

Process implementation and change
Process definition
Process assessment
Process and product measurement

Software Engineering Tools: The subareas of Software Engineering Tools are as follows.

Software tools
Software requirements tools
Software design tools
Software construction tools
Software testing tools
Software maintenance tools
Software configuration management tools
Software engineering management tools
Software engineering process tools
Software quality tools
Miscellaneous tool issues

Software Engineering Methods: The subareas of Software Engineering Methods are as follows.

Numeric methods
Formal methods
Prototyping methods

Software Quality: The subareas of Software Quality are as follows.
    Software quality fundamentals
    Software quality management processes
    Practical considerations

Knowledge Areas of Related Disciplines: The subareas of Knowledge Areas of Related Disciplines are as follows.
    Computer engineering
    Computer science
    Management
    Mathematics
    Project management
    Quality management
    Software ergonomics
    Systems engineering

C.4 Software Requirements

Software requirements are governed by the IEEE 12207 standard. IEEE has a comprehensive process definition for the software requirements area.

C.4.1 Software Requirements Fundamentals

The software requirements fundamental subarea is divided into the following subareas:

C.4.1.1 Definition of a Software Requirement

Product and process software requirement: Software requirement must provide information for both product and the process to build that software product. For example, a Web-based information system may have a login page. The product information may include the form and fields as well as how the login functionality is structured. The process information to make this functionality may include information about which programming language and which front end will be used to make it.

Functional and nonfunctional requirements: Functional requirements include information about the product features and how they work. Nonfunctional information includes information like security, performance, and usability.

C.4.1.2 Emergent Properties

Quantifiable requirements: The requirement specification should provide information about the total number of requirements as well as size and scope of requirements.

System requirements and software requirements: In IEEE standards, a system requirement is defined as a complete set of inputs and outputs for a transaction between all actors including the human operator, the software application, and any physical instrument or device that will be involved in completing that transaction. A software requirement on the other hand discusses inputs and outputs from the software application alone.

C.4.2 Requirements Process

The Requirements Process subarea is divided into the following subareas:

Process models: This area describes information as to what process model is used for requirement elicitation and requirement management.

Process actors: This area describes information about who will be actors for any transaction in the software application and what their role in that software application transaction is.

Process support and management: What supporting mechanism is available for managing requirements (version control, quality control, etc.).

Process quality and improvement.

C.4.3 Requirements Elicitation

The Requirements Elicitation subarea is divided into the following subareas:

Requirement sources: From where have the software requirements been sourced and can the requirements be validated?

Elicitation techniques: What elicitation techniques will be used (questionnaire, interviews, meetings, document exchange, and existing documentation)?

C.4.4 Requirements Analysis

The Requirements Analysis subarea is divided into the following subareas:

Requirement classifications: Can requirements be classified into many classes? What could those classes be?

Conceptual modeling: Could requirements be modeled into a conceptual system?

Architecture design and requirement allocation: Could requirements be allocated into different design parts? What kind of architecture will be employed for designing the application?

Requirements negotiations: Is any negotiation required with customer for trade-offs in designing the application?

C.4.5 Requirements Specification

Software requirements specification subarea is divided into the following subareas:
   System definition document
   System requirement specification
   Software requirement specification

C.4.6 Requirements Validation

The Requirements Validation subarea is divided into the following subareas:

C.4.6.1 Requirement Reviews

Prototyping: What kind of prototype will be designed based on requirements?

Model validation: If the design model will be validated, what method will be used to validate the design?

Acceptance tests: Will acceptance tests be made based on requirements?

C.4.7 Practical Considerations

The Practical Considerations subarea is divided into the following subareas:

Iterative nature of requirements process: Will iterative methodology be employed in case all/any requirements are not clear or there are changes in requirements?

Change management: How will requirement changes be managed?

Requirements attributes: Will attributes of requirements be defined and measured?

Requirements tracing: Will any technique be used for tracing requirements vis-à-vis software design?

Measuring requirements: Will requirements be measured using any metrics for design/construction/testing?

C.5 Software Design

Software design is defined in the IEEE 610 6-12 standard. The Software Design subarea includes software design fundamentals, key issues in software design, software structure and architecture, software design, quality analysis and evaluation, software design notations, and software design strategies and methods.

Subareas of these subknowledge areas are given below.

C.5.1 Software Design Fundamentals

The Software Design Fundamentals subarea is divided into the following subareas:

General design concepts: What design methodology will be used for designing the application?

Context of software design: What context (previous design experience, customer preference, etc.) will be used for designing the application?

Software design process: What methodology and processes will be adopted for designing the application?

Enabling techniques: What techniques will be used for making the design (CASE tools, modeling tools, etc.)?

C.5.2 Key Issues in Software Design

The Key Issues in Software Design subarea is divided into the following subareas:

Concurrency: Will the design permit concurrent running of business processes in the application?

Control and handling of events: How will the control flow of events be handled during transactions in the application? How will events be handled in design?

Distribution of components: How will the application be broken into components?

Error and exception handling and fault tolerance: How will fault tolerance be implemented in the application design? How will exceptions be handled in the application?

Interaction and presentation: How will users of the application be interacting with the application (input/output devices)? How and where will information be presented from the application (computer screen/printer/any other output devices)?

Data persistence: How will data persistence be achieved? Will any client part of the application be used for data persistence?

C.5.3 Software Structure and Architecture

The Software Structure and Architecture subarea is divided into the following subareas:

Architectural structure and viewpoints: How will the logical, physical model of the application be designed?

Architectural styles: Which architectural design will be adopted to model the application?

Design patterns: What pattern will be used to model the application?

Families of programs: If application can be divided into parts, which will form the complete application after integration of all parts?

C.5.4 Software Design Quality Analysis and Evaluation

The Software Design Quality Analysis and Evaluation subarea is divided into the following subareas:

Quality attributes: What quality attributes will be used for modeling the application?

Quality analysis and evaluation techniques: How will the quality of the design be analyzed and evaluated?

Measures: What metrics will be used to assess quality of the prepared design?

C.5.5 Software Design Notations

The Software Design Notations subarea is divided into the following subareas:

Structural descriptions: How will the design structure be represented (UML/any other design language)?

Behavioral descriptions: How will the behavior of the application be represented (use cases)?

C.5.6 Software Design Strategies and Methods

The Software Design Strategies and Methods subarea is divided into the following subareas:

General strategies: What strategies will be used in designing the application?

Function oriented design: Will the design be function oriented?

Object oriented design: Will the design be object oriented?

Data structure oriented design: Will the design be data structure oriented?

Component based design: Will the design be component based?

Other methods.

C.6 Software Construction

The Software Construction subknowledge area includes software construction fundamentals, managing construction, and practical considerations.

C.6.1 Software Construction Fundamentals

The Software Construction Fundamentals subarea is divided into the following subareas:

Minimizing complexity: How will the complexity of the application be minimized (application partitioning, encapsulation)?

Anticipating change: How will changes in design be handled (normalization, general purpose component implementation)?

Construction for verification: How will construction be verified for defects (if verification is in built)?

Standards in construction: What coding standards were used in construction?

C.6.2 Managing Construction

The Managing Construction subarea is divided into the following subareas:

Construction models: What methodology will be used for software construction (agile/waterfall)?

Construction planning: How will construction be planned (resource allocation and iterative development)?

Construction measurement: What metrics will be used for construction for assessing quality, schedule performance, and budget performance?

C.6.3 Practical Considerations

The Practical Considerations subarea is divided into the following subareas:

Construction design: What trade offs were taken in construction design (combining two or more requirements into one, splitting one requirement into two or more, functionality achievement through work around, omitting a functionality, etc.)?

Construction language: Does construction language have any limitation in achieving the required functionality?

Coding: Could standard coding practices at some places not be followed?

Construction testing: Could unit/integration testing not be performed for some reason?

Reuse: Could reuse of components not be done for some reason?

Construction quality: How will quality of construction be ensured?

Integration: How will components be integrated to each other?

C.7 Software Testing

Most areas under software testing are covered in IEEE 610 and IEEE 982. The Software Testing subknowledge area includes software testing fundamentals, test levels, test techniques, test-related measures, and test process.

C.7.1 Software Testing Fundamentals

The Software Testing Fundamentals subarea is divided into the following subareas:

Software testing terminology: What testing terminology will be used for the project?

Key issues: What key issues can be expected and how they can be tackled?

Relationship of testing to other activities: How will testing activities be related to requirements, design, and construction activities?

C.7.2 Software Testing Levels

The Software Testing Levels subarea is divided into the following subareas:

Test target: What level of testing will be desired?

Testing objectives: Unit testing, integration testing, performance testing, system testing, user-acceptance testing, alpha testing, beta testing, regression testing, and usability testing.

C.7.3 Software Testing Techniques

The Software Testing Techniques subarea is divided into the following subareas:

Tester intuition and experience: Has software tester experience level been documented?

Specification-based testing: Will testing be based on specifications or will exploratory testing be done?

Code-based testing: Will only software code will be tested (white box testing) or will black box testing also be done?

Fault-based testing: Will negative testing be done or just positive testing?

Usage-based testing: Will testing be done based on how the application will be used by end users?

Nature of application-based testing: What kind of testing will be performed (functional/nonfunctional)?

Selecting and combining testing techniques: Will a single testing technique be used or a combination of testing techniques?

C.7.4 Software Testing-Related Measures

The Software Testing-Related Measures subarea is divided into the following subareas:

Evaluation of program under test: How will the application be evaluated for testing effectiveness (number of bugs found/not found during testing)?

Evaluations of test performed: How will the testing activity be evaluated (number of bugs found per hour)?

C.7.5 Software Testing Process

The Software Testing Process subarea is divided into the following subareas:

Practical considerations: Test process management IEEE 12207, test documentation IEEE 829, independent verification & validation, test reuse, effort estimation IEEE 982

Test activities: Test planning IEEE 1008, test bed preparation, test execution, defect tracking

C.8 Software Maintenance

Some of the standards used for software maintenance include IEEE1219 and IEEE12207. Subareas under Software Maintenance include software maintenance fundamentals, key issues in software maintenance, maintenance process, and techniques for maintenance.

C.8.1 Software Maintenance Fundamentals

The Software Maintenance Fundamentals subarea is divided into the following subareas:

C.8.1.1 Definitions and Terminology

Nature of maintenance: Preventive/breakdown/remedial/enhancement

Need for maintenance: Reasons for maintenance (bug fixing and enhancement)

Majority of maintenance costs: Cost breakdown of maintenance

Evolution of software: Software evaluation for doing maintenance (maintenance required/not required)

Categories of maintenance: Migration from old platform/Web enablement

C.8.2 Key Issues in Software Maintenance

The Key Issues in Software Maintenance subarea is divided into the following subareas:

Technical issues: What are the key issues during maintenance?

Management issues: What are the management issues during maintenance?

Maintenance cost estimation: What are the estimates of costs for maintenance?

Software maintenance measurement: What metrics are used for maintenance work for its effectiveness (if goals of taking maintenance work met?).

C.8.3 Software Maintenance Process

The Software Maintenance Process subarea is divided into the following subareas:

Maintenance processes: What processes were followed for maintenance work?

Maintenance activities: What activities were performed for maintenance work?

C.8.4 Software Maintenance Techniques

The Software Maintenance Techniques subarea is divided into the following subareas:

Program comprehension: If a detailed planning was led out for maintenance work?

Re-engineering: Were the same methodology and technology employed for maintenance work as were used for software construction?

Reverse engineering: Was the source code changed for maintenance or was maintenance done using only the exposed interfaces of the application?

C.9 Software Configuration Management

Software Configuration Management (SCM) is a supporting software life-cycle process (IEEE12207.0-96) that benefits project management, development and maintenance activities, assurance activities, and the customers and users of the end product. Subareas in SCM include management of SCM process, software configuration identification, software configuration control, software configuration status accounting, software configuration auditing, and software release management and delivery.

C.9.1 Management of SCM Process

The Management of SCM Process subarea is divided into the following subareas:

Organization context for SCM: In what context will SCM be used on the project (maintaining versions of software, building software, keeping versions of project documents, etc.)?

Constraints and guidance for SCM process: What constraints will be imposed on the SCM process (user access, privileges for read/write)?

Planning for SCM
    SCM organization and responsibilities: How will SCM organization be set up? Who will be responsible for what activities for maintaining SCM system?
    SCM resources and schedules: What schedules will be followed for maintaining SCM system?
    Tool selection and implementation
    Vendor/subcontractor control
    Interface control
SCM plan
Surveillance of SCM
    SCM measures and measurement: What metrics will be employed to manage the SCM process?
    In-process audit of SCM: Can SCM system be audited online/offline?

C.9.2 Software Configuration Identification

The Software Configuration Identification subarea is divided into the following subareas:

Identification of items for SCM control
    Software configuration
    Software configuration items
    Software configuration item relationship
    Software versions
    Baseline
    Acquiring software configuration items
Software library

C.9.3 Software Configuration Control

The Software Configuration Control subarea is divided into the following subareas:

Requesting, evaluating, and approving software changes
    Software configuration control board
    Software change request process
Implementing software changes
Deviations and waivers

C.9.4 Software Configuration Status Accounting

The Software Configuration Status accounting subarea is divided into the following subareas:
   Software configuration status information
   Software configuration status reporting

C.9.5 Software Configuration Auditing

The Software Configuration Auditing subarea is divided into the following subareas:
   Software functional configuration audit
   Software physical configuration audit
   In process audit of the software baseline

C.9.6 Software Release Management and Delivery

The Software Release Management and Delivery subarea is divided into the following subareas:
   Software building
   Software release management

C.10 Software Engineering Management

Software Engineering Management can be defined as the application of management activities—planning, coordinating, measuring, monitoring, controlling, and reporting—to ensure that the development and maintenance of software is systematic, disciplined, and quantified (IEEE610.12-90). Commonly, this is what is known as software project management (SPM), but, in IEEE terminology, it is known as software engineering management.

   Major subareas of software engineering management include initiation and scope definition, software project planning, software project enactment, review and analysis, closure and software engineering measurement.

C.10.1 Initiation and Scope Definition

The Initiation and Scope Definition subarea is divided into the following subareas:
   Determination and negotiation for requirements
   Feasibility analysis
   Process for review and revision of requirements

C.10.2 Software Project Planning

The Software Project Planning subarea is divided into the following subareas:
   Process planning
   Determine deliverables
   Effort, schedule, and cost estimation
   Resource allocation
   Risk management
   Quality management
   Plan management

C.10.3 Software Project Enactment

The Software Project Enactment subarea is divided into the following subareas:
- Implementation of project plans
- Supplier contract management
- Implementation of measurement process
- Monitor process
- Control process
- Reporting

C.10.4 Software Project Review and Analysis

The Software Project Review and Analysis subarea is divided into the following subareas:
- Satisfaction of requirement determination
- Review and analysis of performance

C.10.5 Software Project Closure

The Software Project Closure subarea is divided into the following subareas:
- Closure determination
- Closure activities

C.10.6 Software Engineering Measurement

The Software Engineering Measurement subarea is divided into the following subareas:
- Establish and sustain measurement commitment
- Plan for measurement process
- Perform the measurement process
- Evaluate measurement

C.11 Software Engineering Process

The Software Engineering Process knowledge area can be examined on two levels. The first level encompasses the technical and managerial activities within the software life-cycle processes that are performed during software acquisition, development, maintenance, and retirement. The second is the meta-level, which is concerned with the definition, implementation, assessment, measurement, management, change, and improvement of the software life-cycle processes themselves. Most of knowledge areas for this subarea are covered in IEEE1220 and IE12207.

Major subareas of the Software Engineering Process include process implementation and change, process definition, process assessment, and process and product measurement.

C.11.1 Process Implementation and Change

The Process Implementation and Change subarea are divided into the following subareas:
- Process infrastructure
- Software process management cycle
- Models for process implementation and change
- Practical considerations

C.11.2 Process Definition

The Process Definition subarea is divided into the following subareas:
Software life-cycle models
Software life-cycle processes
Notation for process definitions
Process adaptation
Automation

C.11.3 Process Assessment

The Process Assessment subarea is divided into the following subareas:
Process assessment models
Process assessment methods

C.11.4 Process and Product Measurement

The Process and Product Measurement subarea is divided into the following subareas:
Process measurement
Software products measurement
Quality of measurement results
Software information models
Process measurement techniques

C.12 Software Engineering Tools and Methods

Software development tools are the computer-based tools that are intended to assist the software life-cycle processes. Tools allow repetitive, well-defined actions to be automated, reducing the cognitive load on the software engineer who is then free to concentrate on the creative aspects of the process. Tools are often designed to support particular software engineering methods, reducing any administrative load associated with applying the method manually. Like software engineering methods, they are intended to make software engineering more systematic, and they vary in scope from supporting individual tasks to encompassing the complete life cycle.

Software engineering methods impose structure on the software engineering activity with the goal of making the activity systematic and ultimately more likely to be successful. They also enable process activities to be measurable. Methods usually provide a notation and vocabulary, procedures for performing identifiable tasks, and guidelines for checking both the process and the product. They vary widely in scope, from a single life-cycle phase to the complete life cycle. The emphasis in this KA is on software engineering methods encompassing multiple life-cycle phases, since phase-specific methods are covered by other KAs.

C.12.1 Software Engineering Tools

While there are detailed manuals on specific tools and numerous research papers on innovative tools, generic technical writings on software engineering tools are relatively scarce. One difficulty is the high rate of change in software tools in general. Specific details alter regularly, making it difficult to provide concrete, up-to-date examples.

The Software Engineering Tools subarea is divided into the following subareas:

Software requirement tools
    Requirement modeling
    Requirement tracing
Software design tools (e.g., UML and CASE tools)
Software construction tools
    Program editors (e.g., Integrated Development Environments like Visual Studio and Eclipse)
    Compilers and code generators
    Interpreters
    Debuggers
Software testing tools
    Test generators
    Test execution framework
    Test evaluators
    Test management (e.g., HP Test Director)
    Performance analysis
Software maintenance tools
    Comprehension tools
    Reengineering tools
Software configuration management tools
    Defect, enhancement, issue, and problem tracking
    Version management (e.g., Visual Source Safe and Perforce)
    Release and build (e.g., ant and cruise control)
Software engineering management tools
    Project planning and tracking (e.g., Microsoft Project)
    Risk management
    Measurement
Software engineering process tools
    Process modeling
    Process management
    Integrated CASE management tools
    Process centered software
Software quality tools
    Review and audit
    Static analysis
Miscellaneous tool issues
    Tool integration techniques
    Meta tools
    Tool evaluation

C.12.2 Software Engineering Methods

The Software Engineering Methods subarea is divided into the following subareas:

Heuristic methods
    Structured methods

Data oriented methods
Object oriented methods
Formal methods
Specifications and language notations
Refinement
Verification
Prototyping methods
Styles
Prototyping targets
Evaluation techniques

C.13 Software Quality

Software quality is now the most important concern on software projects. Even up to the 1990s, quality was considered a secondary concern on software projects. The top concern used to be whether software project deliverables can be met even if they are of secondary quality. After mastering many processes in software development projects, organizations have realized software quality plays an important role and it must be improved. Lower quality software products have many critical defects. Providing customer support for such software products becomes very costly. First of all, preventing measures for defects entering into any stage of software development should be employed. Then, in the testing phase, an attempt should be made to trap and remove defects that entered into the software product. Subareas in Software Quality include software quality fundamentals, software quality management processes, and practical considerations.

C.13.1 Software Quality Fundamentals

The Software Quality Fundamentals subarea is divided into the following subareas:
Software engineering cultures and ethics
Value and costs of quality
Models and quality characteristics
Quality improvements

C.13.2 Software Quality Management Processes

The Software Quality Management Processes subarea is divided into the following subareas:
Software quality assurance
Verification and validation
Reviews and audits (code walkthroughs, management reviews, inspections, etc.)

C.13.3 Software Quality Practical Considerations

The Software Quality Practical Considerations subarea is divided into the following subareas:
Software application quality requirements
Defect characteristic
Software quality management techniques
Software quality measurement

C.14 Related Disciplines of Software Engineering

Software engineering cannot operate in isolation if it has to be practiced. Definitely any discipline for that matter depends on many other disciplines.

These disciplines include computer science, mathematics, computer engineering, management, project management, quality management, software ergonomics, and systems engineering. Software engineering needs mathematics for making algorithms, doing calculations, etc. Software engineering needs quality management fundamentals for solving quality-related matters. Computer science needs software engineering to build software applications. Software engineering needs computer engineering for building interfaces between hardware and software applications. Similarly, other disciplines either depend on software engineering or software engineering depends on them.

Appendix D: Agile Processes for Software Development

The traditional waterfall model poses issues like high risk, long time in delivery, heavy upfront commitment, and inflexible process. Though the waterfall model certainly has advantages and is extremely useful for large projects, organizations and individuals have been in search of alternative approaches for software development that can help in mitigating these issues. Rational Corporation came up with its Unified Process Model for software development projects in search of a better alternative to the waterfall model. Similarly, some other popular approaches include Scrum, eXtreme Programming, Cleanroom software engineering, Microsoft Solutions Framework, Oracle unified method, etc.

D.1 Rational Unified Process Overview

Rational Corporation introduced an alternative life cycle called the Rational Unified Process (RUP). This includes a matrix of processes and workflows that comprise a new way of developing software. The traditional processes of software development are now known as workflows, which span over what Rational called processes. In this model, there are four process areas and nine workflows (Figure D.1).

The traditional software development process model lacked proper integration between project management processes and software development processes. With RUP, this lacuna was removed. It proposed the phases of inception, elaboration, construction, and transition. The six main workflows of business modeling, requirements, analysis and design, construction, test, and deployment along with the three supporting workflows of configuration and change management, project management, and environment pass through these phases during project execution. These workflows are not restricted to any single phase but span across many phases.

Parallel to the phases are the iterations. The iterations during any phase are determined by the need for clarity during the phase. There will be more iterations during any phase where more clarity is needed (Figure D.2).

The initial unified process had some drawbacks. One of them was not having any process definition for production phase of the software life cycle. Rational Corporation thus introduced a new process model and called it enhanced unified process. Now the production phase was added to the existing four phases. At the same time, two workflows were also added to the existing nine

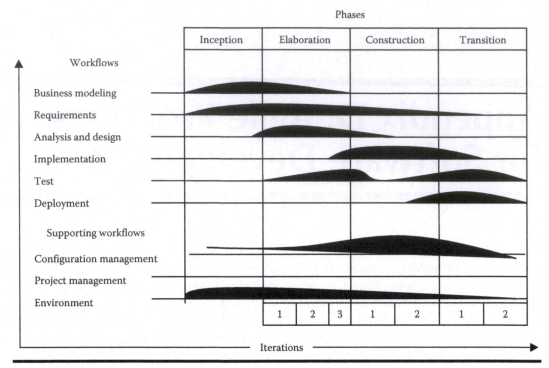

Figure D.1   Rational Unified Process.

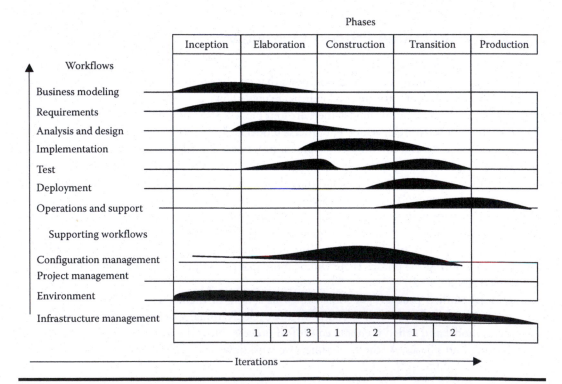

Figure D.2   Enhanced Rational Unified Process.

workflows (Figure D.2). One was the operations and support workflow, which accounts for the work needed for deploying and running the application in the production environment. This was needed as when the software is in development process, user manuals, support plans, and training manuals are to be prepared. The supporting process of infrastructure management was also added. This process allows the operations support team to plan and arrange for the infrastructure, including software, hardware, computer operators, etc., needed to run the installed software system. But more than that, the most important aspect of infrastructure management is to provide resources beyond a single project. Aspects like reuse, resource pooling, consolidation, and process improvement processes are integrated at organization level. The project phases of inception, elaboration, construction, transition, and production are described here.

D.1.1 Inception Phase

The inception phase is where the project scope is defined in the context of project budget and schedule. A project charter consisting of success factors, business case, and financial forecast is established. The business case is elaborated by creating use cases, basic project plan, risk assessment, and project description. To reach the milestone before completing the inception phase, stakeholder feedback on project scope, schedule, and budget is made. Primary use cases validate the requirements. Design and prototype are also validated. A baseline is created to track project budget and schedule. All of these artifacts are validated at milestones to ensure if the project can go ahead. If not, then the project must be scrapped.

D.1.2 Elaboration Phase

In the elaboration phase, the design and architecture of the product takes shape. The milestone after the elaboration phase is known as the life-cycle architecture milestone. The checklist for the milestone includes the following:

1. When at least 80% of the use cases and activity diagrams along with actors have been identified.
2. The software architecture has been created.
3. The architecture has been validated against most of the use cases.
4. A detailed and concrete plan for the entire project has been made.
5. Risk mitigation strategy has been defined.

If the project does not pass through this checklist, the project must be scrapped or redesigned.

D.1.3 Construction Phase

The construction phase is where the software design is converted into software code. It is the most labor-intensive phase in the entire software project. To take care of the large code-building requirement, concurrent engineering and other techniques for rapid application development can be used. If there is a need to get customer feedback on the partial build, iterations can be used.

D.1.4 Transition Phase

Once the product is made, it has to be made available for deployment so that end users can use it. However, before that, the application has to be beta tested to ensure that there are no critical bugs in the application. The application is assessed to validate whether the quality level meets the agreement made during the inception phase. User training also needs to be arranged.

D.1.5 Production Phase

The production phase was introduced in the enhanced model to take care of software processes model after the application is installed and used by end users. Production phase activities involve support and operation activities as well as training for end users so that they can use the application effectively. It also involves rectifying the application when bugs are reported. Enhancement to the application is also made in this phase.

D.2 Engineering Workflows

D.2.1 Business Modeling Workflow

Business modeling is the workflow used by the business engineering team and the software engineering team get to know the real business requirements of the customer and how the proposed software product will help in achieving those business objectives.

Most of the business modeling workflow is done in the inception phase.

D.2.2 Requirements Workflow

Using this workflow, the project team elicits requirements from the customers and end users for the proposed software product. They use techniques like interviews, personal meetings, electronic communications, study existing documents, etc., to get all requirements from end users.

Most of the requirement workflow is done in the inception phase.

D.2.3 Analysis and Design Workflow

This workflow determines how the proposed software product will be implemented. Use cases, activity diagrams, and other tools are used to model the software product. Using these tools, the project team covers all requirements in the product model. The analysis model describes how the proposed product will work against end user requirements. The design model contains all details related to the structure and logic of the proposed product. It also includes information as to how the product will be designed using software components and how these components will be integrated with each other. The design model acts like a blueprint for constructing the product.

Most of the design and analysis workflow is done in the elaboration phase.

D.2.4 Implementation Workflow

Using this workflow, the software design is converted into software code. But before writing the code, organization of the classes, packages, and components is done according to the design document. The components are tested as a unit to ensure that they are perfectly implemented. Once these components have been integrated, an integration testing is done to ensure that integration between the components is working fine.

Most of the implementation workflow is done in the construction phase.

D.2.5 Test Workflow

Once the software system is implemented, it is handed over to the test team. Using test workflows, they perform system testing, performance testing, compatibility testing, and other tests necessary to verify if the software product is working as per requirements. If defects are found, they are fixed. Finally, the product is validated against the requirements using tools like traceability matrix. In this workflow system and beta testing is done.

Test activities span many phases, but most of the work is done during the transition phase.

D.2.6 Deployment Workflow

Once the product is developed and system tested, user acceptance testing is done by end users. User and system manuals are created and end users are provided training to use the product. Finally, the product is installed and is ready to be used.

In the enhanced unified model, a deployment plan has been added in the inception phase itself since all work done on the product through the phases should include supportability and maintainability of the product after the product goes in production.

Deployment activities span many phases but most of the work is done during the elaboration, construction, and transition phases.

D.2.7 Operations and Support Workflow

This workflow was added in the enhanced model after it was decided that the unified process should also support processes when the product goes into production. During the software construction phase, you need to include a provision in the software build itself for good maintenance and operations support. Some of the work belonging to this workflow is done in the construction phase. The remaining work is done in the production phase.

Operations and support workflow span many phases, but most of the work is done during the construction, transition, and production phases.

D.3 Supporting Workflows

D.3.1 Configuration and Change Control Workflow

Artifacts generated during workflow execution during the entire project need to be managed throughout the project. There are iterations and changes in the version of these artifacts. All versions of each artifact need to be managed so that the project team as well as the stakeholders have a complete view of the project and can review these artifacts at any time.

The software code building is done in such a way that the new code created by any developer does not break the current build of the product. The software build has to be maintained at a central location so that developers can check in their new developed code and merge it with the existing build. There are generally many versions of the same product. All of these versions as well as the current version that is being developed need to be kept neatly so that they are available to the entire project team.

Configuration and change control workflow run through all phases of the project.

D.3.2 Project Management Workflow

Project management workflow is where we define the project as well as the iteration plans. As can be seen from the diagrams, there are two levels at which project plans are made. One is at the project level where we have five phases in the project in the enhanced process model. Inside each of these phases there is provision for iterations.

The phase plan consists of measurement plan, risk management plan, problem resolution plan, and product acceptance plan. The iteration plan consists of fine-grained planning within a phase and consists of time-sequenced activities and tasks pertaining to the phase within which the iteration exists. At any given point of time, there are two parallel iterations going on. One is the current iteration plan and the second is the next iteration plan. This is so because the project manager has not only to take care of the current activities but has also to keep working on the next iteration so that there is no time lost between the two iterations. During iteration planning, use cases or scenarios are created. Some other tasks include problem resolution, risk mitigation, change request incorporation in the software product, work on object classes, etc.

The work products (artifacts) of a project plan include iteration assessment, project measurement, periodic status assessment, work order, and issue list.

Project management workflow spans the entire project and covers all phases and iterations.

D.3.3 Environment Workflow

Environment workflow controls and directs all activities that are to be done for a project. It provides all the tools and methods that help the project team work on the project. Apart from the supporting tools and methods for the project, this workflow also defines the ways to refine the unified process itself. This ensures that over time the process of executing projects matures, resulting in better quality, better resource utilization, and project schedule shrinkage.

D.3.4 Infrastructure Management Workflow

This workflow was included in the enhanced model when the production phase was added in the existing unified process model. This workflow spans all phases of the development life cycle. This workflow ensures that the proper tools and methods are provided during operations and maintenance of the product in production.

D.4 Rational Unified Process in a Nutshell

The traditional waterfall model had many shortcomings. The unified process model has tried to eliminate those shortcomings. Apart from these shortcomings, representation of the waterfall model also lacked flow of activities that go through different phases of the project. The unified process model has addressed this issue by introducing workflows in the process model.

D.5 Cleanroom Software Engineering

In the electronics industry, cleanrooms are used to prevent defects entering into the product when semiconductor circuits are fabricated. The same name was used when a process model was developed to make software products where defects are prevented rather than removed during the software development process. This results in certifiable software products with reliability.

There are four major process areas in cleanroom software engineering: incremental development, software design specification, code verification, and statistically sound testing.

D.5.1 Incremental Development

Each increment of a software product is developed separately in a project and is then tested in a simulated production environment. If testing of the new increment of the software proves that it is working satisfactorily, only then does the next increment of development take place. This testing is done against a pre-established quality standard. Each increment is developed using complete iteration over all phases of the software development.

D.5.2 Formal Method for Design and Specification

Software design and specification is based on the box structure method. The software application is expressed as a mathematical function. The software design is compared against the specification to check whether the design is correctly using the functional specification. The rules for functions of the system are defined by the box structure method at three levels of abstractions: behavioral view, finite state machine view, and procedural view. In other words, they are defined as black, state, and clear boxes. At the black box level, the interaction of the system with the application environment is defined. The state box defines the movement of data across the application. The clear box defines the procedures present in the application.

D.5.3 Correctness Verification of Developed Code

A team review is conducted to assess correctness of the developed code. Mathematical verification methods are used for the verification process. This ensures that code errors are detected quickly and rectified.

D.5.4 Statistically Sound Testing

Even though a defect-preventive approach is applied right from system analysis and design, some defects are introduced in the application. An independent testing is performed to remove these introduced defects.

D.6 Scrum

Scrum is an iterative incremental model and was introduced for software development projects. Sometimes, it is also used for maintenance or program management. Scrum is characterized by one cross-functional team that does the entire software development. The process phases overlap and thus are not distinct. Development is done in iterations that are known as "sprints" and cover the complete development life cycle. The project manager is known as a "scrum master." The stakeholder is known as a "product owner" and the development team is simply known as the "team." A sprint typically lasts between 2 and 4 weeks and the duration is entirely determined by the team. During each sprint, an executable code is developed. The features that go into the development of each sprint are determined by the product owner. These features are taken from a feature repository called the "product backlog." At the start of an iteration, a planning meeting is held, where it is decided which features will go in the next iteration. The team then determines if it is feasible to commit to all or a partial list of features. Depending on the feasibility, they commit to develop a list of features in the next sprint. Once the sprint starts, the features are never changed. Once the sprint completes, the team demonstrates the product to the product owner.

Scrum is a methodology that does not require a structured approach to software development. No documentation is needed. Everything is done very informally. Communication between the customer and team members is done verbally. There is little risk as the product is delivered to the customer after each iteration of less than 4 weeks.

D.7 Extreme Programming

EXtreme Programming (XP) is very similar in approach to Scrum for developing software. XP is defined by activities like coding, testing, listening, and designing. The project team is generally small, consisting of up to 12–15 members. XP is characterized by 12 practices. These practices include pair programming, planning game, test-driven development, whole team concept, continuous integration, refactoring, small releases, coding standards, collective code ownership, simple design, system metaphor, and sustainable pace. These practices can be compared to traditional software development terminology.

D.7.1 Extreme Programming in a Nutshell

XP suits smaller software development projects. During system metaphor practice, a story is told that actually forms the requirement. Based on the system metaphor, a planning game is arranged where the project (iteration) plan is discussed. Based on the planning game, test-driven development starts. The development is based on small release concept. The iteration lasts from a few weeks to a maximum of 5–6 weeks. At the end of the iteration, a fully functional and executable release is demonstrated to the customer. If the products meet customer expectation, the team may move to the next iteration. If not, suggested changes are made and again sent to the customer for approval. Some of the techniques used during system design include refactoring and simple design. During coding, techniques like coding standards, pair programming, and collective code ownership are used.

D.8 Oracle Unified Method

Oracle Unified Method (OUM) is a modified version of the Rational Unified Process. It has phases of inception, elaboration, construction, transition, and production, the same as in the enhanced unified process. The workflows are known as project processes. These processes include project management, business requirements, requirement analysis, analysis, design, implementation, testing, performance management, technical architecture, data acquisition and conversion, documentation, organization change management, training, transition, and operations and support. There are iterations inside each of the phases. At the top of the phases are milestones to denote the successful conclusion of each phase.

Project phases in the OUM model are similar in scope to the ones present in the enhanced unified process model. These phases are described in detail in Section D.1 earlier in this Appendix. Let us discuss now the process of the OUM model.

The business requirement process deals with the tasks of requirement elicitation using standard elicitation techniques. Here the work products include business objectives, goals, and detailed and documented requirements. In the requirement analysis process area, the documented requirements are converted into use cases. Work products include use case model, user interface prototypes, and a high level description of the proposed system architecture. In the analysis process area, requirements are further refined to form the analysis model. The language used to make the analysis model should be closer to the development language rather than any business user language. The work product from this process area is the reviewed analysis model, which also includes class diagrams. In the design process area, the system architecture is represented as a set of classes, objects, and components that will be constructed during the implementation process. The work product of the design process area is the reviewed design model that forms the basis for actual construction. Using iterations, the project team develops the software code using the reviewed design model. Each component developed should be unit tested to ensure it meets design specifications before it is taken for integration with other components. After integrating the components, testing is done to ensure that the components are working properly with each other as per requirements. In the testing process area, the system is tested to verify that it meets requirements. It involves doing system, integration, and many kinds of nonfunctional testing. The performance management process area is closely related to the technical architecture process area. Both these areas ensure that the overall performance of the developed application meets end user performance requirements. The technical architecture process area ensures that the software product being developed has the required capability for running in production environment without any problems. The data acquisition and conversion process area ensures that appropriate tools and methods are used for data to be extracted from legacy systems, and these data are appropriately formatted, converted, and sent to the suitable storage devices. These data then become suitable to be used with the new product being developed. Often due to lack of proper documents, a good application is not properly used by end users. Then again in case of any maintenance needs, the application could not be enhanced or defects removed as there was poor documentation about the design and implementation of the application. The documentation process area ensures that these things do not happen and good quality documentation is available for operations and maintenance of the application. It is very important that processes required to execute projects should be refined and should mature over time. This requires change across the organization. Any change thrust upon the employees is resisted. A proper mechanism is required so that these changes are accepted by the people and thus the adoption rate is high, which in turn will make it easier for the people to go about their tasks as per the new process norms. This aspect is taken care of in the organization change management process. From time to time, retraining of staff is required so that they have the required skills to execute projects. The training process area addresses all issues related to training aspects.

OUM works in conjunction with Oracle Project Management Method (PJM). PJM consists of three phases: project start-up phase, project execution and control phase, and project closure phase. Combining PJM with OUM results in a complete mechanism that can execute any software development, maintenance, or implementation project. The combined process model starts with the project start-up phase. The phases of OUM (inception, elaboration, construction, transition, and production) go inside the project execution and control phase. Finally, the project closure phase is executed (Figure D.3).

PJM has 13 process areas that run on top of all processes of OUM. These are bid transition, scope management, financial management, work management, risk management, issue and problem management, staff management, communication management, quality management, configuration management, infrastructure management, procurement management, and organization

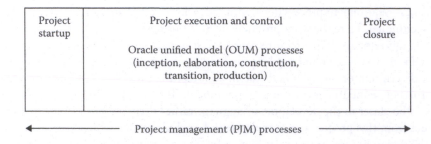

Project startup	Project execution and control Oracle unified model (OUM) processes (inception, elaboration, construction, transition, production)	Project closure

◄──────── Project management (PJM) processes ──────────►

Figure D.3 Combined OUM and PJM processes.

change management. These processes either define boundaries under which OUM processes should operate or they facilitate execution of OUM processes by providing a platform.

D.9 Microsoft Solutions Framework

Microsoft Solutions Framework (MSF) consists of five process areas, namely, envisioning, planning, developing, stabilizing, and deploying. To check that these process areas are complete, there are milestones (gates), namely, vision/scope approved, project plans approved, scope complete, release readiness approved, and deployment complete.

MSF incorporates the best elements from both the waterfall model and the spiral model. The milestones concept has been taken from the waterfall model while the incremental iteration concept has been taken from the spiral model.

MSF has three disciplines, namely, project management, risk management, and readiness management. These disciplines control and govern MSF process areas. The project management discipline has been conceived from and aligned with major project management disciplines like Prince2, or prescribed by institutions like the International Project Management Association and the Project Management Institute.

D.10 Process Tailoring

Each and every project is unique in its scope, objective, and mission. Projects differ from each other in many respects. However, there are standard process methodologies that can be used to plan, monitor, and control projects. Project managers try to fit project objectives and requirements into any of these process models. It is not always possible, however, to fit the project into any standard process model. In such cases, the process has to be modified so that it fits the needs of the particular project. This process is known as process tailoring.

The advantage of process tailoring is that it allows fitting nonstandard elements of a project into a process model. The disadvantage is that once the project is over, the data from the project becomes nonstandard and so is not of much use. Statistical quality control methods need previous project data to be used for future projects. It has to be kept in mind that statistical process control techniques have become extremely useful tools for software projects, and so usefulness of previous project data has become very important. Here it is also important that project data of only similar projects be used for future projects. So if you have data from a project that was executed using very different kinds of process standards, then these data will not be of much use. This is because these data cannot be compared with data from projects that followed other process standards. For instance, suppose a project required that the effort estimate be made using a method supplied by the customer, but this method is not used anywhere except by this customer. The effort estimate data for the project thus cannot be used for any future project even though the future project may have similar scope and project objectives.

Process tailoring, therefore, has this major limitation. However, there is a solution to overcome this problem. Instead of tailoring any process to any extent, we can tailor a process within a defined limit. There is another option for tailoring. Many popular process standards have some predefined tailored processes or variations of the parent process standard. For instance, the Rational Unified Process standard has variations such as open unified process (used by open source developers), essential unified process (simplified model), unified process for education, enterprise unified process (for larger-scale projects), etc. Using a predefined tailored process ensures that even though a project has been executed using a tailored process, its project data will still be relevant for future projects when those projects are going to be using the same predefined tailored process model.

Appendix E: Impact of Offshoring on Standards

Offshoring is, no doubt, influencing the way software development projects are being planned and executed. Project teams can no longer depend solely on verbal communication. Proper and elaborate documentation is the norm now. While this improves the quality of communication and, in turn, improves process quality, it also increases turnaround time. For any change to be successful, the first requirement is to communicate the change clearly to all concerned. Once the change request is approved, changes can be made to the documentation in such a way that it is understandable to everybody. Even the first draft of any work plan needs to be written in a language that is easy to understand by teams located at different sites.

Apart from communication and turnaround time, the other problem is concerns about quality. Customers do not feel comfortable about quality when their partners are located far away. On-time delivery is another concern, which is only heightened due to the increase in documentation.

Can process-driven project management help in mitigating these concerns?

E.1 Communication Concerns and Solutions

For the discussion here, it is assumed that only electronic and voice communication are allowed for all projects. Paper-based communication has not been considered here at all.

No doubt distance, different time zones, different cultures, and many other factors wreak havoc on communication among teams situated at remote locations. These concerns can be mitigated by adopting a common language and way of communication. For team members who have no prior experience working on offshore projects, training in communication may be needed. There is some good news here. Most professionals in locations like India have good experience in working on offshore projects. They have learned how to communicate on these projects. So for them, communication is not a problem. Any team may comprise one or two professionals who are new to such projects. They may need some training. Overall, project teams have experience and so the inexperienced professionals can quickly learn from their team members. Experienced team members can also help them in handling their communication.

Experience has shown that there is a steep curve involved when a majority of team members have no prior experience. But, if only a few have no experience and the majority is conversant, the project does not face any challenges as far as communication is concerned.

Of course, when the customer is from a country like China, Japan, or any European country where English is not the language of communication, then language is definitely the biggest challenge for any project. On those projects, learning the language of communication is the topmost priority.

The other issue of communication is turnaround time. How to deal with this challenge? E-mails are not foolproof. They take time to be delivered and sometimes cannot be delivered. It may even take 1–2 days before it is known that the e-mail was not delivered. E-mails are also not synchronous. Nevertheless, they are very important as they are more formal than other communication channels. They are more reliable than any other alternative mode of communication. But, for instant and real-time communication, instant messengers have no competition. They are cheap (most of the time, free). Team members keep themselves online on these messengers so that, if any team member wants to communicate instantly, they can do that easily. Desktop sharing, too, is a good tool for accessing resources located on a remote computer. Web demonstrations are a good tool for conducting knowledge transfer sessions.

Then there are online applications like forums and wikis to share knowledge. Central configuration management systems can also be used for sharing documents.

So, how does a standard process come into the picture for project-related communications? Well, standard processes help in making these communications meaningful to every team member on the project. The same terminology and documents are used by everybody. The same processes are followed by everybody. Things are done the same way on all locations. This reduces chances of communication errors. Standards play an important role in communication when projects are outsourced to offshore locations.

E.2 Quality Concerns and Solutions

Quality is the top concern on software projects. When the project is moved offshore customers have concerns about quality because they have doubts about the capability of the offshore project team. They are also concerned about the turnaround time required to fix any quality issues.

By certifying all business processes with a standard like CMMI or ISO or IEEE, service providers demonstrate to the customer that they have standard business processes and that they will apply them so that the customer's project will also have those process standards. Software products developed using such high quality standards will definitely have good product quality. Once customers are assured about the quality of processes, they can trust the service provider. Thus, process standard quality plays an important role in mitigating the quality concerns of customers.

E.3 On-Time Delivery Concerns and Solutions

Distance, different cultures, different productivity levels, and some other factors make customers insecure about on-time delivery of projects. How to convince customers that their projects will be delivered as per the schedule that was agreed upon? Again standard processes come in handy. Since the project plan was made with certainty because most of the project details were made clear at the beginning of the project, the regular deliveries and reports will be done on time. This is because the offshore project team will be working with detailed processes with well-defined schedules. Only when some parts of customer requirements are not clear can the project schedule deviate; otherwise, known deliveries will be made with certainty. Well-defined processes make accurate schedules, as project size and productivity factors have been calculated well in advance. Making deliveries on time becomes a lot easier.

E.4 Tips for Offshore Projects

With the added stresses of differing cultures, languages, and time zones, managing a global team requires specific considerations. Here are six tips for making your global software development efforts work.

More companies are looking toward globally dispersed software development teams to solve project staffing problems and make critical time-to-market deadlines. This trend is a fundamental change in how software projects are organized and implemented. Using the idea of "concurrent engineering" to deliver projects faster, you break up a project into smaller, less complex pieces and hire staff scattered throughout the globe who work asynchronously around the clock. This is not the same as adding more people to a project at a later stage to finish the project faster. What it means is that, if you are able to break the development (construction) work in such a way that it allows many teams to work simultaneously without hindering the work of other teams, then development work will be very fast. This is one fascinating factor that contributes to the success of offshoring of projects.

Culture affects global teams in many ways, from what is acceptable to project team members, to how overtime and vacations are used. For example, it is a typically American attitude that if the project is running a week late, project members will forgo or reschedule their vacations. This is not common in European countries where vacations are more important than meeting project deadlines.

Communication can be tricky—especially if not everyone on the team speaks the same language. But even if the language is the same, what we say may not express exactly what we mean. When everyone is located in the same place, we have many opportunities for informal communications to clarify what we said in person or e-mail. Body language also helps co-located teams to remove barriers while communicating. In global projects, developers have few—if any—face-to-face communication opportunities to clarify what is said.

Communicating across time zones is another challenge. Although working asynchronously can help a team progress faster, not everyone is available at the same time. This may slow down communication and decision making. It is difficult to find common meeting times, whether for project meetings or formal technical reviews. A project manager or team lead working on such a project must balance organizational skills, communication, and tools to make the project work. In my experience leading globally dispersed teams, six rules of thumb have made my teams more productive and effective.

1. *Define complementary processes and agree on the meaning of important terms*: Global projects are generally composed of teams that do things differently. Some differences are cultural, while others stem from management styles and strategies. What is certain is that each team's reaction to the other teams' processes and terminology will not be the same.

   Product development processes do not have to be the same, but they do need to be complementary. By complementary, I mean the outputs of each group's processes should match the expectations of the other groups.

2. *Use configuration management systems and defect tracking systems*: When using these systems, it is important to make sure everyone uses them in the same way. Everyone on the project needs to know where the source files are stored, what their state is, and what can be done with them.

3. *Formally inspect requirement documents with all development teams*: Getting the requirements right is key to project success, no matter what kind of project you are leading. In a global project,

it is even more critical. Because it may not be easy to talk to the person who has the necessary information, it is critical to write down, review, and track requirements. It is especially useful to keep requirements in a repository so people can go to one place to continually verify what is going on with the requirements.

Requirement reviews must also be more formal. You cannot simply do a casual walk-through with whoever is available or do an informal review over coffee. Formal reviews should include one representative from each team. These participants sign off that the requirements are correct and ready for their team to implement.

Electronic whiteboards can be particularly useful if you need to discuss design or architecture issues and draw pictures. Normal video communications may be most useful for standard project meetings, rather than meetings focused on carefully reviewing a technical document for defects.

4. *Provide all team members with project plans*: Project leaders sometimes forget that not everyone has access to—or knows—all the intricate pieces of the project schedule. In a global project, this can lead to project failure. Once the project plan is developed, everyone needs access to it. Joint development of the project schedule will ensure all the hand-offs and milestones are well understood and articulated by everyone. At the very least, I recommend the major milestones and their commitment dates be pulled out of the schedule and disseminated to the entire global team by e-mail. It is even better to have the whole schedule and project plan available online in a workgroup tool.

5. *Organize project teams by product feature*: I have seen global teams organized by product development function and by product feature. Although it is possible to have developers in one place, writers in another, and testers in a third, they may find it harder to do the actual work of product development. On the other hand, if teams are organized by product features, then all developers, testers, designers, etc., working on the same product feature are located on the same site, or, at least, are part of the same subproject. In such a case, communication inside the team will be effective and chances of miscommunications will be remote as team members are well versed with the same features and know what other team members are talking about.

6. *Use collaborative tools to bring the project together*: Especially in a global project, collaborative workgroup and workflow tools let people see all of the documents in one place. Workgroup and workflow tools such as Lotus Notes help bridge communications gaps of time and language and lessen the effects of cultural differences on processes.

E.5 Future Trends for Project Offshoring

Changing needs create opportunities for new products/services. Changing business scenarios create opportunities for new ways of doing business.

Normally, political boundaries determine limitation for growth of any business. In free economies, there is virtually no limitation for any business' growth. On the other hand, no private business is allowed in a truly socialist economy. In some other economies that come in between these two extremes (most of the countries in the world have political environments that are a mix between these two extremes), some barriers are enacted which limit growth prospects for any private enterprise. In recent times, many countries have started opening their gates to foreign investors. This has led to the rise of many global enterprises. The trend of global business houses has created concepts like global markets, local markets, global sourcing, global suppliers, etc.

The software industry has also witnessed this trend. Software projects have started getting offshored because of cost factors. Some countries that benefited from this trend have started investing heavily in upgrading technology, government deregulation, tax reduction, upgrading education system, etc., as this is a high-growth and high-potential market. Thus, they not only offer lower costs for these projects but have also become more competitive and quality-conscious, providing, as a result, better quality processes and products.

This trend is going to continue in the future because it makes good business sense to get things done less expensively and with better quality. Governments will also keep wooing foreign companies by providing facilities and changing policies to make their country better positioned for getting these projects.

Appendix F: Review Question Answers

Part I

Chapter 1

1.1 A project is an activity undertaken to accomplish a stated goal, using limited budget and resources, to be completed within a specified time span. A project has a starting date and a finishing date. The stated goal could be to create or modify a product or service, it could also be to do some research and provide a report as the outcome of the project. Software projects are different from other kinds of projects in many ways. Software projects largely involve manual effort to create software products. The manual effort required on these projects requires specialized skills on the part of the people involved on the project team. Software projects also require a great deal of creativity on the part of the people working on them. To create databases, units of source code, software architecture, etc., definitely requires a great deal of creativity when hard specifications are not provided (and are not possible, as well) to do these tasks. Due to lack of hard specifications, the person responsible for doing these tasks requires his own creativity to accomplish them. Due to involvement of a great deal of creativity, it is difficult to make a good estimate of effort required to do these tasks. This factor makes it a tough task to create accurate project schedules as it is not known in advance as to how much time it will take to finish a task.

1.2 Software development projects are difficult to handle because of some unique characteristics of such projects. The foremost challenges faced on software projects are unclear requirements, soft specifications, and changing requirements. Unclear requirements and soft specifications lead to problems of uncertain task durations; changing requirements lead to adjusting project plans. These factors make it extremely difficult to create a plan for a software project. And, when a software plan is made after much thought, it will fail during execution due to the factors mentioned earlier.

1.3 Due to unclear requirements, changing requirements, and soft specifications, software projects often fail to meet the expectations of stakeholders. To mitigate these problems some strategies can be implemented. Instead of taking all requirements in one go, we may take only a few of the requirements and completely make the software product only for these requirements. Then take a few more requirements and make a software product on top of the first product. Incrementally, we can build the complete software product this way. This will eliminate the risks associated with unclear and changing requirements. To eliminate the risks emanating from soft specifications, we can deploy functional consultants who have extensive experience in the industry for which the software product is being made. These functional consultants can help in the functional design with hard specifications, so that no ambiguity is left in the software functional design. The software design consultants then can create hard specifications for implementing this design into software construction.

1.4   Software projects are used to make or modify software products. When a new software product is needed then a software product is built from scratch. This kind of project is known as a software development project. On the other hand, an existing software product sometimes needs to be modified due to changes in business environment, technology obsolescence, etc.; this kind of project is known as software maintenance project.

1.5   Projects need to be initiated, planned, controlled, executed, and, finally, closed. Accordingly, we have project processes like project initiation, project planning, project monitoring and control, and project closure.

1.6   A software project involves three basic types of process, viz., project management, software development, and organization level processes. The project management processes include project initiation, project planning, project monitoring and control, and project closure. The software development processes include software requirements, software design, software construction, software testing, software deployment, and software maintenance. The organization level processes include program management, process improvement initiatives, and process standards. To become a successful software project manager, it is essential that the person must have knowledge and experience in managing all these processes.

Apart from managing processes, the software project manager also needs to handle expectations of customer/stakeholders effectively. He should also be able to manage his team as well as the suppliers.

1.7   Measurement and control of costs, productivity, and schedule for the project is required at frequent intervals to keep these major project metrics under control. To do it, some techniques and measurement methods have been devised by organizations and project management experts over the years. We have graphs, Pareto charts, cause and effect diagrams, scatter diagrams, check sheets, histograms, control charts, etc., measurement methods available to measure and control project processes. Some of these methods, like Pareto charts, scatter diagrams, and cause and effect diagrams, help in identifying root causes of problems, so that appropriate control measures can be taken. Check sheets, control charts, and histograms are used to find deviations in the processes, so that they can be corrected.

1.8   Project initiation is the place where project feasibility, project scope, etc., are determined. To do these things, you need to make a rough estimate for costs, effort, and schedule duration. This is possible only if you have some rough idea about software development tasks to be done on the project. During project planning, requirement specifications, project scope, and, optionally, start and finish dates need to be gathered as project inputs. Based on these inputs, complete project schedule, project costs, and other project planning components like communication plan, configuration plan, resource plan, and supplier plan are prepared. Again, at this stage, complete ideas about software development processes like software design, software construction, software testing, and software release, which need to be used across the project, are required. These processes are the project tasks to be completed to make the software product. When the project execution starts, these project tasks (software development processes) need to be monitored and controlled, so that the project can be kept within control in terms of project costs, product quality, and project schedule. All these project tasks need to be completed before project closure.

We can clearly see that software development processes fall within the boundaries of project management processes.

Chapter 2

2.1   The project charter is the high-level document describing what the project stakeholders are looking for out of the project in hand. Generally, the project charter does not delve into project details, rather, it is a statement that contains the stakeholders' vision for the project. For instance, a project charter for a software project could be to achieve 100% accuracy in order management for a business house as well as to cut order management costs by 25% from existing costs involved in order management activities.

2.2   Project objectives are the list of tasks describing how the project charter can be achieved. In the example given for project charter in answer 1, a list of tasks which will help in achieving 100% accuracy and 25% reduction in order management costs can be prepared. These tasks can include cutting offline work from order management and making the order management process a complete online activity, and introducing checks into the order management process, so that no errors will occur in taking and processing the customer orders.

2.3   Project scope defines what is required to be done on the project to accomplish project objectives. The outcome of project scope preparation is a detailed document which is also known as project deliverables. Project scope is often a bone of contention between the customer and the software vendor/project team. That is why project deliverables should be well defined, so that there should not be any area of dispute or ambiguity when the project deliverables are actually made and delivered. If any project deliverables have any ambiguities or disputed areas, they should be sorted out during project initiation. The project scope should not only describe the deliverables in detail, but expected quality level should also be well-defined, as it influences project scope considerably.

2.4   Software projects are inherently difficult. Problems stemming from soft specifications and unclear requirements mean visibility into the project is very poor. During project initiation, this lack of visibility can hamper efforts to define rough project effort, cost, and schedule. Misunderstanding between the project team and project stakeholders thus becomes a common occurrence. Lack of confidence in the project from the stakeholders is also not uncommon. The project team itself can find it difficult to convince the stakeholders about their competence.

In fact, all these problems during project initiation can lead to a turbulent project execution later, which ultimately leads to project failure.

2.5   Project scope is essentially a list of deliverables, which are agreed by the two parties, viz., the project stakeholders and the project team. But even if the project team delivers the promised functionalities in the software product, stakeholders may not be happy with the quality of the software product. The software product can contain critical defects that may prevent the end users from using it effectively. These defects can even cause monetary losses to the customer. So, software product quality is a must.

But achieving stringent quality norms is a hard and laborious task. It will also be costly and may consume enormous amount of time. Obviously, achieving very high software product quality may not be necessary or required for all software products. So, the project scope document must specify what level of software product quality is required, so that amount of project work can be determined.

2.6 At project initiation level, making an elaborate project plan is impossible because a large number of project-related information is not available. However, rough estimates about project costs, effort, number of resources required, and project schedule are desirable. The project team should make initial and rough estimates about these project-specific details. During initiation, the project team can present these rough estimates to project stakeholders. If the project stakeholders have some specific demands after seeing this rough estimate, then these demands can be incorporated, and the project initiation phase can be signed off.

Chapter 3

3.1 Function point analysis (FPA) technique tries to find out effort and cost estimates for a software project by finding out how many functions will be needed to create the required functionality in the software product to be made. Depending on the number of functions, complexity, and number of interfaces, the unadjusted function point is calculated. A value adjustment factor is applied to get the final FPA estimate.

In the initial stage of a software project, there will be many assumptions about various aspects of the project. So, at that point, FPA calculations will be crude and far from accurate due to these assumptions. Once the project is on its way and these assumptions have mostly been converted into solid project details, then the FPA effort estimate will be close enough to being accurate enough.

3.2 The COCOMO (Constructive Cost Model) for estimating effort and cost for software projects was proposed by Barry Boehm. He studied execution data from a large number of previously-executed software projects and found that there are environmental and internal influencing factors (known as attributes) that affect effort required on a software project. He incorporated these attributes into his famous COCOMO effort estimate model.

One advantage of the COCOMO model is that it can be applied at any stage of the project. For this, there are three versions of the COCOMO model. In the initial stages of a software project, when project specific information is mostly not available, industry average values for all the attributes are applied. This version of the COCOMO model is known as Basic COCOMO. During the middle stages of a project, when almost all of the project specific information is available, then these attributes are applied to calculate effort estimate. This version of COCOMO is known as Intermediate COCOMO. The third version of COCOMO, which is used to calculate effort estimates for various phases of the project, is known as Detailed COCOMO.

3.3 When data for past projects are not available, then both Wide Band Delphi and COCOMO models can be used. Neither of these models use past projects data in deriving effort estimates. COCOMO modeling uses current project attributes as well as industry trends attributes in effort calculations. In Wide Band Delphi, team members derive effort estimates after going through some brainstorming sessions. For these sessions, only current project attributes are used for estimation work.

3.4 Generally, project schedule for software projects is considered to be a constant. This because it is believed that, even if you add more resources to a project to make project schedule shorter, it does not result in shorter schedules. This assumption is not true. Using concurrent engineering techniques, tasks can be split into many smaller tasks, which can be done in parallel to each other, while at the same time as they are independent from each other. Many independent teams can be deployed to complete these parallel tasks. This technique will result in making the project schedule shorter. Since many teams will be involved in such an arrangement, a larger pool of resources will be needed to do these tasks. At the same time there is a larger overhead due to the introduction of many layers of management, which stems from the large number of people included by using many teams. This means the project's budget will be higher, in comparison, than it would be in a situation where parallel task processing was neither sought nor employed, thus keeping the management for the project on just one layer.

3.5 Project scope is a list of deliverables that are to be made during and after project completion. There should also be a rider on these deliverables; the quality aspect. This rider should clearly state what level of quality is acceptable for the software product being made. A high level of quality requires more effort. Indeed, if stringent quality is required, as in the case of life-critical applications, then effort could be several times higher compared to the effort required to develop a general purpose application. It is commonly accepted that a project undertaken by a group of students as a class assignment to develop a software product could have a development speed of 5000 lines of source code per person per month. When an industry strength software product is developed by a professional project team then the development speed sharply drops to the tune of 1000 lines of source code per person per month. This drop in development speed is due to extra effort in building high quality, defect-free software products. This extra effort goes in reviews, inspections, and testing to ensure that quality of all work products throughout the development cycle remains within agreeable limits.

Chapter 4

4.1 The most critical risks on a software project include resource unavailability, skill shortage, technology obsolescence, incorrect effort estimate, quality, escalating costs, requirement changes, misunderstanding, and miscommunication. Each of these risks have potential to jeopardize a software project.

4.2 The best strategy for tackling risks on software projects is to keep some buffer so that, when any risk occurs, the buffer is consumed and the project schedule remains intact. This is true for all risks which can impact project costs, quality, or project schedule. So, we can have a buffer in the project schedule for schedule related risks. We can have a budget buffer to tackle budget-related risks.

For technology-related risks, we can research and make sure that any aspect of the software product will not become obsolete for its projected lifespan.

For quality-related risks, we can have a comprehensive quality assurance plan. Each work product should be reviewed and tested to make sure that quality level throughout the development life cycle has excellent quality, and, thus, the final product will also have above expected quality level.

4.3 Risks are unpredictable by nature. They can suddenly occur at time during the project. But, at the same time, some risks are more likely to occur at a specific time than other risks. It is important to not only make a prioritized list of risks, but to keep this list updated so that the most likely risks at any point in time are kept on top of the list, that way, if they occur, the project manager is ready to take appropriate action to mitigate it.

To make a risk management plan, first of all, you need to identify and list all risks that can impact the project. Each risk can have an impact that can be mild to severe on the project. Note the severity level of each risk; high severity risks have more severe impact on the project. Therefore, these risks should also have higher priority compared to lower-severity risks.

The prioritized list of risks should be reviewed frequently and order of risks should be sorted so that the most likely risks in immediate future are kept on the radar.

4.4 Projects need to deliver the agreed-upon deliverables within the agreed-upon budget, schedule, and quality level. If any of these limits are violated, then the project will fail. There may be many risks associated with occurrences impacting any of these limits. A project manager must be able to tackle these risks successfully or else the project will be in trouble. If a project is going to be safeguarded from these risks, a good risk-mitigation strategy should be in place. For instance, highly skilled resources are highly in demand. To retain them, a comprehensive retention plan is adopted by all employers in the IT field.

4.5 To mitigate the risks posed by changing requirements, either an iterative product development strategy or a comprehensive change request policy is adopted for software projects. In iterative models, only a few requirements are taken at a time for development and complete development is performed for those requirements. When the cycle of developing a software product for those requirements is complete, then the next batch of requirements can be taken for development. Since these iterative cycles are short (a week to 5–6 weeks), it is possible to incorporate all requirements even with some changes.

The other strategy is to enforce a stringent change management policy so that, whenever changes are requested in requirements, an impact analysis is performed first. This analysis will show how much reworking will be needed in already-made software design and written source code. If the customer agrees to go ahead with the additional amount of time and cost involved in doing those changes, only then those change requests will be incorporated.

Chapter 5

5.1 Configuration management systems are vital parts of any software project. They are the central repository for all project documents, requirement specifications, software designs, source code, testing artifacts, etc. As a project progresses, a large number of versions of these artifacts get generated to take care of change requests, defect fixes, etc. So, they also contain all versions of these documents and artifacts.

A large number of software projects involve many teams working on the project from many locations. A centralized management system helps them work together by keeping all project artifacts at a central location and providing secured access to all project teams.

5.2 A good configuration management system should have a secured access mechanism, so that only authorized people can access it. The system should be able to be audited frequently to make sure that all the artifacts it stores are safe and are not tampered with. It should also have a foolproof reliability, so that all the stored artifacts do not get corrupted. It should have a role-based security, so that only authors of project artifacts have the rights to edit or delete any stored artifact. All other users should have access to view or download the artifacts. Continuous integration of software builds should be provided, so that developers can check in their source code whenever they finish their already-tested units of source code.

5.3 When a new piece of source code is integrated with a software build, it can lead to many problems if the source code to be integrated is not clean (has defects, compiling issues, etc.). If the software build is not tested frequently for defects and compiling errors, it will be very difficult to debug and find defects when the build becomes large. Good practice is that, whenever a new piece of source code is added to the main build, the build should be tested for compiling issues and defects. This way it can be made sure that the build is always clean. This kind of testing performed each time a new piece of code is added is known as smoke test.

5.4 For most purposes, a centralized configuration management system is a better option than a decentralized one. A centralized system works on the principles of "one version of truth."

This kind of environment promotes accuracy of information, immediacy (information in real time), faster information delivery, etc. On the flip side, there can be security issues with this system. If many teams are working from many locations and if access is provided to them through internet, then security issues can definitely arise. A totally secure connection and access permission is needed in such scenarios.

A decentralized system, on the other hand, is comparatively secure. But if many teams are working from many locations with their own configuration management system, then all those disparate systems will need to be synchronized frequently using some sort of connection among them. This will pose security issues. Since each system has its own repository of project artifacts, then one version of truth may not be always possible. Moreover, each system may be different from each other (different vendors, different versions, etc.). Integration and synchronization among them will be very difficult in such a scenario.

5.5 When a software vendor makes a software product, he keeps adding new functionality in the product over a period of time. Each time a major version of the software product is released, all artifacts related to that version of the product need to be kept at a secured place for reference in the future. If any patches are to be developed in future for the defects found in that version, then the reference documents belonging to that version can be retrieved and defect fixing can be done. Similarly, if reverse engineering is required at any time in future, these reference materials can come in handy.

Most of the configuration and version control management systems come with a facility to make branches in file system. Each branch can be configured to contain all artifacts belonging to a particular version. When a new version of the software product is initiated, it is a good idea to create a new branch, so that all existing artifacts are copied from previous version. If this is not done, then all required copies of artifacts will need to be copied manually, which may take considerable amount of time.

Chapter 6

6.1 Project plans typically consist of a project schedule, communication plan, risk plan, supplier plan, quality plan, effort and cost estimates, etc. Software projects also configuration management plans as part of the project plan. The schedule plan itself can be divided into tasks related to the chosen software development life cycle. Depending on the software development life cycle, the project plan itself varies considerably and, when this happens, then other plans get affected considerably.

When a traditional waterfall model is adopted for the project, then all of the planning components will be outlined in all details and much in advance. But, for iterative projects, concrete planning is done only for the next iteration while rest of the plans for future iterations are done tentatively.

6.2 Software projects are, after all, an undertaking to produce or modify a software product within a given time span starting from a fixed date, with limited budget and resources. To be successful, the project must be completed within specified limits. If no planning is done for the project, then it will not be known in advance if the project will be completed within these limits. Only when projects are done in an orderly manner will the outcome be controlled. If no project plan was made, then the amount of budget and resources to be consumed on the project will not be clear, nor will the time in which the project will be completed. Due to these factors, a detailed project plan is a must.

6.3 Software project planning is done with many details included. There are a number of project components for which planning is done. These planning components include communication, configuration, resources, project schedules, effort estimation, cost estimation, and quality planning. If there are suppliers involved on the project, then supplier planning needs to be done.

Planning for all these components also has an effect on the software development life-cycle method adopted on the project.

6.4 Top-down project planning is employed when the software product to be developed has a definite release date. In such cases, beginning from the start date, there is a fixed amount of time in which the software product needs to be developed. Since the time duration is fixed, only a limited amount of software features can be developed.

Some of the inputs in such cases include start date, end date, project duration, software requirements, software development life-cycle method, and service level agreements.

6.5 Bottom-up project planning inputs include software development life-cycle method, project scope, software requirements, and service level agreements.

6.6 To tackle risks, project plans include buffers. For risks impacting schedule, a schedule buffer is provided. For risks impacting budget, a budget buffer is provided. For quality risks, a quality plan is provided.

6.7 In iterative models of software development, planning is done at three levels. The topmost level is where a complete product development roadmap is conceived. It is more like a charter for long range planning. It is made after a thorough study of the market, where there is need for a product to fulfill a gap, etc., and a full executive management buy-in is sought (in the case of software product vendors). In the middle level is the plan for major version releases of the software product. This is done on or around a yearly basis. This planning is done after getting the market feedback for tapping immediate market opportunities. At the bottom is the iteration level planning. This corresponds to minor releases of the software product. Generally, they are done on a quarterly basis.

Iterative planning is also done for other kinds of projects. In those cases, the project planning can be done at only two levels; even though the complete roadmap may be present, no planning is required to be done at that level. The product manager may be involved only in the middle and iterative levels of planning.

Chapter 7

7.1 On software projects, not only are schedule and cost to be monitored but quality of the products is also extremely important.

7.2 Sometimes, a project task may be slipping; this could be for many reasons like lateness of a precedent task, an item being reworked, or the unexpectedly increased amount effort required. This situation can be controlled by adding some more resources to the slipping task, so that it can be done in a shorter span of time. Similarly, a job may be completed earlier than the planned date. In that case, some resources from that task can be moved to another task.

Movement of resources on a project in anticipation deviations on the project schedule is known as resource leveling.

7.3 Any project task will have a planned schedule and budget associated with it. When the project gets started, we can put in the baseline dates and budget for this task (same as planned). When the task begins, we can measure the consumption of budget and elapsed time against actual work being done. Suppose we need to write 5000 lines of source code in 30 days.

There are two developers involved in writing the source code. Salary of one developer is $4000 per month and that of another $5000 per month. After 15 days time, a work progress measurement was taken. It was found that 2000 lines of source code was done. The ideal situation would have been 2500 lines of code by this time. In percentage terms, we can say that the schedule is lagging behind by (2500 − 2000)/2500% = 20%. For writing 2000 lines of code, the developers together should have taken 2000/5000 × 30 = 12 days. So, budget is being consumed more than planned by (15−12)/30% = 10%.

Project schedule is tracked from the planned schedule to the actual progress on the project against time. To make the tracking easier, there should be some well-defined marks on the schedule so that, when they are achieved, a definite report about the project can be made. These marks on the schedule can be done using major and minor milestones. Major milestones should denote completion of major phases on the project, for example, software design phase completion and software testing completion.

7.4   Deviations in project schedule can be remedied using many techniques. Some of the popular techniques include overloading of resources, partitioning of tasks, and performing tasks in parallel, but not all kinds of tasks are amenable to these techniques. For instance, a software design cannot be divided meaningfully among many software designers if the design is supposed to be monolithic in nature and not a modular one. Similarly, if the software design is large, and it is being designed in a modular architecture, then the tasks cannot be divided below the module level. So, there is a limit to the extent of the divisibility of tasks. Whenever it is possible to further divide a task, the divided tasks can be processed in parallel by adding extra resources on the project and thus correcting any deviation in the project schedule.

In case of overloading of resources, they can be asked to work overtime to complete their assignment in time.

If none of these measures are feasible, then we can consume time from the project schedule buffer. Project schedule buffers are safety valves in the project schedule, so that when any deviation occurs, the project buffer can be consumed.

7.5   There could be many reasons why a project budget deviation occurs. One could be simply because the tasks could not be completed on schedule and extra time is needed to complete them; this will involve extra budget for the project. In some other instances, project budget could be affected due to rise in salaries of project personnel. Then, cost of tools or services can rise unexpectedly and project budget can be affected. These personnel-related deviations in project budget are irrespective of project schedule.

To tackle these deviations, we can keep a buffer in the project budget. When these deviations occur, we can consume from the project budget buffer.

7.6   During project planning, we make a quality plan regarding the overall quality of software products and work products. In the quality plan, there are tasks (reviews/testing) that measure the quality and, if any defects are found, revision is to be done on those products. Sometimes, number of defects found during such tasks can cause the project schedule to deviate if the allotted revision time is not enough and more time is needed. In such cases, the project schedule buffer can be used.

Chapter 8

8.1   Project data are extremely useful for future projects. This is due to the fact that effort estimation on a project in the early stages is very difficult. Agreement between the customer and the development team can become difficult because of these problems. No side is sure about what the effort and costs required for the project could be. Similarly, it becomes difficult to make a good plan for the project. Using previously executed project data, it is possible to do process selection, project sizing, determine required quality level and number of resources required, determine project schedule, etc. In fact, the entire project can be planned with little effort.

8.2 Before we think about archiving project data, it is of utmost importance that we care about where the project data is coming from, the accuracy of the data, the formats the data have been recorded in the project attributes (industry, project size, use of application, etc.), and such details. The first task should be to cleanse the data to make sure that it is pure. The next thing to do is to find the formats of all data and then convert them into a uniform format. Finally, the attributes should be studied, so that the project data could be placed in an appropriate project data category.

8.3 Project closure is the stage where all development activities will come to an end. Activities like project data archiving, lessons learned, resource release, and source code management are performed during project closure.

8.4 Data for lessons learned reside in many places like in memory of team members, emails, project management systems, and configuration management systems. Extracting and cleaning this data is a tough job. Once it is done, the data should be formatted and then aggregated in a uniform manner. Only then it is useful.

There is a large difference between data and meaningful information. Jumbled, without format, and without context, data is simply useless. On the extreme side, arranged, well-formatted, relevant, and context-sensitive data, which can be termed as information, is extremely useful even if it does not contain much data. This concept should be kept in mind when a lessons learned list is made.

8.5 Any project needs resources, budget, and time for their execution. In software projects, resources in the form of software professionals are, in fact, the most costly. They should be used very efficiently, so that the project costs can be kept in check. When any resources are no longer needed on a project, they should be released immediately so that they can be assigned on other projects.

Part II

Chapter 9

9.1 Software projects have typical phases like software requirement development, software design, software construction, software testing, software release, and software maintenance. Depending on the kind of process model selected, these phases may overlap or might be rigidly separated from each other. Similarly, the phases may be completed sequentially, in loops or spirally.

9.2 Software development is mostly a human activity with negligible amounts of automation. So many people think that statistical process control (SPC) cannot be used on software projects successfully. After all, SPC methods work with processes where precise process data are available. This data then can be compared with a standard set of data, and results can be analyzed to find process areas for improvement so that the existing problems due to faulty process areas will not happen. SPC techniques work well to measure data when data comes from machines. It is because process steps with machines are repeatable, and thus all process data coming from machines have a definite pattern. Finding a set of data that deviates from this pattern is easy and, thus, finding the cause of the error is also easy. The same cannot be said about activities performed by human beings. Humans cannot do things the same way again and again.

Since software projects are a mostly human activity, measuring process data, finding a problem area, and then fixing it is difficult. Nevertheless, with maturity of software engineering techniques, software processes have become more repeatable. Now, it is possible to predict quality, effort, schedule, and budget for a software project with accuracy. So, SPC processes can be applied on software projects. In the development process, checks can be applied at many places so that work products can be checked for defects, and all found defects should be immediately removed. Similarly, process checks can be applied so that process deviations, in terms of schedule or budget, can be checked and controlled immediately. In all these areas, SPC methods are extremely useful.

9.3 Concurrent engineering deals with dividing work into parts, which can be processed or executed in parallel so that project schedule can be significantly reduced, and thus project duration can be made shorter. To do this, we need to make provision for dividing a task inside a process by designing the previous process in such a way that the next process can be easily divided. For example, if we need to divide the construction process in a software project, then we need to make the software design modular, so that the software construction can be easily divided into separate modules and thus work on these modules can be done concurrently.

9.4 Different phases of software development produce different work products. The requirement phase produces requirement specifications, the design phase produces design documents, and the construction phase produces source code.

9.5 The software development cycle produces many products. The metrics deployed on the project need to measure quality of these work products to ensure that it is maintained throughout the development process. Reviews are conducted to ensure the quality of the work products. Requirement specifications, software design, and software construction are reviewed and tested, to ensure that there are no defects.

Chapter 10

10.1 Requirement gathering can be done using many means and methods. Requirements from end users can be elicited using techniques like interviews and questionnaires. Indirect requirements can be gathered from customer feedback, complaints, polls, etc. Requirements can also be gathered from customer support, end-user tests, etc.

10.2 Requirement development process flow entails gathering requirements, formatting requirement data, aggregating requirements, maintaining hierarchy and relationship of requirements to each other, and, finally, prioritizing requirements.

10.3 During requirement development, a lot of quality aspects need to be checked. The relationship between requirements, dependency of requirements, hierarchy of requirements, etc., need to be checked. Formatting of requirements also need to be checked. Apart from correctness, other aspects like maintainability, testability, and reliability also need to be checked.

During requirement management, the most critical aspect to be checked is to assess the impact of change on the entire development cycle. At the same time, the right version of the requirement also needs to be checked to ensure that no processes downstream use wrong version of the requirement specifications.

10.4 Software development is initiated only to fulfill the demands put by the customer requirements. In fact, if the development team is engaged in doing anything else, then this will be a waste of time. Now, requirements cannot be converted into a finished software product in one go. First, an appropriate software design is made based on which the source code will be written. If the requirement specifications are not made properly or some information is missing, then software design cannot be made properly. Subsequently, the software source code would also be not made properly.

For all these reasons, properly formatted and correct requirements are needed.

10.5　Requirement management is all about managing change. Whenever any changes are made in any requirements, the entire project gets affected. Many already-completed work products may need to be reworked; many planned work products need to be revised. This leads to a thorough change in project plan.

The requirement management process flow involves receiving the change request, doing impact analysis on the project, making a proposed revised project plan, sending it to stakeholders, getting approval from stakeholders, and implementing the new project plan.

Chapter 11

11.1　Software design involves making a software architecture and a software design that will convert the requirement specifications into an appropriate design for the proposed software product. The software design can include use cases, activity diagrams, and entity relationship diagrams. From design documents, the software construction can be made properly only if the software design is good and implementable.

11.2　The most obvious constraints while making software design include implementability, reliability, modularity, economic construction ability, and reusability. Construction testing activities are very labor-intensive, and thus costly, activities. If software design is not modular, then the software construction activities cannot be divided and done in parallel. If software design does not lead to an economic software construction, then the total cost of software development will become exorbitant.

11.3　There are many techniques available to make good software designs. Some of them include software reuse, structural models, modular models, system design, and object-oriented designs. In the early days of software development, structural software designs were prevalent with programming languages including COBOL, PASCAL, and FORTRAN being used. With the advent of the object-oriented paradigm, object-oriented designs became popular and the programming languages used included Java, C++, and many other object-oriented programming languages.

11.4　Software designs can be reviewed to make sure that their quality is acceptable. The review can take into account whether or not the design is testable, reliable, modular, and implements all requirement specifications, or whether design consists of nonrequired features. If the review process finds any defects, then they should be fixed in the review process itself.

11.5　The design life cycle involves finding the best design for the given requirement specifications, creating the designs, reviewing the designs, and finally fixing any defects found.

11.6　There are basically two methods of software design, viz., top-down and bottom-up. The top-down design is used when a centrally-controlled configuration of the software system is desired. In top-down design, the software architecture is always balanced, and there is no chance of imbalances in design. In the top-down approach, the top structure of the software is designed first, and then the internal parts of the software are designed later. Some of the benefits of top-down design is that the main considerations of software design like performance, reuse, and scalability are always part of the central theme of the software design, and thus the design is very stable even when the design is later changed for any reason. The limitation of this design is that it suits only for traditional way of doing things like being used only with waterfall model for software development. This is a risky model for building software.

The bottom-up method of software design is used when the smallest units of software components are built first, and the software design and, in fact, the entire software development are built incrementally. This is new way of building software, and all agile models of software development are built this way.

Chapter 12

12.1 Common activities performed during software construction include: analyzing software design specifications, converting the design into source code, unit testing pieces of source code, integrating pieces of source code, and, finally, doing integration testing of the main build each time a new piece of code is added to it.

12.2 Both static and dynamic testing of the source code are performed during software construction activities as quality control measures. Dynamic tests include unit and integration testing. Static tests include finding dead code, unused variables, datatype mismatches, and source code standards deviations.

12.3 There are some methods for rapid application development, for example, concurrent engineering techniques, rapid application development tools, code reuse, and service-oriented architecture.

12.4 Pair programming is a technique which is used with extreme programming. For each development assignment, instead of one developer, two developers are assigned the same task. While one developer writes the source code, the other developer looks after the functional aspects of the assignment. They rotate their roles at defined intervals. This practice makes sure that the developers not only write source code, but they also understand the larger picture of their task by understanding the functional aspects of the pieces of source code they write.

12.5 It is very important that the written source code should be legible, easy to understand, simple, modular, and should be strictly under a framework. The modular design enables construction teams to work independently from each other and in parallel, so that the entire source code writing exercise can be completed in a shorter duration by employing more people on the divided work. The reliability aspects of the source code ensure that there are no major defects in the software product. The simple aspect ensures that the source code is not complex and thus is free from tendency of developing defects. Simplicity and legibility also ensure that the source code is easy to maintain. The developers who are assigned to the maintenance of the source code will be able to understand the source code written by some other developers and will be able to make appropriate changes in the source code. The source code should also contain ample comments, so that the source code will be easier to understand.

12.6 Some of the popular review methods used in software construction include desk checks, peer review, code inspections, and walkthroughs. Desk checks are the most informal and preliminary way of checking code. A developer informally asks any of his colleagues to check his code for defects. Peer reviews can be done formally or informally by one or more colleagues to check source code. Walkthroughs are done formally by calling a meeting and reviewing the source code. If defects are found, then they are marked for removal.

Code inspections are the final and most formal method of code review. Its main purpose is to certify quality of the source code. The certification is when a decision can be made on whether or not a piece of source code can be integrated with the main build or whether the code can be frozen for further development and to be handed over to the testing team for testing the application.

Chapter 13

13.1 Software testing is an activity that should be kept apart from software development to keep it unbiased and uninfluenced. When testing is done in close proximity to software development, then the development team tries to influence the testing team and thus testing activity becomes biased and thus its effectiveness diminishes. This results in the development of a poor-quality software product.

A good solution for this kind of problem is to make the testing function independent from development. In fact, the testing should be done by some independent agency. This kind of arrangement is known as independent verification and validation.

13.2 It is said that software testing costs money but not testing costs even more! How absolutely true is this observation! Software development lasts for a few months to a few years, but software maintenance lasts for the entire life of the software product in use. This life could be from 5 to 6 years to even 20 years or more. So even if software maintenance costs are 10% of the cost of software development per annum, total cost of maintenance often surpasses the cost of software development. This exorbitant cost of software maintenance is a nagging problem for software developers. Ultimately, it is the developers who have to bear the maintenance costs. Customers also become wary of buying software products from those software developers who have poor quality software products.

Keeping cost of software maintenance low is possible only when software defects can be minimized in the software product during development. So, effective and rigorous software testing becomes the only option to get out of this situation.

13.3 Software testing can broadly be classified as dynamic and static types. The static type can further be divided into requirement review, design review, code review, etc. Dynamic testing can be further divided into four levels: unit, integration, system, and user-acceptance testing levels. System and user-acceptance testing can be further divided into functional and nonfunctional testing. Nonfunctional testing can again be divided into performance, security, usability, portability, etc., kinds of testing.

13.4 The first thing that should be done for any testing phase or testing project is to study the testing requirements for the project. It will involve analyzing the requirement specifications, design documents, testing requirement documents, etc. Then, based on the requirements, a test plan needs to be made. The test plan may include analyzing specification documents, designing test cases, writing test cases, writing test scripts, executing test cases, preparing test reports, analyzing test reports, logging defects, evaluating defect fixes, and closing defects.

13.5 Automation brings many benefits. Cost of operation gets reduced, operation execution gets faster, repeated, and boring work is not done by humans and is taken care of by automation tools; costly human resources can be taken away from mundane tasks and can be deployed on critical tasks, human errors can be avoided, reporting can be made better and automated, etc. Software testing tasks have same benefits mentioned earlier when they get automated.

13.6 The defect life cycle deals with all aspects related to defects. When the test team executes test cases, some of the test cases fail. These failures are due to any kind of defect. A defect report is logged in a defect tracking system by the testing team. The defect tracking administrator verifies the defect and then assigns it to a developer. The developer fixes the defect and changes the status of the defect to fixed. The fixed defect is then verified by the test engineer. If he finds that the defect is fixed, then he closes the defect. If he finds that the defect is not fixed properly, then he reopens the defect.

Chapter 14

14.1 During software development, all efforts are put toward ensuring that most of software defects are removed before the software product goes to production. But still, many defects escape into production and are found by the end users.

Software products are used to perform business and other functions for which the software product was made; when these intended functions change, the software product no longer supports the new or changed functions. Sometimes, the software product or the hardware or software components with which the software product is used become obsolete. Again, in these circumstances, the software product becomes unusable.

Due to all these reasons, the software product needs to be changed to make it usable again. That is the reason software maintenance is needed.

14.2 Reverse engineering, forward engineering, and reengineering are the three techniques for software maintenance. In reverse engineering, the existing code base of a software product is studied and all aspects of the programming and design are analyzed and grasped. Based on this knowledge, new extensions in the software product are developed. In forward engineering, instead of studying and analyzing existing source code, the new parts of the software product are developed solely by the knowledge of documentation or by the development team that built the software product. This technique is used when the development team who developed the software also does the maintenance. Reengineering is used to develop similar components from existing components. That is why this technique is also known as reuse engineering.

14.3 The maintenance life cycle starts with getting the list of defects to be fixed and required changes to be done in the software product. This can be termed the requirement list. Out of this list, it is not possible to make all requirements in one maintenance cycle. So, a selection will be made from this list for which maintenance will be done. A detailed project planning will be done based on this selected list of requirements. Once the software is developed and thoroughly tested, it needs to be patched to the production instance. After applying the patch, the production instance will be tested by the end users. Once it is found satisfactory, then the software maintenance project is closed.

14.4 When a software product is developed, it is implemented in a production environment. The end users start using it; as long as there are no defects or no changes are required in the existing software product, everything is fine. But, when maintenance is needed either to fix defects, or change a functionality, or both, then the software design and source code will need to be changed. Due to complex or badly designed source code, changing code may be difficult or may be too laborious a task.

To ensure that this kind of difficulty does not arise during maintenance, some precautions can be taken during the software development stage. This kind of precaution is known as putting maintainability in the software design and source code.

14.5 Some common maintenance process models include the quick-fix model, Boehm's model, Osborne's model, iterative enhancement model, and reuse-oriented model. As the name suggests, the quick-fix model works on the principle of immediately fixing defects whenever they are traced. In this model, the maintenance team does not wait to gather a long list of defects and then planning to fix them in one batch. Boehm's model works on the ROI principle in that the only changes considered for implementation are those justified by their ROI. Other changes are not implemented and may be discarded. Osborne's model stresses that the maintenance plan should be followed strictly as demonstrated in the model. The four steps in the model include first gathering the maintenance requirements, then a maintenance project plan alongside a quality assurance plan should be drawn up, then, during project execution, measurement of work products should be carried out, and, finally, corrections in the work products should be done to correct deviations. The iterative enhancement model works in the same way as any iterative model works for software development. Maintenance work should be done by taking a bunch of requirements, doing the entire development process, and then taking on some more requirements. This process continues until all requirements are implemented. The reuse maintenance model works on the principle that, before any maintenance project plan is drawn up, care should be taken to make reusable components instead of just developing components, so that components can be reused through out the project and thus project cost and duration can be reduced.

14.6 Releasing software involves making decisions about what kind of release to be made, what markets to release to, user training, product implementation, and which version of the software to be released.

Part III

Chapter 15

15.1 Suppose a software development team makes a good plan and starts building the software product thinking that they will build the product first and will then test and fix defects to make it a good-quality product. When they finally developed the software and gave it to the testing team to test, the testing team came up with a large number of defects. The development team started fixing those defects, but the number of defects were so large that the defect fixing continued for a long time. Finally, the project manager discussed this with the project stakeholders. The stakeholders decided to scrap the project and start the project all over again by giving the project to a software service provider instead of doing it in-house. Later, the service provider's team was able to finish the project in time and in-budget with immaculate software product quality. They were able to do it because they had vast experience and they had a good process plan with the built-in quality assurance that helped them to develop software product with required quality.

This is true for any project case. Without having a good quality assurance plan built in to the software project, it is difficult to produce a good-quality software product.

15.2 Product quality is assessed after it is produced by taking measurements of its attributes like physical dimensions, internal chemical composition, and aesthetics (smell, appearance, etc.), and if all these attributes are found to be satisfactory, then the product quality is considered good. Otherwise, the product quality is considered bad and points to the fact that the product contains defects.

Process quality, on the other hand, ensures of project activities comply with the process model that was adopted for the project. This compliance ensures that whatever the process model has envisaged to be can be achieved by doing things the way it is defined there; those objectives can be achieved. Generally, the objective is delivery of the project within the agreed-upon budget and time. It also ensures that the quality of the software product will be good, as these process models also include quality assurance.

15.3 There are many standards for software development projects developed by different organizations and individuals. The foremost of them include Capability Maturity Model (CMM) and Capability Maturity Model Integration (CMMI) by the Software Engineering Institute of Carnegie Mellon University; ISO 9003 by International Standards Organization, IEEE-SWEBOK by the Institute of Electrical & Electronics Engineers; Rational Unified Process by Rational Corporation (IBM). Oracle Corporation and Microsoft Corporation have their own versions of software development models; Eclipse has their own version named Unified Process Model.

15.4 When a software project is undertaken without sticking to a standard process model or best practices, there are bound to be some surprises to the stakeholders and the project team down the line. If the project team consists of experienced people, then they will be able to do their assignments in their own ways. But, in the absence of a proper process model, everybody will do their work in their own ways and in their own schedules. Even if they are given task deadlines, there will be issues like incompatibility among components being developed and some tasks getting delayed. The most difficult aspect will be invisibility across the project. Nobody will know what is going on with the different project tasks. In such a scenario, tracking and controlling will simply be impossible. Definitely, such projects are bound to falter at delivering within budget and schedule.

One more aspect about such projects is that they cannot be planned well. There will be no upfront information regarding project cost and time estimates. This situation is simply not acceptable in a competitive business environment.

15.5 There are essentially three layers of processes that go into a project. The bottom-most layer is the development life-cycle processes, like software design and software construction. On top of this layer is the project processes, like project initiation, project planning, and project monitoring. The topmost layer is the process improvement and program management layer.

15.6 Software projects must be planned and controlled to achieve the desired target of creating a quality software product within limited budget and time. If any of these targets could not be achieved, then the software project could be in trouble. Sometimes, due to either internal or external problems, the software project may be abandoned. Sometimes, it may be due to some external factors over which the stakeholders do not have control (bad economy, changing market trends, natural disaster, etc.) that the project is abandoned. Sometimes, due to organization's own problems, the project may be abandoned.

But, in many cases, the project is forced to be abandoned due to internal problems on the project. Bad project management, poorly-skilled project team, unclear requirements, or too-frequently changing requirements can make a project so problematic that the project needs to be abandoned. These kinds of situations can be managed. Bringing well-trained and experienced people on project, finding and establishing best practices for projects, controlling changes in requirements, reducing risk by using an agile model for software development, etc., are some of the techniques that can prevent such disasters.

Chapter 16

16.1 CMMI framework is not a specification; rather, it is more like a guideline. It does not specify exactly how SDLC processes should be executed; it describes what things are important in each SDLC phase but does not specify in what sequence these things should be done.

So, the CMMI standard is applicable to any SDLC model be they waterfall, extreme programming, or any other model of software development. This is why we also have a concept like process tailoring, wherein any defined process model with well-defined process areas is changed to suit specific project requirements. CMMI supports process tailoring.

Moreover, the main thrust of the CMMI model is on process improvement rather than on specifying SDLC process steps. That is why the organization level process improvement areas are stressed more than the low level SDLC process areas.

16.2 CMMI has five process areas for SDLC processes. These areas are requirement development, requirement management, technical solution, verification, and validation. Requirement development deals with gathering, refining, formatting, and relating requirements to each other. Requirement management deals with allocating, prioritizing, and selecting requirements. It also deals with handling change requests. The technical solution area deals with software design and software construction. The verification area concerns doing static tests for software design and software construction. The validation area concerns doing dynamic tests at various levels (unit, integration, system, and user acceptance) and doing different kinds of tests (performance, functional, security, usability, reliability, portability, etc.).

16.3 ISO standards focus entirely on improving quality of process areas to improve quality of work products. In fact, they do not have any process area that deals with improving quality of work products through some work to be done directly on the work products. In CMMI, there are two process areas known as verification and validation which deal with improving product quality through testing work products and final products, finding defects, and then removing those defects. ISO does not have any similar process area.

16.4 IEEE process standards have concepts similar to CMMI when it comes to SDLC process areas; they are more guidelines than specifications and they do not enforce how the SDLC process areas should be carried out. They just define what activities are performed in each major areas.

IEEE standards are well-suited to many SDLC process models like agile, waterfall, and others. The SDLC process area can be easily tailored for the needs of specific projects.

16.5 Systematic Testing and Evaluation Process (STEP) is a content reference model rather than a process reference model. So, STEP can be implemented in any way suitable to the organization and not in a strict phase implementation. The STEP model is the accompanying testing process model, which goes with any agile model for software development. All the process improvement areas in STEP can be categorized as either quantitative or qualitative areas. The qualitative areas include test process utilization and customer satisfaction. The quantitative areas include test status, test requirement, defect trends, defect density, defect removal efficiency, and defect detection percentage.

16.6 Deming has proposed a process improvement technique, which is applicable to any industry. He proposed that the technique should have four steps, viz., Plan, Do, Check, and Apply (PDCA). First of all, the organization should plan for process improvement.

Then, this plan should be implemented (Do) on a pilot basis. Once implementation is complete, results should be checked (analyzed). If the pilot project results are encouraging, then the process improvement plan should be applied organization wide.

16.7 Test maturity model (TMM) was conceived to complement the CMM as CMM lacked process improvement areas for software testing. Similar to the structure of CMM, the TMM model has five levels of maturity processes, and each level has many process areas. Level 1 is identified by ad hoc measures for testing process. By level 2, there should be test policies and goals defined. By level 3, the testing processes should be clearly linked with the development processes. By level 4, the organization should be using measurements and metrics to control test processes. By level 5, the organization should be able to take initiatives to improve test processes.

Chapter 17

17.1 If the project size itself is small, then it does not make sense to break it further. That means an iterative model is not needed for small projects. All the requirements can be taken for development in one go.

However, if some of the requirements are not clear or the development team does not know how to convert them, initially, then an iterative model can be used.

17.2 Selecting the right process model for a software project is always challenging. However, it is of utmost importance that the right process model should be selected. Project factors that determine process selection include project size, complexity, area of maturity, team location, documentation level required, and organization maturity.

One aspect of process model selection is the ability of the model itself to support different kinds of project and development processes. While iterative models support risk reduction, incremental development, less management overhead, and better communication, they also have drawbacks like slower development and location constraint. In the case of the waterfall model, the benefits include high speed of development and no location constraint. One more benefit of the waterfall model is the utilization of gains in software engineering like process improvement and knowledge management. But, at the same time, the drawbacks of the waterfall model include high management overhead, excessive documentation, and high risk.

Based on the benefits and drawbacks for a project, the project team can decide on process model.

17.3 Plan-driven software development models have the biggest benefit in that everything is well-planned on the project. Then, these models allow for process improvement, which, in turn, result in higher productivity and quality. When software is to be developed at a higher speed, these models support concurrent engineering, and, thus, many teams can be formed and assigned development tasks, which can be done in parallel to each other. These models also allow teams to work from any location. Thus, benefits of offshoring such as lower costs and skilled manpower can be realized.

17.4 Agile, or iterative, models are a new phenomenon. Once organizations started to realize the limitations of the traditional waterfall model, they started looking for alternative options. The typical problems they faced on their projects were unclear requirements, requirement changes, large upfront risk, etc. Agile models eliminate all these problems. By doing incremental development, requirement changes can be incorporated in the next iteration in the development. Similarly, unclear requirements do not need to be touched until they become clear. Since the development team keeps demonstrating the product in a working condition after each iteration, the stakeholders feel more confident about the project and can play with the developed parts of the software product to see if this is what they were looking for. Meanwhile, the development team is busy developing software for next set of requirements.

17.5   Waterfall-model-based projects are notorious for budget and schedule overruns. The problems on these projects are large risk exposure, upfront investment, invisibility into the project from outside (what is going on the project, how much work has been completed, if the software design and construction are going smoothly, etc.), etc. In fact, waterfall model projects can be considered to be a monolith operation from outside. The software product for which the project team was instituted can be visible only after the project runs for its entire duration (sometimes as much as 3–4 years). Only after this long span of time can the project's stakeholders see the software in action. This is, indeed, a big risk, making all that investment commitment in time and money some four years back and then finding that the delivered product does not function as expected.

These are the biggest drawbacks of waterfall-model-based projects.

17.6   Agile models are maturing fast, and project teams are using them more and more. The current drawback of agile models is their comparative immaturity. They have around only for a short while. So, if somebody wants to adopt best practices and is looking for best practices related to agile models, he will be disappointed since there are no empirical data available which can demonstrate what is a best practice for any process related to the agile models. However, data may become available in future.

Currently, agile models dictate that the project team should be located at the same site as that of the customer; the project team cannot be located at some other site; the communication among team members should be only verbal and face to face. Due to these requirements, the project team cannot be enlarged if high speed development is required. Similarly, concurrent engineering cannot be employed. Benefits of offshore development can also not be taken.

Part IV

Chapter 18

18.1   Software projects are different from other kinds of projects in that, for software projects, the specifications for work products are not rigid. This necessitates constant interaction among customers, project teams, and suppliers. Without proper and constant communication, people will never understand what is required of them. Only after good communication can the communication gaps be eliminated, and people will be on the same page.

18.2   Software project teams consist of highly trained and skilled software professionals, but it does not mean that they are responsible and disciplined. In fact, office politics, motivation issues, long working hours, etc., are the kinds of issues that keep coming, and the project manager needs to handle these issues tactfully. Software professionals have large salaries and they have high demand in the market. Every project faces the risk that a team members will leave the project in the middle and join some other organization because of higher pay. Office politics and motivation issues can be attributed to manual and unchallenging work.

18.3   Software project teams need to be constantly in touch with the customers and end users because the requirements given by the customer are not specific. From these software requirements, business analysts make requirement specifications. These specifications may or may not be the exact requirements end users are looking for, as business analysts may not be able to capture exactly how the end users may be thinking about their requirements. Moreover, despite so much advancement in the software development industry, the software specifications (requirements, design, and construction) are not exact. So, every new feature added to the software must be shown to the customer to know if this is what they were looking for.

There is one more challenge to software projects related to customers. Customers do not know what actually goes on in the project and may have or develop some incorrect expectations. Getting these expectations right is a big challenge.

18.4   Project teams from software services suppliers may be located at offshore locations. They may have cultural, language, productivity, and other differences from the in-house project team. They may also have higher organizational maturity level. The bottom line is that they need to deliver the same of quality component that is expected by the customer. Their operations may be cheaper, but on-time delivery cannot be compromised.

Again, due to lack of rigid specifications, communication between the in-house project team and the supplier's team is of paramount importance. The supplier's team must understand what is required to be delivered.

Chapter 19

19.1   Software projects are executed in environments that demand tight deadlines, high levels of skill, and understanding specifications, and, working accordingly, communicating clarifications and guidance, etc., are some of the typical tasks. Project assignments are also demanding, and, often, team members need to work overtime to finish their assignment on time. At the same time, the project manager needs to do a lot of work to ensure many things.

Often, training may be needed for some team members. Arranging training on time is important. Similarly, there are junior team members who need mentoring. Some assignments may be too complex or labor intensive, and project team members may need to get help in completing those assignments.

19.2   The obvious means of motivation is the monetary benefit that each team members gets but this is not the only factor that can motivate. Apart from salary and other monetary benefits, the project team members should be given incentives like free training, skill development opportunities, challenging assignments, promotion opportunities, and good workplace ambience, can motivate team members. Good relationship building, cheerful disposition of managers, recognizing team members whenever they achieve something important, etc., are some other measures that can motivate the project team.

19.3   When people work on projects, they learn a lot of things. When they leave the project or the organization, all this learning is lost. The new person who replaces him will have to spend some time on the job to learn all these little things, which add up to a substantial learning curve for anybody. For example, a customer who likes to get an immediate response in a certain manner is known only to people who have worked with that customer for some time. The new person will not know this little secret to pleasing the customer. Similarly, if a particular tool on the project needs to be set up before it can be appropriately used, the information is known only to people who have worked on the project for sometime. Similarly, making a good design for a software product is known to the person who worked on that project.

How can these little secrets be saved even when a person leaves? A knowledge management system can capture some of these little facts. When a person leaves, these important pieces of information are not lost as they now reside in the knowledge management system.

19.4 Communication management deals with exchanging information between project teams, suppliers, and customers using communication media. When communication is done among many teams, it is important that the communication should be in a structured way. The best way is to use standard templates, this will ensure that there are no communication gaps or miscommunication. The more layers of management, the more structured and formal the communication should be.

19.5 Software project organization structure will depend a lot on the kind of project, project size, development speed, development model, and way of execution (outsourced/contracted out/offshored, etc.). If the development model is incremental integration with iterative model and speed of development is a concern, then a timeboxing structure will be needed. Here, more than one project team may be involved. If the project is offshored, then there will be project teams located at far-flung sites with a need for comprehensive infrastructure for communication. On projects where cross-functional expertise is required, a matrix organization is more appropriate. Larger project size invariably involves bringing many layers of management.

19.6 On large projects where communication is more formal and impersonal, it is difficult to know which team member has done his job well and which did not. To evaluate the performance of team members effectively, it is important to have good performance measurement metrics available, and ensure that they are used effectively.

Some popular techniques for performance evaluations include self-appraisal, peer reviews, and managerial appraisals. In the appraisal, the most important things to capture are whether an individual has performed well on the job or not, has worked well in the team or not, has supervised his junior members well or not, has mentored anyone or not, and what his worth was on the project. Based on his worth, he should be given appropriate pay raises, bonuses, promotions, etc.

Chapter 20

20.1 Sometimes, customers have the right expectations from the software project, but, most often, there is a mismatch between customer expectations and reality. In these cases, the project manager must set the right tone from the very beginning of the project. If his expectation about project schedule is wrong then the project manager must present the project schedule to the customer with good explanations of how much time is realistic for each kind of activity on the project and why the project should take so much time. If the customer has incorrect expectations about the project budget, then the project manager must explain about the cost involved in each activity convincingly. If customer has incorrect expectations about quality, then the project manager must convince the customer about why a certain level of quality is achievable with the given technology, time, and process constraints.

20.2 Projects are never set in a fixed mold. There is always scope for degrees of change from the agreed-upon contract. Besides, the customers always come up with requests, and the project manager may find it difficult to fulfill those requests.

In such situations, the project manager must evaluate the impact these changes and requests may have on the project. Based on the assessment, he can return to the customer with feasibility of acceptance. At this juncture, he can negotiate with the customer, justly the project goals, customer requests, and his own interests.

Sometimes, when there are many problems faced on the project, the project manager may not be able to finish the project as originally planned. In such situations, the project manager must make a realistic assessment and negotiate with the customer to cut down some features so that other product features can be finished on the project.

20.3 Project deviations are the most obvious cause of worry to project stakeholders and the project team. Despite good intentions and honest efforts, deviations in budget, schedule, or quality may arise. In such situations, the project manager must have a recorded evidence to show for himself as well as to explain the causes, which derailed the project schedule or budget to the customer.

To tackle project deviations, the project manager must keep some buffers in the project plan so that, when any deviations happen, then he can use time from that buffer. This way, the project schedule or project budget will not deviate in the overall project plan.

20.4 To be completely objective is a desirable state. Unfortunately, no project or people on the project can be 100% objective. So assessment of work performed, quality of work, performance of people, etc., are never assessed at face value. There is always some amount of subjectivity, and, thus, objective assessment is never possible.

So, when it comes to giving a report to, or negotiating with the customer, the customer may have their own reservations, judgments, etc. If the project manager and the project team have developed a good rapport with the customer, then these adverse assessments can be mitigated to some extent.

Chapter 21

21.1 The software industry has come a long way since its beginning. Nowadays, there are good software service providers (suppliers) who not only help on software projects but possess some specialized expertise as well as offering their services for fees which are lower than what it would cost to do it in-house. So, most modern-day large software projects involve suppliers.

Managing these suppliers requires in fields like a wide range of expertise law, contracting, managing, evaluating, etc.

21.2 The supplier agreement should have legal clauses, penalty clauses, service level agreements, severance of service conditions, confidentiality agreements, etc. On many software projects, the supplier may get access to confidential and critical information, and, thus, it should be ensured that this information is not abused or leaked. Some software projects themselves are of high strategic importance, and, thus, disclosing any information about the project may harm interests of the customer. There should be elaborate service level agreements, so that the service offered by the supplier can be managed properly. There should be penalty clauses, so that if the supplier fails in any service level agreements and the customer suffers any losses, the supplier could be penalized.

21.3 When a customer seeks services from service providers, he can try to find out if any suitable suppliers are available who can do the job. For this purpose, customers can use Request For Proposal (RFP), Request For Quotation (RFQ), or Request For Information (RFI) techniques to get information about suppliers, their competencies, and how they can do the required job. RFIs are the most preliminary forms that are used to learn about suppliers.

RFQs are forms that are used to get quotation from suppliers for any suitable job. RFPs are forms that are used to get complete proposal with project planning, and all other details about the way things will be carried out during the project.

21.4   When a customer evaluates bids from many suppliers, he will try to see competencies for the given job. There past record, customer references, project team profile, cost (bid amount), long-term stability of the supplier, etc., for each of the bids. He will then compare the bids based on his evaluation of each bid. Based on this comparison, he can then select the best bid.

21.5   When a project is to be offshored, there will be many considerations before doing so. The considerations include cultural differences, productivity, language, time zones, and infrastructure. Before the project is offshored, it must be ensured that the project should not suffer due to these differences and that appropriate measures are taken. Before the offshore team takes over, they should be given training and existing knowledge about the project should be transferred to them.

Part V

Chapter 22

22.1   The project team uses tools to do their work and, when they are finished with their work, they need to report it. If the tool is a standalone tool, then the person will need to get data from the tool, paste it into his report, and send it to the project manager and other team members as required. This way of doing things is not desirable. First of all, authenticity of the report becomes questionable. Then, the productivity of the person goes down. Then, if the person does not report at that time, it is difficult to know status of his work. Report of his work in this case is almost offline.

    The benefits of working online are obvious! It provides instant access to information in real time, improves productivity, improves transparency, allows automatic reporting of results, provides access to information to many people, etc. So, if the tools used by project teams are integrated to the main project tools (configuration management, test management, etc.), then information and status about all project tasks will be visible to project managers and other people who need to know the information. For these reasons, if a new tool is being used on a project, then it must be able to be integrated with existing project tools.

22.2   Tool support is very important as, whenever there is some problem with the tool, the tool support staff can provide assistance. If a project tool becomes obsolete then, first of all, you need to get in touch with the tool vendor to get support for the tool in future. If this is not possible, then discuss alternatives with the vendor. If the vendor has closed down, then some service providers can still provide support for the tool. If this avenue is also not possible, then tool documentation can be useful. If there are a lot of problems with the tool and there simply are no avenues to get help, then it will be better to get some alternative tool.

    Before buying any tool for the project, the project manager must ensure that the tool should be supported by the vendor. Even when the tool's life ends, the vendor should continue to provide support for the tool.

22.3   There are many costs involved in purchasing, maintenance, and training for a tool. The purchase cost itself has many components. If the tool is an enterprise tool, then it may have a server cost component and a number of seat cost components. Total purchase cost will be the sum of these two costs. Then, there will be support cost for the tool. Generally, support cost is a percentage of the server cost and is incurred annually. Apart from that, there may be some incidental support costs. Finally, a cost is involved in providing training for the tool. This cost may include cost for training and the time spent by the project team members for attending the training.

22.4 Most of the software projects start on a smaller scale. When the early versions of the software being developed grow to some stature and get some good market response, the stakeholders get more confident. They expand the project team to develop more features at a greater speed. So, scale of the project team goes up.

   If the project team is using some tools that cannot scale well to meet the needs of project team, then the project team may be in trouble. The expanded project team may not be able to use the tool appropriately. So, the tools must have the ability to scale, so that they can support bigger teams.

Chapter 23

23.1 When software developers write their code, they need to do many things like compiling their code, running a debugger to check and fix their code, using a text editor to write their code, using a version control tool to manage different versions of their source code, and accessing a database. If, for each of these activities, they are using separate tools that are standalone, then their productivity will go down substantially. For each activity, they may need to start the program, do the appropriate work in the program, close it, then start the other program and do their work there, etc. If they are provided with an integrated tool that can take care of most of their needs without resorting to many separate tools, then it will be a lot easier for them to do their work. Such tools are known as integrated development environments (IDEs).

23.2 On software projects, a lot of defects are detected during testing cycles. These defects are then fixed by the developers. Once a fixed defect is verified to be fixed by a testing engineer, then the defect is closed. Otherwise, the defect is reopened, so there is a complete life cycle of defects.

   A defect tracking tool helps in managing the defect life cycle. From defect logging to defect fixing, defect fix verification, defect closing, and defect reopening, the tool helps in managing the entire defect life cycle. The online tools are capable of supporting distributed teams who may be working from many sites.

23.3 Computer-Aided Software Engineering (CASE) tools help in performing many activities during development life cycle. Some CASE tools help in requirement development. Some other tools help in design development. Some designs are made in a CASE tool; many CASE tools are capable of generating skeleton source code, which helps in software construction as this generated code helps in enforcing programming standards. Some CASE tools also help in converting one design into another. For example, if a use case diagram is made in a CASE tool then, without any effort, the use case diagram can be converted into an entity relationship diagram.

   CASE tools are very productive as many activities during development life cycles can be automated using CASE tools.

23.4 Requirement management deals with providing a hierarchy of requirements, clubbing requirements, establishing relationship among requirements, prioritizing requirements, requirement selection, etc. Various requirement management tools help in doing these activities even though not all activities are supported in one tool. So, sometimes, a combination of tools is used. Still, the requirement management tools are not mature enough, and thus many project teams do not have many options and thus end up doing many of these tasks manually.

Index